ADDRESSING RAPE REFORM IN LAW AND PRACTICE

Addressing Rape Reform in Law and Practice

Susan Caringella

COLUMBIA UNIVERSITY PRESS  New York

Columbia University Press
Publishers Since 1893
New York   Chichester, West Sussex

Library of Congress Cataloging-in-Publication Data
Caringella, Susan.
Addressing rape reform in law and practice / Susan Caringella.
p.   cm.
ISBN 978-0-231-13424-8 (hard cover : alk. paper) —
ISBN 978-0-231-13425-5 (pbk. : alk. paper) — ISBN 978-0-231-50875-9 (e-book)
1. Rape—United States. I. Title.
HV6558.C367   2009
345.73'02532—dc22
2008026476

Columbia University Press books are printed on permanent and durable acid-free paper.
This book is printed on paper with recycled content.
Printed in the United States of America

c 10 9 8 7 6 5 4 3 2 1
p 10 9 8 7 6 5 4 3 2 1

References to Internet Web sites (URLs) were accurate at the time of writing. Neither the author nor Columbia University Press is responsible for URLs that may have expired or changed since the manuscript was prepared.

To my mother, who taught me not to be a victim,
and to my padre, who taught me compassion for all who are.

After researching rape and sexual assault for years, many of us build a seemingly impermeable shell that is sometimes alarmingly effective. Yet, from time to time, something about a case strikes like a lightning bolt to remind us of the utter atrocity of these crimes, like babies, only months old, found with objects in their vaginas or rectums or with HIV or gonorrhea in their throats.

We must never end the struggle for justice for all those victimized by these vile crimes.

Contents

Acknowledgments

Like any author of a book like this, I owe a great deal of gratitude to a multitude of people. My deep gratitude to Kris Mullendore, former ADA, current professor, and good friend, who read and responded at great length to early as well as late versions of the chapters of this book. Her meticulous and keen comments helped me turn the book around at early stages and correct and polish legal arguments in the final product. My deep appreciation also goes to Lynn Chancer, for working with me so that we would both get published by a company from our "top ten" wish list and for offering me unswerving encouragement and endless support.

My sincere appreciation goes to Deborah Schneider, literary agent (and sister) extraordinaire, who suggested so many contract changes that my editor became fearful of losing me as an author. My appreciation also goes to the late John Michel, my original editor at Columbia, who believed in this project so strongly that he wrote me from his hospital bed despite his grave suffering. My gratitude goes as well to my current editor, Lauren Dockett, for picking up my manuscript midstream and facilitating the successful completion of this project. And my sincere appreciation goes to the copy editor of this book, Sarah St. Onge, for her keen eye and mind.

I would also like to express my gratitude to two almost editors: George Ritzer, of Lexington Press, who promoted the earliest version of this work, and Elizabeth Knoll, of Harvard University Press, both for showing me the value of being focused and for promoting my confidence in pursuing this endeavor.

My heartfelt gratitude goes to Claire Renzetti, who serves as a role model of commitment to the profession, to those who work within it, and to the ideals of justice and equality. My profound thanks also to Walter DeKeserderdy, for his insightful comments as well as his model of productive commitment to ending "woman abuse" in all its forms and manifestations.

Others deserve special recognition, too. Emily Lenning tirelessly tracked down sources and annotated articles for this book. Amanda Counts deserves gratitude for her ever ready, thorough help with Web work and annotations. Drew Humphries' interest, encouragement, and enthusiasm helped spur me on. Marjorie Zatz's admiration for my perseverance in perfecting the manuscript helped keep me going. Laura Fishman's model of determination in the face of obstacles shored up my own resolve.

Other colleagues, too, like Nicole (Nicky) Hahn Rafter, Susan Miller, and Kim Cook, all helped to advance this work in their own significant ways. Lewis Walker and Pat Martin (cochairs) and David Hartmann (current chair) of the Department of Sociology, Ronald Kramer (director, Criminal Justice Program), Douglas Ferraro and Elise Jorgens (former deans of the College of Arts and Sciences), and Subhash Sonnad (professor and chair of the Sabbatical Leave Committee), all of Western Michigan University, merit special thanks for their tangible support in the form of giving me release time to write. Karen Rice deserves special mention, too, for her indefatigable cataloging of references as well as other typing and assistance that helped bring this project to fruition.

My gratitude also goes to Kathy Savage, the epitome of rape victim turned survivor and fighter, who resolutely pursued one of the first successful test cases of using DNA evidence to prosecute a rapist, and to all the others, both known and unknown to me personally, who, in an amazing multitude of ways, fight and survive the horror and trauma of rape and sexual assault victimization.

My parents, John and Marilyn, and my sister DonnaLee, and special friends like Pat Peppler and Bob Deets all deserve special recognition, too, for staying with me, schlepping me around, and even feeding me when I wasn't able because of several surgeries. And my further thanks go to so many others who understood my "booking" and seemingly perpetual absence.

I must also acknowledge my late Satanya and my Querida Rudita (aka Rudi), who lay ever by my side, patiently and unendingly waiting, or walking and wading (obliviously, with Post-its stuck to their fur) through the piles and piles of drafts, rewrites, reorganizations, reconceptualizations, and so forth, over the years it took to complete this work.

Finally let me share a quote from Churchill that is posted on my computer, my refrigerator, my office desk, and elsewhere: "Writing a book is an adventure. To begin with, it is a toy and an amusement; then it becomes a mistress, and then it becomes a master, and then a tyrant. The last phase is that just as you are about to be reconciled to your servitude, you kill the monster, and fling him out to the public" (Rhodes James 1974: 7883).

ADDRESSING RAPE REFORM IN LAW AND PRACTICE

Background to Rape Reform | ONE

Challenges surrounding the discrepancy between social ideals of equality and justice and the reality of discrimination against minorities and women defined social movements focused on civil and women's rights in the 1960s and 1970s. But these movements also spawned gaps between their own abstract ideals and practical possibilities. This book is concerned with one of these discrepancies, namely, the rise of a rape reform movement that was legislatively ambitious but in many ways ineffective. Through the 1970s, a rape reform movement did prevail in securing changes in rape laws across the United States. These legislative reforms, however, which began with the model in Michigan in 1974 and were enacted to varying extents in every jurisdiction a decade later, were accompanied by two unintended consequences.[1]

UNINTENDED CONSEQUENCES

One by-product of rape reform was that precisely because all state jurisdictions altered legal codes, the salience of rape as a social problem tended to dwindle. In retrospect, victim advocates, the public, and other constituent bodies seemed placated by the flurry of legislative resolutions aimed at redressing the persecution of rape victims in place of the prosecution of rapists. Concomitant with this, the liberal and radical feminist reform movement that was so engaged in critique transformed into more of a social service delivery bureaucracy that grew dependent on government funding to survive, which seriously dampened its critical edge (Miller and Meloy forthcoming: 286). In point of fact, the antirape movement drew less and less attention from feminists as the issue of rape drew less attention in the aftermath of legislative changes and was replaced by a growing concern about domestic violence. Feminist scholarship and activism concerning rape and sexual assault have been dissolving over the many years since the early dynamic days.[2] Some have even characterized feminist inattention to sexual violence as stultifying "stagnation" since these early years (Mardorossian 2002: 1).

The second unintended consequence of rape reform laws is equally noteworthy, and understandable given the conciliative effect of sweeping legal change. Once reforms were enacted on the books, relatively little attention was paid to the impact of laws in action. Yet even the limited research on reforms has shown that results have fallen far short of objectives. For instance, reforms have failed to increase reporting, arrest, and/or conviction rates; they have similarly failed to remove consent and resistance standards and the influential role that past sexual history evidence plays at trials (see chap. 3).

Consequently, reforms have largely served a symbolic and educative function (Chappell 1982; Osborne 1985; Polk 1985). This frequently observed conclusion, though, underestimates the success of reforms. To say that attitudes about rape shifted because the laws changed is to say a great deal, especially if we pause to appreciate pre–reform era beliefs about rape victimization. Nonetheless, the reforms implemented in day-to-day discretionary decision making have been tainted by persistent problematic attitudes, as the many women—and sometimes men[3]—who are victims of rape and sexual assault continue to be twice victimized (Burgess 1975).

EXTANT MODELS OF REFORM

The limited assessments of the practical impact of rape reform laws, though, inspired a subsequent group of feminist scholars, albeit only a few, to put forward alternative models of rape reform. These are, in the main, academic treatises that are more philosophical or idealistic than practical or realistic. Scholars like Estrich and Schulhofer are joined by others like Pineau (1996a),

Reeves Sanday (1996), and Burgess-Jackson (1999) in crafting proposals for further change in rape law. The two notable books for systematic and creative recommendations in this realm are *Real Rape* by Susan Estrich (1987) and *Unwanted Sex* by Stephen Schulhofer (1998). That Harvard University Press published both texts reflects the importance this subject has been accorded in social science and legal circles. What both books underscore is that rape, unless sensationalized through occasional high-profile cases, is not taken seriously despite decades of legal and social change. Simple rape—or nonaggravated or "he said, she said" rape—is still not taken seriously (for elaboration, see "He Said, She Heard" and "She Said (She Felt), He Heard (Thought)" in chap. 7). The similarity between these two works and this book is that all three conclude that the legal system persists in unfair treatment of women who are raped or sexually assaulted in spite of massive reforms repealing discriminatory standards in legal codes. Even more important, these two previous works—kindred with the book here—point beyond the identification of such failures to delineate new reform models aimed at remedying the injustices diagnosed in rape case processing.

Estrich's book was a hallmark in establishing that rape reforms affected only so-called real, rather than simple, rape. The distinction between the two, according to Estrich, was that "real" rapes are stereotypic, aggravated, stranger rapes as compared to the majority (three-quarters or more) of "simple" acquaintance or date rapes that do not involve additional injuries, accomplices, weapons, and so on.[4] *Real Rape* was groundbreaking not just because Estrich identified that reforms affected only "real" rapes but because she proffered an alternative legal framework especially targeting criminal culpability. The crux of Estrich's "negligent liability" model was that unreasonable mistakes of consent to sex (made by defendants) should confer criminal responsibility for rape. Her innovative thinking went on to make the analogy between economic crimes and sexual assaults, pointing out that if money, rather than sex, were being sought in deceitful interactions, the behavior would be considered criminal. In essence, she argues that sex procured by false pretense should be criminal, just as money procured by deceit is fraud.

Schulhofer's "sexual autonomy" model is more theoretical and philosophical, as well as more extreme or radical compared to the conceptualizations that Estrich and I advance. Schulhofer's paradigm goes beyond affirmative consent reforms like those familiar from the highly publicized Antioch College Sexual Assault Code, which calls for positive indications of assent to sex acts at every stage of sexual encounters. He argues for observable, "actual words or conduct indicating affirmative, freely given permission to the act of sexual penetration"

(1998: 283). Going still further, he asserts that the right of women and girls to sexual autonomy is the right to be free from any and all circumstances of coerced permission as defined in this way and, even more, free from any "unwanted sex," as his book title designates.

BUILDING FROM PRIOR MODELS

My model uses Estrich's landmark approach as a springboard but goes beyond her work in several respects. First, I expand the notion of negligent liability to encompass criminal recklessness in addition to criminal negligence. Second, I extend the host of legal changes to encompass rules of evidence that judges and juries are allowed to consider and jury instructions pertaining to the principles juries must apply in rendering verdicts. Examples of such changes include the shifting of the burden of proof when the consent defense is used, the introduction of presumptive involuntariness, nonagreement, and the de jure articulation of the irrelevance of drinking, dancing, and dress style to case findings.

The model espoused in this book views "affirmative consent" (where the presence of "yes" has to be shown to refute rape charges), not to mention Schulhofer's "sexual autonomy," as a demanding edge of reform, justified under only tightly defined circumstances (i.e., only when the defense wants to introduce the consent or mistake of consent defense to an accusation of rape). The integrity of Schulhofer's model is incontrovertible; at the same time, though, its practicality is questionable. Calling for a new right for women (sexual autonomy) when long-standing rights are yet to be fully accepted, let alone fully realized, seems an unworkable strategy. Asserting a policy perspective that calls for a right that goes beyond a policy (like affirmative consent) that is not socially and politically accepted constitutes a questionable tactic. The lack of popular support for an affirmative consent policy is evident in the national ridicule that attended Antioch College's affirmative consent policy, as well as in the fact that only three states have enacted affirmative consent into law over the thirty some years of reform.

It is for these reasons that the model laid out in this book is neither as radical as Schulhofer's nor as radical as the lesser but still demanding affirmative consent law approach. But there is more. I devised my model to be one of political compromise, because I think this renders it more acceptable both publicly and politically. It makes the changes I advocate more realistic and achievable.

THE BOOK'S MODEL: REFORMING RAPE REFORMS

Middle-Ground Strategy

The directions my model maps out represent a middle ground between a weak and an extreme reform position. The weak position sees reforming the law as, by and large, an ineffective measure for problem resolution, accomplishing not much more than minor or symbolic results. On the other hand, one type of extreme reform position holds that virtually any/all legal change will be effective; in fact, legal change is often seen as a panacea, with no recognition of the discrepancy between law enacted and law in action. So-called liberal terminology is often associated with such perspectives. Another type of extreme position views only those stances that are radical departures from the status quo, for example, affirmative consent or sexual autonomy (or strict liability, see chap. 5), as reforms viable to accomplish any real change. My approach is somewhere in between these positions, incorporating the bulk of rape reform laws, for example, shield legislation and the repeal of corroboration, resistance standards, and so on, but going further than these reforms through the modification of rules of evidence and jury instructions the better to synchronize the reforms on the books with the reform in action in order to accomplish real change. Proposals emanating from this book would correct for historic discrimination by better aligning rape prosecution with other criminal prosecution but not go so far as to create unique privileges or rights (for victims) in rape cases.

My middle-ground model can be conceptualized as a form of feminist (left) realism. Left realism is a theoretical position (in criminology) whose adherents typically address or reappropriate the real issues of serious street crime and victimization that earlier critical theorists tended to overlook in their efforts to expose the rampant crimes and enormous victimization by the rich and powerful, for example, state, organized, white-collar, corporate, and transnational deviance and criminality. Left realists and feminists have benefited one another, with feminists influencing left realists by inserting pivotal concern about women as a subjugated group, just like class and racial/ethnic minorities, while left realists have drawn critical attention and political agendas back to street crimes, among them those affecting women. Some left realists have broadened their perspectives by incorporating pragmatic solutions to the real problems to which feminists call attention, such as those surrounding the violent victimization of women (DeKeseredy, Alvi, and Schwartz 2006; DeKeseredy, Schwartz, and Alvi 2006).[5]

Patriarchy, like capitalism, is a structure that molds gender inequality and the more individualistic pain and suffering that men's violence inflicts on women. Real, pragmatic gains (and not just tinkering types of insignificant changes) can be realized within extant (infra)structural (and superstructural) arrangements. Put differently, the feminist contribution to left realist criminology can be drawn on as a way of realizing a critique of the broader structures of inequality and domination/subordination while offering pragmatic, viable, and palatable ways to change the institutional and microlevel manifestations in gender relations and woman abuse.

There are other lenses through which to elaborate the view of my model as a middle-ground position between the weak or symbolic and radical reform stances. First, I present the model in the critical recognition that while new laws can make a significant difference, passage itself does not guarantee changes from past laws and practices; that is, the model does not suffer from the naïveté of seeing changing law as a cure-all. Second, my model accepts existing rights of females and victims. This stands in contrast to Schulhofer's stipulation of females' new right to sexual autonomy. Third, my model, while extending beyond reforms implemented to date, is nonetheless predicated upon historically accepted or extant, and not new or altered, legal rights and principles. This is true in terms of substantive law, (e.g., notions of criminal culpability: mens rea), and procedural law (e.g., jury instructions). It is worth underscoring in this context that my model accepts historically established rights of defendants as well. More specifically, the Fifth and Sixth Amendment rights—against self-incrimination, to a public trial by a jury of peers, to counsel, to confront one's accusers, to call witnesses on one's own behalf, and so on—stand respected. I am also protective of the constitutional principles underlying the criminal legal system's workings, specifically those of fundamental fairness for all parties to a case, of due notice about law, about criminal definitions and legal obligations, and about the Fourteenth Amendment's guarantee of equal protection under the law for all parties to a case.

My model is also far-reaching, incorporating recognition of, indeed focus on, simple rapes and sexual assaults between acquainted parties where drinking, dating, dancing, and so on, are involved. It is broad as well in addressing substantive as well as procedural legal changes in statute and in processes that were previously neglected in reforms that stopped short at changing the law on the books.

Viability

The model here should be more palatable and hence, I argue, more viable than more extreme models. In other words, the proposed new model is more probable to see enactment that corresponds with objectives and implementation that makes a significant difference. This is important because one additional problem with previous reforms is that they pertain predominantly to de jure law, and this is where all the rape reforms of the past three decades have faltered: they have failed to deal with the de facto practices involved in the implementation of laws, however well or badly written. Based on extant legal rights and procedural principles and informed by existing practices that go hand in hand with the implementation of reform law, my model ought to be more readily accepted by constituents and legislators alike and hence more likely to be put into law and practice.

Lynn Chancer's work suggests a feminist context for appreciating how my model represents a compromise strategy beyond binary choices like the weak and extreme reform stances that can open new inroads or, in other words, is viable and potentially effective. In her book *Reconcilable Differences* (1998), Chancer describes how binary, "either/or" extremes in feminism have yielded debates that can more productively be resolved through analyzing differences to find common points of view. In parallel fashion, my model can be seen as a conciliatory tactic that attempts to resuscitate rape reform from the quagmire that has settled between the camps that hold reforms can do little good anymore and the camp that insists reforms must be extreme to do any good whatsoever.[6] Detailing an innovative array of changes that stay within the parameters of established legal rights and standards, with an eye toward regular criminal procedures, holds out the promise of a midpoint where the poles may meet and join forces to make a positive difference in combating rape victimization.

In this broader social context, then, *Addressing Rape Reform in Law and Practice* delineates a host of de jure and de facto problems with rape reform laws on the books and in practice. It moves beyond the limited academic literature on this subject by both analyzing existing reform laws and proposing a new model of rape and sexual assault law informed by the history of previous reform approaches' successes and failures. At the same time, this book builds on the very few other theoretical approaches promulgated by scholars who have gone beyond critique to offer solutions for rape reform law. Moreover, my recommendations go beyond the legal model I advance to address pragmatic, organizational changes that influence daily implementation practices of law. Such changes make implementation with integrity more likely by targeting such things as informal decision making, compliance, and funding possibilities. My model is situated between the either/or positions of the liberal rape reform and radical feminist stances that have dominated approaches to this subject. My intention is to chart a new direction for sexual assault prosecution that prioritizes fairness in law and in implementation practices. This is simply crucial for it is de facto practices that are pivotal and overlooked, an omission that has undermined the forging of authentic change in how rape and sexual assault are adjudicated.

Victim advocates, politicians, legislators, criminal justice officials, and the public ought to approve of the model for a number of reasons. It is designed to appease all these constituent groups and afford greater protection and justice for rape and its victims because it builds on successes instead of minimizing them. Symbolic, educative functions mean that some attitudes have changed; this is why there is evidence of the actual de facto removal of some discriminatory requirements, for example, resistance standards, and why we've witnessed a modicum of enhanced prosecution and conviction, as well as a measure of greater comparability between the ways rape and other crimes are handled in some jurisdictions (see chap. 3). This translates into improved outcomes and better treatment for rape victims. The model also is informed by the failures of reform. Instead of bemoaning that reforms didn't work or that changing rape law cannot solve the problems of discrimination against rape victims, the ensuing chapters develop step-by-step alternatives to remedy the problems that have persisted despite the best reforms. To put it in another way, relatively few works go beyond critique alone to map out the next wave of strategic moves, models, or paradigms. This is precisely the subject matter of this book.

The importance of statute change cannot be gainsaid. The law is a powerful, if not coercive, tool that can be harnessed in the struggle to alter the way we think about and treat rape and sexual assault. As Berliner put it, "the law can and should play a normative role in condemning [deceptive or threatening] behavior" (1991: 2703). The law is viewed by most as the ultimate account of what is right, good, and proper versus what is wrong, bad, and offensive. And this account is largely taken as neutral, configured to provide equal protection of all societal members' best interests. This is how law so often gets taken for granted, or perceived as inherently, unquestioningly right, or becomes hegemonic. Because of this, the law can be a persuasive influence on attitudes: those of the public and those of criminal justice personnel. Criminal justice officials are supposed to be accountable to the public and influenced by any shift in the public's attitudes toward the cases they process through the legal system. Criminal justice personnel are also likely to internalize some of what they must practice on a daily basis. These factors combine to facilitate making the law in action more closely mirror the law on the books.

Comprehensive Change

The comprehensive nature of the model strengthens the potential for its proposals to be effective. Suggesting changes beyond the legal model in order to render change more viable and implementation more efficient in meeting goals (than previous reforms achieved) is one consideration that makes for comprehensiveness in change. Another lies in the comprehensiveness of the model itself.

The paradigm of reform is broad and detailed in terms of both its theoretical base and its incorporation of substantive and procedural law, for examples, rules of evidence and juror instructions, as written and practiced. The breadth of the paradigm extends beyond extant law yet does not stray from it to create law outside of existing legal principles; for instance, the model broadens conceptualization of what constitutes sexual assault, specifically sexual assault by duress and sexual assault by fraud or guile, within the purview of existing legal doctrine. Similarly, it extends the legal doctrine of mens rea from homicide offenses to rape. The focus, too, is extended, from reform that in the past was applied predominantly to the stereotypical stranger-out-of-the-bushes "real" rape to a systematic set of reforms aimed at the bulk of rape, which is "simple," or date, acquaintance, nonaggravated rape. The way the reforms are interlocking and mutually reinforcing further strengthens the model. It safeguards against corrupt influences like sexist beliefs and reluctance to change, because the reforms are set up in such a way that each component props up the others in reciprocal fashion, that is, each part of the model complements what precedes and follows it, and in quite an explicit manner. This should help close the loopholes that previous reforms left wide open, letting discrimination in requirements, standards, and victim/case treatment continue to prevail. An additional feature of the model fleshed out in the following chapters that would facilitate the accomplishment of objectives concerns building up visibility and accountability for criminal justice decision makers, particularly for the informal decisions, for example, plea deals, that are routinely made. The last chapters suggest several concrete ways to ensure a better match among the goals, means, and end results of reform maneuvers.

Devising a paradigm of reform to serve as a model for the states is really nothing new. The federal government does it all the time: federal rules of evidence, federal sentencing guidelines, federal rules of criminal procedure, the model penal code, and so on. These exert a good deal of influence on the laws states develop individually. In addition to the obvious advantage of a national example to influence state law is the added benefit of greater consistency in changes across jurisdictions, as well as, once again, the reinforcing potential of one jurisdictional change on another.

It is important to reinvigorate rape reform to pursue progress for rape victims. In the interests of fairness, justice, and crime prevention and control, we simply must level the playing field. Victims remain at serious disadvantage, suffering a veritable host of injustices and discrimination. To say that balancing the scales to promote greater equality for rape victims is long overdue is an understatement. Defendants enjoy special privileges, like requiring victims to have resisted, like legally impugning the character, truthfulness, and reputation of rape victims with their past sexual activities and even past interactions (even if not involving coitus), and like the need for them to express nonconsent—which is not required in other crimes and prosecutions. It is high time to give victims a fair shake, to dismantle the zealous overprotections for men accused of this crime, which have been buoyed up by the myths about false accusation, ulterior motives, and so on, commonly embraced when rape charges are levied. Because of such factors, rape continues to be, as the FBI claimed over thirty years ago, the "most notoriously underreported offense in the country" (1975: 15). The unique barriers those victimized by rape face dissuade them from reporting and prosecuting offenders; the effect is that they are discriminated against: denied access to and protection from the criminal justice system. Just think about the Kobe Bryant case. The publicity and resultant trauma were so overwhelming that the alleged victim finally had to retreat and withdrew her charges. The physically disabled have been empowered to sue to gain access to courts; rape victims, disabled for different reasons, are entitled to similar recourse (Lane 2004: A1). Leveling, balancing, and seeking comparability are not efforts to seek privileges or advantages for victims. Rather, serious changes are desperately needed in order to counterweigh what has been a gross level of inequality and unequal access to legal protection for a crime that is "particularly difficult to prosecute" (Temkin 2002: 238; also see Adler 1987; Du Mont and Myhr 2000; Estrich 1987; Fairstein 1993; Hunter, Burns-Smith, and Walsh 2000; Vachss 1993). If a "serious imbalance between the rights of criminal defendants and the rights of crime victims" (Kilpatrick, Beatty, and Howley 1998: 1) characterizes adjudication of crime in general to the point of arguing for a constitutional amendment (as with victims' rights legislation), the degree of "imbalance" between the rights of the accused and the rights of victims in rape cases cannot be gainsaid.

POLITICAL CLIMATE AND BACKLASH

The dire need to rectify such inequity is even more pronounced given the regression and erosion of gains brought about by the reign of the conservative religious right and the backlash against the civil rights and feminist movements in general and the rape reform movement in particular. In many quarters across the country, backlash criticism of exaggeratedly overreaching protection for victims, of excessive vilification of men, and of the criminalization of uncomfortable sex by feminist rape reforms has replaced concern about reforming rape law. A new generation of young women thinks equality has arrived and that women need no special help or special protections. This third generation of alleged feminists condemns second-wave feminist and rape reform movements for their allegedly radical tenets. These new myths have to be addressed. As Allred and Somers recently put it (when commenting on the Kobe Bryant rape case), fallacies about rape and rape law are so pronounced that it is "time to reread Susan Brownmiller's *Against Our Will*" (2004: 63). I would go much further: we must confront and correct these new backlash myths about rape, rape law, and rape victimization before they wreak more destruction in the struggle for equality and fairness for all. A new wave of changes will go far in such an effort.

Legal Change Sweeps the Nation | **TWO**

Rape reforms aimed to achieve layers of objectives. A primary goal was to promote the prosecution of rape offenders in place of the persecution of rape victims and thus to eliminate the double victimization of rape victims. In order to accomplish this, reforms sought to remove the unique requirements and standards that accompanied carnal knowledge statutes. Carnal knowledge laws define rape as "carnal knowledge of a female, by a man, not of his wife, forcibly and against her will." The rape reform movement's attempt to educate the population and criminal justice officials alike went hand in hand with repealing requirements in order to dispel myths and replace discriminatory attitudes with the facts and realities of rape victimization. The hope was that if sexist attitudes, legal practices, and statutory provisions were dislodged, rape offenses would be treated more comparably with other acts of criminal violence. The effort to reach comparability with other violent, assaultive offenses was designed to bring about increases in reporting, arrest, prosecution, and conviction for rape. In other words, the rape reform movement tried to bring the views and treatment of rape in line with other crimes of violence, where victims were not treated with such suspicion and themselves put on trial. The attempt was to make the crime of rape less difficult for victims to charge, for prosecutors to pursue, and for judges and juries to recognize. Reform strove to reduce the inordinately high rates of attrition, where more than 90 percent of cases ended without conviction. The hope was that ultimately would-be rapists would be deterred from committing rape and sexual assault because of the reporting, prosecution, conviction, and punishment of the men who rape.

OVERALL CHANGE

Because so much of the trauma for rape victims has rested at the legal system's door, reform efforts pivoted around legislative alterations. Fully thirty-six state rape statutes underwent change between 1976 and 1978 alone (Field and Bienen 1980: 153). By the early 1980s virtually all states had altered their rape legislation.

The state of Michigan enacted the earliest and most radical rape reform legislation in 1974. The law, referred to as the Criminal Sexual Conduct Code (CSC) (Public Act [PA] 328), set the model for many other states to follow in enacting change in forcible (*sic*) rape statutes.[1]

Michigan's governor signed the Criminal Sexual Conduct Code in 1974; it became effective on April 1, 1975 (BenDor 1976: 149). The law defined graduated steps or degrees of criminal sexual conduct (CSC). Instances of CSC in the first and third degrees are crimes of criminal sexual penetration, and occasions of CSC in the second and fourth degrees are crimes of criminal sexual contact. CSC in the first degree (CSC1) and in the second degree (CSC2) are differentiated from CSC3 and CSC4 by aggravated conditions of (1) victims who are minors; (2) blood affiliation, same household, or power/authority/trust position of assailant; (3) commission of another felony; (4) the presence of weapons; (5) force/coercion or victim incapacitation along with injuries; or (6) force/coercion or incapacitation and multiple offenders. CSC in the third degree (CSC3) and in the fourth degree (CSC4) are not accompanied by such aggravating circumstances.[2] The code's other features, such as the removal of discriminatory requirements, are discussed in the following sections.

REMOVAL OF UNIQUE REQUIREMENTS

In some states, the changes were sweeping; in others, they were nominal. One salient change entailed repealing or relaxing unique requirements and standards.

Corroboration

Requiring corroboration in addition to a victim's testimony is unique to rape; that is, corroboration is not necessary for the prosecution of virtually any other crime. Over the years, most jurisdictions repealed corroboration requirements. In the case of Michigan, a de jure corroboration requirement did not exist on the books; however, it was so universally applied that reformers determined such a requirement really did operate in the criminal justice system, despite the lack of law stipulating that this was the case (Cobb and Schauer 1977; Michigan Women's Task Force on Rape 1974). Reformers approached this problem resourcefully. They removed the de facto requirement of substantiating evidence for a rape victim's complaint by legislatively specifying the lack of a de jure requirement. In other words, the reform in Michigan got rid of the de facto corroboration requirement by stipulating the lack of its de jure existence (PA 328 sec. 520h). Most states followed suit, removing corroboration demands where they existed (Schulhofer 1998: 30). Some states, however, retained these demands, if in compromised ways. Some states hedged, for example, by "qualifying this by saying that the victim testimony itself 'must be convincing to the point the rational fact finder could find the defendant guilty beyond a reasonable doubt' (Kentucky) or that the victim's testimony is sufficient 'unless the testimony is inherently improbable or incredible' (Maine)" (N.O.W. Legal Defense and Education Fund and Cherow-O'Leary 1987: 80). It is charitable to see these kinds of reform legislation as a compromise, given that they leave the back door so wide open.

Consent and Resistance

Consent and resistance requirements, likewise unique to rape, have also been repealed or relaxed in many jurisdictions. The modal change is that "resistance to the utmost" "throughout the entire duration of the attack" is no longer demanded so that judges and juries may consider resistance that falls short of this level. Bailey and Rothblatt state that even where resistance standards have been retained, resistance to the utmost is a concept that has grown "obsolete and outdated" (1973: 278). LeGrand comments that "good faith resistance, measured in relation to the total circumstances of the alleged attack" (1973: 620) replaced "to the utmost" standards. Victim resistance remains a part of statutes in some states, among them, Alabama, the District of Columbia, Idaho, Kentucky, Mississippi, and Wyoming (N.O.W. Legal Defense and Education Fund and Cherow-O'Leary 1987: 80). Schulhofer claims that "the great majority of states retained (and still retain) some form of resistance requirement, but the requirement was softened considerably.... Nearly all states began to abandon the old insistence on resistance 'to the utmost.' In effect, 'reasonable' resistance became sufficient" (1998: 30). In some jurisdictions the requirement has been done away with all together. In Michigan, for instance, the law states explicitly that "a victim need not resist" (PA 328 sec. 520i). States such as Alaska, Iowa, Minnesota, New Jersey, Ohio, and Vermont have similarly done away with resistance demands (N.O.W. Legal Defense and Education Fund and Cherow-O'Leary 1987: 80).

Many states have moved to a degree or step structure whereby rape and sexual assault are graduated along a continuum of crime severity, in large part in order to raze discriminatory resistance and consent standards that doubly victimize rape victims. Objective crime circumstances are delineated that automatically determine the existence and degree of sexual assault offenses. This stands to replace reliance on the determination of victim resistance to indicate force, which is in turn used to indicate nonconsent and the "against her will" aspect of traditional carnal knowledge legislation. Objective circumstances, like the existence of a weapon, additional injuries, and/or aiders and abettors, can be documented as evidence to charge different levels of sexual assault crimes without resistance, as in Michigan. Reliance is on the characteristics of the offense rather than on victim behavior (such as resistance). This not only makes rape prosecution more similar to that of other criminal offenses, and hence fairer, but also streamlines criminal justice processing and allows flexibility in charging that better reflects the seriousness of different rape and sexual assault crimes.

Past Sexual History and Character Evidence

Perhaps the most frequent reform is referred to as "shield" legislation. This alters the laws on rape that permit the defense to interrogate victims in open court about any and all past sexual activity. Most jurisdictions have in one way or another restricted this disparaging practice. Using character or reputation evidence of a victim's previous sexual involvements is no longer allowed to impugn the credibility of the victim—if the sexual activities have not been with the defendant. This evidence has also been used to demonstrate a victim's alleged promiscuity or to demonstrate her proclivity to consent to sex. Michigan's model reform states that past sexual activity is irrelevant and therefore inadmissible under a wide set of circumstances (PA 328 sec. 520j). If the defense wants to introduce this type of evidence, an "in-camera," or private rather than public, hearing is held with the judge, who determines its relevance and subsequently its admissibility. The model CSC Code provides that sexual character evidence is permitted only:

(1) To the extent the judge finds that the following proposed evidence is material to a fact at issue in the case and that its inflammatory or prejudicial nature does not outweigh its probative value:

    a. Evidence of the victim's past sexual conduct with the actor.

    b. Evidence of specific instances of sexual activity showing the source of origin of semen, pregnancy or disease.

(sec. 520j)

Michigan provides an example of what Searles and Berger (1995) categorize as "more" restrictive laws that "create a general prohibition" with "allowable exceptions." The "less restrictive" shield laws "allow admission of evidence of the complainant's prior sexual conduct after determination of its relevance" (227). Sexual behavior with the accused has conventionally been considered legally relevant, and admissible regardless of its actual irrelevance.

Cautionary Jury Instructions

Chief Justice Lord Matthew Hale admonished juries in 1680 that "rape is an accusation easily to be made, hard to be proved, and harder to be defended by the party accused, tho' never so innocent" (1971: 635). This has echoed through courtrooms for centuries.

Reforms have discouraged the cautionary instructions judges issue before juries begin their deliberations that warn jurors about how difficult it is for a man accused of rape to defend himself. As Estrich points out, juries have always been told that they must be convinced beyond a reasonable doubt of the defendant's guilt; giving special instructions in cases of rape is therefore as unnecessary as it is unfair (1987: 54). The National Organization for Women summarizes that, since reforms, "special instructions for juries increasingly have met with disfavor" (N.O.W. Legal Defense and Education Fund and Cherow-O'Leary 1987: 80). Tong explains that, "unable to find any real reasons for distrusting female testimony more than male testimony, most states have banned the mandatory and even discretional reading of these instructions" (1984: 105). Virtually all states now have eliminated this practice (Schulhofer 1998: 30).

Prompt Complaints

Reforms have also eliminated the fresh or prompt complaint requirement that demands victims of rape, alone among crimes, report right away or lose their access to the legal system. While a few states still have promptness requirements (ranging from three to six months; see N.O.W. Legal Defense and Education Fund and Cherow-O'Leary 1987: 82), in practice, prompt reports remain important for convictions (Estrich 1987: 53–54).

REDEFINITIONS: VIOLENCE AND DEVIATE OR CRIMINAL SEXUAL CONDUCT AND SEXUAL ASSAULT

The rape reform movement pinpointed many of the problems with rape prosecution as stemming from the view and treatment of rape as a sex crime. The "rape as sex" view is believed by many to beget the myths and corollary discriminatory legal obstacles already noted. Because of this, rape has been redefined in many jurisdictions. About half the states maintained the term "rape" (twenty-nine states; see Field and Bienen 1980: 154), while slightly less than half adopted different terms for different rape and related offenses. "Sexual assault" is, of course, one popularized variation in terminology. Others are "criminal sexual conduct," "deviant sexual conduct," "criminal deviate sexual behavior," "sexual assault," and "sexual battery." A salient difference between sexual assault and what is typically understood to be rape derives from the distinction between what have traditionally been considered sexual assault crimes and what has been termed "carnal knowledge" or "forcible rape." The former often criminalize acts other than vaginal penetration by the penis—for example, penetration with objects—and criminal contact short of penetration, as well as including other sorts of victims, for example, males and spouses.

The attempt has been to redefine rape as violence in order to get away from the term "rape" and all the loaded connotations, requirements, attributions, and adversities it carries. Redefining rape as criminal violence, or replacing the rape-as-sex view with the notion of rape-as-violence, is designed to make rape and/or sexual assault offenses as serious, legally and sociologically speaking, as other offenses that are violent in nature. The thinking is that if rape is defined as sexual violence, society, the law, and the criminal justice system will all be more likely to treat it as the heinous and harmful behavior that it is.

I should note that some sexual assault is not violent in physical terms, and we need to be careful to include these crimes in definitions specifically, and not just crimes of rape as penetration, which rape-as-violence tends to connote. We don't want to lose sight of the true range of sexual assaults, which includes crimes of contact in addition to vaginal, oral, and/or anal penetration. While defining rape as a crime of violence can be problematic for the potential to lose sight of other offenses of sexual assault, it should also be noted as problematic in its tendency to lose sight of the sexual nature of the criminal violation. The commonality, irrespective of rape, sexual assault, type of penetration or contact, violence or force, and so on, of course, is the lack of consent to any of the offensive *sexual* violations of the body.

OTHER LEGAL CHANGES

Gender Neutrality

Most jurisdictions have redefined crimes to cover a broader category of victims. The vast majority of states have gone to sex-neutral designations in reforms, in order to encompass male victims of sexual assault, as well as female offenders.

Victim Anonymity

Providing victims privacy through anonymity is another feature of reforms. The victim's identity is commonly withheld by organizations, like the media, as a matter of course and sometimes statutorily ordered. For instance, in Michigan the statute mandates that the name of the victim (and offender) be withheld upon request until the offender is arraigned (PA 328 1974: 4 sec. 520k).

Victim Polygraphs

In a few states, the police and/or prosecutors are prohibited by law from requesting that a rape victim take a polygraph (lie detector) test, in order to spare the victim additional anguish. But this has frustrated police and prosecutors, who believe that a victim polygraph helps them pursue criminal charges. Michigan law serves as an example of a type of compromise. It reads, "A law-enforcement official will not request or order of victim to take a polygraph examination or lie detector test. A law-enforcement officer may allow the victim to take a polygraph/lie detector test if the victim requests it or inquiries about the results of the accused's test. Victims will be informed if actor's test indicated that accused may not have committed crime" (Michigan Compiled Laws 776.21).

Statutory Rape

Most states specify a minimum age under which intercourse automatically becomes rape. The crime is recognized whether this is called statutory rape, as is customary, or some degree of deviate or criminal sexual conduct. The range in age is thirteen to eighteen (Berger, Searles, and Neuman 1988: 351). The reasoning behind criminal designations on the basis of age is that youth and teenagers cannot form meaningful consent. Moreover, youth constitute an obviously vulnerable population. Another popular change relating to the age of rape victims relates to young boys in particular. In thirty-five states, gender-neutral language has been enacted in order to encompass young male victims under statutory rape laws (American Bar Association 1996: 87).

There has been a tendency in reforms to lower the age at which statutory rape is automatic. For example, statutory rape might now pertain to youths who are less than sixteen, rather than twenty-one or even eighteen years of age. The reasoning behind this is that sexual values and standards have been changing, and the law needs to recognize consensual teenage sex when similarly aged, older teens are involved (Field and Bienen 1980: 171; N.O.W. Legal Defense and Education Fund and Cherow-O'Leary 1987: 81). A number of states have addressed the issue of statutory rape vis-à-vis consensual teen sex by enacting reforms that stipulate age differences between males and females. In other words, statutes proscribe sex acts when the male is three or more, four or more, or five or more years older than the female aged, respectively, sixteen, seventeen, or eighteen. These law are gender neutral, employing the words "minor" and "defendant," and so apply to same-sex or to female offender statutory rapes as well (see Davis and Twombly 2000).

Punishment

Some states not only specify automatic crimes but also specify automatic enhancements in the severity of the crime charge and/or the possible penalties for rape when rape victims are under certain ages. For example, in Michigan if the victim is under thirteen, or between thirteen and sixteen when accompanied by certain additional crime circumstances (e.g., the perpetrator is related to or in a position of authority over the victim), the potential charges are exclusively the most serious charges of CSC in the first or second degree (PA 328). Berger, Searles, and Neuman calculate that penalty enhancements of this nature are automatic in sixteen states (1988: 351).

It is important to point out that, contrary to public perception, so-called feminist rape reforms did not reach for higher levels of punishment in rape cases overall (Field and Bienen 1980; Snider 1985). This is due to the longstanding knowledge that juries are reluctant to convict in cases where penalties seem overly harsh. And harsh penalties are a pronounced tendency in rape statutes.

As Estrich (1987) notes, reformers strove more for certainty than severity of punishment. The reform laws frequently stipulated conditions of criminal events that determined severity levels along with progressive scales that specified crime seriousness matched with corresponding punishment levels. These left discretionary latitude for decision making by opening the door to lesser crimes and punishments, to counteract the reticence juries (or judges) may feel in rendering convictions. While degree structures permitted differential, and lesser, punishment levels, what often happened instead was that "pro-control" (Snider 1985: 344) or "law and order" criminal justice personnel, governmental officials, and particularly politicians usurped rape reform advocates to determine tougher sanctions in some jurisdictions.

Marital Rape

The spousal exemption to charges of rape is yet another feature of reform legislation. Marriage has until very recently been construed, both legally and socially, to give men the right to sex, any and all sex, at any time, in any place, with their wives. Marriage has been seen as a license for men to hit, to rape, and to hurt women. A man has been imbued with the right to sex with his wife, and the wife can never say no to her husband or have any recourse, no matter how violent the sex. Historically speaking, women consent to sex when they marry, and that consent is intractable. Scholars on marital rape usually point to Sir Matthew Hale when describing the origin of such law. He stated, "The husband cannot be guilty of rape committed by himself upon his lawful wife, for by their mutual matrimonial consent and contract, the wife hath given up herself in this kind unto the husband which she cannot retract" (cited in Kennedy Bergen 2000: 223).

Reforms have repealed the marital exemption that coexisted with carnal knowledge or "forcible" rape statutes. Some form of marital rape is now recognized in all states.[3] Kennedy Bergen has most recently summarized that in "18 states and the District of Columbia, and federal lands, the law grants husbands no exemption whatsoever from prosecution." In the remaining thirty-two states, "there are still some exemptions from prosecuting husbands for rape" (2000: 224), that is, there are still rights and protections for men at the expense of wives. The legislation that recognizes marital rape often requires the filing for divorce or the legal separation of the couple or the condition that the couple is living apart (Field and Bienen 1980: 165). This, of course, leaves married women who live in the same residence as their husbands unprotected. Some states explicitly exclude marriage as a defense to rape charges (as opposed to removing the exemption), while a few others provide for a separate crime of "spousal rape" (National Center for Victims of Crime 2004b).

REFORMS IN CANADA, ENGLAND AND WALES, AUSTRALIA, AND NEW ZEALAND

Research on rape reform laws passed in other countries is most readily available for other English-speaking countries. The similarities in reforms to those just described and to one another are striking.[4] Corroboration requirements have been repealed or formally stated to be nonexistent (for Australia, see Gregory and Lees 1999; for Canada, see Du Mont and Myhr 2000); shield legislation has been enacted (for England, see Temkin 1995 and Adler 1987; for Canada, see Sheehy 2000 and Du Mont and Myhr 2000); degree structures have been put in place (for Canada, see Du Mont and Myhr 2000); jury cautions have been removed (for Canada, see Du Mont and Myhr 2000); prompt complaint requirements have been repealed (for Australia, see Gregory and Lees 1999; for Canada, see Du Mont and Myhr 2000); male victims and marital rape have been legally recognized (for England, see Temkin 1995); and victim anonymity has been provided (Adler 1987).

The extant body of literature on rape reforms in Canada discusses how they have been quite similar to those in the United States, including the model Michigan reform (Field and Bienen 1980; Osborne 1985; Snider 1985). The reforms in Australia and New Zealand have also introduced "radical changes" (Temkin 1995: xx, citing the act amending the Canadian Criminal Code passed in 1982, the Crimes [Sexual Offences] Act of 1991 (Victoria), and the Crimes [Amendment] Act of 1989 [New South Wales]; also see Adler 1987).

Du Mont and Myhr (2000), commenting on the similarity to the Michigan circumstances, report that the Canadian Parliament

expunged rape, attempted rape, and indecent assault from the Criminal Code in favor of three levels of sexual assault: sexual assault (Section 246.1, now 271); sexual assault with a weapon, threats to 3rd person, or causing bodily harm (Section 246.2, now 272); and aggravated sexual assault (Section 246.3, now 273). In addition, this legislation negated the possibility of a consent defense in the presence of force, threats of force, fraud, or the exercise of authority. The law specified that "no corroboration is required for a conviction and the judge shall not instruct the jury that it is unsafe to find the accused guilty in the absence of corroboration" (Section 246.4, now 274). The rule of the recent complaint was also repealed

(Section 246.7, now 277). Furthermore, it was established that the complainant's sexual history with men other than the accused could not be introduced as evidence except in very specific circumstances (Section 246.6, NOW 1987: 267).

(1110–1111)

Temkin suggests that England and Wales were slow to change. She sees this as owing to how common law and practice did not discriminate quite so harshly against rape victims. There was no corroboration requirement in common law, and England did not insist on the high levels of resistance demanded by U.S. law. Nevertheless, England, too, reacted to criticisms leveled by women's groups about the mishandling of rape and its victims. England's first reform enacted restrictions on the admissibility of past sexual history early on, in the 1976 Sexual Offences (Amendment) Act (Adler 1987: vii). This law provided for victim anonymity as well as curtailing the admissibility of evidence on the victim's character. It wasn't until more recently, in the 1990s, that further change came about, in 1991, with the recognition of marital rape, and in 1994, with the recognition of male victims of rape and the expansion of the definition of rape to encompass anal penetration (Temkin 1995: xx).

Gregory and Lees (1999) describe the changes in New South Wales, Australia, passed as a package of reforms in the Crimes (Sexual Assault) Amendment Act of 1981 (Lees 1996: 112). Gregory and Lees note that the reforms "outlawed questioning about past sexual history" and made all types of such evidence inadmissible (1999: 208). Other features of Australian law reform are the repeal of the corroboration requirement and the relatively strong provision that judges warn jurors against being prejudiced if the victim did not make a prompt report (ibid.). A unique feature of Australian reform prohibits victims from giving evidence of their virginity. This is a novel reform attempt to make irrelevant the victim's past sexual conduct.

Adler spotlights shield type laws in her discussion of reform in England, comparing it with Australia, Canada, and the United States. She discusses how shield laws that are more restrictive and stipulate specific conditions of admissibility in statute are necessary. She sees these as better than those that leave conditions of past sex conduct admission open to judicial interpretation, that is, she sees statutory restrictions as preferable to leaving the matter up to judges. This is because even the former, more restrictive reforms have been found to be ineffective in precluding judges from allowing the questioning of victims about their sexual past across these jurisdictions (Adler 1987: 144–145; Temkin 1995).

OTHER VICTIM-ORIENTED DEVELOPMENTS

Civil Suits

Suing in civil court presents an alternative means to redress rape victimization. Civil suits can be employed in addition to, or in lieu of, criminal court proceedings. There are a variety of ways that suits occur. First, victims can sue assailants for punitive damages, pain, and suffering. The standard of proof is lower in civil courts than in criminal courts. In civil litigation, the burden is to show with a "preponderance of evidence" rather than to show beyond a reasonable doubt (as in criminal matters) that the person is responsible for the act (see chap. 11 for discussion of different standards). Victims have used the civil avenue more in recent times, as states' recognition of the harm suffered by rape victims has grown. Twenty-nine states have now allowed civil suits for damages in rape cases (N.O.W. Legal Defense and Education Fund and Cherow-O'Leary 1987: 83).

Another avenue for pursuing civil remedies is tied to universities. Victims have successfully sued for negligence when universities have failed in providing a safe environment. Bohmer and Parrot (1993) furnish clear delineations of the types of possible suits here. They describe suits based on tort law, such as premises liability claims (144–152), where responsibility is attributed for unsafe places; and those predicated upon "intentional infliction of emotional distress," where the "way the university handled the victim's complaint was sufficiently insensitive as to intentionally cause her emotional distress" (152). They also describe claims of victims against institutions as based on contract (safe educational environment) and based on civil rights claims and detail suits of other third parties, such as fraternities, for alcohol violations, for failing to secure or follow party permits, and for facilitating rape (155–156). Further, victims may also sue the parents of the perpetrator, if the latter is a minor (O'Gorman Hughes and Resnick Sandler 1987: 7).

Carrington and Nicholson (1984) expound on third party suits, stating that victims can sue third parties "whose simple or gross negligence caused or facilitated the criminal act" (3). The NOW Legal Defense and Education Fund reports that third party suits against others have included "landlords, owners of hotels and restaurants and supermarkets, who may have contributed to the occurrence" (N.O.W. Legal Defense and Education Fund and Cherow-O'Leary 1987: 83).

Federal Law: The Violence Against Women Act

Another avenue of redress for victims of sexual assault was passed at the federal level in 1994. It is referred to as the Violence Against Women Act, or VAWA.

Joseph Biden (D-Delaware) originally introduced the VAWA legislation in 1990. The Senate Judiciary Committee, chaired by Biden, began hearings in June of that year (Reeves Sanday 1996: 240). Four years later, Congress passed the act, and President Clinton signed it into law on September 13, 1994. The VAWA is best summarized by Biden. As he put it, "the Violence Against Women Act is intended to respond both to the underlying attitude that this violence is somehow less serious than other crime and to the resulting failure of our criminal justice system to address such violence.... The act is intended to educate the public and those within the justice system against the archaic prejudices that blame women for the beatings and the rapes they suffer; ... and to ensure that the focus of criminal proceedings will concentrate on the conduct of the attacker rather than the conduct of the victim" (1993: 38).

The Violence Against Women Act is Title IV of the Violent Crime Control and Law Enforcement Act of 1994. It has seven subtitles (A through G), each of which has numerous sections or chapters. The first chapter of subtitle A, "Safe Streets for Women," addresses rape. The chapter doubled the federal penalties for those with one or more prior "sex crimes" convictions, regardless of whether the convictions were sustained in state or federal courts. It also mandated restitution and authorized funds for victim counselors at the federal level. The second chapter "authorized to be appropriated" (1994: 1916) grants to "strengthen effective law enforcement and prosecutor strategies to combat violent crimes against women" (1910). The third chapter provides for grants to the secretary of transportation and of the secretary of the interior to improve lighting, camera surveillance, and security phones in public transportation and federal/national parks. Chapter 4 restricts the introduction of sexual history and "sex predisposition" (1919) evidence in federal criminal and civil proceedings. Chapter 5 allots funds for rape prevention and education in general, as well as funds for programs targeting runaways, homeless and street youths, and children who are sexually abused. This last chapter provides for the confidentiality of victim-counselor communication.

The second subtitle, "Safe Homes for Women," tackles domestic violence. The most salient provisions provide for interstate enforcement of protection order violations, grants for presumptive arrest policies or policies that "encourage arrest" (1932), and grants for domestic violence shelters, youth education, community programs, and family programs and services.

Subtitle C, "Civil Rights for Women," is the most heralded, and most critiqued, dimension of VAWA. It specifies the "Civil Rights Remedies for Gender-Motivated Violence Act" (PL 103–322 1994: sec. 40301, "Short Title," 1941). It makes violence against women a violation of women's civil rights, when attributable "at least in part, to an animus based on the victim's gender" (sec. 40302[d][1], 1941). It also establishes concurrent federal and state jurisdiction in such matters (and encourages the protection of anonymity for rape victims). It must be indicated immediately that this civil rights remedy was ruled unconstitutional by the U.S. Supreme Court the first time it was tested (see chap. 4 on failures). MacKinnon (2001) explains that defining violence against women as sex discrimination puts this violence within the purview of the Fourteenth Amendment's equal protection under law clause. Reeves Sanday observes, "According to Biden, if women have to change their lives to accommodate the fear of rape while men don't, that's not equality" (1996: 241).

The rest of the VAWA's provisions (subtitles D through G) make possible enhanced punishment for repeat offenders at the federal level, compensation and restitution for victims in criminal and civil litigation, and improved local, state, and national record keeping and research. "Compensatory and punitive damages" (to reimburse victims for monetary losses and to punish offenders through imposing monetary orders to pay victims for their suffering), "injunctive" relief (like protection orders) "and declaratory relief" (defining something to be against the law before the commission of the specific act, like defining rape a violation of civil rights) (1941) are now all possible. The act grants more protection to victim anonymity in both sexual and domestic assault cases. It also provides allocations for improvements in "mechanistic" crime prevention or environmental circumstances, ranging from, for example, subway lighting to funds for education, training, and prevention purposes and funds for hotlines, shelters, and crisis centers and from funds for youth and community educational programs to funds for in-service training of law enforcement, prosecution, and judicial personnel.

Victims' Rights

There have been a number of initiatives regarding the rights of crime victims. Rape victims have figured solidly in these. There are state and national decrees on victims' rights, pronouncing, for example, the right to be informed of delays and postponements, the right to be separated or protected from the accused during court processes, the right to make a victim impact statement, and the right to be informed of the release of rapists from prison. There have also been innovations for child victims of sexual assault, including, for instance, the use of videotaping or closed-circuit television for child victims' testimony and closing off the courtroom to spectators when public courts are used (Whitcomb et al. 1994: 6). Victim rights have also extended to reimbursement, often by the state, for the costs of, say, medical exams and injuries. At the federal level, the Victims of Crime Act (VOCA) passed in 1984 allocates monies to states to provide for victim compensation, particularly for the crimes of rape, domestic violence, and child abuse (Koss et al. 1994: 224).

EXTRALEGAL DEVELOPMENTS

The most widely known changes stemming from the antirape movement of the last thirty years are mostly of an extralegal nature. Some of the more frequent types of innovations that have cropped up should be familiar. Starting in 1972, rape crisis centers spread across the country; they now number over 550 (Odem and Clay-Warner 1998: 42). These centers have hot lines, provide counseling and advocacy for rape victims, and employ personnel to accompany victims to hospitals, police departments, and courts. Sexual assault programs also, for example, serve as community watchdogs over the agencies that handle sexual assault crimes, collect statistics on the treatment of sexual assault crimes, speak out publicly about the treatment of victims, and provide public service through giving talks about rape to different groups and even developing public service ads for television. Community, regional, and state task forces monitor cases and agencies, as well as meet, research, and make recommendations to criminal justice and government bodies about how to improve the treatment of rape victims, offenders, and cases. All these groups and others have joined parallel victim advocate groups and law and order campaigns to lobby for changes to serve victims better and enhance the goal of justice (thought by some to mean heightened punishment) in relation to sexual assault crimes. Feminists and other reform advocates have taken on the task of educating communities about the myths and facts surrounding sexual violence, developing and mainstreaming programs and materials in schools from the elementary through the university levels. Medical evidence kits have been developed and provided to hospitals to facilitate the collection of all the necessary evidence for prosecution and conviction and to preserve the chain of evidence in rape cases. In-service training has accompanied a move in many police and prosecutor offices to devise specific units for rape and sexual assault cases, where select officers/attorneys specialize in order to become experienced experts in the criminal processing of rape offenses.

SUMMARY

This listing of the impressive array of developments is not exhaustive, and neither are the developments themselves mutually exclusive. This is true in terms of extralegal services and in terms of other victim-oriented developments like suing possibilities and federal as well as state-level legislation. What it all means for victim and case treatment, though, remains an empirical question, to which the next chapter turns.

Failures and Successes | **THREE**

"In August 12, 1974, the governor of Michigan signed into law a bill titled 'Criminal Sexual Conduct.' A wrenching change from the old state law, it represented the first comprehensive attempt by a state to break away from century-old myths and legal traditions surrounding the crime of rape. The new statute had barely made the distance to the governor's desk, passing its final hurdle in the legislature at 5:30 A.M., July 13, near the end of the last marathon session. Had it not been for a small, sleepless group of dedicated feminists, lobbying all that night, this experimental law might still be in committee. Instead the new law went into effect April 1, 1975, and *the real work of reform had just begun*" (BenDor 1976: 149, emphasis added).

BenDor's comment that the real work begins after passage of reform statutes is not commonly recognized, yet its importance cannot be gainsaid. The burgeoning research and literature on rape of the past quarter century leave several gaping holes. One of the most understudied areas is precisely the examination of effectiveness of the vast rape reform measures passed across the country in the mid-1970s and 1980s.

The limited research that has been undertaken over the years to assess what has happened in the aftermath of rape law reform points to success as well as failure in achieving reform objectives. There is evidence that the changes established through the rape reform movement did improve the lot of rape victims (Marsh, Geist, and Caplan 1982). Substantive statutory and procedural rule changes have enhanced the criminal justice system's handling of sexual assault crimes. There are indications from research that in some aspects of reform law, in some jurisdictions, the historic discrimination against rape cases and rape victims has been at least partially abated. The weight of the evidence, however, suggests that these measures fall short of achieving the goals reformers envisioned (as described in chap. 2). One reason for failure that should be noted at the outset is that not all jurisdictions revised all aspects of their rape statutes. (Michigan's far-reaching changes remain more of an exception than the rule in rape reform law.) This means that many states still maintain antiquated laws and procedures that segregate rape cases for prejudicial treatment. And there are a myriad of problems with even the best of laws, as I detail throughout this and subsequent chapters.

The title of Susan Estrich's book, *Real Rape*, provides one sort of summary relating to how the reforms on rape failed. After careful legal research, Estrich interprets that despite new laws it is still only the stereotypical rapist-out-of-the-bushes rape that the criminal justice system treats seriously. The system continues to slight "simple," or nonaggravated, acquaintance and date rape, as well as nonaggravated rapes like those where there are no gangs or weapons or additional injuries. We should bear in mind, though, that so-called real rapes are now taken more seriously, even though simple rapes are still not being pursued. At least reforms have facilitated this result.

REQUIREMENTS

Discriminatory requirements not only continue to exist in law in some jurisdictions; they persist in practice, or are operative in a de facto manner, in many jurisdictions, even some of the best. This is because discretion permeates the criminal justice system. That is, because criminal justice actors all enjoy decisional options at virtually every stage of case processing and because there is not a great deal of visibility, accountability, and/or control over the exercise of this discretion, the laws on the books look different from the laws in action. This is especially pronounced in the examination of outcomes attending rape reforms.

Corroboration

Corroboration requirements provide the first example. First, recall that in some states reforms merely qualified the need for corroborative evidence rather than removing it completely. Second, although corroboration evidence may not be required de jure, it continues to be extremely influential, tainting decision making in cases of rape (Caringella-MacDonald 1985, 1988; Clark and Buchner 1982; Myers and LaFree 1982; Osborne 1985; and, especially for medical corroboration, Weninger 1978). Research in Kalamazoo, Michigan, provides details, showing that prosecutors rely on evidence additional to victims' complaints in charging and plea-bargaining decisions. Prosecutors cited evidential problems twice as often in sexual (all CSC) as opposed to nonsexual assault cases as the reasons for denying prosecution altogether (Caringella-MacDonald 1988). This research found that pragmatic factors, such as victims' decisions not to proceed with charges, characterized the reasons for denying prosecution for nonsexual assault, while lack of evidence in addition to a victim's complaint (corroborative evidence) was significantly associated with CSC case denials (ibid.). Clark and Buchner (1982) found corroborative evidence to be required in the majority of the seventeen cross-national jurisdictions they investigated. It is also interesting to observe Osborne's analysis of cases in Canada in this regard. She found that judges thought that corroboration is "a rule of good sense, albeit not a rule of law" (1985: 53). This means that cases are still not often pursued unless there are eyewitnesses, crime scene photographs showing violent destruction, blood, bite/burn marks, semen, and other types of corroborative evidence. Spohn and Horney quote a comment by an Atlanta lawyer that punctuates the issue: "You still win or lose on your corroboration" (1992: 163).

Consent and Resistance

The research on consent and resistance is a bit more equivocal but still disappointing. First, resistance is still a requirement in many jurisdictions. Second, while the requirement has been widely relaxed and even abolished in some places, victim consent and credibility have been found to remain disproportionately at issue in rape prosecutions when evidence of resistance is lacking. The question of whether a victim consented or agreed to sex, of course, arouses the most disbelief. Research in the reform state of Michigan, however, found that evidence of resistance alone was not a determinative factor in prosecutors' charging and plea-bargaining decisions. This is to say, prosecutors did pursue cases in the absence of evidence of resistance, although in its absence they were likely to doubt victims' credibility more in sexual assault than in nonsexual assault cases (Caringella-MacDonald 1988). Estrich (1987) reports that consent remained at issue in all degrees of CSC crimes in Michigan, as well as in the state of Washington, another of the strong reform jurisdictions. In the Kalamazoo, Michigan, research, prosecutors noted credibility problems such as implausible accounts and suspected ulterior motives, making consent an issue in the sexual assault cases twice as often in the nonsexual assault cases (Caringella-MacDonald 1988).

Spohn and Horney (1992) provide an insight about the lack of notable change in corroboration and resistance requirements. They comment that corroboration and resistance were never that important for the types of rapes that the criminal justice system typically handles in the first place. So-called real rapes, where strangers and aggravating circumstances exist, present lower thresholds or less need for corroborative evidence and/or victim resistance. Hence the reform laws were more symbolic than real in the changes enacted, since the requirements weren't heavily relied upon in the bulk of the types of rape cases processed. To expound, research suggests that eliminating requirements like those for corroboration and resistance benefit only a particular kind of the fewer simple rapes that are pursued, namely, the rapes of that type that are nonaggravated. But it is stranger rapes—which are fewer in number in comparison to date/acquaintance, nonaggravated, simple rapes—that are most often punished and for which the need for corroboration or resistance is less pronounced. Overall, the bulk of the research suggests that abolishing the resistance requirement has not led to increased prosecution and conviction for nonaggravated rape or for acquaintance or date types of rape cases.

Past Sexual History and Character Evidence

The failure of reforms to eliminate the introduction of previous sexual activity and character evidence is also somewhat equivocal. The strong leaning in findings, however, is toward a negative interpretation, given reform goals.

On the positive side of the ledger, challenges to rape shield laws have failed in state and federal courts, on the basis of the Fourteenth Amendment right to equal protection (Sasko and Sesek 1975, citing the Ohio American Civil Liberties Union [ACLU]) or, more commonly, on the basis of the Sixth Amendment right to confront one's accusers (ibid., citing the Ohio ACLU and L. Herman 1977; Spohn and Horney 1992: 28, citing Berger 1977, Haxton 1985, Loftus 1982, Rudstein 1976, Tanford and Bocchino 1980, and S. Williams 1984). Colorado's strong shield law was upheld under the recent challenge in the high-profile Kobe Bryant case (where the defense argued—albeit unsuccessfully—that barring questioning about the alleged victim's sexual history before and after the sex acts involving the defendant violated the constitutional right to confront one's accusers and have a fair trial). Michigan's model (one of the most restrictive) shield law has been upheld by state appellate courts (Spohn and Horney 1992: 28, citing *People v. Dawsey* 76

Mich. App. 741, 746, 257 N.W.2d 236, 237 [1977]; and *People v. Hackett* 421 Mich. 338, 356, 365, N.W.2d 120, 128 [1984]). The U.S. Supreme Court has also upheld the constitutionality of the restrictive Michigan shield provision on past sexual conduct evidence (Spohn and Horney 1992: 29, citing *Michigan v. Lucas* 114 L Ed, 205 [1991]). The federal rules of evidence on shield restrictions in rape cases have been upheld in federal courts as well.

But not all states have strong prohibitions in the first place. And whether prohibitions/shields are strong or weak (Searles and Berger 1995: 227), evidence of sexual activity is insidiously, if not blatantly, interjected regardless of shield provisions. The practice of investigating the past sexual activities and character/reputation of victims was uncovered in Michigan under the model reforms (Caringella-MacDonald 1988; Marsh, Geist, and Caplan 1982). Marsh, Geist, and Caplan (1982) reported that the officials they surveyed actually admitted they hadn't changed their courtroom tactics with respect to sexual/character evidence. Spohn and Horney report that such evidence was still seen as important in all three of the strongest reform jurisdictions they investigated, namely, Michigan, Illinois, and Pennsylvania (1992: 155). They further disclose that officials believed that even one singular prior sexual encounter between a victim and offender stood a fifty-fifty chance of being admitted, in spite of the strong reform prohibitions. The belief that past sex connotes "sluttiness," dishonesty, lesser harm, or consent serves to reify that rape is a "stranger-danger" crime and that acquaintance, date, or marital rapes are not properly treated as criminal offenses, or at least not serious ones. Spohn and Horney point out a further problem. They interpret that the reform provisions about past sex/character really only pertain to the very few cases where acquaintance rape gets prosecuted, the defendant argues consent, and the case actually goes to trial (1992: 166). This is a tiny minority of rapes.

Virtually all researchers who comment on past sex evidence reach the same conclusions: such evidence is believed relevant to consent and is routinely worked into case proceedings (Adler 1987; Berger, Searles, and Neuman 1988; Dusky 1996; Estrich 1987; Temkin 2002). Research in Illinois, Florida, Idaho, and Canada found that the influence of such evidence persisted (Bienen 1983; Hayler 1985; Nicoll 1979; and Osborne 1985, respectively).[1]

A recent development is indicative of the continued relevance of past sex, despite reform efforts. This development also shows how the backlash against reforms has eroded previous gains. In New Jersey, a state notable for affirmative consent reforms (see chap. 6 for elaboration), where the law provides some of the strongest potential protections for victims, a Supreme Court case (*New Jersey v. Anderson Garron*) ruled that the 1994 amendment to the prior sexual history provision that restricts the introduction of such evidence is unconstitutional. The court declared that even prior interactions between the victim and the defendant are relevant. As noted by Justice Coleman in one dissenting opinion, "under the Court's holding today, it will be virtually impossible for a woman to prove that she was raped by a man whom she had previously expressed interest in, flirted with, or even dated, even if she never engaged in sex with him prior to the assault occurring" (www.vpico.com/articlemanager/printerfriendly. aspx?article = 112620, accessed March 4, 2005). This couldn't be more regressive or contrary to reform.

Cautionary Jury Instructions

There are several issues attending the repeal or replacement of the Chief Justice Hale variety of cautionary instructions to juries. Although the Hale cautions are not generally advised anymore, sometimes other instructions are supposed to be given but are not read to juries before deliberations. Juries should to be instructed that corroboration and resistance are not required for findings of guilt and that past consensual sex does not mean sex in the current instance in jurisdictions passing these types of reforms. But this does not always happen. Spohn and Horney found through their interviews, for instance, that some judges so informed juries and some did not. In addition, some prosecutors routinely requested judges to issue these instructions to juries, while others failed to do so (1992: 163–164).

New instructions have begotten other problems too. Berger pointed out some time ago that in California, where judges are required to give instructions that past consent to sex with the defendant does not intend consent in the crime charged, this practice still puts a negative spotlight on the victim instead of on the offender (1977: 97). And victim scrutiny is tantamount to victim doubt in cases of rape.

The repeal of cautionary jury instructions has led to other problems as well. Tong reports that criminal justice actors may request and rely on psychiatric exams and victim polygraphs in lieu of cautionary jury instruction (1984: 106). This, of course, is conducted in an alleged attempt to get at the truth in the case; translated, however, this means it is intended to reveal victim consent. It appears that the tactic has grown in popularity. Defense attorneys are increasingly, and successfully, trying to introduce victims' medical and psychological records, as was attempted in the widely publicized Kobe Bryant case. And, as Giannelli (1997) expounds, this goes even further in some jurisdictions, where some trial courts have the authority actually to order the psychiatric or psychological testing of victims.

Prompt Complaints

In similarly unsuccessful fashion, the prompt complaint requirement that so many jurisdictions have written out in reforms (N.O.W. Legal Defense and Education Fund and Cherow-O'Leary 1987: 82) may continue to influence decision making and outcomes in rape and sexual assault prosecutions. Once again, discretion allows police to unfound (decide no crime occurred), prosecutors not to proceed, and judges/juries to dismiss/acquit when victims take what these actors believe to be too long to come forward to charge men with rape. Estrich notes that promptness of complaint continues to be an issue in the model reform state of Michigan (1987: 53–54, 90). Spears and Spohn, too, found that even in the model jurisdiction of Detroit, Michigan, cases were more likely to be charged when victims filed complaints within *an hour* of the rape (1987: 512). This gives an idea of what "prompt" can be construed to mean in some sectors.

ENHANCEMENTS IN CRIMINAL JUSTICE PROCESSING

The second and primary area that has been assessed in the limited research on the aftereffects of statute alterations relates to whether rape cases are now more likely to be processed or, conversely, whether attrition (case mortality) has diminished. Here, as elsewhere, the results are somewhat mixed.

Reporting

Research on the frequency with which victims report rape since the reforms has found both a lack of change and increases in rates of reporting rape offenses to police. Berger, Neuman, and Searles's nationwide research (1991), along with Marsh, Geist, and Caplan's Michigan research (1982), report that victims did not bring sexual assault crimes to police any more often in the aftermath of rape reforms. By contrast, Spohn and Horney's 1996 assessment of six jurisdictions and Bachman and Paternoster's 1993 study of jurisdictions nationally reported some increase in the rates of victim reports.

Police

Marsh, Geist, and Caplan (1982) found that arrests had increased, although only slightly, in post-reform Michigan. They also found, however, that the rates of unfounding complaints by police did not undergo any change. They concluded that the lack of diminution, or the stability, in these rates meant failure for reforms. Basically, this means that police arrested more suspects yet continued to send the same proportion of victims home by unfounding/dismissing their rape claims. Polk's (1985) analysis in the California reform jurisdiction lends support to negative interpretations. He failed to find as much as a slight increase in the rates of arrest. He specifically reported that clearance rates (the vast majority of crimes cleared by police are cleared by arrest) did not rise in the wake of reforms.

Prosecution

Findings regarding rape prosecution rates are again both positive and negative. One positive finding is Polk's (1985), in California. He reported a slight increase in post-reform filings for felony (more serious) rape charges. Marsh, Geist, and Caplan (1982) also found an increase in charging for the most severe, first-degree CSC cases. Spohn and Horney's (1996) examination in six jurisdictions found an increase in cases bound over for trial, although the magnitude was small.

Loh's (1981) research showed no change in prosecutors' charging habits. And Marsh, Geist, and Caplan's positive finding in 1982 that CSC 1 filings increased is contradicted by their own further analysis of Michigan data, as well as by Chappell's 1982 research in Wayne County, Detroit. The further analyses showed that only "real" as opposed to "Mickey Mouse" or "bad" rapes (Chappell 1982: 10)—namely, CSC in the second, third, or fourth degree (all of which are less likely to involve strangers)—were most frequently pursued. In other words, the increase noted turns out to hold only for "real" or "good" or readily convictable rape cases (the authorizations for CSC 1 were more than double those for CSC 2, 3, and 4 combined in Kalamazoo, Michigan; see Caringella-MacDonald 1988). Spears and Spohn's research found that "victim behavior, character and credibility" continued to influence prosecutors' charging decisions, regardless of the "case seriousness or evidentiary strength" of cases (1997: 519). Leive's study of the 1993 Senate Judiciary Committee's survey of eight states reports similar results, revealing that prosecutors dismissed 89 percent of rape cases before even pleas, let alone trials, took place (1994: 199).

Conviction

Mixed results attend the research on increases in conviction rates, too. One assessment uncovered evidence of some enhancement in overall conviction rates in the years after reform (Caringella-MacDonald 1984). Marsh, Geist, and Caplan

(1982) also discovered enhanced conviction rates, but only when original charges were for the most serious charges of CSC. Lower degrees of CSC were still viewed with suspicion and bargained down to even lesser crimes in order to achieve convictions. Loh finds the growth in conviction rates to be negligible, describing a similar pattern to Marsh, Geist, and Caplan's. He refers to this pattern as "Truth in Criminal Labeling" (1981: 28). By this he means that convictions were more often sustained for rape charges after reforms, instead of being reduced to non–rape charges. Spohn and Horney's (1992 and 1996) research was the most negative, finding no significant changes in conviction rates after reform.

The most positive result was found in comparisons of traditional versus model law jurisdictions. This research showed Michigan to fare better in overall attrition rates—the flip side of conviction rates. In other words, there was less attrition of cases from police report to conclusion in the reform state jurisdictions than in traditional rape law jurisdictions (Caringella-MacDonald 1984).

Sentencing

The research on sentencing after rape reform is also largely discouraging. Spohn and Horney (1996) report no significant effects of reform in relation to enhanced rates of imprisonment. And while Bachman and Paternoster state that there were slight increases in the number of acquaintance rape arrests that resulted in imprisonment, they discuss a "large acquaintance discount," where there is a "very small change in the likelihood that an individual who raped an acquaintance would be imprisoned" (1993: 573–574).

The reforms that graduate punishment levels according to the definitions that provide for varying steps of sexual assault crimes can be seen in a positive light in that they allow a range of sanctions to correlate with the severity of sexual assaults. As previously noted, however, many reforms were incorporated into so-called law and order initiatives and erred in the direction of punitiveness, setting penalties at high levels that could exacerbate the problem of juror hesitancy (Allison and Wrightsman 1993; Snider 1985). Since it appears that predominantly the higher levels of "real" rape crimes are the cases being pursued and for which convictions are being sustained (Caringella-MacDonald 1985; Chappell 1982; Loh 1981; Marsh, Geist, and Caplan 1982; Spohn and Horney 1992, 1996), only the highest levels of punishment are being considered. This could be influencing the less than satisfactory conviction rates: convictions and hence sentencing might not improve under reform because the high degrees and high-penalty cases are those being pursued, and this has been shown to generate reticence in findings of guilt and sentences of imprisonment. Michigan provides a case in point. CSC in the first degree carries a maximum sentence of life imprisonment, whereas second- and third-degree CSCs carry up to fifteen-year maximums. These are quite different considerations for adjudication and possible outcomes.

COMPARABILITY TO OTHER CRIMES

The objective of having sexual assault offenses match other violent and/or as-saultive offenses in terms of case treatment has not been completely realized, either. On the positive side, comparability in the treatment of rape and other violent crimes has been found in police arrest rates, as described by Marsh, Geist, and Caplan (1982) in Michigan. Success has also been found in the rates of charging and plea bargaining by prosecutors in CSC versus other assault offenses in Michigan (Caringella-MacDonald 1985). Success has further been indicated in conviction or, conversely, attrition rates for rape versus other crimes in California (Galvin and Polk 1983). Moreover, research in Michigan revealed that even though CSC cases did not present as much evidence as did those for other assault crimes, they were authorized for prosecution more often than were nonsexual assaults (Caringella-MacDonald 1985). Furthermore, CSCs were not reduced to lesser level (authorized) charges any more (neither in proportion nor in magnitude) than were nonsexual assault offenses (Caringella-MacDonald 1985). Still further, the percentage of cases plea bargained did not significantly differ between sexual and nonsexual assault offenses in the model state site (Caringella-MacDonald 1985). And prosecutors cited problems with evidence as reasons for reducing charges in roughly 50 percent of all cases, both CSC and non-CSC (Caringella-MacDonald 1985). Another optimistic finding was that victim precipitation (blaming victims for provoking or bringing the crime upon themselves), although noted in sexual assault cases (and more often than in nonsexual assault crimes), was still attributed in a small minority of the cases (Caringella-MacDonald 1985).

But further findings range from mixed to negative. A mixed interpretation, for instance, comes from Kalamazoo, Michigan, where there were no observed differences in the proportion of sexual versus nonsexual assault cases reduced or dropped out of the system. The negative result was that the magnitude of reductions differed. The overall amount of charging decrease was significantly greater for CSC cases, as was the degree of charge diminution through plea bargains. In fact, the degree of reductions (or amount to which the number and severity of counts were lowered) in the charging decisions was nearly twice as high for sexual as opposed to nonsexual assault offenses (Caringella-MacDonald 1991:

5). Pointing to failure in other locales are Clark and Buchner's 1982 findings. They report that in the majority of the seventeen cross-national jurisdictions they studied, rape cases were not as likely to end up in convictions as were other violent criminal offenses.

REDEFINITIONS: SUCCESSES AND FAILURES

The antirape movement's strategy to redefine rape along the lines of other violent and/or assault crimes in order to cast off old attitudes, laws, and practices about what constitutes rape and who constitutes its victims has led to some improvements. One kind of success has been that rapes other than the stereotypical stranger-out-of-the-bushes rape have been brought to court and resulted in judicial and juror determinations of guilt and sentences of imprisonment. Spohn and Horney (1996) found no differences of any significant magnitude between acquaintance and stranger rape outcomes. Bachman and Paternoster (1993) report similar findings with national data. Weninger reports from his research in Texas that a "mix" of cases went to trial, including not only acquaintance rapes but also rapes where victims "voluntarily encountered" assailants (1978: 392). Even radical feminist Andrea Dworkin acknowledged that "increasingly, incursions against women are prosecuted as rape; that rape is now a crime against the woman herself; that the use of force is enough to warrant a prosecution (if not yet a conviction); that a date, a friend, an acquaintance, will be prosecuted for the use of force" (1997: 210).

Issues remain, however. The strategy to criminalize date, acquaintance, non-aggravated, or simple rape comes with at a price; for example, it is taken less seriously than so-called real rape and less likely to see a positive result. This must temper positive evaluations and accolades and must inform future efforts if further progress is to be made on the front against sexual assault against women.

Broadened Definitions

The reform measures that opened up definitions to include acts other than vaginal penetration by a penis accomplished several things. Reform definitions of penetration and contact offenses encompassing oral, anal, and object invasions of the body have led to arrests, prosecutions, and convictions. The problem, however, is that even the most outrageous of cases involving these types of acts have not always led to successful outcomes. The Glen Ridge case serves as a prime example. The victim was of a mental age of around eight. She was gang-raped by five young men, while eight others sat and watched—in chairs lined up for viewing ahead of time. The victim was vaginally penetrated by penises as well as by a broom and a baseball bat. Amazingly, victim consent and desire were still alleged in the court proceedings, as well as in the press coverage of this case.

OTHER LEGAL PROVISIONS

Critical assessment leads to an identification of both failures and successes in each of the other reform changes delineated as well. The measures have made some gains but hardly ever without concomitant disappointment that detracts from a reading of accomplishment.

Gender Neutrality

Gender-neutral language in laws enlarges the scope of victims and offenders. This feature of reform extends protections for males, while it simultaneously extends the possibility of indictments for females. Most states incorporated this change, and this was a positive result, but not without a downside. The problem is that trying to make rape and sexual assault laws gender neutral erases the "unique indignity" suffered primarily by women (Estrich 1987: 81).

Victim Anonymity: Privacy Versus Out to Shout

Reform law provisions for protecting victim privacy by prohibiting disclosure of victims' names until arrest or criminal disposition have been steeped in controversy. The attempt to shroud victim identity was born out of concern about the condemnation attendant with rape victimization. Nancy Ziegenmeyer took this head-on when she decided to come forward with her story in 1990. She went public with her account of her experience, a "stranger-danger" rape, and detailed her trials and tribulations as she moved through the cumbersome and lengthy criminal justice processes. She told her story to the editor of the *Des Moines Register* in Iowa, who published a five-part series of articles (by reporter Jane Schorer) on the rape. The gutsy 1991 story (under the editorship of Geneva Overholser) won a Pulitzer Prize for Public Service. Nancy Ziegenmeyer was straightforward about wanting to counteract the stigma for all women by identifying, instead of hiding, her name and her rape. She understood that trying to conceal one's identity after rape perpetuates the belief that rape is somehow different, lesser, or a dirty little secret. Privacy provisions have been criticized for perpetuating such notions.

Many raped women, however, justifiably feel that having their identity known will bring about a second kind of victimization. As Deborah Denno articulates, the stereotypes surrounding women and rape can be either dispelled or reified by public identification of raped women (1993: 1125, citing Marcus and McMahon 1990–1991: 1020, 1030–1036). Patricia Bowman was one such woman who was smeared in the press. In the televised Kennedy Smith trial, she was the "blue blob" on TV who sought to have her anonymity protected. But, contrary to journalistic convention,[2] news agencies, television stations, and magazines all referred to Bowman by name. They claimed that her identity was already known, that is, in the public domain (Denno 1993: 1128), because one or two sources had revealed her identity. The media therefore asserted that there was no reason to follow the convention, because there was nothing left to protect. Questions about the victim's lying about the rape, having ulterior motives, given the involvement of a Kennedy, and the like were all given press. The victim's name in another case, namely, the Kobe Bryant case, was "accidentally" released by unknown court personnel, and controversy again ensued as some of the media made her identity known to the public. Questions about lying, ulterior motives, and on and on attended the coverage of this case as well.

Another set of debates about rape victims' right to privacy has arisen in light of the rights of accused rapists. Denno cites Alan Dershowitz speaking on behalf of the accused in rape cases, who explains that withholding victims' names steps on the civil liberties of the accused (Denno 1993: 1129, citing Dershowitz 1984: 10). Relatedly, the ACLU has argued that the practice steps on the right of accused parties to confront their accuser (Sasko and Sesek 1975, citing the Ohio ACLU). Moreover, the media are wont to claim that having to suppress rape victims' identities infringes on the First Amendment right of freedom of the press.

So, the good news is that law reform and custom come together to withhold rape victims' names from the press in order to protect victims' privacy and shelter them from further stigmatic victimization. The bad news is that it is not usually up to the victim, that so-called accidents happen, that the press frequently publicizes identities anyway, that further harassment and/or blame often ensue, and that the practice has come under constitutional fire.

Victim Polygraphs

That victim polygraphs are problematic is obvious: they focus prejudicial attention on rape victims. Even though "a handful of states" (Dusky 1996: 386) has outlawed officials from requesting that victims take a lie detector test, some victims want to take a polygraph to strengthen their cause and aid in the pursuit of criminal charges and penalties. Michigan's compromise tactic—allowing polygraphs but only upon request by victims—is laudable, but how realistic it is, and how it may get mangled in practice, is anybody's guess.

Not only are polygraphs sufficiently unreliable to be proscribed for use in court, the state of being a rape victim is sufficiently traumatic to render any such test a failure. Dusky conveys that rape victims are commonly in states of fear, guilt, heightened blood pressure, sporadic or heavy breathing, and so on, precisely the conditions the polygraph is designed to detect—to uncover criminals, not to verify victimization. From a victim advocate point of view, the polygraph can be seen as a setup, designed to guarantee failure. What is worse, Dusky reports that "when ABC's *Prime Time* surveyed more than two hundred rape crisis centers around the country, they found that in seventeen states rape victims said that police threatened them with arrest or charges of perjury if they failed the exam"(1996: 386). So a rape victim who reacts naturally to becoming a crime victim may find herself charged as a criminal in the attempt to pursue prosecution of a man who raped her.

Contrast the situation of the victim, whose constitutional right not to incriminate herself can be seen to be violated in this instance, with that of the accused. He is informed at the outset about his rights, before interrogation; while she, who comes forward on her own, to report a most intimately personal and often violent victimization, is not informed of hers. This is because, a victim, in fact, doesn't enjoy such rights, so there is nothing of which she could be informed. What is more, the accused enjoys the right to an attorney for counsel (provided by the state, if need be), while the victim has no such assistance or guidance and is exposed to criminal accusation. The asymmetry could not be more manifest.

Statutory Rape

The alterations of laws on statutory rape have both broadened and limited the kinds of females who can be victims. Some (Delgado 1996) applaud new provisions for limiting statutory rape by recognizing female agency at younger ages, while others (Oberman 1994) decry the exploitation that is fostered by the decriminalization of some categories of victims. More specifically, because teen sex is rampant (53 percent of fifteen- to nineteen-year olds have had sex; see Oberman 1994: 21, citing Henshaw 1992), and because girls indicate that they want and consent to sex at younger ages than in the past (for example, at sixteen, seventeen, and eighteen years of age; see Oberman 1994), some reforms have reduced age limits on statutory rape to fifteen or sixteen (instead of, for example, eighteen or twenty-one). Many see this as progressive change. To move protections for some females out of the statutory rape category, however, opens up problems, particularly those stemming from exploitation. This is because so much teen sex involves males who are typically three, four, five, ten, or more years older than the girls (Oberman 1994: 18–19, citing Males 1992: "70% of teen births, pregnancies and sexually transmitted diseases are from men over 20"). The reforms that have altered rape law such that the age difference between the male and female has become the decisive factor for statutory rape determination can be seen as positive in this light. This may broaden protections for young women in new ways. Such changes still reduce some of the old protections, however, and so remain controversial.

In terms of sanctions for statutory rape, enhanced punishment for youthful victims is an improvement in going after same-household, incest, and child victims who need the law's protective arm. With youth as with older victims, however, the reluctance to convict in the face of more severe punishment is a trade-off that must be seriously contemplated.

The punishments that have been altered in rape reforms have tended to be "get tough," or law-and-order, enhancements. Gradation of degrees of sexual assault and corresponding punishments could, however, curb this tendency. But again it is disproportionately the so-called real rapes that get processed and punished and, further, handled at the higher degrees with longer prison sentences, which also means a greater possibility of acquittal/dismissal. Degree structures can also be positive, though, because they enhance prosecutors' plea-bargaining positions (See chap. 16).

Marital Rape

Recognizing female agency, desire, and willingness or the lack thereof, not to mention the violent domination and exploitation of women who are married, should be applauded in the changes that define marital rape to be a crime in all fifty states (Kennedy Bergen 2000: 224). Society, or at least law, has finally conceded that marital rape is not an oxymoron. Married women are not simply the property of men. The marital rape laws across the fifty states represent great strides in recognizing that rape and sexual assault are different from consensual sex, because of the violence, force, and/or coercion, and acknowledging the right to say no despite marital status. This concedes that a marriage license is not a license to inflict sexual violence or to rape or sexually assault a woman.

As Kennedy Bergen has pointed out, though, not all laws are equal. Only eighteen states and the District of Columbia have completely removed the marital exemption in rape (2000: 224). In the remaining thirty-two states, some protections or exemptions for husbands remain. Finkelhor and Yllo use the category of "partial exemption" to describe the law in some of these states, where husbands can only be charged with rape by their wives if they are living apart, legally separated, or have filed for divorce (1985: 141–143).

Kennedy Bergen describes how some of the laws afford even less protection by negating wives' nonconsent to sex acts under certain conditions where "wives are most vulnerable and legally unable to consent—for example, when they are incapacitated from drugs or alcohol, mentally or physically impaired, or unconscious" (2000: 224). Thus, under what would be aggravating circumstances for nonwives in some reform law states, for example, victims being unconscious or incapable of consent, in other jurisdictions would not be crimes for wives under the same set of (aggravating) circumstances. The possibility of any level of criminal rape charge is annulled by virtue of a marital relationship in these instances.

The attitude apparent in these exceptions is tied to another problem. Only cases involving the most violent, perverse, or brutal rapes in marriage are ever reported, not to mention prosecuted or ending up in conviction. Russell gives the example of these non-"ordinary" kinds of rapes as those involving "tire irons, dogs, strangulation, or death threats" (1985: 79). Underscoring a related problem, she later observes that "in some states, so-called lower degrees of rape are not considered crimes in cases of wife rape: for instance, rape imposed by force but without the wife's suffering additional degrees of violence such as kidnapping or being threatened with a weapon" (1998: 76). Lest there be doubt that rape—even with aggravating conditions—still is often not viewed as rape when husbands and wives are involved, consider the following story published in *USA Today*. The article reports that "a man kidnaps his estranged wife, rapes her, accuses her of an imaginary affair, and chokes her to death; a reporter writes that he 'made love to his wife,' then strangled her when 'overcome with jealous passion'" (Jones 1994).

Yet a further issue is that some states have differentiated marital rape from all other rape and developed a distinct crime category for it. What is more, some states treat marital offenses as lesser crimes, to the point of defining spousal sexual assault as only a misdemeanor.[3]

And there is more woeful news. In twelve states, the exemption for marital rape has been extended to cover unmarried men who cohabit with women, or "voluntary social companions" (Finkelhor and Yllo 1985: 149). The latter category actually extends rape immunity to men who rape a woman with whom they have had previous consensual sex.

The good news is that Kennedy Bergen's more recent count puts the number of states that have extended exemptions for married couples to cohabiting couples at only four (2000: 224).

SUCCESSES AND FAILURES IN REFORM LAWS ABROAD

Some outcomes from other countries have been interpreted in a positive light. Just as in the United States, however, successes have not been without qualification. Where evaluations are available, mixed results, at best, attend reforms in Canada, England and Wales, and Australia.

Successes

On the positive side, reforms have been noted to improve the lot of victims in England and Wales, with victims experiencing less trauma (Gregory and Lees 1999). Gregory and Lees are clear that the most helpful aspects of reforms have put female criminal justice officials and specialized units in charge of rape cases in criminal justice and medical agencies. They also bring in research that confirms there were more arrests and convictions in New South Wales (Australia) after reforms. Their interpretation is that the different evidential standards and procedures make "complaints more actionable" (1999: 208, citing Allen 1990: 230–231). Lees's earlier work on England also points out that reform "led to a significantly higher proportion of cases going to trial and a conviction rate of 82 percent" (Lees 1996: 112, citing Allen 1990: 231). Another rather optimistic finding from England comes from Adler's research. She found that whether or not the victim voluntarily accompanied the defendant to the eventual crime scene did "not, by itself, correlate with the verdict" on a rape charge (1987: 112–113).

Gregory and Lees bring in the example of the Lloyd and Walmsley's 1989 Home Office Study to discuss evidence of some other types of reform success from England. The Home Office research showed that more nonstranger rapes resulted in conviction in 1985 than in 1973. Gregory and Lees point out that the greatest increase in the acquaintance (or nonstranger) rape convictions fell in the subcategory of "intimates"—a positive result indeed. Additionally, the increased convictions involved were cases that occurred indoors. Gregory and Lees comment that conviction on the basis of factors like this stands against erroneous stereotypes and so represents a measure of progress. Soothill's study, although focused on the media, also contains court data that replicate the result that rape cases in English courts increasingly include crimes that occur in private, or in-door settings, and that involve acquaintances (1995: 173).

The remaining positive research result comes from Canada. Hinch reports that the rate of police unfounding of that which they refer to as "open territory" victims (Clark and Lewis 1977), or who deviate from "feminine" or "good girl" stereotypes, declined markedly after reforms. Those cases involve the types of victims who typically are the most blamed for bringing about or deemed to de-serve the crimes they suffer. They entail, for example, victims who drink, who have active past sexual histories, who hitchhike, and/or who are from the low-er/working classes, are single mothers, and so forth. Hinch found that the un-founding of such complaints dropped from 97 percent (in 1970) to 38 percent in 1982 (1988: 245). Despite the magnitude of the drop, 38 percent is still not a low proportion of cases. To interpret this as evidence of success would be charitable, but it is nonetheless progress worthy of spotlight.

Failures

As in the United States, the limited research on the impact of rape reforms in other countries falls more on the side of failure. In England and Wales, for exam-ple, Gregory and Lees (1999) rather surprisingly found that there was not only an absence of an increase in or even a steady state of case processing but actually an overall decline in conviction rates of reported rape cases after reforms. They calculate that 24 percent of reported cases culminated in conviction in 1985, and that this fell to a 10 percent conviction rate in 1996 (2–3, citing Home Office Sta-tistics). They carefully examine the changes in the criminal justice system that coincide with reforms. In their interpretation of this devastating change, they note that the year "1985 was just before the Crown Prosecution Service (CPS) as-sumed prosecution of criminal cases, a task formerly undertaken by the police" (3). They posit that the "police reflect the status quo; predominantly white, male and conservative in outlook; they are themselves part of a macho culture which is profoundly anti-feminist. Any attempts to introduce radical changes in the way in which cases of male violence are handled by the police must therefore confront two major obstacles: the first is the 'enemy within,' i.e., resistance from police culture; the second is the 'enemy without', which is the refusal of the other major players in the criminal justice system, from the Crown Prosecution Ser-vice to the Court of Appeal, to accept … a fundamentally new approach to the problem of male violence" (3). However badly the police handled rape cases, the criminal justice agents like prosecutors and courts appear to do a worse job. The researchers, however, mine the data further to show that it was actually the types of cases pursued that lowered convictions. More acquaintance, non-"real rapes" were being brought forward, and so convictions dropped.

Gregory and Lees also explore further the data from Walmsley and White's Home Office study. Although they noted the 1973–1985 increase in convictions for acquaintance (and indoor) rape, there was an decrease in convictions for rape cases overall (1999: 92–93). More, this reduction in convictions for all rape cases happened at the time of increased reporting of rape charges (ibid.). Gregory and Lees go on to say that police and prosecution were both more "timid" (93) in the pursuit of rape cases in the later years. They propose that it was "reaction to the high acquittal rate in cases of non-stranger rape" that "effectively brought this development" (going forward with acquaintance rape complaints) "to a halt" (93).

Gregory and Lees clarify that the positive development brought to a halt was the prosecution and conviction of the more specific category of intimate as opposed to simply acquaintance rapes. Their research found that "no criming" (the British equivalent of unfounding) occurred in 35 percent of stranger rapes, 51 percent of acquaintance rapes, and 61 percent of intimate rapes (1999: 96). Moreover, their research showed conviction rates falling off along the same continuum: 45 percent for stranger rapes, dropping to 30 percent when one considers convictions for lesser charges; 24 percent for acquaintance rapes, falling to 18 percent when reversals on appeal are factored in; and 0 percent for rapes involving intimates (96–97). Again, police, prosecutors, and courts are all to blame for not implementing reforms with integrity, but police and prosecutors at least initially tried.

Wright's 1984 study of six counties in England also showed attrition to be a problem in rape case processing. He cites the problems to be "no criming" by police, the dropping of charges by prosecutors (not incidentally, he reports that prosecutors withdrew charges more often than victims), and lenient sentencing commonly consisting of probation or fines. Wright concluded that rapists who actually get sent to prison must be surprised at their unusual misfortune (400).

Temkin (1995) reviews the research on shield provisions in England, as well as Australia and Canada. She concludes that shield reforms intended to protect against reliance on sexual history and character evidence are largely ineffective when discretion to determine the admissibility and probative value of past sex conduct is left to judges, as opposed to being specified in legislative statute. The questioning is allowed, victims are put on trial, their credibility is impugned, and jurors grow more and more biased. Temkin elaborates that when judicial discretion has been replaced with "firm limits" (308) of law, victims fare much better.[4] Adler adds that the problem is that even if it is disallowed, lawyers bring up sexual history questions and introduce it by "indirect evidence, innuendo and suggestion" (1987: viii).

Adler's research depicts other failures in England. She describes how overt signs of violence and injury "over and above the rape" are needed if rapists are to be convicted (1987: 113) and concludes that not a single conviction was obtained in the cases she examined where there was a lack of corroborating evidence (156), despite the lack of this requirement in even common law. And, she summarizes, stereotypes about rape continue to influence the severity of charges as well as the severity of sentencing in rape case outcomes (viii).

Adler also studied the provisions for victim anonymity. Apparently the hope was that provisions would protect victims' identities, as well as "alter the quantity and, above all, the quality of press reports relating to the rape" by limiting "access to the raw material for the sort of titillating rape reports" the press usually produces (1987: 63). Unsurprisingly, no such change in stories was effected (Adler 1987, citing Hay, Soothill, and Walby 1980; Soothill 1995). Worse, Adler conveys that sensationalized press coverage actually increased. Soothill's (1995) parallel finding informs that (despite the courts' increased processing of private and acquaintance rapes), the media covered primarily stranger, gang, public place, and serial rapists.

The research on Canada's reforms shows "checkered success" (Sheehy 2000: 227), but, in the main, failure. Perhaps the best finding is that acquaintance rape cases, "including current or previous partners" (Du Mont and Myhr 2000: 1109), went forward in the courts more often after reform. The remainder of the findings in Du Mont and Myhr's research, as well as in the other research on Canadian reforms, falls to the failure side of the ledger. The research consistently points to essentially no overall change in the aftermath of reform law (Du Mont and Myhr 2000; Hinch 1985, 1988). Attrition rates are reported to be high and, conversely, conviction rates low in rape case processing. Du Mont and Myhr are comprehensive in their citations of the research over some "three decades" that shows that "few sex offenders are arrested and charged, and still fewer are prosecuted and convicted of sexual offenses" (1111).

Studies on the effects of reform in Canada also consistently point out that the nature of the cases that do proceed through prosecution and—to a lesser extent, of course—conviction are the most serious and aggravated crimes of sexual violence. For instance, Yurchesyn, Keith, and Renner (1995) report that the rather few cases that make it to court are those where there are weapons present, and/or observable threats or use of violence on victims, and/or extensive injuries to victims. The other factor they mention is drinking on the part of the victim, which garners press attention and public reproof (73).[5] That discriminatory requirements continue to be relied upon guarantees that it is the most stereotypical, rather than the most common, rapes that get processed through criminal legal systems. The research in Canada has further found, for example, that corroborative evidence, such as witnesses, is still sought and, indeed, is needed (Du Mont and Myhr 2000: 1111; see Hinch 1988); that resistance by victims makes prosecution more likely (1127); and that the failure to file prompt complaints hinders prosecution (1119), in spite of the fact that reform specifically deems such factors irrelevant.

Shield legislation, too, is problematic in Canada. Sheehy's interpretation of "checkered success" points up that while shield revisions have attempted to preclude questioning victims about past sexual encounters, defense attorneys manage to "obtain women's personal records to achieve discreditation and intimidation" (2000: 227). Hinch discusses how lawyers still manage to introduce evidence of victim's sexual activity despite reform prohibitions (1988: 244). He also highlights how some of the provisions in the Canadian shield law have been found to be unconstitutional. He describes that the proscription of reputation evidence has been ruled unconstitutional as it interferes with the defendant's rights to a "full defense" and "fair trial" (ibid.).

Stereotypes that render some women "illegitimate" rape victims persist in Canada as well (Du Mont and Myhr 2000; Hinch 1988; Yurchesyn, Keith, and Renner 1995). Du Mont and Myhr conclude that "negative stereotypes and false beliefs about women who have been raped" persist despite reform law in Canada (2000: 1130). Hinch reports that victim precipitation continues to hold sway (1988: 243). He also notes that justice officials still disdain victims who drink, those who have had sex in the past, those who hitchhike, and those who come from lower/working classes (245–247).

Hinch catalogs a number of other reform disappointments in the Canadian context. Victims suffer at the hands of the police in Canada in a couple of ways. First, victims who either refuse or fail polygraphs find their charges dismissed (Hinch 1988: 241). The second injustice is novel—and atrocious. Several victims police disbelieved, who had been drinking and who reported rape, ran into not just the unfounding of charges but criminal charges against themselves. Hinch found that police charged these victims with "being drunk in public" (246). He remarks that "the implication is that being victimized while intoxicated does not constitute legal victimization, and unconsented sexual touching while intoxicated does not constitute violation of the law. Only the act of being intoxicated in a public place is illegal"(246).

The other set of problems that Hinch enumerates boils down to difficulties with sexual assault versus rape definitions. Hinch states that using the term "sexual assault" instead of rape has been problematic in Canada because this practice downgrades the seriousness of rape. He expounds that police and prosecutors constitute the front line in defining what sexual assault will mean. They do the defining by the decisions they make about pursuing cases (1988: 241–242). And the cases that police and prosecutors follow through on turn out to be the stereotypical aggravated rapes, ignoring all the while the kinds of rape that are more common though unsanctified in cliché. No change in the characteristics of the cases that are charged, prosecuted, and ultimately convicted materialized in Hinch's inquiry. Male-driven definitions construct the nature of the legal definitions of sexual assault, which are misleadingly biased and inaccurate in relation to what occurs, and that should be legally recognized.

Avenues for and Attitudes About Victims | **FOUR**

OTHER AVENUES FOR VICTIMS

Interrogating the effects of the developments described on rape victims, rather than on the criminal legal system, reveals, once again, mixed results. There have been some improvements; however, some of the initiatives have had no demonstrable impact on victims directly or on attitudes about them.

Civil Suits

While monetary compensation and restitution can help rape victims heal and get on with their lives, civil suits are not a very realistic option in the majority of cases. First, assailants often do not typically have many assets, so it's not often worth going through a civil proceeding. Further, victims may not have the necessary assets to hire attorneys. Additionally, victims and offenders may often be related, making civil suits an untenable option. Still further, victims may not want to face the rapist again or relive the rape as proceedings drag on. Yet more, victims do not want to be interrogated about past sexual relationships and activities, which is an allowable practice in civil court. It is significant to note that victims generally sue only as a last recourse (Bohmer and Parrot 1993: 161). This is because of the unlikely returns and excessive costs.[1]

And civil suits suffer from more than their failure as an option for rape victims. Defendants, too, can sue. They can sue, and increasingly have done so, for defamation of character, libel, and/or slander because of rape accusations. They intimidate victims out of proceeding with suits, threatening to smear the victim's name and reputation in public. Bohmer and Parrot point further to defendant suits for "abuse of legal process" and "intentional infliction of emotional stress" (1993: 144, 157). Bohmer and Parrot also describe how fraternities have turned the tables and become plaintiffs, suing universities for violations of due process in the handling a rape complaint (157–156).

Alternative avenues to the criminal justice system, particularly in the case of college students, are worth singling out. Students who are sexual assault victims can use university mechanisms for redress. Yet these avenues are also extremely limited. The university may expel or suspend assailants, which may help the victim feel safer on campus for a brief time and perhaps yield some sense of justice being served. These outcomes, however, are not only limited but, in fact, rare. The most recent case at the University of Colorado yields ample evidence of what many would see as patterned rape (by university-sponsored athletics) that still winds up blaming victims, getting rationalized away, and eventually being dismissed. Federal-level appeals are planned to challenge that the University of Colorado was legally responsible for the rapes that occurred there. Even though the university recognized or admitted that rapes took place on university property, it is arguing for a reversal of opinion, contesting that it was not in the purview of the university's responsibility to prevent the rapes (Vaughan, Ensslin, and Abbott 2005: 1). Bohmer and Parrot (1993) and Reeves Sanday (1996) talk in this regard about how even the isolated successful cases are often overturned on appeal.

Federal Law: The Violence Against Women Act

Many of VAWA's specific provisions open up actual new roads for redressing the violent victimization of women. The expansive reach of VAWA's coverage, spanning federal, state, and local, ranging from criminal to civil, and involving the allocation of hundreds of millions of dollars in funds for services, programs, and personnel training, stands as a significant gain for women. Congress recommitted to such activities when it "reauthorized the VAWA in October of 2000, ensuring that the grant programs will continue" (Valente et al. 2001: 300). Because monies are still being allocated and because of the rest of VAWA's provisions, there are other advantages to VAWA as well. For instance, VAWA's financial support for gathering and publishing nationwide statistics and ongoing research helps to prove that violence against women is neither isolated, nor infrequent, nor only a women's issue. Additionally, training criminal justice personnel, mounting programs, and funding hotlines, crisis centers, and domestic violence shelters should all be commended for the relief they concretely give violently victimized women.

A line of resistance, however, that inevitably arises with any governmental act, program, bill, or the like concerns money. Dollars usually jump-start critical attention, and there have been alarms about the $1 to $2 billion allocations over the years since the 1994 Violence Against Women Act went into effect (projected in Frazee et al. 1995 and U.S. Senate 1993: 68–72).[2] Yet the dollar amounts are actually relatively small in comparison to other governmental expenditures. The federal government, for instance, spends approximately $400 billion on defense (Eitzen and Baca Zinn 1997: 455, 458), and this before wartime budgets under President George W. Bush. Nonetheless, VAWA's allocations have been controversial, giving rise to the in-fighting that these tight fiscal times engender. And it should be highlighted that domestic violence receives the lion's share of attention and resources in the VAWA, with sexual assault receiving less than 10 percent of the funds (Miller and Meloy forthcoming: 266).

Perhaps the greatest amount of controversy surrounding the VAWA, however, relates to the provision making domestic violence, sexual assault, and stalking into federal crimes, deeming them to violate civil rights protections, because of gender animus; in other words, making such offenses crimes of gender bias, or hate crimes. This would have allowed women to sue for damages in federal court for crimes of discrimination. When this was passed it was heralded. As Frazee and coauthors have commented, "along with the Civil Rights Act of 1964 and the Americans with Disabilities Act, the Violence Against Women Act stands as one of this country's greatest civil-rights achievements" (1995: 42). To declare acts of violence against women to be against federal civil rights law is momentous. It gives stature and seriousness to woman abuse. Or, as Senator Biden put it, this "elevates such offenses to a more visible, 'first-class' status and thereby may provide the impetus to reverse a currently unacceptable situation" (1995: 101). Biden goes on to say that this act begins reversing a culture that "normalizes rape as the mistakes of errant youth or negligent men" (103). MacKinnon comments that this behavior is now "called in law what it is in life: sex discrimination" (1991: E5).

It turns out, though, that all this was too good to be true. In *U.S. v. Morrison et al.* (529 U.S. 598) in May 2000, the Supreme Court ruled that the civil rights remedy of the VAWA was unconstitutional (Valente et al. 2001: 299). The argument was that this part of the federal VAWA legislation stepped on states' rights in an exercise of federal power beyond that granted in the U.S. Constitution, because the jurisdictional basis for the provision was that the violent victimization of women substantially affected interstate commerce. Rape and domestic violence are state-level crimes unless it can be established that they sufficiently impact interstate commerce. Advocates marshaled evidence to show how violence against women affects women's earning abilities, their abilities to raise a family, state welfare services and costs, medical care and the delivery of other services, and more. These dimensions were all shown to have connections to governments, both state and federal, and all these agencies, services, and funds were shown to affect interstate commerce, thus violence against women was found to fall under the jurisdiction of the federal government. This obviously was not compelling enough, as the court overruled the provision, finding that a national economic impact is not the same as having a substantial effect on interstate commerce, which would have had to be established for the act to be based on the exercise of the commerce clause powers, and so it was found that the provision did not fall within federal powers under the Fourteenth Amendment.

The original precedent-setting case that undercut the VAWA provision for the federal-level civil rights remedy was *Brzonkala v. Virginia Polytechnic and State University* (from the Western District Court of Virginia within the Fourth U.S. Circuit Court of Appeals). The case included a claim filed under the VAWA federal protection against gender-motivated crimes involved the rape of Christy Brzonkala. Brzonkala was a student at Virginia Polytechnic and State University who was raped by two male students in a dorm while a third male student looked on. Only one of the students, Morrison, was found guilty under the university's sexual assault policy. The school suspended him, but the suspension was retracted upon appeal. Christy filed suit in federal court under the VAWA. The seven-to-four ruling by the Fourth Circuit Court of Appeals in *Brzonkala v. Virginia Polytechnic and State University*, which the Supreme Court affirmed, was that the VAWA was unconstitutional. The Supreme Court decided that Congress had overstepped its bounds, that violence against women was not appropriately an interstate commerce issue and hence not a federal issue, thus defining a federal remedy for the lack of equal treatment of violence against women and men in state courts was improper (Tracey 2000: 53–61).[3]

There are other problems with the VAWA. First, there are extremely few instances where the new provisions apply. The federal system designed to deal with federal crimes in federal courts and winding up in federal prisons constitutes less than 10 percent of the criminal caseload. The VAWA does nothing to change this. Second, only a tiny minority of rape and domestic violence cases actually get as far as criminal courts; incredibly few are tried in federal courts, as violations under federal statutes, because such cases would have to have federal jurisdictional facts, involving, for example, interstate crimes, where victims are taken across state lines; kidnapping along with rape or battering violence; or rape or battering on federal lands or in federal prisons. Moreover, the only real provisions in the VAWA of relevance here are the increased federal penalties for repeat rape offenders charged in the federal system and the provision for inter-state enforcement of protection orders in domestic violence cases. The notion that crimes are "spruced up" (Gutmann 1993: 44) or made "first class" (Biden 1995: 103) is just window dressing rather than reality or, better yet, just ideologi-cal "gerrymandering" (Woolgar and Pawluch 1985).

An additional problematic aspect of the VAWA concerning criminal charges is that the act uses the term "sex crime" when referring to rape. This is problem-atic, as previously denoted, for a variety of reasons, for example, sex crimes carry a connotation of consent and myths of false accusation. Suffice it to note here that it is sadly ironic that a federal act recognizing the violence against women overstates the sex in its referent, which undercuts said violence.

One further issue deserves highlighting. This relates to the Subtitle A "Safe Streets" section of the VAWA (which allocates grants to improve secu-rity, lighting, and so forth on public transportation and in national parks). The problem is that this neglects the location of the majority of rapes and domestic violence: in the private homes of citizens. While Subtitle B specifically targets "Safe Homes for Women," this is strictly in reference to domestic violence. This means that private residences, where the majority of all rapes occur, are neglected and that the atypical "real" (see Estrich 1987) or "classic" stranger-out-of-the-bushes rape is reified as all rape, or the only true rape. The danger on public transportation or in national parks or crossing state lines or on fed-eral lands or on Native American reservations that the act encompasses pales (the number here is so nominal that it is hard to find) in comparison even to other "stranger" rapes.

VICTIMS' RIGHTS

The importance of the development of rights for crime victims cannot be gain-said. Witnesses have historically been nothing more than witnesses for the pros-ecution. The rights to be treated respectfully; to be aware of the processes going on in a case; to have a voice in terms of the financial and emotional costs of victimization, preferences for outcomes, and so on are all simply decent measures in any civilized society.

The downside of the victims' rights movement and its repercussions for initiatives addressing violence against women, however, can be grave. Perhaps the greatest problem with the victims' rights movement in the U.S. context is that it has developed at the expense of the rights of the accused. Although this need not necessarily be the case, it has been. Partly because of two decades and more of "get tough" crime policy and the wars declared on crime (and especially drugs) in the United States, granting crime victims more rights has meant greater punitiveness for criminal offenders. Given that the United States maintains its infamy as one of the most punitive modern-day societies, if not the most punitive (Currie 1985; Walker 2004), increasing criminal justice sanctioning makes for neither effectiveness nor justice.

COMMUNITY REGISTRATION AND NOTIFICATION

Community registration and notification laws are similarly beset with problems. They have the obvious advantage of keeping track of offenders and letting communities know about rapists in their midst, but the drawbacks must be recognized. Some of the most salient issues concern the tracking, labeling, and extrication of offenders from society for the entirety of their lives. These lifetime sanctions are being imposed on people who have already served the full sentences determined by legislatures, courts, and correctional officials. And offenders can be as young as thirteen or fourteen when this lifetime stigma is imposed. Just as other victims' rights campaigns have been tied to a retribution movement in the United States, community registration and notification laws have been carried out in a fervor to punish, punish, and then punish some more. Furthermore, community notification often strips people who have served their time of any possibility of rehabilitation and reintegration into the communities where they reside. The legal changes themselves, however, are more symbolic measures than effective remedies, enacted for advantage in political maneuvering. Quick-fix measures, like Megan's Law, are far from panaceas, yet they give the appearance of expedient and effective solutions to social issues. Politicians benefit from being allegedly responsive to public concerns, an accolade often gained from their own grandstanding and/or saturated media coverage of specific (and often atypical) cases (like Megan Kanga's).

Another salient reason that community protection laws offer safeguards more illusory than real is that some criminals fail to file/register while others move to different communities, and an overloaded system cannot track or catch them. Furthermore, such policies are tied to the myth of stranger danger. The vast majority of all rapes and sexual assaults involve people who know one another. Further, upward of three-quarters of the assailants in child sexual assaults are family members and relatives (Steinbock 1995: 5). Needless to say, making known the identity of family or relative abusers already known to victims does not contribute much in the way of protection.

EXTRALEGAL DEVELOPMENTS

The spread of crisis centers across the nation has been a godsend for victims. The real failure here is lack of funding and personnel, as the need so outstrips the capability of service delivery. The development of task forces has been an important grassroots force generating awareness, recommendations, and even policies at local levels to help ameliorate problems in rape victimization.

Another type of extralegal development previously mentioned is the introduction of rape evidence kits. The only real downside here is that the system cannot keep up with the analysis of the kits once hospitals have collected them. In fact, Congress passed a bill in 2000 designed to address the horrific backlog of rape evidence kits that have been collected. Despite this, many thousands of victim kits continue to go unanalyzed. The DNA Analysis Backlog Elimination Act (PL 106-546) provided states and localities $125 million over a four-year period for the analysis of rape evidence kits (A. Weiner 2008). Similar measures are being considered to extend the scope of and monies for evidence collection (Rape, Abuse and Incest National Network 2008; Seghetti 2006).

In-service training for police and justice personnel has been a positive extralegal development from the point of view of promoting awareness of the dynamics of rape and the logistics of reforms for practitioners. The degree to which such education becomes internalized by individual actors can be evidenced in the beliefs and attitudes about rape.

ATTITUDES ABOUT VICTIMS

Innumerable measures could be discussed for their ability to improve the plight of women who suffer sexual violence. Perhaps chief among these are measures designed to change beliefs about rape and about women. The reason attitudes are so fundamental is that it is precisely beliefs that always have been, and always will be, tied to how the law, the criminal justice system, and social communities treat the crimes of sexual violence and the women victimized by these crimes.

Criminal Justice Attitudes

Two major pieces of research have directly asked criminal justice personnel about their views on rape reforms. The first was a survey of attitudes that Marsh, Geist, and Caplan undertook in the early 1980s.[4] What they reported from their survey can be characterized as ambivalence. Marsh and her colleagues noted that traditional, prejudicial beliefs about the crime of rape and its female victims persisted, albeit to a lesser extent, after reforms in Michigan. They unraveled that while beliefs about the importance of unique requirements like corroboration, resistance, and past sexual activity basically did not waver in the pre- to postreform eras, prosecutors, judges, and defense attorneys placed less priority on these dimensions after Michigan's CSC Code became law. As for the criminal justice actors' beliefs in rape myths about false accusations, victim provocation, and so on, similar patterns ensued. Marsh, Geist, and Caplan (1982) report that the derogatory beliefs that rape victims fabricate charges of rape, that they are to be blamed for bringing about their own rape, that they desire and consent to rape, and so forth were all in evidence in the survey of attitudes after reforms had been implemented. Such beliefs were less prominent, however, or at least less frequently noted in the postreform, as opposed to prereform, period. Other research in the model state of Michigan, while not directly surveying criminal justice personnel, is worth mentioning for the similarity in results. This research examined police reports and court transcripts and found that while culpability was attributed to some rape victims for such things as going to bars, being out alone at night, and dressing too sexily, this was characteristic of a minority of the cases (Caringella-MacDonald 1988). Further, notions like these about victim precipitation did not exert a significant influence on prosecutorial charging and plea-bargaining decisions (ibid.). This is notable progress.

The second major piece of research directly assessing criminal justice attitudes about rape reform was conducted by Spohn and Horney and reported ten years later (1992) than the Marsh, Geist, and Caplan study. These findings were similarly mixed. Spohn and Horney found that officials still thought resistance and corroboration were important in the aftermath of reforms, even in the strongest reform jurisdiction in Michigan (Detroit). It is interesting to note that officials thought these factors were decisive for juries, which may help to understand the low conviction rate associated with jury trials in Detroit in the postreform period (129). Spohn and Horney also found that despite shield legislation, past sexual relationships between victims and offenders were believed relevant even in the strong reform states of Michigan, Illinois, and Pennsylvania. They conclude that past sex between the victim and the offender was not only likely to be admitted but routinely accepted and unquestioned as indicative of consent (159–160). Victim promptness in reporting crimes was also accepted as relevant by criminal justice personnel and taken as corroborative of charges (115), without any question or thought about its validity as an indicator of rape.

Spohn and Horney's research findings can be characterized as negative or as indicating the failure of reforms, however, simultaneous with the negative findings stands an overall positive result. Spohn and Horney articulate the ambivalence in the following manner. They assess that "judges, prosecutors, and defense attorneys in all of the jurisdictions expressed support for the reforms, which they believe have improved the treatment of rape victims" (159). Countering this, of course, is the finding that reforms had "little impact on the way criminal justice officials evaluate rape cases" (115).

Although Spears and Spohn's (1997) research did not directly ask about officials' attitudes, their follow-up analysis of the subsample of cases in the reform jurisdiction of Detroit is worth noting for, once again, the continuity in results as to the spirit and body of attitudinal reform. What they found was that victim behavior, character, credibility, and promptness in filing charges were all relevant to the prosecutorial charging decision. This finding is punctuated by their evaluation that showed this to be true "regardless of the strength of evidence in the case or whether the crime was classified as an aggravated or simple sexual assault" (501).

Public Attitudes

Carole Goldberg-Ambrose summarized the empirical work on rape reforms and attitudes about rape. She neatly recapitulates that some researchers believe "the changes have thwarted feminist goals; others have found little impact on case processing or victims' experiences; still others have pronounced the reform efforts a success" (1992: 173). This, of course, is precisely what I have so carefully detailed in the chapters so far. What Goldberg-Ambrose concludes is that the greatest force undercutting the success of rape reform laws is attitudes. She states, "There are many obstacles to measuring and achieving rape reform, the most notable being the need to eliminate juror misconceptions about rape and its victims" (ibid.). While there are some indications of improvement in public attitudes, which translates into improvement in juror attitudes, lay, public, juror, and criminal justice attitudes all remain problematic, to say the least.

The opening quotation from a Queens County (New York) district attorney in Hecht Schafran's article about jurors and rape is illustrative of just how awful public attitudes can be: "In March, 1992 police in Queens, New York, arrested a man in the act of raping a 61-year-old homeless woman. The grand jury wanted to know why she was outdoors at two in the morning" (1992: 26). The false beliefs about the crime of rape, about rape victims, and about rape offenders are vast.[5] Succinctly put, the extant research shows an overwhelmingly consistent pattern of people in general believing in rape myths. As Allison and Wrightsman (1993) delineate, women are believed to be responsible for their rape (e.g., to precipitate it or not to resist enough) and to lie about having been raped (whereas instead they wanted and consented to the sex acts), while offenders are believed simply to be motivated by sex drives, acting on normal needs and urges, or mentally deranged. In sum, then, the interpretation that rape reform efforts have failed to rehabilitate public attitudes is inescapable.

The Media

The media must be mentioned in any examination of attitudes in modern-day society, because they are so influential in attitude formation and attitude change. There is a reciprocal relationship between the construction or production of news and other coverage about a given phenomenon, such as rape or sexual assault, and the consumption of media-generated images and stories about that phenomenon. In other words, both the media and the public influence one another, where consumer appeal drives media representations, while media reproductions influence the public's views. Whether the chicken or the egg comes first is less important than recognizing the mutual nature of this influence.

The research on the media and rape typically centers on the nature of depictions of specific rape cases, for example, that of New York Central Park jogger or that of Kennedy Smith, and whether these depictions are sympathetic or antagonistic to rape myths. And just as was the case with the implementation of reforms and with the criminal justice and lay attitudes about rape and reforms, there is evidence of both progress and entrenchment along the lines of victim-blaming/offender-exculpating rape mythology. While media accounts both reinforce and rebut discriminatory beliefs about men and women and rape (see, e.g., Benedict 1992; Caringella-MacDonald 1998; Chancer 1997, 1998; Cuklanz 1996; Fineman and McCluskey 1997),[6] the cases garnering the most attention remain the unusual "stranger danger" gang-rape cases. And questions about victim credibility, consent, lies, and so on are inserted even with rapes all would consider the most vile, for example, the New York Central Park jogger who was left for dead, the Glen Ridge gang rape of a girl with a mental age of eight, and the alleged victim in a Duke University gang rape, where the alleged assailants wrote racist and sexist e-mails that, among other things, boasted about plans to skin some strippers.

FAILURES AND SUCCESSES: A RECAPITULATION

The question is, what do we end up with after all this reform activity and dedicated energy to combat the problems of processing rape through the criminal justice system? On the one hand, success has materialized, for some victims, in some jurisdictions, on some charges. Many observers and researchers have concluded that victims are no longer twice traumatized, at least to the same degree that characterized the past. This success has been attributed variously to the influx of women into the criminal justice system; the establishment of training and specialized units in police, prosecutorial, judicial, and medical offices (Gregory and Lees 1999); educational campaigns; the shield prohibitions and other provisions in reforms (as discussed at length here); the support and advocacy of crisis lines; sexual assault centers; evidence kits; and victim confidentiality provisos.

Make no mistake: gains have been achieved by the legislative reforms, educative strategies, watchdog groups, and so forth. It is just that successes have been partial and ushered in so incompletely. And, unfortunately, ultimately the weight of the evidence falls on the side of failure. A summary of the results yields qualification after qualification: Although requirements may have been diluted and appear not to be relied on to the same extent as in the past, the unique requirements are still relevant. Although there have been some increases in rates of reports, arrests, prosecution, conviction, and punishment, they have not often been systematically achieved or of consequential proportion. Although increases have been evidenced, they pertain only to the most heinous "real" rapes. Although some comparability has been found between the treatment of rape and sexual assault and other crimes of violence and assault, lack of parity still looms large. Although new degree structures and definitions have been put in place, they have not corrected for historic problems. Although there is a modicum of change in some beliefs in some areas, it appears that criminal justice, lay public, and media attitudes have not widely or fundamentally changed. Attributions about victim consent, character, lies, and the like continue to crop up, albeit in some jurisdictions, at some stages, and by some personnel perhaps less often or with less vehemence than was true before reforms, these myths persist in coloring discretionary decision making in the legal processing of rape and continue to keep fairness and justice out of reach in many cases, for many victims.

So, it winds up that only the strongest cases, with the most evidence, with characteristics that meet the old requirements, that fit the stereotype of stranger-out-of-the-bushes ("real") ambush (and yet infrequent) rape, that most often end up in conviction. And yet still, even in cases like these (for example, the New Bedford pool table gang rape, where patrons of the "Big Dan's" bar hooted and cheered the gang of rapists to rape the victim more and more, and the Central Park jogger), the media speculates about victims' consent, past sexual histories, and contributory responsibility because of behaviors like dancing or drinking or jogging after dark and persists in painting these as focal features. And the magnitude of victim blaming in the acquaintance rape cases that get publicity speaks to the tenacious power of rape myths. For instance, in the Kobe Bryant case the victim's sexual history (before and after the rape) and mental state were drawn out to raise questions about false accusation, lies, consent, character, and so forth. In the Duke University lacrosse team alleged gang rape, the victim's job as an exotic dancer was used to disenfranchise victimization: to mean that she couldn't have been raped, that she probably consented, that she falsely accused the team members and more. In fact, women at the college donned "Innocent Until Proven Guilty" T-shirts and baseball caps to show their support for their classmates accused of raping a "dancer."[7]

There are a variety of approaches to rape law. They can be grouped together based on commonalities. The first set of similar laws in the typology I develop starts with the historic laws on rape that predate reforms. These are framed by patriarchy and male entitlement. The legal reform measures are a second type of rape law. The radical models (such as strict liability and affirmative consent) that have been proposed and even enacted in a rare jurisdiction or two constitute a third framework of rape law. It is worth repeating that while this third type provides important insights, the radical models tend to be more theoretical than practical, that is, too removed from public and political opinion to be viable. I envision a futuristic model as a fourth type of rape law, one I develop in the subsequent chapters of this book, which is designed to build on reform successes and redress some of the problems that have emerged with the diversity of approaches to the legal processing of rape, in both theoretical and practical terms.

The range in law is from noticeably misogynistic, to sexist, to feminist. Patriarchy defines one end on the continuum, chronologically moving from a complete absence of laws prohibiting rape, through carnal knowledge statutes, on to early (liberal) rape reform legislation, and eventually into more radical negligence, strict liability and (three different kinds of) affirmative consent models. Different kinds of feminism inform the models from early rape reform laws through the affirmative consent paradigms. The model I put forward is situated in the feminist range, but not at the extreme end. It is more middle ground, seeking to compensate for the overprotection of men and the underprotection of women in rape law and policy while not going so far as to write out constitutional rights for men accused of rape or deny the sexual agency of any/all women. My proposed model additionally is also devised to be practical, not just theoretical, so as to be tenable in the politics and practices of criminal justice in the twenty-first century. Some would characterize my work as a "feminist left realist" position (Walter DeKeseredy, personal communication, 2007).

PATRIARCHY AS CONTEXT

The continuum begins with historic patriarchal culture and attitudes that eventually made their way into carnal knowledge laws on rape (recall the definition of the crime here as vaginal penetration of a female by the penis of a man not her husband, forcibly and against her will). By and large, men have historically assumed that they can have sex with women whenever they choose. I conceptualize this kind of belief, and the behavior that emanates from it, to be comprised of three related types of sexist notions. The oldest belief is a presumption of entitlement, the second a belief or presumption of women's desire, and the third a notion about women asking for and/or deserving the forced and often violent sex of rape. These stances do not accommodate the possibility of women's nonagreement to sex. Nonconsent, in fact, is completely overlooked until it becomes focal in the legal layering imposed by carnal knowledge law's resistance requirements and consent standards.

Entitlement, or the righteously held prerogative to free and full access to a woman's body, is observed in the male belief in the right to have sex and to use force and violence in order to do so, whenever and wherever a man has the urge. The extreme end of this kind of belief is seen in the rape of conquered peoples, such as that witnessed in colonization, war, and genocide. And this is not a belief that lies dormant in antiquity. The tragedy is that there are readily available contemporary instances of such entitlement across the globe, for example, in Bosnia-Herzegovina, Rwanda, and the Sudan. What is more, the belief is more prevalent than these extreme or narrow examples would imply. The ascendancy of a male right to female bodies is found in the practice of "bride capture"(Brownmiller 1975: 7). In Brownmiller's classic articulation, "The earliest form of permanent, protective conjugal relationship, the accommodation called mating that we now know as marriage, appears to have been institutionalized by the male's forcible abduction and rape of the female. No quaint formality, bride capture, as it came to be known, was a very real struggle: a man took title to a female, staked a claim to her body, as it were, by an act of violence. Forcible seizure was a perfectly acceptable way—to men—of acquiring women, and it existed in England as late as the 15th century" (7).

The notion of men's entitlement to rape women, and the corollary conceptualization of women as chattel or property belonging to men, has been commonplace in relation to wives and prostitutes and across times and places in relation even to one's own children. It is this historic stance of male license that beckons males to develop and lasciviously indulge their appetites for sex, aggression, violence, power, and control.

A second dimension of belief pertaining to male right and reign over female bodies was further expanded by interpretations that rendered resistance to sexual advances, better said, to hostile sexual takeover, as nothing more than coy invitations to sex or polite cover-ups of "true" desire and consent. Women's resistance is taken as either put up for the sake of appearances or only initially genuine. The notion that rape fulfills women's fantasies to be conquered, taken, or dominated by men is similar to the erroneous beliefs about consent and token resistance. This rationalizes rape, serving to further male sexual entitlement.

This attitude may grow so strong as to morph into a third kind of premise. The subsequent belief is that a woman asks for or deserves the sex forced on her (as opposed to acquiescing to sex). That a woman was drinking, dating, dancing, flirting, or even (just) talking with a man may be cited as justification for rape. The belief is that if a female dates a male, or drinks with one, she is tacitly accepting sex with that man. The belief feeds further into a belief that if a woman desires and consents to any male's sexual overtures, she is more likely to consent to any other male. Belief that a woman desires and consents to male overtures because she has acquiesced to interacting with a specific male is also tied to rape mythology about how women succumb to desire once sex has begun to be compelled. Victim blaming of this nature is a particularly pungent form of the belief in the male right of sexual access, and the corollary rationalization of nonconsent.

A man's liberty, indeed right, to take sex in any way he so chooses persists across the globe even today, as do the supporting premises about rape victim desire, token resistance, and provocation. All these perspectives leave the fundamental issue of women's consent out of the equation. They reveal a complete and cavalier disdain for women's voluntariness, willingness, agreement, or consent. The operative assumption underlying such beliefs is that women want or agree to any and all male sexual acts, even if violently forced on them.

Carnal knowledge statutes reflect and perpetuate all these misogynistic notions. These are epitomized in the corroboration, resistance, and consent standards, past sexual history admissibility, cautionary juror instructions, and so on that exist in various de jure and de facto law today.

The eventual historic route that directly addressed the issue of a female's consent in law centered on requirements for victims' resistance. To recapitulate, resistance has been relied on to demonstrate force, and the presence of force has been required to indicate the lack of consent. The lack of consent in turn has been required in order to show that the resisted, forced, nonconsensual sex against a woman was against her will (according to carnal knowledge statutes). Yet more, resistance to the utmost, throughout the entire duration of an attack, was established as the bar to prove the existence of force and hence the nonconsent of a female. Such standards are unattainable, especially because of differences in males and females: size; strength; gendered socialization about ability, power, passivity, and so forth; the state of mind while being violently, sexually attacked; and male interpretations that conveniently view almost all female resistance as token. Given this, we might be able to begin to understand how men may construe even strong physical resistance as consent. Naturally, if forceful resistance is mangled into consent, it becomes possible to see how mere screaming, running, verbal protestation (saying no), and silent submission can be twisted into evidence of desire by men. In fact, silence or even saying no is not just deemed insufficient but taken as longing for even the most brutal, violent sexual attacks committed by men.

The requirement of resistance can be understood as a requirement that a verbal no must be accompanied by some sort of physical expression of no in order to prove nonconsent. But clearly throughout the history of court cases and legal processing this has not been enough, either. Even the most vigorous forms of resistance, should they cease before the consummation of the act(s) or fall below what a court determines to be "utmost" fight and struggle, are viewed as insufficient expressions of lack of desire or nonconsent. The convoluted logic that resistance is needed to show force, that force is needed to show nonconsent, that nonconsent is needed to show the act(s) were "against her will," and that all this is necessary in order to evince the crime of rape demonstrates how exorbitant the law has been in protecting the types of male entitlement and rationalizations I have just laid out.

ESTABLISHING ELEMENTS OF RAPE:
NONCONSENT, FORCE/COERCION, AND INTENT

The elements of the crime of rape that must typically be proven in order to sustain a rape conviction are the fact of sexual penetration (or contact in sexual assault offenses), the identity of the accused, the presence of nonconsent, and the existence of aggravating circumstance(s) and/or force and/or coercion. Historically, victim resistance also had to be proven, corroborative evidence had to be shown to substantiate a victim's claims, and the victim had to file a "prompt" report of the incident with the police.

Legal scholar Susan Estrich (1987) reports that in defining the crimes of rape and sexual assault, states do not specify that criminal intent, or mens rea (guilty mind), on the part of the accused must be proved. Yet this is customary for other criminal offenses. Estrich notes that the role of intent in rape is virtually nonexistent in the context of the United States. She draws examples from several states (Maine, Pennsylvania, South Dakota, and Massachusetts; see 94–95) to show that some "recent American cases have gone so far as to say explicitly that there is no intent requirement at all for rape.... The Maine Supreme Judicial Court ... and the legislature ... by making no reference to a culpable state of mind for rape, clearly indicated that rape compelled by force or threat requires no culpable state of mind"(94). She continues, "while the matter of the requisite intent for rape was hotly debated in England and Commonwealth countries, it was barely mentioned in American cases. In the older opinion there is some discussion of intent with respect to attempted rape—where the essence of the crime is criminal intent. But in completed rapes, questions of intent or mistake are rarely even mentioned" (94). Instead of intent, states specify nonconsent as an element of the crimes of rape and sexual assault. Consent, or its lack, is rarely defined, however.

Estrich expands on why intent is absent in rape law. She explains how consent, judged in light of force and resistance (as previously described), provides an easier way to protect male interests than does raising the issue of intent in rape cases. Her reasoning is that arguing that a defendant did not intend to rape would be ludicrous in "real rape," that is, stranger-out-of-the-bushes aggravated rape, where less doubt as to consent adheres. The argument would need to be that consent was mistaken and hence that defendant's intent was absent, but this would be difficult to show. This leaves intent as a ploy for the more ambiguous cases, where force, nonconsent, or resistance is harder to show. Only in the desperate or "utterly hopeless on the issues of actual consent, or resistance or force" (95) cases would the defense try to win an acquittal by arguing that the defendant didn't intend to rape the female, that is, that the defendant mistook consent, which nullifies criminal intent (see "The Mistaken Consent Defense," later in this chapter). Because lack of intent is so far-fetched with aggravated, "real" rape, and because of "the doctrines of consent, defined as non-resistance, and force, measured by resistance" (95) are an easier way to protect men from rape charges than is attempting to negate intent with consent in ambiguous (or "real rape," for that matter) circumstances, the issue of intent in rape is submerged. Another way to look at this is that it is easier to defend against rape with such arguments as "she consented," or "he didn't use force," or "force cannot be demonstrated," or "she didn't resist," or "resistance cannot be demonstrated" than it is to defend by means of arguing a lack of intent.

Estrich goes on to elaborate on the problems with replacing intent with consent in rape cases. Not only are such defenses easier and potentially more effective for men, they are further unfair to females in several additional regards. "First, it means that the trial focuses almost entirely on the woman, not the man. Her intent, not his, is disputed. And since her state of mind is key, her sexual history may be considered relevant, even though utterly unknown to him.... Second, the issue to be determined is not whether the man is a rapist, but whether the woman was raped.... Third, the resistance requirement is an over broad substitute for intent. Both can be used to enforce a male perspective on the crime.... [It] requires women to risk injury to themselves in cases where there is no doubt as to man's knowledge or his blameworthiness" (96).

STRICT LIABILITY

Intent is nowhere as clearly irrelevant as under the strict liability doctrine. Here criminal culpability (or responsibility) is rigidly, or incontestably, construed under particular crime circumstances, with no exceptions whatsoever. Criminal responsibility is automatically affixed to actors who engage in certain acts, with no regard for mens rea, criminal intent, premeditation, guilty mind, consciousness of guilt, recklessness, negligence, prior knowledge, or even the severity of the act or its consequences. Strict liability for certain kinds of rape or sexual assault means that consent, whether present or not, whether mistaken or not, whether reasonably believed or not, is never relevant. Therefore consent is never available or allowed as a defense to rape charges where strict liability obtains. This is because the male would be culpable, whether or not he (or anyone else) meant to or knew that he did anything wrong or against the law. The sex acts are unequivocally criminal, regardless of what the female wanted, said, or did; in other words, rape occurred regardless of the woman's consent or the man's honest, or genuine, or reasonable, or unreasonable belief about consent. A commonly understood application of strict liability and criminal responsibility is statutory rape, where the male is criminally culpable strictly because of the female's age, regardless of other factors, no matter what she said, whether she lied, or what he—or other reasonable people—might have thought under the circumstances. Alternatively put, with statutory rape, nothing—not even consent—can vitiate criminal responsibility.[1]

Another illustration of strict liability in responsibility for rape can be seen in statute provisions that criminalize sex act(s) with unconscious victim(s), implicitly recognizing the lack of ability of victims to consent to sex act(s) while unconscious. This prohibition is as old as statutory rape (Schulhofer 1998: 18). Another example is found in statutes that criminalize sex with mentally retarded persons under any circumstances, similarly because of the view that retarded persons are incapable of giving consent.[2]

THE CONSENT DEFENSE AND EARLY REFORM PROBLEMS

It is useful to revisit rape reforms given the context afforded by this chapter. Rape reforms attended to consent, force, and resistance problems by either repealing or relaxing the resistance standard. Recall, some reforms relaxed the requirement by removing the need to show resistance to the utmost and/or through the entire duration of the assault. Other reforms replaced the resistance standard with graduated offenses predicated on objective crime circumstances that were presumptive of force. Different aggravating factors, such as weapons, multiple offenders, and additional injuries (along with higher levels of victim vulnerability, for example, youth or being subordinate to someone in a position of authority) are specified for the various degrees of offenses in the attempt to establish force and nonconsent and eliminate the resistance requirement, thus preventing the defense of consent from perpetually arising in response to rape accusations (Estrich 1987: 85; Bienen 1980: 181; Michigan PA 328). Delineating crime circumstances is a tactic designed to draw the focus away from victim consent and instead place it on the offender's actions and on the conditions surrounding the crime itself, as is typically the case with other crimes.

This, however, did not work, as can be seen in the case of Michigan's model reform. Here consent was overlooked in favor of the emphasis on force, but consent easily crept back in as a defense to any and all circumstances that were supposed to demonstrate the existence of force and therefore nonconsent (Estrich 1987). Michigan, and the state of Washington in following suit, avoided use of the word "consent" to try to get away from all the problematic overtones associated with consent in rape cases (Estrich 1987: 89). But by failing to define the defense of consent or to address it in any way, the defense of consent remains tenable in all degrees of rape in the model state of Michigan.[3]

What this means is that the defense of consent not only can but has been argued under virtually all the elements of the crime. Hence the consent defense and mistakes as to consent (see chap. 11) have remained operative, in practice or in a de facto fashion, and persisted in influencing the judgments of judges and jurors in even the most heinous rape cases. In fact, the defense of consent has succeeded in leading to either acquittals or overturned convictions under such serious conditions as when rape involves weapons or gangs of men. It is in this vein that Estrich describes the case of *People v. Bernard* (360 N.W. 2d 204, 205 [Mich.App. 1984, 85, 90]), where a "Michigan Appeals Court … held that the weapon must actually be in the hands of the one who is committing the criminal sexual act, not held by his accomplice" (1987: 85) in order to sustain a conviction on first- or second-degree CSC (where the weapon constitutes the aggravating condition).

Michigan erred by trying to dodge the issue of victim consent, which allows it to surface and thus remain salient in the minds of judges and juries (Adler 1987; Estrich 1987; Spohn and Horney 1996). In other words, victim consent remains a pivotal issue because judges and juries insist on demonstrations of high levels of force and demonstrations that the victim forcefully said no, either by indicating this behaviorally or at least by protesting with more than a mere verbal no (despite the de jure specification of the lack of a resistance requirement) in order to negate the assertion that victim consented. This shows that there is an acute need to confront directly, rather than skirt, the issue of consent. Sidestepping consent not only allows but now almost demands that the old standards be employed de facto.

A related problem is that reform laws that shift the spotlight from victim resistance to a focus on the accused open a booby trap by raising the question of the relevance of the accused's belief about victim consent. The issue is that courts have interpreted that even if the defendant is dishonest or mistaken, his belief in victim consent can stand as a defense to rape accusations (see the next section in this chapter, as well as chap. 11). Because even the model reform law avoided dealing head-on with consent, and because of the related legal opinion that allows consent to any degree charged (except for statutory rape), and because mistaken consent can be used as a criminal defense, reforms in Michigan, as elsewhere, are still completely riddled with problems for victims and the conviction of rape and sexual assault offenders.

Legal reform could have taken advantage of the open moment in the aftermath of the repeal of resistance requirements, as in Michigan, but failed to do so.

Nonetheless, with resistance requirements gone, and reforms in place that shift focus from victim resistance to offender conduct and crime circumstances, progress could still be made if consent were addressed directly and, perhaps more important, looked at in new ways. Historic practices, as well as new loopholes left open by reforms, could still be closed off, but further changes would need to be made.[4]

THE MISTAKEN CONSENT DEFENSE:
REFORM ESTABLISHING NEGLIGENT RESPONSIBILITY

Chapters 9 and 10 present a detailed discussion of the issue of negligence and criminal culpability; however, a thumbnail sketch about this perspective at this early juncture is necessary to lay out the various legal models fully.

Black's Law Dictionary defines criminal culpability as "blameworthiness…. A person's criminal culpability requires a showing that he acted purposely, knowingly, recklessly or negligently" (Black 1991: 264). It is to the negligent aspect of criminal responsibility that some rape reform scholars turned next.

Susan Estrich's Approach

Susan Estrich (1987) articulates one innovative way to deal with the problems surrounding the issue of consent in rape prosecutions. Zsuzsanna Adler's contribution, *Rape on Trial* (1987), is complementary to this work. Both authors spotlight the problems of consent, especially the defense of mistakes about victims' consent, despite reform efforts. They use their discussion of these problems as a platform to propose ways to redress a myriad of issues surrounding rape prosecution. Adler focuses on the problems stemming from the use of reputation and sexual history evidence, while Estrich features the problems surrounding consent and mistakes of consent in a broader sense (see also Goldberg-Ambrose 1989: 949).

Both scholars discuss the landmark case of *Morgan* (*Director of Public Prosecutions v. Morgan*, [1975] 2 W.L.R. 923 [H.L.]), which was decided in the British courts in 1975. Estrich uses the *Morgan* case to develop her line of thought about how to handle consent in the United States, while Adler's focus is in the British context.

Both Adler and Estrich describe how *Morgan* can be used to fashion an innovative way to conceptualize the issue of negligence in relation to unreasonableness in belief about victim consent in rape prosecution. Their discussion of *Morgan* and a criminal negligence approach to consent defenses can be seen as a type of compromise between the strict liability previously described and the more far-reaching changes embodied in the affirmative consent models that are demarcated in the next chapter.

Adler and Estrich explain that the key issue in *Morgan* was about whether defendants can use mistaken belief in victim consent as a defense against rape accusations. In essence, this case allowed the accused's mistakes about women's consent to vitiate men's culpability for rape. The court found that consent can successfully refute charges of rape, however unreasonable, wrong-headed, "fanciful" (Adler 1987: 1), foolish, or incredible men's (mistaken) belief in consent might be. As Adler summarizes, "the crux of the judgment was that a man cannot be convicted of rape if he genuinely believed that the woman was consenting to sexual intercourse, however fanciful and unreasonable the grounds for this belief" (ibid.).

This case involved four men who were out drinking together and looking for a woman or women with whom to have sex. One of the men invited the others to his home to "have sex" with his wife. He warned that she'd resist but that she liked "sex" this way. The original court convicted the four men. The appellate court (the House of Lords) ruled that the mens' mistaken belief in consent, or their negligence or unreasonableness in interpreting the presence of consent, was not a sufficient basis to deny the charges and absolve the men of criminal responsibility for rape. The House of Lords, while not defining that negligence or unreasonableness, found enough for a determination of guilt for rape and eventually upheld the original convictions of the men, but only because the court deemed that no one (no jury) could honestly or reasonably believe that a wife would give consent to her husband's three drinking buddies, especially since she put up a struggle against the men (Estrich 1987: 93). Instead of addressing negligence in making mistakes, *Morgan* left a dangerous legacy, wherein even unreasonable mistaken belief in consent could be taken to negate intent and successfully absolve men of rape charges. As Kadish and Schulhofer summarize, "in England,... the prosecution must prove that the defendant either knew consent was absent or was willing to proceed 'willy-nilly', not caring whether the victim consents or no" (2001: 358).

Despite the possibility or hope that upholding the convictions in *Morgan* could have left open, in another British case that followed *Morgan*, the case of *Regina v. Cogan* ([1975] 3 W.L.R. 316 [CA]), a conviction was reversed precisely because of the *Morgan* ruling against a negligent liability model for rape. In other words, the court sustained that even unreasonable belief in consent is sufficient to defend against rape accusations successfully. *Cogan* also involved a husband giving "permission" to a friend to have intercourse with—or, put more accurately, to rape—his wife. The husband, a violent man, threatened his wife, penetrated her, and invited his friend to do the same, while the woman was clearly distressed, trying to turn away while sobbing (www.buffalo.edu/law/bclc/web/

ukcogan.htm). In *Cogan*, the court ruled that just because the belief in consent could be deemed to be unreasonable (where a husband "gave" his wife—who was crying in protest—to a friend; see Estrich 1987: 93), the unreasonably taken consent does not make the sex/the case a criminal one involving any offense(s) of rape (Adler 1987: 1–2; Estrich 1987: 92–93).

It is worth restating that these decisions leave open the possibility that if a man believes there was consent, no matter how unreasonable this belief may be, there is no rape. This basically means that a man can mis-TAKE consent whenever he wants and not be held responsible for committing any crime.

As for consent and negligence in interpreting consent in the U.S. context, recall that the intent of the accused is set aside for the relative ease of (successful) defense as to victim (lack of resistance and) consent. In other words, intent is left in abeyance because of the preference for protecting male interests with the rather facile demonstration of the defense of consent. Whether reforms sidestep consent (as Michigan's does) or persist in requiring resistance to demonstrate force and hence nonconsent, problems are obvious for rape victims.

Victims, however, fare better in the United States than across the Atlantic in terms of how/when/what mistakes might mean. By and large, courts have determined that if a man honestly and reasonably (see below) deduces victim consent, that consent can be taken as existent and stand as a defense to rape charges (Kadish and Schulhofer 2001: 358). But if mistakes are unreasonable, they will not typically excuse culpability.

Estrich delves into the details about mistakes by addressing negligent liability. She uses a U.S. case to lay out her view of how negligent liability in mistaking consent should confer criminal culpability. She describes a case involving honest but unreasonable mistakes as to consent. She asserts that not only should unreasonable mistakes be insufficient to exculpate but even honest, unreasonable mistakes should not vitiate criminal responsibility for men charged with rape. The case Estrich cites is from Massachusetts, where an (arguably) honest mistake of consent was nonetheless unreasonable or negligent and should have been sufficient for a finding of guilt and a criminal conviction. Although a conviction wound up being the outcome, the honest-but-unreasonable consideration was not the standard used (although her point is that it could and should have been). The case was *Commonwealth v. Sherry* (Supreme Court of Massachusetts, 386 Mass. 682, 437 N.E. 2d 224 [1982]). Kadish and Schulhofer (2001) provide the details of the case. A nurse went to a doctor's apartment for a party. She was drinking and socializing when she was pushed into a bathroom with another doctor, subsequently pulled by the arms out of the apartment by the host, carried by a third doctor to a car where she was held in the front seat, and driven unwill-

ingly with the host and two other doctors to a summer home owned by one of
trio. Once they arrived, she asked to be taken home but was instead carried into
the house. The woman smoked marijuana with two of the doctors, and then all
four walked around looking at the home. While in one of the bedrooms she was
sexually assaulted. She protested while the doctors undressed her; she protested
and said "no" and "stop" when they each forced intercourse on—raped—her. She
said she didn't resist further because she was numbed by fear. The men thought
she agreed both to going to the cabin and to engaging in the alleged sex. Estrich
describes some details of the case that led the men to think this, for example, the
woman went upstairs to sleep after the "sex" and out to breakfast with the doctors
the next morning on the drive back to town. The victim did consent to the drinking and smoking, acts that typically disenfranchise women from victim status.[5]

Estrich argues that the men's belief about consent was unreasonable, even if
honestly misbelieved. She goes on to note that it was the multiple actors, rather
than the unreasonableness in mistaking consent, that led to the men's conviction
(when, in fact, it should have been the unreasonableness of taking consent as
present that should have proved the legally sufficient basis for conviction).

Estrich's ultimate recommendation is that in cases like *Morgan*, *Cogan*, and
Sherry, the unreasonableness of mistakes should be seen as negligence, and negligence should bestow, not vitiate, criminal responsibility for rape. A woman's
struggle or simple verbal protestations should be enough to make it clear that
she does not consent, and this makes belief in consent unreasonable, which is
negligent on the part of the man and therefore criminal; this should be sufficient
for sustaining conviction for rape.

Critical Appraisal

Estrich's formulation has been criticized for being in error and for being vague.
Henderson thinks Estrich is wrong that U.S. courts don't address intent vis-à-vis
the issue of victim consent (1988: 211). Schulhofer tends to agree in some passages
that Estrich overstates the case in contending that the courts do not recognize negligence in rape prosecution (1998: 258). Henderson goes on to object that Estrich
is similarly wrong to think that a focus on intent will translate into a focus on
offenders and take attention away from victim behavior, which will in turn shift
focus from victim resistance and thus consent (1988: 211). Henderson thinks that
the opposite will obtain, that is, that interrogating negligence and mistakes will
reintroduce the resistance requirement as a measure of reasonable mistake.

The problem of vagueness in Estrich's proposal is apparent in several places. For instance, she does not precisely spell out the conditions under which

negligence would be fair to impute. She states only here that "the threshold of liability—whether phrased in terms of 'consent,' 'force,' and 'coercion' or some combination of the three—should be understood to include at least those non-traditional rapes where the woman says 'no' or submits only in response to lies or threats which would be prohibited were money sought instead" (1987: 103). There are two different problems here. First, the statement leaves a good deal of ambiguity as to any sort of formula or definition of negligent culpability, which is the crux of the contribution in her model. Second, allowing for some "combination of the three" is seriously problematic since most states already require a showing of both nonconsent and force or coercion. This is not something to advance or even tacitly accept. The expression of nonconsent or the presence of force or coercion ought to be sufficient, each in and of itself, to constitute rape (see chap. 8 for an extended analysis of this). Requiring both is an unjustifiable burden in rape prosecution. And any statement about the direction reforms should take ought to chart out that either nonconsent or force/coercion alone is legally satisfactory to establish the crime.

Estrich, too, glosses over what would make mistakes unreasonable. She offers that if the same old sexist definitions prevail, then what is considered reasonable will be problematic (as it is determined from a male point of view). She doesn't tell us, however, how to get a nonsexist "woman's point of view," which she includes in the definition of what is reasonable. She merely states the need to use a woman's point of view and does so quite tersely. And although she so significantly points out how interpretations of various scenarios are made through a gendered lens, she doesn't actually tell us what a woman's point of view of reasonableness, acquiescence under force, and so forth might be. This is problematic given how important a woman's point of view and reasonableness are to rape and sexual assault determination.[6]

SUMMARY

The main lessons for reforming rape reforms from this look at the law's history is that consent and intent should not be overlooked (nor be redundantly required) and that intent or its absence (or negligence as to intent) can confer criminal responsibility. Simultaneously, the law needs to be clear that nonconsent and force/coercion (or threats thereof) are redundant with regard to establishing the criminal offenses of rape/sexual assault. Finally, it is worth reiterating that what makes mis-TAKE of consent unreasonable must, too, be addressed in reforming rape reforms.

A different approach to handling the issue of consent is struck by reforms that stipulate a requirement for affirmatively given consent. Affirmative consent reform law in rape entails the requirement that a female's positive assent, agreement, or permission to the act(s) of sexual contact or penetration be demonstrated. Antioch College's policy requiring affirmative, verbal consent before each and every sex act may be the most familiar example.[1]

Instead of looking at whether the victim resisted or indicated nonconsent or said no, affirmative consent flips matters and looks for the woman saying yes. In the absence of evidence establishing "yes," the case is rape. In other words, the prosecution needs to show that there were no indications of freely given consent to the sex acts in order to prove sexual assault. (The defense then would need to establish reasonable doubt about the existence of indications of consent to any sex acts in order to excuse criminal responsibility for rape.) Antioch's affirmative consent policy specifies the standard that "the act of willingly and verbally agreeing to engage in specific sexual contact or conduct" (Reeves Sanday 1996: 265) at each progressive step of sexual engagement up through penetration is required for consensual sex; otherwise it is sexual assault.[2]

NEW JERSEY'S LAW

The requirement that consent be verbally or physically given, that "yes" be said or shown, rather than "no," was upheld in law in the state of New Jersey. In 1992 a New Jersey Supreme Court decision upheld the affirmative consent rule and defined that in the absence of "freely-given permission of the victim" sexual penetration was sexual assault (Reeves Sanday 1996: 265). In New Jersey, the consent that must be shown can be expressed either verbally or through behavior or actions by the victim. Reeves Sanday quotes the law to explain that "permission can be 'indicated through physical actions rather than word.' The court claimed that permission would be determined 'when the reasonable person would have believed that the alleged victim had affirmatively and freely given authorization to the act'" (283). In the New Jersey case referenced here (*State in the interest of M.T.S.*, New Jersey Supreme Court 129 N.J. 422, 609 A.2d 1266 [1992]), a juvenile penetrated another juvenile without her consent "involving no more force than necessary to accomplish that result" (Kadish and Schulhofer 2001: 339). In this case, the courts directly removed the force requirement (Schulhofer 1998: 44, 96), allowing that "physical force or coercion could be satisfied by proof of nonconsensual penetration" (Kinports 2001: 756) and nonconsensual penetration existed where freely given assent was not in evidence.[3]

Consent, affirmative or otherwise, is fairly consistently defined in these kinds of rape statutes as agreement to sex acts that is freely or willingly given. (The matter is far from this simple; see the next two chapters, which take this up in some detail.) The two other states with affirmative consent policies are Wisconsin and Washington (Schulhofer 1998: 40). Wisconsin defines consent as "words or overt actions by a person who is competent to give informed consent indicating a freely given agreement to have sexual intercourse or sexual contact" (Reeves Sanday 1996: 282). Reeves Sanday quotes the Wisconsin definition, citing a 1980 Wisconsin Supreme Court case that determined a "demonstration of affirmative consent is required" in that state, rejecting a defense argument that parties can enter into consensual sexual relationships without "freely given consent in words or acts" (1996: 282).[4]

Statutory definitions of consent, which can be used as a defense to a rape accusation, should not be construed as equivalent to an affirmative consent requirement. There is a difference between affirmative consent, where the yes has to be demonstrated (at each stage and/or to the penetration), and the defendant using the legal defense of consent to try to mitigate his culpability by arguing that it was not rape (forced sex) because she agreed to it. The difference between defining consent in statute and requiring the presence of an affirmative, positive yes is the difference between (his) ex post facto protestations and her (constant) indications that she is agreeable to the acts (lest the acts be deemed criminal ones). One is a far cry from the other.

The value of affirmative consent is that it sets up sex in a positive rather than negative way, so the parties involved expect one another to be honest or forthcoming about their sexual desires. Such communication can reduce all sorts of risks in sex and make for more enjoyment and potentially perhaps for better, more fulfilling relationships. As argued in the case of Antioch, affirmative consent policies can function to sensitize, train, and educate males and females alike to be sensitive to and respectful of their partners; want(s), wish(es) and will(s).

Those who promote affirmative consent policy, such as Reeves Sanday (1996), Pineau (1996a), and Schulhofer (1998) (see next two sections of this chapter on Pineau and Schulhofer), put forward a more compelling reason for the standard. Affirmative consent is designed to promote communication about sexual matters and mutual respect and gratification, in place of male-dominated definitions, roles, expectations, and stereotypes about sex and sexual fulfillment. The Antioch policy is quite specific about this and about how such a standard is designed to educate as much, if not more, than anything else.

Another reason for the standard is that men and women understand and interpret force and coercion, as well as free and willing consent, in different ways. As Estrich points out, definitions of force originate in the schoolboy estimations; as Schulhofer sees it, "force" is usually defined as that which goes beyond what is required for penetration. This is a gendered conception, sculpted according to a male model of physicality and force—what I would reference as entitled, bullying, aggressive/assaultive, and/or violent behavior. Anything short of these levels does not receive recognition as force or even as coercive, threatening, or menacing behavior. This translates into meaning that women who feel forced are not legally recognized to have been forced or compelled unless there is physical violence. An affirmative consent standard insists that men, and the law, pay attention to women's definitions and experiences of force and coercion (by requiring expression of the opposite: willful agreement), even if not under the condition of actual physical violence (from a male point of view).

On the flip side of the coin of understanding force/coercion is understanding consent, which is also interpreted differently by men and women. Affirmative consent policies recognize the lack of force or coercion as only a first step in sex. As Reeves Sanday (1996) sees it, we need to go beyond inadequate "no means no" reform speak, for this doesn't get at women's definition of the situation sufficiently. The focus should turn toward eliciting yes to all sex acts. The next step (beyond an absence of aggression) requires that men seek out and ascertain women's positive approval, agreement, consent, or permission for sex acts before acting in sexual ways.[5] This is a higher standard than just the absence of force/coercion in interpretations and is intended to ensure voluntary willfulness in sexual activities.

Affirmative consent advocates also address the failure to utter positive assent or anything at all, in the case of silence. Reeves Sanday explains that we need to recognize that silence does not constitute a willful yes. Silence can mean that the victim feels uncomfortable, or threatened, or coerced, or fearful that sex will be forced with violence if she doesn't give in. Reeves Sanday refers to "frozen fright" (1996: 283) in regard to silence, where women may be too scared to say or do anything to communicate their lack of consent because they feel terrorized.[6] If a woman is in a state of frozen fright, there are probably coercive elements at play, making her failure to say no (or yes or do anything else) a fact that should be extraneous or irrelevant to prosecuting the crime and instead be seen to evince the crime by proving force/coercion.[7] The point for affirmative consent policy is that anything short of a clearly expressed voluntary (noncoerced) positive or affirmative indication of desire or willingness to engage in sexual activities (by a competent individual) constitutes an insufficient basis for establishing consent and therefore constitutes sexual assault. The scenarios of silence point to an understanding of the rationale underlying this.

Critical Appraisal

An oft-cited criticism is that much of what affirmative consent policy attempts to reach is uncomfortable sex. And, as Schulhofer notes, even affirmative consent law does little in scenarios where women "acquiesce in a man's demands" (1998: 96).

While it is certainly true that many women have given in to sex, participating in, for example, "wrestling matches," "petting sessions," or sexual activities that went "too far," when they would rather not have (Gaitskill 1994), the legal point is whether the woman "gives in" or concedes. I contend that this is what should demarcate criminal rape and sexual assault from other noncriminal sex. Affirmative consent law tries to make expressed agreement the standard, and acquiescence acceptable only if positively, demonstrably, not passively indicated. The problem is that a woman can acquiesce without saying anything. Much sex that is agreed to occurs without expressions of "yes," "I want to do that," or the like. An awful lot of consensual sex takes place in silence. This is problematic given affirmative consent law that would find sexual assault in the absence of an expressed demonstrable affirmative response.

Affirmative consent statutes also fail to define what "freely given" consent means. Without definition, anything could tenably undermine the "free" part of "freely given consent." Schulhofer notes that acquiescence and lack of "freely given" consent, as in the case of silence, can be influenced by coerced "emotional demands or social pressure ... psychological appeals ... even by vulnerability resulting from a powerful 'crush'" on a man (1998: 97). The question is, do factors such as a crush or psychological appeals in the company of silence (the absence of a yes) make for rape? Do these things make for coercion? Do such factors make even an expressed yes unfree? In other words, do these things make consent coerced?

It is true that sex that is not fully desired or wanted should be considered in light of rape reforms and that matters need to change so that the extent of "uncomfortable sex" can ultimately be diminished, but I would assert that this is a matter more for education than litigation. The overly broad reach of law that tried to extend criminal sanctions to "uncomfortable sex" or sex that is acquiesced to in silence when there are no aggravating circumstance, force, or coercive physical threats only—not emotional demands, psychological appeals, and so on—is clearly beyond what criminal courts are likely actually to implement or uphold. If even acquaintance rapes that are aggravated by weapons, multiples offenders, additional injuries, and so forth—differing from "real" stranger-out-of-the-bushes rapes only because the victim has some passing knowledge of the offender—are not taken seriously by the criminal legal system, how can sex that is acquiesced to in silence or where there is simply a lack of the expression of yes (in the absence of force, threats, implied threats, power/authority differentials, etc.) be expected to be recognized, let alone sanctioned, by the legal arm of the (male) state?

A veritable litany of other problems attends the affirmative consent reform approach. Look at the experience of Antioch, for instance. The affirmative consent policy drew national attention, and mockery in most circles. "You've got to be kidding," "now look what those crazy feminists have done," "now those radical man-hating feminists have ruined sex for us all"—these were the types of exclamations that rang across the country and splattered the headlines. This radical policy gave legitimacy to backlash criticisms that were previously gross exaggerations. Now the criticisms weren't so far off the mark. Seeking affirmative consent for sexual activity is not very realistic about sex, either. People aren't going to start having foreplay or intercourse with a lot of talk or question-and-answer sessions just because of new policies. It is unrealistic—in fact, to many fairly ludicrous—to think about the questions: "Can I touch your boobs now" "Do you mind if I suck your vagina?" "Shall I penetrate you now?" People just don't have sex this way. As Schulhofer so eloquently puts it (in assessing Reeves Sanday's "verbal-permission rule"), the result would be "imposing a degree of formality and artificiality on human interactions in which spontaneity is especially important" (1998: 272).

A good deal of the ridicule and rejection of Antioch's policy stems from this staging dimension, which is an attempt to deal with offenses of contact that are short of penetration. The effort to fight the type of thinking, evident in the Kobe Bryant case, that agreement to kissing, fondling, or petting mean agreement to penetration is well intentioned. But the means are problematic. Given the public reaction to affirmative consent policies, and especially the highly sensationalized coverage of the Antioch policy, it would seem that it is more readily acceptable when the onus is on the female to stop the male—for example, saying "no," "don't," "stop," at each stage—than when it is on the male to check for yes. And just getting this further kind or level of acceptance (of "no" being enough) would be a stride in progress all by itself.

Silence under affirmative consent law is of obvious concern. While it is, of course, true that silence should not be taken as consent, the call for affirmative consent is not as likely to solve problems as a focus on the factors associated with the crime itself would accomplish. I say this because it would generally be easier to document the circumstances that surround the crime that implicate nonconsent than to prove that the victim did not in any way indicate her consent. The problems with focusing on rape victims are more than evident by now, and affirmative consent reforms cannot eliminate such problems, for example, juror belief in the defendant's side of the argument or taking his side when he says she indicated consent. In fact, the policy requiring the demonstration of victim consent draws focus in all cases on issues of victim consent, whereas with some other reforms that would draw attention to crime circumstances such as force and coercion instead of victim articulation of consent, this would be true for only those cases where the accused rebuts charges with a defense of consent.

Another problem is that it is not terribly realistic to expect juries to convict in cases where, as the prosecutor in the Glen Ridge case told the jury, the victim doesn't have to say anything, and even if she just lies there, guilt can be properly assessed if she didn't say yes, even in the absence of any other aggravating conditions (Reeves Sanday 1996). Furthermore, as Schulhofer comments, "most courts are still willing to infer consent from passivity and silence, without any affirmative signed consent" (1998: 272). Isn't a determination of guilt more likely if the scrutiny went to, for example, whether or not there were multiple offenders and whether or not the female was incapacitated in some way (both these circumstances obtained in the Glen Ridge rapes, where the jury was told that the victim didn't have to say anything at all because the law required a yes)? As Schul-hofer notes, affirmative consent left to judges and juries to decide leads to reliance only on the "traditional categories of physical intimidation" (1998: 97). As previously pointed out, and as Schulhofer expounds, the affirmative consent reforms made little impact because they (referencing Wisconsin and Washington) failed to specify "the kinds of pressure or coercion that would prevent 'freely given' consent" (40). If narrowly construed, "traditional categories" of "schoolboy" (Estrich 1987) force/coercion would be relied on. And, "if broadly read, the requirement to freely given consent would create criminal liability whenever a woman's acquiescence was influenced by emotional demands or social pressure" (Schulhofer 1998: 97). Schulhofer goes on to comment, "this approach would convert a seemingly consensual encounter into a criminal assault not only in cases of economic duress or abuse of institutional authority but whenever the defendant knew—or should have known—that the woman's participation was induced by psychological appeals" (97). The failure to differentiate legitimate from illegitimate pressures or to define freely given accord invites all kinds of ambiguity. And ambiguity is an issue for fairness and justice. Schulhofer, for example, condemns such ambiguity for violating the fair notice doctrine in criminal law.

Still more, focusing on the female's expressions or actions has always been problematic and would, in all probability, continue to be so. Old issues, like "he says she gave demonstrable permission, that she cued him affirmatively," or "anyone would have understood her behavior as positive assent," or "all his friends would have interpreted consent, too," and all the other mis-takes about (freely given) consent can so easily creep back in, irrespective of the fact that reforms mandate looking for a yes rather than looking for a no.

A related problem lies in the reasonable person standard in interpreting whether consent is voluntarily affirmatively given. This stipulation does not solve the problems of a "reasonable man" standard. What exactly constitutes "reasonable" is discretionary, as well as derived from a male—not a neutral, let alone female—point of view. If permission is to be found "when the reasonable person would have believed that the alleged victim had affirmatively and freely given authorization to the act," as was used in the case in the Glen Ridge case in New Jersey (Reeves Sanday 1996: 283), is anything really accomplished? Isn't it just as likely for a male to claim he picked up on "yes" even though she didn't say it (recall that verbal permission is not required in New Jersey; physical action can dictate free agreement)? Thus the "he said, she said" dilemma is not necessarily dismantled. While affirmative consent policy can be understood to attempt to make mistakes about consent more difficult to establish (as reasonable), mistakes themselves are not defined or dealt with directly in any way.

Because of this, the reasonableness of mistakes might not be affected (men "mistake" consent under all kinds of conditions; consider the Glen Ridge case, where the young men involved said the young women—whose mental age was about eight—really wanted and agreed to sex and penetration by objects with the gang of young males).

Yet a further, and related, drawback is found in the strong tendency to reinforce the age-old male-aggressive/female-passive model of sexuality.[8] Men must check for the yes or willing consent, yet women express and interpret consent and nonconsent, agreement, volition, freedom, and coercive pressure in light of culture, socialization, and experience. This is to say that males and females understand "affirmative consent" or expression of agreement in gendered ways. The affirmative consent reforms thus make little headway in this regard because they merely substitute understanding a yes in place of understanding a no; both remain contoured by gender roles. And the reforms here do little to affect the male definitions prevailing in understandings.

PINEAU'S "COMMUNICATIVE SEXUALITY" INNOVATION: COMBINING AFFIRMATIVE CONSENT AND STRICT LIABILITY

Lois Pineau (1996a) offers a rather extreme approach for dealing with the problem that consent issues present for rape prosecution. Her unique model calls for three changes that she views as solving the particular problem in more "simple" date rape contexts. First, she defines that any/all non-"communicative sex" constitutes date rape. Second, she argues for strict liability for date rape. And, third, she maintains date rape should be a misdemeanor crime rather than a felony.

In her "communicative sex" approach, Pineau proposes that dating couples must express their wishes and desires to one another throughout the sexual encounter and that what the woman understands about whether she freely gives consent is what should determine the presence of consent or lack thereof. In other words, consent is to be derived from the woman's point of view about the experience, wherein the sex partners talk and act freely, in ways that impart understanding about affirmative versus negative feelings regarding each part of the sexual encounter. Pineau puts it this way: "Persons engaged in communicative sexuality will be concerned with more than achieving coitus. They will be sensitive to the responses of their partners. They will, like good conversationalists, be intuitive, sympathetic, and charitable.… Their concern with fostering the desire of the other must involve an ongoing state of alertness in interpreting her responses" (1996a: 19–20).

Pineau's position is that communicative sex must be established—from the woman's point of view—to legitimate sex. Without communicative sex, the acts are date rape. This can be likened to an affirmative consent model. The phrase "can be likened to" takes into account the difference between the Antioch model and Pineau's. In her book on the Pineau model, Leslie Francis states in her introduction that "the Antioch policy is so appropriate as an illustration of the consensual sexuality that Pineau defends, that we sought approval from the college to include it in this volume" (1996: xviii). As Scholz observes, however, "the Antioch policy also differs in an important way from Pineau's version of communicative sexuality. According to the former, consent must be obtained every step of the sexual encounter for each encounter. It is on this latter point that Pineau and Antioch differ. There is, in other words, no presumption of consent for declared lovers under the Antioch policy" (1998: 243). Pineau defends her view (presumed consent for declared lovers) by stating that this is encompassed because "negative response is still given full credence" (Scholz 1998: 243). Regardless, if a woman charges date rape, what would have to be shown to disprove it with Pineau's model is that sex was "communicative," without pressures or restraints to coax affirmative response(s) throughout the sexual episode.

Pineau's second premise regarding strict liability would mean that criminal responsibility for date rape exists regardless of what the man thought about consent. As Pineau sees it, the accused's criminal intent, mens rea, his state of mind, or beliefs—reasonable or not, honest or not, mistaken or not—are irrelevant to the crime and his criminal responsibility. The man would be guilty whether or not he knew he did anything wrong. As Pineau puts it (in a response to Harris), "this means that if it is established that a person violated the law, he may be guilty whether he meant to do so or not" (Harris and Pineau 1996: 116). Pineau sees strict liability as the way to get around the problem of "reasonable" or "honest" mistakes as to consent (not to mention the unreasonable mistakes or negligent liability model as advanced by Estrich). What the defendant may have meant to do just doesn't matter. Francis puts it well. Her characterization of Pineau is that "it is not reasonable for women to agree to coerced or pressured sex (or, therefore, for men to believe that women have agreed)" (1996: xii–xiii). If you engage in sex under specific conditions, you are to be convicted, period.

Pineau advocates the strict liability model for nonaggravated rape. She promotes this with the logic that "this clearly dispenses with the need to establish *mens rea*. ... Since rape convictions often fail because *mens rea* is defeated, and since *mens rea* may be defeated in many jurisdictions on the basis of a man's 'honest belief' in a woman's consent, and since 'honest belief' is all too easy a defense in the present ideological environment, elimination of the *mens rea* is an obvious and effective strategy" (Harris and Pineau 1996: 116).

The third premise in Pineau's model stipulates that the strict liability that would only be for nonaggravated or date rape become a misdemeanor crime. Pineau justifies this by contending that the conviction rate would be higher if date rapes were defined as less serious offenses. She also thinks that such a definition would be necessary in order for the strict liability model to be acceptable.

Critical Appraisal

Because Pineau's model is similar to affirmative consent reforms, it suffers from many of the same problems. But, further yet, the ambiguity in her scheme is seriously problematic. First, how are "communicative sex," " respect," "sensitivity," and "fostering desire of the other" to be discovered and demonstrated? If affirmative consent is too high a bar, how can communicative sex be realistic? And if nonconsent is difficult to show, can demonstrating noncommunicative sex be any easier? Second, Pineau does not define "pressure" that would negate "communicative sex." What constitutes pressure? What makes pressures nonlegitimate or unreasonable? How can this be determined? Who is to make the determination? Third, as Pineau herself says, it must be established that the person violated the law, but she does not talk about what law, how it is violated, what conditions of pressure, and so on must be in evidence. Again, under what conditions—for example, violence, pressures, force—does law violation pertain in her scheme? Is she saying that the "pressures" she sees as negating communicative sex (the much higher standard than consent) are supposed to count in defining behavior as law violating?

Pineau goes on to say that if a man violates the law, then a man's belief or state of mind or thinking about what a woman might or might not have wanted or consented to becomes irrelevant. Francis summarizes Pineau along this line saying that strict liability or disregard of the defendant's intent or state of mind obtains where the woman "was in fact not consenting to the activity" (1996: xvii). But nonconsent is still problematic. How is a woman's nonconsent to be determined? A further issue with Pineau's premise about eliminating intent as a factor and defining date rape as noncommunicative sex (to ameliorate the problems of consent, mistakes about consent, and the reasonableness therein) is that intent is not the issue, consent is. As I described in chapter 5, proving intent as an element of the crime of rape has not, in this country, been seriously problematic because of the favor accorded defendants through the resistance requirement and consent standards.

In nonaggravated/date rape (where there are no aggravating conditions, force, or physical threats or some sort of pressure that makes communicative sex untenable according to Pineau's model) where Pineau would insert the strict liability clause to establish that someone violated the law of rape, what has to be established is nonconsent (or noncommunicative sex). Hence the issue of a woman's consent remains focal. Focusing on disputed communication about consent, not to mention respecting "being intuitive, sympathetic and charitable" in communicating about having sex, brings us in circular fashion back to the same old problems about victim focus and blame and consent in rape, date or otherwise.

Pineau means consent to be focal, with her assertion of communicative sexuality from a woman's point of view, but sees this to solve instead of exacerbate the problems of consent. Not only is this not the case, but a further problem concerns how a defense of "she communicated freely with willingness" can be argued when the woman is obviously saying, by virtue of registering charges, that from her point of view—which is what counts—there was not communicative sex, there was not consent, there was instead (coercion or some kind of pressure and) date rape? Defense would seem impossible, and false conviction possible, given this scheme.

Harris extends this critique yet further. She states that "making nonaggressive sexual assault a strict liability crime means, in effect, that even if it would be completely impossible and unreasonable for the man to believe that the woman was engaging in the sexual act against her will,... he would still be convicted" (Harris and Pineau 1996: 120). In other words, even if a man was sure and it was impossible for a reasonable person to believe that the woman was not consenting, he would still be convicted. This is a problem for justice.

Some of these problems are due to a failure to define terms in a system that is about conceptualization. Other problems can be found in the definitions that Pineau offers. Her definition of sex versus date rape, for instance, doesn't go much beyond sufficiently communicative sex and the "intuition, charity, and sympathy" of good conversationalists in an "ongoing state of alertness" (Schulhofer 1998: 85). This definition of the qualities of good conversationalists is hardly universal, and rape, date or otherwise, is hardly about having good conversational skills. Moreover, communication about, over, or during sex activities manifests some of the worst, most lacking communication skills that we ever see or experience, even when great conversationalists are the parties involved.

Some of the problems may be due to definitional issues, some may be matters of interpretation, but in any case the problems are tied to a further ambiguity or, better stated, contradiction. Pineau recognizes that the law would maintain its own standards, not hers. But she implicates actual or real change in other passages of her text rather than this sort of philosophical meandering. Her model is theoretical, not necessarily realistic or practical, even by her own estimation; yet it is somehow supposed to lead to actual change. For instance, Pineau says date rape should be a misdemeanor only in order to render her model acceptable and possibly lead to actual legal change. But then she states things like there is a difference "between *accepting a paradigm* and *imposing a paradigm*" (1996: 128; emphasis in the original) and that there is a difference "between having a right and enforcing the use of that right" (Harris and Pineau 1996: 129). She further states that "if communicative sex is to be taken as the norm, that is not the same thing as legislating it" (Pineau 1996: 128). This is confusing, if not contradictory.

Nonaggressive date rape where consent is allegedly coerced or the result of nonreasonable or nonlegitimate pressure raises a host of other concerns in the way Pineau presents her model. First, she fails to define the crime(s) of nonaggressive date rape. Second, it would seem that date rape could be aggressive (coerced or pressured) if Pineau doesn't think the communication was open enough. In Pineau's view, yes doesn't always mean yes. This winds up leaving the assessment of the acceptable means of talking about agreement to sex to Pineau alone, which is to say that it leaves the legal judgment to her alone. At a minimum, this cannot possibly conform to the legal standard of fair notice to men regarding what the law sanctions. And this is not to mention the problem of false convictions inherent here. Furthermore, if we have problems prosecuting sex that isn't consented to, what good can proposing that some sex that is consented to (where there may be some communication but not enough) is not rape?

Pineau's model positing that even some consensual sex is crime does no favor for even the date rape victims about whom she is concerned. This route will surely provide little help to the solution of the problems of rape. Another issue is that contending that even some consensual sex is crime strips women of sexual agency. This is as unjustified as it is ill advised. Commenting on the problematic nature of sexual agency in Pineau's system, Schulhofer says that Pineau doesn't recognize anything beyond "the obligation to promote the sexual ends of one's partner" as legitimate motive. Schulhofer notes "curiosity, financial gain, a desire to impress peers, and an interest in adventure or rebellion … social status, … personal self-esteem, or financial security" (1998: 84–85) and "procreation, emotional intimacy, and physical pleasure" (85, citing Chamallas 1988) as possible motivations for sexual involvement.[9] These should all be considered in definitions because they can be a respectable part of the regard for a woman's sexual autonomy. Summarizing criticism of Pineau's work, particularly in the denial of women's sexual agency, Schulhofer concludes, "this sort of solution is neither practically workable nor politically realistic. And more basically, it should not command support even in theory. The goal law should pursue is just the reverse—to protect and enhance autonomy, not restrict it" (88).

Other issues attend Pineau's third premise on making nonaggravated date rape a misdemeanor. The invasion and devastation of rape are never simple, low-level misdemeanor harms. Misdemeanors are typically thought of as nuisance offenses. And the types of rape that Pineau would classify here are not just the lesser crimes of sexual contact, such as grabbing a woman's breast. They are crimes of penetration that are allegedly less serious simply because the couple was acquainted or dating—for whatever length of time—before the so-called miscommunication. It is commonly understood in the literature that the trauma suffered from intimate, date, and acquaintance rape can be greater than that suffered from stranger rape, because of, for instance, the violation of trust and the undermining of judgment and self-esteem (see, for example, Campbell 1989; Koss et al. 1988; Sampson 2008; Miller and Meloy forthcoming; Sampson 2008). It is incredibly misguided to think that the simple, nonaggravated date rapes to which Pineau refers will be handled in some improved manner should they become misdemeanors. They are already handled in a diminished, minimized, inequitable fashion in their present status as felony offenses.

Harris (Harris and Pineau 1996) contends further that if date rape were to be treated as a strict liability misdemeanor, there would be resistance to implementing such law. Prosecutors would hesitate to charge, and juries to convict. Schulhofer (1998) sees it similarly. He warns that when legal boundaries are extended, as in Pineau's provision for legal sanctioning of "unreasonable" or coercive or pressured sex to which a woman has consented, laws will not be enforced. Harris takes this yet a step further and insightfully observes that there would be backlash against the women who charge men with such crimes. This would be because the status of the crimes would make people view such charges as simply frivolous, more frivolous than date rape might already seem to many.

Pineau responded to these criticisms, justifying her recommendation to make nonaggravated rape a misdemeanor offense. What she anticipates is that this would increase convictions, since there is less reluctance to convict with lesser—misdemeanor—crimes. While this may be true, downgrading acquaintance rape to misdemeanor status oversteps the boundaries. Pineau elaborates that other reforms have failed to recognize the problem that the law is only a punitive tool and thus often overly harsh. She thinks we should use the law less and punish less. Again, this may be true, but she goes too far vis-à-vis acquaintance rape. And again there is a contradiction. Making acquaintance rape a misdemeanor is not exactly using the law less, although it may reduce the punitiveness of law. In fact, given Pineau's thinking (about overcoming hesitancy to convict with more severe punishment), it may be using the law more.

Pineau continues her justification with consideration of wife battering. She asserts that sanctions like intervention and treatment are used more often, so that abusers are interrupted, stopped, watched, counseled, and so on, which is probably more effective than prison time. While I agree that we may be overly punitive and that a harsh level of punishment affects conviction rates, not all reforms and reformers were unaware of this problem, and some endeavored to reduce prison time for rape for precisely this reason (see Snider 1985). Yet rarely is rape (as opposed to sexual assault) reduced to the misdemeanor levels she suggests, which would be an excessive reduction. It is beyond the scope of this book to respond very fully to the claims about spouse abuse, but let me just say that our "interventions" and "treatment" and lack of punishment have left quite a bit to be desired here, too.

The essence of the problem is that Pineau's model wouldn't work—even in theory. It's too radical, the removal of a consent defense, as would be entailed with strict liability rape, would never fly, and the affirmative/communicative model would permit miscarriages of justice for men. (If a woman makes the date rape charge, she is saying that sex was noncommunicative and nonconsensual, and since the model posits that communicative sex is to be determined from a woman's point of view, the case is closed, and the guy's convicted. The model is a closed system). Injustices are also fostered on the other side of the ledger, because of date rape—even nonaggravated—would be only a misdemeanor.

So it seems that whether the attempt is to attach strict liability to aggravated rape or nonaggravated rape, there are enormous problems. For these reasons, strict liability as a legal strategy for rape has little to commend it. There are many other, more promising strategies that would be more palatable to the legal and lay communities and could accomplish a great deal more for women, and men as well.

SCHULHOFER'S "SEXUAL AUTONOMY" INNOVATION: BEYOND AFFIRMATIVE CONSENT

Schulhofer posits an extremely different approach to the problem of rape and sexual assault that further extends the purview of affirmative consent reforms. He contends that the only way to get away from all of the sundry problems attending the legal response to sexual assault is to reconceptualize fundamental rights, and hence violations, that the law is supposed to safeguard. He asserts that the law should protect women's right to sexual autonomy, or sexual self-determination. Put differently, Schulhofer argues that crimes of rape and sexual assault constitute violations of women's right to give or withhold meaningful consent, or freedom of choice, about sexual activities. He persuasively describes how women are, or rather should be, entitled to control their own bodies and men's access to them. He states that in order for any sexual contact to be allowable, women have to give uncoerced "permission," free from any restraints or compulsions of any sort whatsoever. Permission to sex must be voluntary, or "affirmatively and freely given."

Schulhofer provides perspective on the wide margin of difference between rape laws and reforms and his own model, stating that "rather then asking whether certain sexual advances unjustifiably impair freedom of choice, we had asked only whether the conduct is so bad that is equivalent to violent compulsion, whether it is tantamount to rape" (1998: 102). He claims that "the issue of sexual autonomy must be addressed directly, not as a byproduct of the endless and hopelessly confusing definitional debates about the meaning of force" (98). He continues, "Many philosophers insist that autonomy requires even more. For a person to be fully self-governing, they suggest, requires not only that she be free of interference with her choices, but also that she be able to select from a wide array of reasonable alternatives when making any particular decision" (105–106).

Schulhofer's conceptualization of the right to sexual autonomy is well stated in his comment that, "like our rights to physical safety, to our property, our time and our labor, the right to choose—or refuse—sexual intimacy deserves the protection and support of society and its laws" (1998: 282). He further states that, "just as nonviolent threats to take property amount to criminal extortion, nonviolent coercion to induce consent to unwanted intercourse should constitute a serious criminal offense" (280).

In the discussion of the violation of sexual autonomy rights, Schulhofer naturally includes traditional force, coercion, and threats of physical injury, but he goes beyond this to include virtually any and all other restrictions that might impinge upon freely given permission and the constraint of reasonable options for purposive behavior. For instance, he declares that "the effective protection of sexual autonomy requires standards to identify sexual demands that are improper even when they do not constitute threats in the classic sense"(1998: 36). He contends that if threats (as differentiated from offers) endanger free choice in the sexual activities of a person, the threats are coercive, wrong, and impermissible (124–131): "In a regime that prohibits not only physical force but *all* unjustified impairments with autonomy, an impermissible threat is, by definition, an improper interference with freedom of choice.... A wrongful threat intended to induce sexual compliance is coercive in itself, just as a wrongful threat intended to obtain money is sufficient in itself to constitute the criminal offense of extortion. If a threat is completely trivial ('Comply or I'll drink your soda'), there is no reason to treat it as anything other than jest; whether the man seeks to obtain money or sexual acquiescence, the threat must be one intended to induce submission" (131). This goes beyond affirmative consent reform law previously discussed, as Schulhofer is asserting a radically new right, beyond at least any previous articulation of legal rights. This is so as affirmative consent requires "only" a positive indication of yes to the sex acts, whereas Schulhofer's model claims the new right of sexual autonomy for women.

Schulhofer, like Estrich and like Pineau, further maintains that what constitutes free choice, restraint, duress, pressure, and so on is to be determined from the women's point of view. If a woman feels or believes she has submitted unfreely, that she has been pressured into granting permission to her body, violation of her right to sexual autonomy has transpired. What is more, it is up to the man to ascertain the presence of unpressured, legitimate, free permission for sex. This dimension is like the affirmative consent reforms previously described. Justifying his proposal, Schulhofer asserts that it is high time to "move away from the demand for unambiguous evidence of her protests and insist instead that the man had affirmative indications that she *chose* to participate.... We can insist that any person who engages in intercourse show full respect for the other person's autonomy—by pausing before he acts, to be sure that he has a clear indication of her actual consent" (1998: 272–3; emphasis in the original).

In sum, Schulhofer's approach to enhancing legal protection for women in matters of sex and sexual violation involves reconceptualizing the harm of sexual assault as a violation of the basic right to self-determination in sexual activities, as defined by each woman in each sexual episode, wherein the man has the responsibility to assess how the woman feels about her freedom to give consent (in the absence of all pressures) to acts involved in each sexual episode. Schulhofer's larger framework affords broader safety and security that would clearly allow more types of sexual offensiveness to be deemed criminal.

Critical Appraisal

Schulhofer's approach merits some of the same criticisms he raises with regard to other reformers and types of rape reform. For instance, the vagueness or lack of definitions he takes issue with in regard to force, coercion, and implicit threat can be seen to attend his notions of "freely given," "affirmative" words or conduct of "consent" or—still more problematic—"permission." The lack of concrete distinction is most pointedly evident in one of his comments pertaining to concepts critical to his model. He states that "protection from coercion and the protection of autonomy are closely related and thus sometimes hard to tell apart" (Schulhofer 2001: 150). Delimiting one phenomenon from another is an onerous task, one that needs to be tackled head-on. Yet what Schulhofer (rather skillfully) does is redraw the lines (by talking about violation of sexual autonomy in the absence of affirmative sexual permission) without acknowledging that line drawing about sexual violation versus consensual sex remains a task yet to be clearly accomplished.

Schulhofer intimates that terms like "implicit threat" (1998: 78), "nonviolent abuse" (88), and "moral, psychological or intellectual" (89) coercion may be too broad (transforming sex into rape on the basis of bad feelings), but he is at fault for the same lack of precision. He sees terms like "psychological" coercion or "pressure" as permitting an overly broad interpretation of sexual assault where a man simply lies to have sex. Yet he posits that anything that interferes with a woman's sexual autonomy, including phenomena as broad as "nonviolent coercion," should be a "serious offense" (280). The problem is that it is not clear how any of the just noted phenomena differ from one another.

The constant reference to "permission" and use as a synonym of "consent" is a particularly bothersome feature of Schulhofer's work. Permission connotes more acquiescence to a request than meaningful consent. It has more of an association of conceding to be acted upon, or "done to." A type of free acquiescence differs, albeit slightly perhaps, from willful agreement.[10] Permission is problematic because it reinforces a binary view of the male to female, which is to say the dominant to subordinate. This is a view that binds male to aggressiveness (or at least assertiveness) and female to passivity. Permission to have sex, as taken by males and yielded by females, is not a very emancipatory view of sexuality. In fact, such a view has the potential to fit in neatly to a conception of woman as property (sexual property where a man owns a female or a female concedes to be given to or taken by a man). The danger is that regression to old views and associations is probably more likely than progression to new views, for example, linking women with sexual agency and autonomy.

The problematic posturing on "permission" is one of the rare instances where Schulhofer seems constrained by the problem of hegemony or unwittingly bound in by ideological assumptions that normally serve males. The only other instance arises in his discussion of no meaning no. Schulhofer says that women cannot always say no when they mean no or when they do not desire sex (1998: 263–264), that women do not always know what they want (261), that "'no' doesn't always mean 'no'" (260; see also 264), and that women give out "mixed signals" (263) because they are "equivocal" about sex (260). Given all he says indicating that women can't manage a no and given his view that at least some women say no when they mean yes or when they are "feeling unsure or not feeling ready, not just yet" (261), arguing for change that would require women to say yes seems unreasonable.[11] If women can't say no, which is proper social convention (which he suggests) even if they mean no and even if women are too "shy or inhibited to indicate their interest" in sex (267), how likely is it that they will feel comfortable saying yes, not to mention indicating that they are feeling uncoerced, free, autonomous, and respected about their "permission" for sex? "Yes" is meant to be a higher standard and can be well justified, as Schulhofer, Pineau, Reeves Sanday, and a few others so convincingly argue. The problem raised by scholars, including Schulhofer by his own admission, is that yes is a harder standard than no and women can't always even manage no. And if women say no when they mean yes, how are they going to muster the gumption actively to say yes when they want to?

While Schulhofer's work is as incisive as it is impressive, it suffers from a related problem, one that he keenly articulates about other rape reforms: his view is so radically different from extant conceptualization, let alone law or conceptualization about constitutional rights, that it is unlikely to have much practical impact. Liberal, as opposed to radical or radically different, notions and reforms didn't succeed in making actual change (e.g., courts, by his own description, still rely on only "traditional categories of physical intimidation" [1998: 97]), so what is it about his model involving the right to sexual autonomy that would prompt change more effectively?

Arguing that the law be extended to protect choice in sexual intimacy isn't likely to go very far, when women are still fighting, and increasingly fighting, to maintain some semblance of choice about whether we will allow our bodies to bring another human being into the world, for whom we will be responsible for decades. Arguing for the right to have sex and pleasure is surely a more arduous task that fighting against sexual attacks. The former right for sexual self-determination seems less pressing than the right to be free from violations and injuries inflicted by others. The law is already accepted for its role in protecting against physical harm, the problem is that the harms of sexual assault are yet to be fully protected against in the practice of law. Arguing for a whole new right, that is, to sexual autonomy to choose according to one's desire, pleasure, or notion of fun, in place of arguing for the more effective protection of an old right, that is, to be protected from physical harms, intrusions, and violations, just seems overly optimistic or excessively hopeful, especially in these times of conservatism and backlash against all things liberal, not to mention radical.

Goldberg-Ambrose levels a critique against Estrich that can be directly applied to Schulhofer. She says that Estrich (1987) neglects to "suggest any means, other than her own prodding, to achieve the restructuring of rape law" (Goldberg-Ambrose 1989: 951). This is true of Schulhofer too. Unlike Estrich, however, he provides a model statute that would, if enacted, codify the types of changes he recommends and in time possibly even the altered understanding of sexual interaction that his book promotes. Herein though lie other problems with several of his tenets.

First, he provides his "Model Criminal Statute for Sexual Offenses" (1998: 283–284) after the end of his last chapter, just before his notes and index, which is to say as a separate section at the end of the book. The statute is a stand-alone appendix, rather than something discussed elsewhere in the book. A model law that would allegedly address the concerns in his chapters should be clearly integrated with the text and address how each of the sections of his proposed statute would provide for the realization of the objectives he lays out in the text proper. The gap that is left between the reform directions he advances and the model law he attaches at the end of the book leaves his work open to the weighty criticism of vagueness that he attributes to extant laws and extant scholarship.

Several other problems stem from Schulhofer's model statute. He says that the word consent "means that at the time of the act of sexual penetration there are actual words or conduct indicating affirmative, freely given permission to the act of sexual penetration" (1998: 283, sec. 202[b]). His model continues, "consent is not freely given ... whenever" (sec. 202[c][8]) circumstances like victim age, threats, and so on are present. The work would be improved if Schulhofer used words like submission or compliance, or nonvoluntary acquiescence, instead of consent (see the next chapter here for elaboration) when he contrasts sexual assault to consensual sex. This would avoid diluting the word "consent." It would also facilitate developing a connotation that would be consistent with criminal offenses, as distinct from consensual sex. Moreover, using a word/words different from "consent" would diminish the association of "consent" with all the traditional problematic connotations, such as consent and resistance. Differential referents such as those just offered (and elaborated in later chapters) would also serve to acknowledge women's agency to want, even initiate, freely agree to, and consent to sex, which is so integral to Schulhofer's notions about the right to sexual choice and sexual autonomy.

Schulhofer's model law provides for four degrees of sexual offenses, all of which are crimes of penetration. This means that crimes of criminal sexual contact, short of penetration, are nowhere recognized in his model. This is an obvious shortcoming. These types of offenses could conceivably be encompassed by his provision that sexual offenses entail violations of "any other right of the victim" or where offenders may "inflict any other harm that would not benefit the actor" (1998: 284, sec. 202[c][5][v]), but he ties these considerations only to the offender's knowledge of victim consent. We really do not know if or how they pertain to acts of nonpenetration since these are nowhere delineated and since Schulhofer is remiss in connecting his statute appendix to any discussion or parts of his text. The ambiguity is compounded by his use of the terms "sexual assault" and "sexual abuse" to refer to degrees of crimes, although his definitions are restricted to crimes of penetration (when they could and should pertain to sexual assault and sexual abuse short of or different from penetration).

A further issue is that Schulhofer's appended statute never defines the jurisdictional law in regard to the difference between first-, second-, third-, and fourth-degree felonies. What the differences in degrees would mean is, I suspect, differences in punishment levels, but we do not know.[12]

Under the umbrella of victim-offender relationships, Schulhofer specifies a broad spectrum of criminal circumstances (unlike Estrich's model of reform, which neglects this dimension). He specifies "parent, foster, guardian, or other supervisory or disciplinary authority over the victim" and those in positions of power over victims, as in, for example, institutionalized or controlled/restricted environments or physical or psychological treatment settings. While his chapters pertaining to such matters are compelling, and laudable, what is missing is an enumeration of other relatives and household members who deserve to be singled out because of their relationship with or supervisory, disciplinary, authoritative or otherwise superordinate position they have over victims. I am thinking here about relatives such as brothers, uncles, grandfathers, and other household members like mothers' boyfriends—who are not infrequent offenders—who do not necessarily fit into any of his classifications, such as guardian or supervisor.

Schulhofer's model criminal statute is replete with other wide open areas and language, which require illustration and defense for comprehension as well as to be practical in import. His statute specifies sexual offenses, for example, if "bodily injury" is inflicted "on a person other than the victim" (1998: 283–284, sec. 202[c][5][i]) or if a defendant "commit[s] any other criminal offense" ([c][5][ii]). Referencing anyone, or any person other than the victim, is an overly broad substitute for specifying those persons, for example, who are in proximity to a victim or to whom a victim would care about enough to make her submit. Schulhofer's own distinction between threats that are consequential and those that are not (recall his example of "comply or I'll drink your soda" as an inconsequential threat, indeed a "jest" [1998: 131]) should make him sensitive to the need to differentiate consequential from inconsequential others (in terms of threats to injure someone else or to commit some other crime). In parallel fashion, Schulhofer's model code states that if defendants threaten to "accuse anyone of a criminal offense" ([c][5][ii]), or threaten to "expose any secret tending to subject any person to hatred, contempt or ridicule, or impair the credit or business repute of any person" ([c][5][iii]), or threaten to "*violate any other right* of the victim or *inflict any other harm* that would not benefit the actor" ([c][5][v]; italics added), it would be a sexual offense. It is vague, for instance, as to what "any other right" might mean and unclear as to what "any other harm that would not benefit the actor" is meant to reference.

The problem of imprecision in language, such as "any" other person, "any" other threat, and the like, is compounded by the fact that such expansiveness in definitions would, in all likelihood, beget challenge instead of popularity. Resistance to reforms designed to enhance victim protection and prosecution should be well known by now. Defining criminal offenses and offenders with such a broad brush makes criticism and resistance more effortless and obstructs, in place of opening, paths to needed future changes. This, juxtaposed with the rather radical calls for legal recognition of the new right of sexual autonomy and for affirmative consent/freely given permission to sex acts, renders Schulhofer's considerable contributions less likely to have any real impact.

Schulhofer's affirmative consent and sexual autonomy model is unlikely to be widely adopted. This is not to say that his contribution is trivial, for his work is perhaps the best of the genre. Overall, it challenges sexist dogma, while simultaneously opening up alternative conceptualization. The work goes a long way in educating about the nature of sexual assault, and this is anything but trifling. More precision, however, would go a long way toward clarification and hence, at least, toward education and awareness.

SUMMARY

While there are certainly drawbacks, like feasibility, to the affirmative consent models reviewed here, aspects of affirmative consent commend them for further reform efforts. Specifically, if affirmative consent standards were used only in particular instances such as "he said, she said" scenarios, where consent is at issue, perhaps some such standards would be more viable, that is, acceptable to the public.

Consent and Voluntariness, Agreement/
Nonconsent and Involuntariness,
Nonagreement

RECOGNIZING BACKGROUND FACTS

We need to recognize that regardless of specific reform direction or recommendation, a definitional distinction has to be drawn somewhere so that it is possible
to distinguish volitional sex from criminal rape. Drawing a line in the sand cannot be avoided. All reforms may draw it differently, with differing conceptualizations of relevant elements and definitions of same, but they all have to dichoto-
mize criminal sex from acceptable sex in some way at some point. The road to the
distinction is often tortuous in detail, making rape reform thinking inaccessible
to many (from the public, to practitioners, to even some academics). Recognizing
that a black-and-white distinction is inevitable helps to move us forward to assessing the relative merits and drawbacks to the different models and/or reforms
enacted or posited. A list of the words that wind up defining rape and sexual assault as differentiated from sex points up the importance and finickiness of line
drawing. Think about the following words and phrases: "against her will," "nonconsent," "unreasonable belief," "honest mistake," "negligently mistaken," "misleading," "capacity to harm," "ability to inflict," "belief in ability," "belief in threat,"
"affirmatively given," "coercive," "implicit threats," "voluntary permission," "emo-

tional appeals," "pressure," "persuasion," "fraud," "deception." Different laws, proposals, and scholars have variously used all of these to draw lines.

Schulhofer makes an interesting observation on the task of line drawing. He maintains that, when all is said and done, ambiguities still remain: "no standard can eliminate all factual uncertainty or swearing contests between witnesses" (1998: 271). "He said, she said" will thus ever be with us. Yet we must strive to make ambiguities less; that is what all the definitional attempts are about. To this, I would add that the construction of meaning and the ability to make one's construction prevail are at the root of a lot of the ambiguities. In other words, what he creates, or takes, or interprets the situation to be about and what she thinks happened or interprets as the meaning of his words and behaviors in a given situation are not phenomena that are equally likely to be believed. There is a historically grounded proclivity to give credence to male, not female, constructions. And this is what definitional demarcations try, and must continue to try, to alter.

We need to be cognizant of another truism so simple it is often forgotten. Without aggravating circumstances, cases essentially boil down to disputes about "he said, she said." And these (nonaggravated, nonstranger) "simple" rapes are the vast majority, roughly three-quarters, of all rape cases. It is of paramount importance to underscore that these cases are the most unaffected by rape reforms. Put differently, one of the largest impacts of all the changes in rape legislation materializes in taking "real," or aggravated, rape more seriously, leaving little impact on "simple," technical, "he said, she said" rapes and sexual assaults. Yet encompassing simple rape and sexual assault was what a lot of the legislative redefinitions and reconceptualizations were about in the first place.

A further fact that we need to appreciate up front is that there is, and will always be, discretion in the criminal legal system's processing of cases. This, too, is an unavoidable fact of life. Discretionary decision making is what determines implementation of any reform provision; it is, on the one hand, what delivers individualized justice and, on the other, what allows for discrimination. And with rape and sexual assault, it is discretion in implementation that explains the failures and the dismissal of "he said, she said," simple, date/acquaintance rapes.

While some reforms were well written, while some aspects of some laws have been positive in impact, and while some solid scholarship has advanced reforms, the original and persisting problem of discretion in the decision making routinely involved in enforcing reform laws has not been seriously contemplated. The work on reform for rape and sexual assault offenses continually reconceptualizes the phenomena and readjusts the line in the sand with different definitions, formulas, and perspectives. Yet the scholarship on reforms, while substantiated theoretically (from criminology, to philosophy, to sociology, to feminism and more) and legally (through analyses of statutes and case law), is cognitive and intellectual in nature, while the problems with reforms stem from actions, irrespective of cognitions, of those responsible for handling rape complaints. And the research on reform has shown that old-fashioned attitudes about females lying about rape, asking for rape, and so on influence discretionary decision making to undermine reform goals. Thus the reform conceptualizations have in many ways failed to reach or convince practitioners and the public, while these legal and lay populations (as jurors) handle cases no differently from the way they did in the past. The new ways of defining rape have not been seen as legitimate enough to translate into practice via the decisions that determine outcomes. Alternately stated, rape reform scholarship, educational efforts, and legal changes have failed to convince enough people that the traditional ways of thinking about rape are wrong, outdated, and unjust. Changing language, definitions, and lines in the sand is absolutely necessary but merely a first step. It must be followed up with changes informed by experiences from this first set of reforms and directed at both laws on the books and laws in operation on routine, daily bases.

A further fact about rape has to be recognized and articulated at the outset in the creation of any new model. This is that rape is a unique crime, in that it conjoins violence or physical force or coercion and sex. The reform movement's attempt to eliminate common law connotations and the attendant problems in adjudicating rape by defining rape as a violent, and not a sex, crime has led to a new problem: the tendency to erase the sexual nature of rape.

A related unique feature of rape is that it is the only crime where all cases entail physical contact. With murders, robberies, and assaults (the three other violent crimes or "crimes against the person" defined by the FBI), physical contact is not inherent in the commission of the crime. For example, weapons ranging from guns to knives, scissors, and ice picks allow someone to commit these other crimes without ever directly touching the victim. But with sexual assault crimes, the nature of the crime itself by definition involves touch or physical battery. Offensive physical invasion of a sexual nature contours the unique character of rape.

The protection of the body is perhaps one of the highest precepts that the law embodies. The relevance of this axiomatic legal protection from physical harm is that rape reforms often miss the point, that is, they overlook the unique nature of sexual assault. The best of the new models for reform in rape neglect to see that the defining feature of rape is physical, sexual contact or penetration as injury. Redefining rape as a violent crime, as a violation of sexual autonomy (Schulhofer), as communicative sexuality (Pineau), as a human rights violation (Human Rights Watch 1995), as sexual assault, as just another assault (without reference to sex; see Tong 1984), as a property crime like robbery (see Burgess-

Jackson 1999), or as an extortion crime (see Estrich 1987) entails reconceptualization as reform. To the tendency of reforms only conceptually to redefine the crimes, add the problem that these new definitions tend to background if not erase the unique offensiveness or "indignity" (Estrich 1987) of rape and sexual assault on the body (Cahill 2001).

Despite the initial problems associated with reform that this backdrop brings to the fore, the positive function of legal reform in educating official and lay populations alike should not be underestimated—as has been the case. The advantageous outcomes of reforms have been that at least so-called real rape has been taken more seriously and treated less discriminatorily vis-à-vis other crimes; for example, the corroboration requirement and resistance standards have been found to have disappeared de facto in routine practice in some jurisdictions. It is now time to learn from this and make changes for the future, for all rape but most especially to target in second-wave reforms what got left behind or was unaffected (Bryden and Lengnick 1997: 1199), namely, nonaggravated, simple, acquaintance, and date rape. In order to do this, reforms have to be informed by the practices corollary with the implementation of any new legal enactments.

What follows in this and subsequent chapters offers an alternative model of rape law reform that is informed by the characteristics and issues attending rape and its prosecution through the legal system that I have described above. I present this model in six parts over the subsequent six chapters. The specific problems I attempt to remedy in the model developed are, for example, the failures surrounding the prosecution of simple rape and sexual assault, the historic reliance on woman's consent, the issues that arise with force, consent, and intent, the allowance for consent and the (un)reasonable mistake of consent as criminal defenses, the process of arguing consent defenses especially in "he said, she said" cases, and the neglect in attention to lesser sexual assault offenses involving nonphysical threats and deceptions. As I will discuss later, my model also attempts to avoid the problems and harvest the benefits associated not only with rape reform laws but also with those that the more theoretical models of affirmative consent, strict liability, and sexual autonomy raise.

CONSENT AND NONCONSENT: A CONTINUUM

Several factors complicate the task of demarcating sexual assault as a crime from sex in general. One is the problem that consent poses in identifying rape and changing rape law. The criminal conduct involved in sexual assault under conditions of nonconsent is conduct that can and does routinely occur under noncriminal conditions of consent. As Mullendore observes, one of the difficulties surrounding consent in rape arises because sex acts can be consented to, but when rape is alleged, the consensual aspect appears as consent to criminal battery (injury) or at least is hard to differentiate, especially in the less severe cases (e.g., where there are no weapons, aiders and abettors, or injuries in addition to the rape itself). The issue becomes how to recognize nonconsent to sex when there are no (obvious) aggravating circumstances or "whenever it is 'one on one' behavior where the 'mimicking' of consensual procreative sex clouds the issue" (Mullendore, personal communication, 1998).

In order to address these and other problems in conceptualizing and prosecuting rape, it is useful to differentiate the range of potential responses to (noncriminal) sex acts. The positive kinds of responses that are implicitly included in the notions of consent can be conceptualized along a continuum. That to which consent refers can be seen in words like "agree," "concur," "and accord."[1]

The range begins with desire, sometimes ardent or enthusiastic, that can translate into initiating sexual behaviors and may lead to mutual participation in and/or willing voluntariness, agreement to sex acts initiated by another. Again, responses like agreement and concurrence must, definitionally, be freely, volitionally, genuinely, or willfully given (i.e., absent force, injury, etc.). It is important to recognize women's sexual agency and the purposive and sometimes passionate behaviors surrounding sex activities. The continuum starts here, in order more accurately to depict women's roles when they are fervent, active, and enlivened by sex, stepping far outside antiquated stereotypes of mere passivity or indifference.

It is important to underscore, too, that for volition to be present a person must be legally capable of giving meaningful consent. This is to say, to consent the person must be of legal age and sound of mind, which is to say not incapacitated by mental illness or by alcohol or drugs (voluntarily, surreptitiously, or involuntarily administered) or be unconscious or asleep.[2]

To give consent or to assent to sex, a person must also have the requisite knowledge about that to which they are agreeing. Voluntariness, agreement is not only meaningless under the conditions of violence and threats, it is meaningless under the condition of deception. Consent must be knowingly given. Two definitions are helpful here. Berliner cites *Webster's Dictionary* on consent in this context, stating that consent is "capable, deliberate, and voluntary agreement to or concurrence in some action" (1991: 2689 n. 14). Berliner also provides a definition of "knowing": "A person acts knowingly ... where he [sic] is aware of such nature or that such circumstances exist" (2691 n. 26). In other words, the person is conscious of the context and behaviors to which he or she concedes or agrees, in the absence of any sort of coercive forces or deception as to the nature of the act or situation. Henceforth, wherever the words "consent" and "agreement" are used, it should be with the understanding of the qualifiers of "capable," "knowing," and "voluntary" attached.

Moving along the continuum, we come next to a level of agreement slightly lower than voluntary, capable, knowing passionate participation and lower than mere capable and knowing voluntariness, agreement. This would be voluntary, uncoerced "permission" (Schulhofer 1998) or acquiescence. Though perhaps less ardent or mutual, this is an alternative articulation that could also belong in the realm of consent. Alternatively stated, freely chosen acquiescence, or conceding to sex, is the next point on a scale of concurrence. Permission and acquiescence can be seen as a type of reaction that is not as strong as passionate participation or voluntariness, agreement but nonetheless retains or yields agreement. Acquiescence might entail giving in, conceding, acceding, or assenting to sex acts. Permission to sex acts can be seen as a similar type of less enthusiastic response, where someone allows her(him)self passively to be acted upon or "done to." It is important to reiterate that any type of acquiescence or permission as that described here must occur in the absence of force, restraint, duress, threats, fear, compulsions, impairments (like alcohol or drugs), constraints, intimidation, or pressures or must not take place as a result of the authority/power position of the actor. It is the exceptional case where a woman voluntarily, freely, competently, knowingly participates or agrees or acquiesces or gives permission to sex acts under any of these conditions. Therefore, an exceptional case must be made and a differential standard and process must be developed to accommodate such rare, unusual, but possible scenarios. (Chapter 11 describes this in detail.)

Some volitional yielding to sex might be viewed as still a different kind of assent. The yielding may be carelessly done, done uncaringly, or occur indifferently, with little concern one way or the other or perhaps just with resignation. It is important again to bear in mind with this distinction that the disregard or lack of interest must still be free from threats, fears of safety, and so forth (as will be set forward in these chapters).

A LINE IN THE SAND

Drawing a line between sex and sexual assault is quite obviously not without its difficulties. Schulhofer's concept of sexual autonomy intimates that any sex that is "unwanted" should be criminalized. But Miriam Lewin's (1985) treatment of unwanted sex is quite different and problematizes this very premise. Her subtext is akin to the "wrestling matches" and "petting sessions" mentioned in chapter 6. Blurriness creeps in when one contemplates sex that is capitulated to but not necessarily desired. Lewin's discussion of "unwanted intercourse" creates a category that renders overly simplistic the line of demarcation suggested by Schulhofer.

Lewin asserts, "unwanted intercourse occurs when a reluctant partner is induced to acquiesce against her (his) will by psychological pressure from the would-be lover, but without the use of or the threat of force" (1985: 184). The point relevant for this discussion of a continuum is that there is no coercive power forcing the yielding. Hence the "unwanted sex" that is given into may not be desired sex, but it is accepted sex, where there is acquiescence. The trade-off is perceived to be worth the capitulation. This falls within what I am depicting here as volitional consent, specifically acquiescence or permission, even if half-hearted. If there is deception or force or threats of safety or a fear that harm is afoot, the act(s) would fall outside the "acceptable," noncriminal, nonsexual assault realm. One line is drawn at this (and further elaborated through the rest of this chapter).

I think the phrase "against her will" is extremely ill advised in this light. Choosing to surrender to sexual advances or requests because of psychological pressures or emotional appeals does not make for sex "against her will" or a criminal offense of rape or sexual assault. And the phrase "against her will" is associated with carnal knowledge law, which is associated with traditional kinds of force, injury, and so on.

I suggest that the phenomena Lewin mentions are better thought of as persuasions, rather than pressures, comprised of statements like, for example, "I'll break up with you if you don't have sex with me," "I'll do it with someone else," or "I won't love you." (These persuasive attempts are differentiated from duress and fraud, elaborated in chapter 12 of this book.) In my view, persuasion and psychological or emotional pressures or appeals are not consequential enough threats of injury to enjoin the protection of criminal law. Another line must be drawn at this.[3]

IMPLICIT COERCION AND CONSENT

The line for meaningful consent, then, is drawn at voluntary, capable, knowing acquiescence or permission in the absence of violence, force, threats of consequence, duress, and fraud (see chap. 12 on the last two dimensions). This excludes persuasion, psychological pressures, or emotional appeals. On the far side of the line lies submission under involuntary conditions. By involuntary conditions I mean submission because of such phenomena as physical violence, force, or threats; the dismissal of expressed nonconsent; fear of injury in the face of noncompliance; blackmail; being defrauded about the identity or nature of the actor or acts or contexts; being physically pinned in, held down, or otherwise constricted; having control stolen; or having options for escape limited.[4] These are all tantamount to coercive forces that create conditions of involuntariness, which is to say circumstances and behaviors that are inflicted on individuals, not freely chosen by them. This precept, that compulsion negates volition, was established as long ago as Aristotle (Baker 1999: 53). The wisdom stands the test of time.

Agreement or volition stops at submission under any manner of such force, threat, or compulsion. Where force, coercion, duress or power/authority, or false pretexts or deception (see chap. 12) engender submission, coercion of some nature is either explicitly or implicitly present, and consent cannot rightfully be taken to exist. Compliance under explicit or implicit compulsion is involuntariness, nonagreement. Yielding one's body or obeying demands because of threats stated or implied by coercive conditions and/or fear of any kind of harm is succumbing to coercive circumstances, which is antithetical to willing, volitional participation in or agreement to sexual activities. Agreement intends willingness, which is only a real choice in the absence of constrictions, controls, or coercive pressures. Surrender in such scenarios cannot be deemed to be within the purview of volitional agreement or volitional (versus coerced) acquiescence.

Where peril is intimated, harm is menaced, and women are put in fear, but no obvious violence or physical force is used, there is coercion and there is rape, although this may be murky to some. This is because of the confusion of sexual assault with "unwanted sex" (see Lewin 1985), where there is no coercion, or that between physical coercion or threats, on the one hand, and, on the other, persuasions or psychological pressures/appeals, where there is again no threat and, in this case, no crime. The relevant point with these very common but less directly violent rapes is that when a woman fears harm from the situation she is confronted with or is told to fear that force will be used or that harm will result if she does not capitulate to a man's menacing demands, sex acts turn into rape and sexual assault, and what might have been voluntariness, agreement or consensual sex is transformed into sexually assaultive injury and physical theft of a woman's body, integrity, and dignity. The theft and use of a woman's most private and personal body parts—her genitalia—is one of the ways in which rape can be understood to humiliate, demean, rob, and physically as well as psychologically injure females in a manner that can never be undone. The Criminal Law Revision Committee describes the British case of *Olugjoba* (QB 320, 1982) in the context of a discussion of drawing lines. They state that "the Court of Appeal, in *Olugjoba*, held that threats of force are not the only kinds of threat that may negative consent. It drew a distinction between consent, on the one hand, and 'submission' or 'reluctant acquiescence' on the other, but left unresolved the ambiguous issue of how the two states of mind were to be demarcated" (2000: 55–56). Whether the victim consented would be left up to the jury to decide (on a case-by-case basis). Temkin points out that this is problematic because this court decision model of consent (as contrasted to, for example, a legislative definition of consent) means that there are no conditions, even such as blatant violence or injury, where consent would automatically be absent or unavailable as a defense, because it is up to the jury in each case (2002: 92). I would clearly agree, and the model I am offering both defines consent (see below) and the conditions that negate its tenability, demarcating volitional versus reluctant acquiescence that is involuntary (unless proved otherwise by the defense; see chap. 11).

My contention is that (1) submission is not consent, voluntariness, agreement, voluntary acquiescence, or permission under any kind of violence, force, or consequential threats or deceptions; (2) threats are different from psychological pressures, persuasions, and emotional ploys or appeals, and the former make for crime while the latter do not; (3) acquiescence, however recalcitrant, if given knowingly and capably can be voluntary consent under exceptional circumstances, that is, only under some particularized conditions (see chap. 12 for how consent defenses can be available or are unavailable); (4) these premises mean that if violence, force, coercion, duress, or fraud are demonstrated, nonconsent need not be demonstrated in court, as this would be redundant in almost all or most typical cases. Conversely, if nonconsent were demonstrated, the prosecution would not need to prove force or the like (see the next chapter).

Burgess-Jackson elucidates issues along these lines in an article entitled "A Theory of Rape" (1999). As he sees it, most rapes aren't physically "forcible in the sense that they leave the victim no choice. In many cases of rape, probably the vast majority of them, the victim is *given* a choice by the rapist. She is presented with two or more options, one of which is submission to sexual intercourse. ... The alternative to submission—death or physical injury, for example—is less desirable from her point of view. This phenomenon ... I call 'coercion'" (94; italics in original).

Burgess-Jackson continues to describe physical force or compulsion and differentiate this from psychological compulsion, namely, where the rapist creates a situation that makes it in the best interest, or makes it the best alternative, for the victim to go along with his will because of threats (1999: 94). He defines psychological coercion simply: "to compel by threat" (95). The difference between this (compelling by threat) and psychological pressures or lies, which are sometimes referenced as "psychological coercion," requires comment. Burgess-Jackson's definition is advantageous in its specific reference to (largely) physical threats, where psychological coercion exists if bodily (or property, as he extends it) injury is menaced if the victim refuses the will of the rapist. Coercion, then, excludes emotional, intellectual, or psychological appeals such as pressures, ploys, or lies, as I previously differentiated, but includes psychological coercion where the rapist makes it in the rational interest of a victim to comply given fear of alternatives. This may be an obvious point. Since this discussion, however, is about definitions that differentiate rape and sexual assault from sex, all considerations about inclusion and exclusion merit attention.[5]

He Said, She Heard: Implicit Threats

Another definitional differentiation can benefit from clarification. It is advantageous to keep force and coercion conceptually distinct from one another. We need to guard against the slippage between force and coercion. *Black's Law Dictionary* is again useful as it distinguishes between force and coercion. *Black's* defines force as "power, violence, compulsion or constraint exerted upon a person or thing" (1991: 444). Coercion is a more encompassing term. It refers to "compulsion; constraint; compelled by force or arms or threat" (177). This means that coercion would cover both acts and threats to act. In order to avoid cumbersome and confusing terminology, hereafter "force" will be used exactly as *Black's* defines it—as physical violence exerted on a person or a thing—and "coercion" will be used to refer to threats to act.

The slippage between force and coercion creates even more confusion when explicit and implicit coercive threats to use force are discussed as "implicit force." Schulhofer, for instance, describes how implicit force has not been seen as sufficient to establish rape in some jurisdictions. He states that "many courts do not recognize a man's indirectly intimidating conduct or the frightening character of a situation as sufficient, even when the circumstances leave the victim in fear of immediate harm" (1998: 74–75). This "implicit force" would be better discussed as implicit coercion or implicit threat, wherein force is characterized as physical or applied and coercion is characterized as the threat of force. Threats or coercion can be either explicitly stated or implicitly involved in a situation. Once differentiated, we need to recognize further that implicit threats can be as "equally powerful and intimidating" (Schulhofer 1998: 75) to a woman as explicit threats can be. Schulhofer observed that this was easily recognized as far back as the 1940s. He notes how "a woman surrounded by 'four big men' would fear injury and need not resist, even though they did not tell her they were going to do anything to her if she refused" (75). "This approach, recognizing both explicit and implicit threats as forms of force, is now widely accepted, at least in theory" (76). I should add that behaviors can be threatening without words. For example, behaviors as simple as raising a hand, clenching a fist, or pointing to a gun are clearly threatening absent any vocalization. A rapist doesn't have to say out loud "I will use this knife," as he brandishes it, or "I will hurt you worse" in order for the threats to be real and in order for a victim to receive and heed them. Hands near someone's throat imply strangulation as a possible course of action, even in the absence of words or additional gestures.

Estrich, too, considers implicit coercion or "threatening situations" (1987: 86). She states that "nonconsent goes unrecognized ... where women plainly do not consent but where traditional force or explicit threats are not used" (86–87). Several case examples are illustrative. In the case of *State v. Alston*, Estrich (1987) describes how the defendant, who had been physically abusive to the victim in their past cohabiting relationship, found the victim, demanded to know where she lived, threatened to "'fix' her face" if she didn't honor his "right" to have sex one more time, proceeded to grab the victim's arm and take her to a friend's house, where she protested, but he took his "sex," which is to say raped her as he "pulled her up from the chair, undressed her, pushed her legs apart, and penetrated her" (61). The court conceded nonconsent, but the jurors did not convict in this case because they were not persuaded that there was evidence of enough force to justify a finding of the crime of rape (60–63; Kadish and Schulhofer 2001: 332–333).

In the case of *Rusk v. State* (406 A.2d 624, 628 [Md. Ct. Spec. App. 1979] rev'd, 424 A.2d 720 [Md. 1981]), the victim and defendant met at a bar; he asked her for a ride home, she obliged, he asked her upstairs, she repeatedly declined, and he took her car keys to strand her late at night in an unfamiliar neighborhood, whereupon she followed him to his apartment after several commands from him. She asked if he was going to kill her if she did not do what he wanted. She cried, he put his hands around her throat, which he interpreted as a "heavy caress," and she interpreted as "lightly choking" (Estrich 1987: 64). Although the appeals court upheld the lower court conviction on the grounds that the victim's fear was reasonable in this case, they, too (like the Special Appeals Court that reversed the original conviction), were skeptical that any real force was in evidence (65).

Evans is another case that illustrates court interpretation of force and threats, explicit and implicit. In this New York case, the defendant gave the victim a ride from LaGuardia Airport into the city. The victim was described by the court as "unworldly," "naive," and "gullible" (Kadish and Schulhofer 2001: 346, citing *People v. Evans* [Supreme Court, New York County, Trial Term 85 Misc. 2d 1088, 379 N.Y.S. 2d 912 (1975)]). The assailant pretended he was a therapist doing a scientific experiment on women's and men's reactions to one another in a singles bar. The defendant took the victim to a singles bar and then to one of his alleged offices, whereupon he advanced on her, pulling her onto a bed. She rejected his sexual advances, indicating nonconsent. He said, "Look where you are. You are in the apartment of a strange man. How do you know that I am really a psychologist.... I could kill you. I could rape you. I could hurt you physically" (347, citing *People v. Evans*). He then changed course, pretending that she reminded him of a lost love, which earned her sympathy for a moment, but then he grabbed and allegedly raped her. The court was not convinced it was rape, because they did not find "forcible compulsion nor threat beyond a reasonable doubt" (348).

In *Goldberg v. State* (41 Md. App. 58, 395 A.2d 1213 [Md. Spec. App. 1979]), the victim went to an isolated building that was the defendant's "temporary studio" (Estrich 1987: 67–68). The defendant was posing as a modeling agent. He advanced on the victim, who expressed nonconsent, saying she didn't want to "do that stuff" (68). She said she was fearful because of the isolation and because of how much larger the defendant was than she (67–70). The appellate court insisted on some demonstration of force or physical behavior of nonconsent—or resistance (not verbal expression of nonconsent)—in order to find for rape (68), and thus did not uphold the conviction.

In *Commonwealth v. Berkowitz* (641 A.2d 1161 Pa. 1994), the victim stopped in on an acquaintance in a dorm room while she was waiting for her boyfriend. The defendant began kissing and fondling the victim, who said no. The victim began to cry, "no, I gotta go, let me go," but the defendant "got up and locked the door," pushed her on the bed, and penetrated her, although she continued to protest "no" (Schulhofer 1998: 70). As Kinports reports "in the court's words, the victim 'stated' 'no' throughout the encounter with the defendant but found insufficient evidence of the 'forcible compulsion' required by the state's rape statute" (2001: 793, citing *Commonwealth v. Berkowitz* 6641 A.2d 1161, 1164 Pa. 1994). The original conviction was reversed on appeal because the court interpreted forcible compulsion to require more than victim nonagreement.

Not only are these cases indicative of implicit and explicit coercive threats, they showcase the prominence and persistent requirement of force over and above (in order to prove) nonagreement. They simultaneously showcase how coercion—explicit, not to mention implicit—is not enough for court determinations of rape.

Kinports contemplates these issues. She first cites Dressler's work to point out that force is viewed as tantamount to violence and that using "nonconsent" to define rape "trivializes the concept of forcible rape and the harm" that victims suffer (2001: 795–796, citing Dressler 1998: 423). In other words, force and violence, not nonconsent (and not coercion, I might add), are necessary to define the crime of rape. Despite recognizing this, however, Kinports next goes on to explain how the intrusion and pain of "nonconsensual" intercourse is itself violent (795–796, citing West 1994: 125, 150). Quoting Dorothy Roberts, she comments that "as Roberts points out, creating distinctions between 'seemingly nonviolent sexual coercion' and 'sex accompanied by physical violence' tends to 'obscure the common nature of both'" (796, citing Roberts 1993: 381), which in turn obscures the harm of both forms of violation. Although "there may well be a difference 'between forcible and nonforcible nonconsensual intercourse,' it is 'not the difference between violent and non-violent rape,' but rather 'it is the difference between lots of violence and not as much violence, or lots of force and not much force.'" (796, citing West 1994: 163).

It is noteworthy that perceptions of rape victims who give in to rapists' demands when given the alleged choice of greater harm if they do not took a sharp downward turn in the Kobe Bryant case. The defense raised the specter of a problematic new way of combining considerations of consent and submission. The defense was going to attempt the argument that the victim "consented to submit." Submitting is different from acquiescing, with the former happening under fear of greater harm/injury if a person does not give in and the latter pertaining to a situation where a person gives in voluntarily—which is to say, without constraint, force or threat. The blurring of lines in the construction "consent to submit" is nothing more than a strategic defense ploy playing on the semantics I argue matter so greatly. Semantics matter because, if this tactic is ever successful, a new category of defense could be opened up, wherein a new definition could be constructed to condemn victims (who allegedly agree to give in to sex acts) and to exculpate offenders who threaten victims to get them to give in to the crimes of sexual assault and rape (so defined because of the threat/compulsion/coercion that forces the yielding).

In most instances, yielding—through silence, passivity, cooperation, or even indications of "okay" or "yes"—under conditions of forcefulness or coerciveness is not genuine or real consent. And so the level of giving in described by "consent to submit" would begin a new continuum—say, of nonconsent—ranging from victims' surrendering under conditions of force, duress, and so on up through victims' resisting vocally or physically, even brandishing their own weapons. Regardless of where it falls on the continuum, however, the nonconsent is real, and the rape is really rape.

She Said (She Felt), He Heard (Thought): Implicit Consent

Whether consent is fervent, emotionally strong, animated, rationally calculated, or desperately or carelessly conceded, the problem is that it is so rampantly presumed or inferred, rather than assessed, where it may not exist. The issue is tied to the assumption that laws have implicitly made about women, sex, and rape. The operative assumption is that consent is constant, or implicitly (omni)present. In other words, the presupposition is that women always agree to sex. "Always" translates to mean—to men—that all women, at all times, in all places, are desirous of, interested in, and consenting to all sexual overtures by men—which means all men. The fact of the matter is that all women do not always want sex—even with a particular man, let alone all men.

A relatively recent case in Canada (*R. v. Ewanchuk* [1999] 169 D.L. 4th 193 [Can.]) illustrates how strongly implied consent can bias cases. The case involved a seventeen-year-old girl who had a job interview with a man. The interview took place in his van. The victim subsequently accompanied him to his trailer. He made incremental sexual advances, whereupon the victim indicated unwilling nonagreement at each move. She said "no," "please don't," "stop," and so on but was fearful that being any more assertive than this would escalate his behavior into a more violent attack. The court simply but significantly stated, "There is no doctrine of 'implied consent,'" which the defendant assumed, apparently from the victim's behavior, for example, accompanying him, not offering more resistance. The court went on to note that "the complainant's conduct may give rise to the defendant's mistaken belief in consent, but it does not undermine the fact of her nonconsent itself. Here, the court found that the accused knew that the complainant was not consenting before each encounter, "thus the defense of mistaken belief lacked the requisite 'air of reality'" (MacKinnon 2001: 853–854, citing 169 D.L.R.4th at 214, citing *R. v. Esau* [1977] 2 S.C.R. 777 [Can.]). The relevant point here is that specifying the absence of an implied consent doctrine in court cases (as well as in de jure law) is needed. This may be one useful way to undermine its perpetuity.

SEMANTICS: CHANGING "CONSENT" TO "VOLUNTARINESS, AGREEMENT" AND "NONCONSENT" TO "INVOLUNTARINESS, NONAGREEMENT"

We need to jettison the word "consent" altogether and replace it with new vocabulary that reflects genuine consent when existent but precludes the frequent and erroneous assumption of consent when absent. This is necessary because sex can be consensual and consensual sex can be a defense to rape charges, so the meaning of "consent" must be preserved yet corrected to be more accurate, which is to say, less presumed, less frequent, and less rationalized into existence when absent. Because using the word "consent" brings up past associations of omnipresent female acceptance and desire, and because of the concomitant un-bridled doctrine of implied consent, the word "consent" has to be avoided alto-gether so as to eliminate the common law and lay connotations that so damage rape prosecution.

Reconceptualizing consent is necessary because of the loaded associations that rape myths layer on everyday interactions, asserting that women want, desire, fantasize about, and precipitate male domination in sex and even vio-lent rape victimization. Semantic change in the pivotal notion of consent can begin the move to disenfranchise these historic damning attitudes. The change must be drastic if we are to shake the enduring and deeply entrenched ideas about consent.

New terminology to mold new connotations should define that only assent that is volitionally made counts as agreement. Words like "agreement" are help-ful insofar as they typically allude to stronger, or less passive, notions of con-sent. (This terminology is also consistent with my attempt to recognize women's real sexual agency and even ardent behaviors.) Altering the word would help to diminish the endemic belief that consent is implied. It would similarly limit the applications where agreement could be legally taken to exist. Translated, this means that agreement would not be assumed and instead would have to be shown, that is, would only be pertinent if the defense mounted it (agreement) as a criminal defense to the charges of rape or sexual assault.[6]

Although "voluntary consent" should be seen as redundant, it obviously is not, owing to hundreds of years of public belief, sentiment, and common law. If "voluntariness, agreement" were to replace "consent," perhaps people would begin to see the earlier redundancy and understand that "consent" alone must always be volitional and free. I chose the word "voluntary," as opposed to "will-ing," to go along with the term "agreement" because of the problems associated with the traditional reliance on the construction "against her will." By using an-other word, I avoid the potential continuation of the meanings associated with this phrase.

By "voluntariness, agreement," I intend agreement to or acceptance of sex acts that is unforced, uncoerced, volitional, freely given, and not in any other way exacted by means of physical pressures, intimidation, or threat to the physi-cal safety or well-being of the woman.[7] It is instructive to contrast the meaning of the words "voluntary" and "involuntary." The clear antonym of the type of voluntariness, agreement I am laying out here is seen in the definition of involuntary as "without will or power of choice; opposed to volition or desire ... under duress, force or coercion" (Black 1991: 574). Submitting involuntarily, then, means yielding or complying under conditions of physical harm or threats of harm that compel a person to do what they otherwise would not do (348, definition of duress) or when "one party is constrained by subjugation to the other to do what his [sic] free will would refuse" (177, definition of coercion).[8] I use "nonagreement" synonymously with "involuntary acquiescence," "involuntary submission," or "involuntary compliance," to reference submission, or surrendering to sexual demands, under specified offense circumstances (see the model array in chap. 13 for circumstances). I treat nonagreement as the opposite of purposive, voluntary choice, genuine or free assent given in the absence of force, coercion, or other involuntary conditions (like duress).

I propose the term "involuntariness, nonagreement" to replace the word "nonconsent" in rape adjudication. I want to emphasize here that I am not suggesting that nonagreement become a part of the definition of the crime or one of the elements of the crime that prosecutors must prove in addition to heinous or forceful or coercive conditions. I am only advocating that we eschew "nonconsent" to eradicate old-fashioned notions and prejudicial practices that have been concomitant with the use of that term.

SEMANTICS: CHANGING THE DEFENSE OF CONSENT TO THE DEFENSE OF VOLUNTARINESS, AGREEMENT

Abandoning the term "consent" in favor of some alternatively articulated conceptualization, like the voluntariness, agreement being described here, is but a first step in changing ideas about consent and rape. Several other specifications need to follow along with this change. Removing the consent defense and replacing it with some alternatively worded defense would be a much needed next step on the road to attacking the horrendous slew of problems about belief in consent in rape. Making the legal defense mirror the semantic change in vernacular by repealing the consent defense and enacting a voluntariness, agreement defense would maintain the feasibility of the defense but eliminate the prejudice it presupposes. This would move the law further toward the fundamental fairness for women, as well as men, that the law is supposed to exemplify.

It is important that rape laws statutorily define "voluntariness, agreement." The failure of reforms, like the model CSC Code in Michigan, to do so (recall that the Michigan statute avoided the word "consent" altogether) has led to successful defenses of consent under even the most egregious crime circumstances.

Tchen makes just such an observation in her comment that "the omission of a statutory definition of consent ... poses a real possibility that the courts will rely on precedents using common law definitions of consent.... This could mean that the 'fiction of implied consent' will be applied, and actions by the victim such as hitchhiking or drinking will be construed by the court as consent" (1983: 1541–1542). It is therefore important to define not only force and coercion, as Michigan did, albeit somewhat limitedly (Michigan's law lists five nonexhaustive circumstances of force/coercion) but also consent—or agreement, in the scheme I am proposing—to preclude the impact of implied consent dogma.

DEFINITION OF VOLUNTARINESS, AGREEMENT

It is instructive to look at de jure statute definitions of consent that fall within the meanings I am carving out here. Wisconsin's definition of consent is "words or overt actions by a person who is competent to give informed consent indicating a freely given agreement to have sexual intercourse or sexual contact" (Tchen 1983: 1543–1544). Minnesota's definition of consent is "a voluntary uncoerced manifestation of a present agreement to perform a particular sex act" (1542).[9] Illinois law states that "consent means words or overt action by a person indicating a freely given agreement to the specific acts of sexual penetration or sexual conduct in question" (1549). These definitions are highly similar in expressing that consent intends volition. A simple definition of voluntariness, agreement is that a capable person knowingly makes a free choice to engage in sex acts and indicates this through words, gestures, or other conduct.

But even definitions that bookend the notion of consent with the concepts "voluntary" and "freely given" do not preclude reliance on implied consent, and ultimately resistance as well. As Tchen remarks "the experience in Florida indicates that even a consent definition using the concept of a knowing and voluntary consent may still allow the courts to use the resistance standard and implied consent" (1983: 1546). She provides an Illinois example of the problem, too, noting that, despite the "freely given" aspect of the Illinois statute, the courts have determined that "voluntary submission by a female ... no matter how reluctantly yielded, amounts to consent" (1550–1551). Voluntary submission may be an oxymoron but obviously has not been viewed in this way by judges in Illinois or elsewhere. Submission is not freely given; it is instead giving in under circumstances less than freely, voluntarily chosen or under compulsion. It represents caving in the face of danger, intimidation, threats of harm, and/or hopeless inevitability. There is nothing voluntary about being forced into fear, nothing resembling free or voluntary choice in "reluctant yielding," nothing free or voluntary about being subdued or vanquished. Submission under force or coercion is no more indicative of voluntariness, agreement to sex than is a pig's ear.

That consent is still attributed to victims who charge rape, in spite of definitions that include the word "voluntary" or "free," means that it is imperative to devise additional ways to disarm the doctrine of implied consent. Using a new concept, such as voluntariness, agreement, with more automatic and potent associations with volition, choice, preference, mutuality, and the like, and articulating what this concepts is meant to include and exclude, is a necessary starting point—but only a starting point—in reforming rape reforms. The same goes for substituting involuntariness, nonagreement for nonconsent. It is an additional step but still just a step.

ELIMINATING THE DOCTRINE OF IMPLIED CONSENT: STATUTORY SPECIFICATION

There are a couple of ways we could go about trying to purge implied consent. Hoping for court decisions (stare decisis, or the doctrine of case precedent) to declare implied consent dead is one way, as the *Ewanchuk* decision in Canada evidences.[10]

The endemic presumption of implied consent sullies the treatment of rape victims. Therefore this presumption must be dealt with head-on to be dismantled. Eradicating the doctrine of implied consent is one way to fight the myth that women ask for, precipitate, deserve, want, or consent to sex and then cry rape. The most efficient way to accomplish this is to specify de jure that consent cannot be presumed. My recommendation is to specify in rape laws that voluntariness, agreement (consent) to sex acts does not implicitly exist and that voluntariness, agreement or consent to sex acts therefore cannot rightfully or reasonably be assumed. Indications of voluntariness, agreement range widely, but however they are expressed, they cannot be presumed. Instead they must be looked for and/or observed to be used to defend against a rape accusation (see chap. 11 for a discussion of how the affirmative consent standard would apply in this situation). And, to reiterate, so as to be steadfast about the meaning, submission, acquiescence, or saying okay or even saying yes under force/coercion does not constitute agreement that is in any way free or voluntary (see below); that is, capitulation is not genuine consent. Berliner makes a germane point here. Her concurrence with the above recommendation can be seen in her statement that "the law can point out that a belief in consent should not be a mere assumption";

it should at the least be "honest" and "reasonable" (1991: 2706). (Berliner's further discussion of mistake of consent is discussed in subsequent chapters here.)

The focus on victim consent and the inference that consent is implicitly present distinguish rape from other crimes. Enacting a provision to dislodge implicit consent would make rape more consistent with other crimes and laws. Think of it this way: police do not automatically investigate nonconsent when other crimes are reported, and prosecutors do not have to disprove consent, or prove nonconsent, to establish other crimes beyond a reasonable doubt. Tchen quotes the House Judiciary Committee in Michigan, where it was stated that "the question as to whether or not the victim 'consented' is not an issue in any felony other than rape" (1983: 1538, quoting House Judiciary Committee analysis of Senate Bill 1207 [June 27, 1974], quoted in *People v. Nelson*, 406 Mich. 1020, 281. N.W. 2d 134 [1970]). Tchen goes on to assert that prosecutors should not have to establish nonconsent "at the outset" of cases (1538, 1548). This uniqueness is neither necessary nor justified.

Rape should be treated like other crimes—for example, murder, robbery, assault—where nonconsent is the prevailing view. In fact, there are so few instances where consent is presumed with other crimes that notice of nonconsent is regularly unnecessary. Attorney Susan Krumholz provides the best example: uniquely in the offense of trespass is there a burden of the complaining party to show notice of nonconsent a priori (personal communication, 1998). In much the same way, stating that consent cannot be presumed in statute would serve notice that consent is not and cannot be inferred or implied or reasonably taken to exist, especially when a woman says no or when any sort of coercive circumstances prevail. This would level the playing field so that the salient assumption would no longer be that she voluntarily agreed to the sex act(s) under such duress and, concomitantly, that she must be lying in her accusation of rape.

In short, consent is never inherently present, and the law must so state. Voluntariness, agreement must be proven one way or the other, either through the prosecution's proof of the opposite—namely, nonconsent (if there is no other criminal circumstance like force)—or through the defense's proof that consent was expressed in some way (see chap. 11).

SHE'S NOT A LIAR: STATUTORY SPECIFICATION

Accompanying the myth that consent is implicitly present and/or that women agree to sex they later report as rape is the belief that women falsely accuse men of rape. Lying, like consent, is not presumed or the frequent belief with other crimes, like robbery and assault, and should not be a frequent belief when rape or sexual assault are reported.

By accusing someone of rape, a woman is saying that she did not voluntarily agree to the sex act(s) that she is registering in her complaint. This is to say that either saying no or (in the absence of the expression of "no") simply being in the presence of duress, force, or compulsion or in a situation where other aggravating conditions, such as weapons or multiple offenders, are present is a sufficient basis for criminal charges of rape. The woman reporting rape is alleging that the act(s) of a crime occurred, which should provide the threshold for police to begin looking for the suspect. This is how other crimes are handled, and rape should be handled in parallel fashion. This is often not the case, however, when victims bring forward allegations of sexual assault. Instead, victims are doubted as liars, most often suspected to have consented to the sex acts they allege to be crimes of sexual assault. Yet victims of other crimes are not suspected of lying, that is, of fabricating charges because of their consent and/or willing participation in the crimes they report. For example, when someone complains of a robbery, the charges are typically filed and investigated by police, who may unfound the exceptional case where they doubt the existence of a crime because of some suspicion about consent, lying, or some other fraud. Consent to share one's money with a criminal is simply presumed to be unlikely. Implicit nonagreement is the operative premise. Even in cases of theft where insurance would cover losses, victims are not presumed to have consented to the theft. Ulterior motives, like financial benefit in the case of insurance, do not automatically arise when someone reports a theft. Yet, in cases of sexual assault, consent is frequently presumed and ulterior motives like malice, resentment ("a woman scorned"), or regret are attributed, even though there is little to gain and much to lose for the person who brings forward charges of rape.[11]

Questioning victim consent means questioning the existence of involuntariness or the woman's allegations about the existence of force, threats, or aggravating circumstances that made her submit to the demands of a rapist. Given the widely known and massive extent of underreporting in rape, it is more likely than not that the minority of rapes that make their way to the criminal legal system are not falsely reported, that is, that what transpired was forceful or nonconsensual, in other words, rape. Since both force/coercion and nonconsent are required, de facto if not de jure, the cases that make their way to the legal system are the stronger cases to begin with. And given that even according to police judgments, the vast majority of rape reports are founded (the figure is commonly put at less than 2 percent unfounded; see Bryden and Lengnick 1997 for a review; see also Dusky 1996; Hunter, Bentley Cewe, and Mills 1998), the belief that victims are lying or falsely claiming rape is what is unreasonable to assume.[12] Kanin adds that two other factors underlying unfounding are uncooperative victim/witness and reporting in the wrong jurisdiction (1994: 1).

The distrust of rape victim accounts is testimony to how ingrained implied consent, and hence false accusation, myths are when rape is at hand. The insidious myth that women implicitly give in to or agree to sex acts and then claim rape needs to be corrected for its atypicality, abnormality, and unreasonableness. In order that women who come forward to report rape do not continue to be so discriminatorily mistrusted and seen as liars, fakes, phonies, or frauds, we need to specify de jure that the person who charges or reports a rape or sexual assault offense cannot rightfully or reasonably be presumed to be lying. Those reporting rape should be presumed to be involuntary, nonagreeing victims to a crime, not willing participants in the sex acts constituting criminal offenses. This is the case with other crimes, and the law needs to state specifically that it is the case in rape because of the assumptions otherwise.

I am arguing that we begin to think of those reporting rape as innocent until proven guilty (guilty by a defense demonstration in a court of law that voluntariness, agreement was present). The magnitude of unfairness to rape victims is evidenced by the fact that there is a need to stipulate that victims are innocent until proven guilty; even criminal offenders enjoy this right. It is only fair to think that those coming forward with criminal charges did not desire, want, precipitate, participate willingly in, or voluntarily agree to being raped, just as it is accepted that other victims did not agree to being beaten up, to having their money or property stolen, and so forth. Those reporting crimes, including those reporting rape and sexual assault, should all be presumed to be unwilling, unwanting, nonconsenting parties to criminal victimization and so to be telling the truth when they report that they were forced, coerced, or indicated nonagreement and only involuntarily submitted to the acts constituting crimes. The importance of this inclusion is that those who report rape are innocent not only of lying or fabricating charges but of committing the crime of filing false police reports. This perspective, that it should be assumed that women who report rape are innocent of filing false police reports and lying, recognizes the legitimacy of women's point of view concerning the existence of force, threats, involuntariness, or nonagreement (see chap. 10 for further discussion of the woman's point of view). This, of course, must be convincing to judges and juries in order to prove rape in court, but it should at a minimum replace the historic male privileged perspective that has so discriminated against women in the past and continues to do so today.[13]

Should there be any remaining doubt as to the necessity of such a provision, consider the following. Tchen mentions how consent has been "implied" or construed when "the issue was not *actual* consent, 'but rather behavior by the victim short of consent that is taken to signal her sexual availability' " (1983: 1524, citing *State v. Myers*, 606 P. 2d 250 [Utah 1980]; italics in the original). "A woman who sends out signals, such as drinking, dancing, or hitchhiking, is assumed to have," then, advertised availability, desire, and/or consent and even to have "invited the rape" (1524). "A victim's 'provocative clothing' or 'sexually promiscuous' behavior are also signals of 'implied' consent that incriminate the testimony of the female complainant and pardon the actions of the male defendant" (ibid.). These are all ungrounded, unreasonable, and outrageous stretches.

Stating in law that those charging rape cannot be assumed to be lying is akin to what the state of Michigan did with respect to the corroboration requirement. Michigan enacted a provision in the CSC Code that denoted the absence of a de jure corroboration requirement in order to eliminate the de facto existence of a corroboration requirement. Specifically, the law spelled out that corroboration of a victim's testimony is not required (PA 328 1974). Stating that victims are not lying or filing false police reports when charging rape is providing a de jure specification to correct a de facto situation.

An additional dimension that justifies the de jure specification that those who charge rape cannot be assumed to lying or falsely charging men is found in a consideration of other criminal offenses in another light. Consent to injury is an untenable legal defense (excuse) in cases of serious (assault and battery) injury or death (Mullendore, personal communication, 1998). We rarely if ever think or assume that those who report serious assaults voluntarily agree to the attacks or injuries. While the legal impossibility of consent to harm could be extended to rape, I am not advocating that the law go this far. This is because consent to forced or coercive sex is tenable, even though highly unlikely. Consent to the injuries of nonconsensual sex is highly improbable but not impossible, just as consent to other physical harms is highly improbable but not impossible. I am not arguing, then, that consent cannot be argued or that "she's a liar" can never be used as a criminal defense, only that women who state that they have been raped do not deserve to be presumed to be liars, cheats, or whores, and this is what consent—implicit or explicit—conveys.

SUMMARY

The following proposals, outlined and discussed in the model for reforming rape reforms in chapters 13 and 14, are designed to change substantive law, in de jure fashion, as well as procedural law, through instructions to jurors.

These changes would reinforce one another, educating fact finders about new revisions in rape laws as cases are adjudicated. Chapters 13 and 14 lay out and expand on these notions.

Summarily, I propose the following for all rapes/sexual assaults, whether involving only involuntariness or involving force or coercion or aggravating characteristics:

1. Substitution of the new, stronger wording "voluntariness, agreement" for "consent" and of "involuntariness, nonagreement" for "nonconsent" in crime definition.
2. Substitution of the new, stronger wording "voluntariness, agreement" for "consent" in the constructions "defense of consent" and "defense of mistake of consent."
3. Definition of voluntariness, agreement as a freely chosen, positive decision to engage in sex acts, expressed in words or actions by those capable of giving agreement willingly.
4. Specification in de jure law that there is no doctrine that allows consent/voluntariness, agreement to be inferred; there is no "implied consent."
5. Specification in de jure law that those who report rape cannot reasonably be presumed to be liars; it is unreasonable to assume that victims falsely report rape/sexual assault offenses.[14]

AGGRAVATING CONDITIONS, FORCE/COERCION, AND NONAGREEMENT

A simultaneous consideration of what constitutes aggravating conditions, force-ful or coercive conduct on the part of the offender, and involuntariness, non-agreement on the part of the victim indicates a need to modify rape law further.[1] Kinports alone elaborates a critical direction for change in her assessment of the redundancy of proving both force/coercion and nonconsent in rape. Few others as much as intimate the connection Kinports elaborates so well in this regard.[2] The problem is that in almost all jurisdictions the prosecution must prove non-consent in addition to force/coercion (Kinports 2001: 756, also citing Anderson 1998). If this requirement is not de jure, it is nonetheless required in practice. As Kinports puts it, "if one, but not the other, is present, the sexual act is not rape" (771). The prosecution must prove nonconsent as well as the crime-defining cir-cumstances or aggravating, or forceful, or coercive conditions (beyond a reason-able doubt) in order to establish the crimes of sexual assault or rape.[3]

Nonagreement should not have to be proven when physical danger or threats are evidenced because it is unreasonable to think that women concede willingly to sex acts under conditions of violence and threats of harm. There may be an exceptional case here and there, for example, involving sadomasochism (see chap. 11 on defenses and affirmative consent), but such circumstances are atypical, rendering the proof of both involuntariness and danger superfluous. Expressing nonagreement should be obviously unnecessary in the face of knives, multiple attackers, threats to physical safety, and the like. And this needs to be clearly stated in law in order to be understood and practiced as clearly in the criminal justice system. Specifically, then, the law needs to state, de jure, that proof of aggravating conditions, force, or coercion is sufficient for conviction and that proof of nonagreement under these conditions is unnecessary.

PRESUMPTIVE NONAGREEMENT

A parallel measure to reinforce how redundant force or coercion and nonagreement are in the face of physical harm or threats should be the specification, again de jure, that involuntariness, nonagreement is presumptive under conditions of force/coercion or certain crime circumstances, for example, gangs, weapons. Put differently, rape statutes would do well to spell out both that nonagreement need not be proven by the prosecution independently of any violence or threats and that nonagreement should rightfully be the presumptive belief about the context of the sex acts in these cases. In other words, unwillingness, nonagreement to sex under harm or threats of harm should be taken as implicit, reasonable, and the operative premise since volitional, genuine agreement is not routine, or likely under such conditions. This is justified under any of the circumstances of aggravation or any type of explicit or implicit force or coercion. This is a slight step beyond stating de jure that consent cannot be presumed. It is stating de jure that not only can consent not be implied or presumed but the opposite—nonconsent—is implied or to be presumed when aggravating conditions or force are present.

The reasonable view dictates a presumption of nonagreement by victims when there is more than one defendant, or when a victim has been physically pounded into submission, paralyzed by fear from the waving of a gun or knife, or suffered injuries additional to those from forced intercourse, or when the victim was asleep, mentally incapacitated, or incapacitated by drugs or alcohol. Succinctly, all criminal circumstances, from those aggravating to those of implicit threats, make the expression and proof of involuntariness, nonagreement unnecessary. To state this in law is necessary to eliminate the redundant legal requirement to prove both force/coercion/aggravation and nonagreement.[4]

The Michigan case of *People v. Hearn* (100 Mich. App. 749, 300 N.W. 2d 396 [1980]) serves as a reminder lest there be any doubt about the necessity to specify that nonagreement is reasonable to assume. As Tchen summarizes, "the defendant and victim were strangers, he used a gun and a knife, and her story was corroborated by her boyfriend, who was also attacked. Even under those circumstances, the Michigan Court of Appeals held that the trial court's refusal to instruct the jury on the defendant's consent defense was reversible error. Apparently, the defendant's testimony alone was sufficient to raise the consent issue" (1983: 1554). So, the jury was supposed to be told about the possibility of the victim's agreeing to the sex, despite the stranger's wielding a gun and a knife and the presence of a witness who corroborated the victim's account and was himself assaulted. In order to counter the erroneous attitude that women, like the one in this case, willingly agree to such "sex," statutes need to spell out that it would be reasonable to assume what should be implicit here: she did not agree under these circumstances. My model would elevate the notion of nonagreement to the level of a legal presumption, a legally reasonable belief, whenever any force, coercion, or aggravating conditions attend the crime. This would stand to reverse the belief/canon of implied consent in addition to the de jure stipulation that consent cannot be presumed. (The defense of consent would still be available but have to be proven; see chap. 11.)

Simple, Date, or Acquaintance Rape and Presumptive Nongreement

A significant problem is that simple rapes, which do not have aggravating circumstances like multiple offenders, injuries, and weapons, are those cases where voluntariness, agreement is most often assumed to exist. Simple rapes (non-aggravated, acquaintance, or date rapes) are typically cases where there is an absence of such extenuating conditions or where generally "only" elements like force, coercion, or victim incapacitation are present. (I deal with those rapes where there is only nonagreement or "no" in the next section.)

Simple rapes are most commonly thought of as involving parties who are acquainted: parties out dining, drinking, or partying; pickups-ups at bars; or parties dating one another. These so-called simple rapes are the majority of the rapes, but they go largely unaffected by reforms. Yet presumptive nonagreement is as warranted with these simple rapes as with aggravated rape; it is, in fact, necessitated to a greater degree because the refusal to recognize nonagreement is so much greater in the absence of observable, physical, or obvious violent force/coercion or aggravating crime circumstances. Summarily, presumptive nonagreement pertains whenever any level, not just an extreme level, of force or threat or aggravating condition obtains, and this is regardless of victim-offender acquaintanceship or dating behaviors.

It is worth underscoring that being acquainted with someone, or dating, or kissing, or drinking (even to the point of incapacitation) does not make the physical or emotional harm of force or violence less injurious, and neither do these make the verbal threats of coercion any less menacing (in fact, acquaintance rapes have been shown to cause greater harm than stranger rapes, because of the personal nature of the violation, the trust betrayed, the subsequent fear of all people the victim knows, and so forth; see Bryden and Lengnick 1997; Katz 1989:31; Miller and Meloy forthcoming). Nor do these circumstances make the victim's submission any more akin to voluntariness, agreement or desire. Whether the assailant is a stranger or a date, whether the victim somehow knows the offender or not, whether she has been drinking or not,[5] no means no, and failing to take the victim's refusal seriously and/or using force or threats to overcome it is unreasonable and serious, not just "simple" crime. Simple rape is really rape, too.

My recommendation (presumptive nonagreement for any force/coercion/aggravation regardless of victim-offender relationship, drinking, and so on) reverses the reasonable expectation vis-à-vis consent and states that nonagreement is what is reasonable to assume under any such circumstances. This is a move toward an equitable starting ground, a counterweight to the privileged status that prejudice against rape victims has enjoyed. It is a swing of the pendulum in the opposite direction, intended to counteract deeply entrenched discrimination against women who charge rape. While some might argue for more initial neutrality in approach to criminal charges of rape, this is neither tenable nor desirable given such deep and longstanding prejudice with rape cases.[6] Furthermore, as MacKinnon so astutely puts the caveat, "the state will appear most relentless in imposing the male point of view when it comes closest to achieving its highest formal criterion of distanced aperspectivity" (1983: 658). This is to say that the law is most male when it is at the best of its "aperspectivity." Neutrality can be substituted for "aperspectivity," meaning that attempting to be neutral, by holding the presumption of involuntariness, or voluntariness, in abeyance, would fall in favor of the historically situated male point of view, which presupposes voluntariness (consent) when rape is charged. Making the statutory presumption one of involuntary sex, or nonagreement to criminal conduct charged, would make the legal handling of rape more comparable to other crimes. I am not proposing is a separate and unequal status for rape offenses; rather, I am advocating a greater equality of rape with other crimes at the outset of criminal accusation and charging.

"Only 'No'": Without Force/Coercion or Aggravating Circumstances
Where Presumptive Nonagreement Does Not Apply

Presumptive nonagreement is not justified in those instances where the victim indicates nonagreement but there is no force, coercion, or other aggravating crime conditions. This is because where force and the like are absent, agreement is routine, or at least as likely, as nonagreement. A legal presumption is thus not justified. In fact, in these instances nonagreement constitutes the element of the crime that the prosecution must prove (in addition to identity and the penetration or contact) in order to establish the criminality of the sex acts.[7]

There is another reason that it would be unreasonable to assert that nonagreement should be presumptive in these types of "he said, she said" nonaggravated, nonthreatening cases of simple rape and sexual assault. Presumptive nonagreement would be unjustified because it is the element of the act(s) that differentiates sex from rape in these instances, and either agreement or nonagreement is tenable. Here, the law should not render legal bearing or weight on that which the prosecution has the legal burden to prove, that is, the nonagreement or involuntariness of the acquiescence. It would be unfair to have the law give one side an advantage before either goes to bat before a judge or jury in such cases.[8]

While nonagreement should be redundant with proof of force/coercion or aggravating circumstances and so should not have to be proven alongside force/coercion/aggravation, proof of involuntariness, nonagreement should still remain an option for the prosecution in lieu of, or in addition to, the proof of the force/coercion. We know that stronger cases result if the prosecution has evidence to establish both elements of nonagreement and force/coercion/aggravation. Recall that some reforms that eliminate consent as an element of the crime remove the need for the prosecution to prove nonconsent (Tchen 1983: 1551). Care must be taken here to avoid foreclosing the option of proving nonagreement as one of the elements of the crime, so that nonagreement, standing "only" with proof of penetration and the identity of the offender, is sufficient for conviction. It is because of this that some advocates have begun to argue for reclaiming consent-based definitions of rape and sexual assault (see Temkin 2002: 177).

Sexual assaults where victims indicate no but offenders inflict no traditional force or menacing intimidation when they proceed to engage in sex acts after victims express nonagreement have been overlooked in the literature (even by Kinports, who addresses the unjustified requirement to prove both). This is problematic, since proof of involuntariness, nonagreement alone needs to be recognized to suffice for conviction. The law must change in order for this to happen, however. While the prosecution's demonstrating the existence of involuntariness, nonagreement alone should be adequate to prove crimes of rape or sexual assault, in the majority of jurisdictions the expression of nonagreement is insufficient to establish sexual assault offenses. The point is that while all sexual assaults involve nonagreement or nonconsent, not all sexual assaults involve violence or coercive threats. Of course, the prosecution would likely elect to demonstrate both force and nonagreement (or the lack of consent) in cases where force/coercion is present, so as to increase chances of conviction, particularly conviction on higher-severity levels of crimes. To emphasize the point, proof of both force and involuntariness, nonagreement are not always redundant because involuntariness, nonagreement can and does exist without force (although force rarely occurs without nonagreement or involuntariness). Demonstrating that a victim indicated nonagreement to sex acts should mean that forceful conditions do not also have to proved, because there are legitimate, "real" rapes and sexual assaults where no violence (in its common connotation) is present and no traditional force is employed or threatened. Kinports details how a few states have explicitly recognized this, noting that "a handful of state legislatures have made nonconsensual, nonforcible intercourse a lesser offense than rape, and the New Jersey Supreme Court held in State ex rel. M.T.S. that the statutory requirement of 'physical force or coercion' could be satisfied by proof of nonconsensual penetration involving no more force than necessary to accomplish that result" (2001: 756–757).

The cases where involuntary submission of victims is expressed but no aggressive or coercive conditions attend the acts may be crimes of a different type but are "real" crimes of sexual assault nonetheless. Simple rapes where involuntary submission is indicated in the absence of any other crime-defining conditions still deserve to be treated more comparably to other criminal offenses (just as "real" rapes warrant treatment comparable to other crimes), even if they are crimes of less severity. The recommendations in my model set out thus far in this chapter constitute a part of the work toward this goal.

NO IS ENOUGH: SHE SAID (NO), HE HEARD (YES, OK, SURE, FINE)

While verbal expression of no should be sufficient to establish involuntariness, nonagreement to sex, a verbal no is, distressingly, insufficient to establish involuntariness (nonconsent) in most jurisdictions (Schulhofer 1998: 271). Nonconsent should be legally recognized where a woman contends that she said no to show that she did not voluntarily agree to, did not give permission to, did not want or desire the sex act(s). This should constitute a legally sufficient basis for defining involuntariness, nonagreement, even when there are no other physical or aggravating crime circumstances such as weapons, additional injuries, or "mere" force/coercion.

The legal recognition of the expression of nonagreement is of great importance since so much of rape is simple rape. Simple rape is when serious or obvious physical force or threat by someone known to the victim does not accompany the sex that is compelled in the absence of the woman's desire, permission, or volitional agreement. It should be a crime if she "just" says "stop" or "no" and he hears "yes," or "okay," or "maybe," or takes consent as implicit, or just doesn't listen at all and proceeds to satisfy himself with her body.

Victims indicate negative responses of nonagreement, nonvolition, and nondesire though conduct, words, deeds, and gestures. They may express nonvolition behaviorally, through conduct like pulling away, putting up body armor to repel and ward off sex acts, screaming, pushing assailants away/off, kicking, biting, and at times even going to the extreme of pulling out a weapon themselves. They may also express involuntariness, nonagreement through verbal protests of "no," "stop," "you're hurting me," "I don't want you to do that," "get off of me," "get out of here," and the like or begging the assailant not to follow through on sex actions. These are all clear indicators of involuntariness or nonagreement. A comment from a case in Wisconsin (State v. Lederer 99 Wis. 2d 430, 299 N.W. 2d 457 [Wis. Ct. App. 1980]) pertaining to (affirmative) consent is applicable to the verbal nonconsent being discussed here. The court stated that "we know of no other means of communicating consent" than through verbalization (Tchen 1983: 1545). This sentiment is positive insofar as it recognizes verbal statements as sufficient to indicate nonconsent and, in this case, crime. The negative side is that it does not recognize other deeds or gestures. The flip side of this somewhat problematic posture is that verbal protests can conclusively indicate involuntariness, nonagreement. That the expression does not have to be behavioral (e.g., physical resistance) and can just be verbal should go without saying. That verbally expressed words of nonagreement make consent untenable, invalid, or inoperative still needs to be defined in law (both de jure law and court decisions), however, since implied consent continues to raise its ugly head in precisely such situations.

It doesn't seem to be so much to ask for women to have the right not to have sex imposed when they do not want or agree to it. All that is being sought is a woman's right to be left alone, not to have someone actively doing something to her against her will. What women desire is not to have to suffer the imposition of *any body*. This should prevail over men's privileged right to have, to take (and to mis-take) sex and actively to impose their bodies and what they want on someone else. Along these lines, we might ask why it is that "just say no" is deemed an effective enough tactic in the so-called war on drugs in this country (the assumption being that drug users and pushers will listen to "no" instead of taking drugs and/or forcing, deceiving, and enticing others to take them), but "just say no" to sex is not sufficient, not taken seriously, and apparently not clear enough for many men to heed or believe that no means no. Perhaps we need better slogans like "just ask" and "just listen" and "just hear no when we say it."

Although most jurisdictions have not recognized the either/or construction of proof of force/coercion or of nonagreement, several have interpreted nonagreement in the absence of force or threats and found this to be an adequate basis for rape (Kadish and Schulhofer 2001: 271). Schulhofer notes Wisconsin, Florida, Hawaii, Missouri, New Hampshire, Tennessee, and Washington as states where nonconsent alone constitutes the crime of rape (1998: 343). This demonstrates that victims' verbal or behavioral indications of involuntariness, nonagreement can be accepted as legally sufficient to satisfy the burden of proof that involuntariness, nonagreement was present and hence the sex acts constituted rape or sexual assault. This bodes well for future change in states that presently do not accept "only" a verbal "no" as establishing nonconsent and the crimes of rape/sexual assault.

Acceptance of behavioral indicators and verbal noes seems the least the law could sanction. Clearly, nonagreement can, and should, be recognized in nonverbal gestures like shaking one's head no and in body language like curling up in a fetal position, covering body parts with hands, inching away, and so on, if these can be demonstrated in court. In point of fact, Schulhofer reports that in a few states body language already can count as evidence of (non)consent (1998: 271–272). Baker articulates that there is no "fixed set of moves that need to be gone through in order to give consent. Consent can be given through words, gestures, body language, or without any speech at all, and it can be differently communicated on different occasions" (1999: 52). As Pineau sees it, we all can understand what is meant by words and by body language in terms of anger, fear, and so on. The problem has been that we haven't relied on this kind of evidence in rape, so we haven't looked for it (Harris and Pineau 1996: 130). But if evidence of involuntariness and nonagreement is sought in words, gestures, and acts, evidence will be found.

NO MEANS NO:
WOMEN SAY WHAT THEY MEAN AND MEAN WHAT THEY SAY

What goes hand in hand with specifying that (1) nonagreement is a sufficient basis to define rape and (2) expression of no is enough to prove nonagreement? The answer is: the statement "no means no." When no is said, no should be understood. To do otherwise is not acceptable or reasonable; in fact, it should be criminal. To accentuate the point, when a victim says no, it is unreasonable and dishonest to infer, imply, or construe consent. Reasonableness means that no means no, and this means that protestations are always genuine (see Adler 1987: 53). Saying no should be sufficient to indicate nonacceptance or disagreement about sexual activity, even when the least of aggravating circumstances are absent, that is, even when there are no coercive or implicit threats.

Remick conveys an excellent idea in her article entitled "Read My Lips: An Argument for a Verbal Consent Standard in Rape" (1993). She defines the consent standard in rape in the form of an admonition. She articulates it as: "Always take 'no' for an answer. Always stop when asked to stop. Never assume 'no' means 'yes.' If her lips tell you 'no' but there's 'yes' in her eyes, keep in mind that her words, not her eyes, will appear in the court transcript" (1106). Although this expression of the concept may be too flippant, it could be considered in developing juror instructions about voluntariness, agreement (See chaps. 13 and 14 on jury instructions). To Remick's sentiment, I would add: women say what they mean and mean what they say.

Estrich's conception of how consent is reasonably and unreasonably interpreted in rape cases is straightforward. The basis that can and should be used to determine nonconsent in any type of rape is the standard that no means no. Schulhofer's comment gels the point that no really means no. He states that "relatively few men will interpret a woman's 'no' to mean that she wants him to force himself on her immediately" (1998: 256). Interpreting that a women's no doesn't really mean no is as baseless as it is disingenuous.

Estrich makes another observation that is significant to this discussion. This relates to women saying no and saying yes. She comments that women may be saying yes to sex now more than they have in the past but that yes may still really belie no or the lack of desire or genuine agreement. What Estrich intends here is that women may not always have the gumption to say no when they want to.[9] Estrich brings up this point to strengthen her premise that men should heed no when women say it. She states that if "more women do feel free to say yes, that provides more reason—not less—to credit the word of those who say no" (1987: 102). This point is well taken. She continues that, because "yes may often mean no," or, as stated better elsewhere (since the formulation "yes may often mean no" may feed into rape mythology), because women don't always say no when they really do not want sex, "it does not seem so much to ask men, and the law, to respect the courage of the woman who does say no and to take her at her word" (ibid.). As she puts it earlier, asking men to think before sex is not asking men to "read a woman's mind, but to give her credit for knowing it herself when she speaks it" (98).[10]

It is clear that judges and juries don't think a verbal no is enough to indicate nonconsent, and men, too—including rapists—likewise dismiss the noes a woman may utter. Some men do not hear or heed such noes until they get translated into physical expression such as screaming, running, kicking, or fighting. Some men disregard no even in such circumstances. Robin Weiner fills out this line of thought. She sees the problem to be that "because both men and women are socialized to accept coercive sexuality as the norm in sexual behavior, men often see extreme forms of this aggressive behavior as seduction, rather than rape" (cited in Kadish and Schulhofer 2001: 362). Here, men turn no into yes through culturally convenient interpretations. Weiner continues that

> miscommunication of this sort may create a situation where submission would be reasonable behavior for a woman but would not indicate voluntary consent. A woman may believe that she has communicated her unwillingness to have sex—and other women would agree, thus making it a "reasonable" female expression. The male might still believe she is willing—and other men might agree with his interpretation, thus making it a "reasonable" male interpretation. The woman, who believes that she has conveyed her lack of consent, may interpret the man's persistence as an indication that he does not care she objects to plans to have sex despite her lack of consent. She may then feel frightened by the man's persistence, and may submit against her will.
>
> (cited in Kadish and Schulhofer 2001: 362)

Weiner's comment is well taken. In the context of this discussion, however, what is key to note in this passage is the terminology "submit against her will." While Weiner aptly notes that there may be differences in the male and female definitions of the situation, problems follow. The formulation "submits against her will" is poor terminology, especially given what the author is trying to convey. Submission, as well as "against her will," both underscore involuntariness, nonagreement. The issue Weiner's work raises cannot just be dismissed as a matter of semantics. Her unfortunate choice of language showcases the importance of semantics as a powerful influence on understanding rape. What is essential in interpreting Weiner's scenario is the fact that a woman's submission against her will should never be construed as voluntary, or as consent, or even as denoting ambiguity in sexual assault. Moreover, if a man persists despite some communicated negative expression and reluctance, what ensues should be called rape. Yet further, if woman feels frightened because of a man's threatening behavior, it is rape. Because the woman thought she conveyed no, because the man persists "because he does not care" or "plans to have sex" in spite of "her lack of consent," a crime of rape should clearly be recognized. It is unreasonable to infer consent under any such conditions. This is not to say that more ambiguous situations do not exist, for example, where the female thought she communicated nonconsent but said and did nothing to indicate this with gestures, behaviors, and the like, so the male continued through to penetration. Few cases that get reported to authorities, however, are so equivocal on the point of consent, as is so often erroneously assumed, inferred, believed, and concluded. Most legal cases are not wrought with the magnitude of ambiguity that people like Weiner raise. (On the flip side, however, an awful lot of cases needn't be handled so unjustly as to erase woman's agency when she does express no.)

It should be recognized that consent to sex should not and cannot be taken as the norm, the presumed state underlying interactions, or the implicit condition characterizing rape/sexual assault scenarios. Implicit consent is why men hear "yes," "sure," "maybe," "let's do it." An assumption of implicit consent is completely unwarranted, and the terminology must be abandoned for the harm that it has created and continues to purvey for sexual assault victimization.

The model for which these chapters are laying the groundwork will address the issues of reasonableness and of male and female definitions and interpretations of rape. For example, a reasonable woman's point of view is to be employed in case processing, which is to say, is to be given credence in defining the presence of voluntariness, agreement , threats, power, intimidation, and the like. Furthermore, jury instructions will indicate to jurors that if they believe the victim expressed nonagreement, this establishes reasonableness, independent of what the defendant says or how he chose to interpret the victim's signals.

SILENCE DOES NOT MEAN CONSENT: AGGRAVATING, FORCEFUL, OR COERCIVE CONDITIONS

Silence, passivity, or the failure to say anything or act in any observable way, in place of gestures or verbal or behavioral expressions of no, when there are no aggravating crime circumstances and/or no force, coercion, or other threats or compulsions, requires separate commentary. Recall that part of *Black's* definition of consent—or voluntariness, agreement , the term being used here—states that "submission under the influence of fear or terror cannot amount to real consent" (1991: 210). Silence may be what obtains with submission under brutalization, fear, or terror. Silence under such circumstances is tantamount to involuntariness, nonagreement. The recommendations just made are that involuntariness should be presumptive and that an expression of nonagreement is unnecessary when force/coercion/aggravating conditions attend the crime. The proof of either nonagreement or any kind of coercive condition is sufficient to establish the crime, and this would hold under the condition of silence. This means that proof of the coercive conditions engendering the silence would be sufficient for criminal conviction. But, in reality, this is not the case, because of the requirement to prove both force/coercion/threats and to prove nonconsent, which silence does not indicate. Schulhofer indicates that "most courts are still willing to infer consent from passivity and silence" (1998: 272). This is problematic since the passivity or silence may be brought about by extremely coercive conditions.

It is important to comment on a particular corollary to silence caused by fear or threats. This is what Reeves Sanday refers to as "frozen fright," where a victim cannot physically act or verbally speak, let alone resist (1996: 283). Fear that induces paralysis of the ability to move or scream or even talk should be quite clear in meaning. It is unequivocally involuntary submission or nonagreement. So silence may quite expectedly occur under conditions of force, compulsion, intimidation, terror, and other sorts of brutalization. "Frozen fright" creates a serious problem, though, when prosecutors have to prove nonconsent, often still judged by resistance, along with the forceful or aggravating criminal conditions.[11]

Schulhofer's discussion of implicit threats and coercion can productively be examined to help ferret out situations of intimidation and fear that would define involuntariness, nonagreement in relation to silent victims. Recall Schulhofer's discussion of implicit (versus explicit) threats that are "now widely accepted, at least in theory" (1998: 75). This context can and should be taken into account in rendering judgments about the existence of coercion (75–78) and hence about involuntariness, nonagreement even when unexpressed, as in the case of silence. Just as involuntariness, nonagreement can be rightfully taken when an assailant brandishes a kitchen knife without saying, "I'll cut your throat with this if you don't submit," nonagreement can be rightfully taken when there is silence under threats that are implicit as opposed to verbal. Schulhofer provides illustration of cases where he discusses how implicit threats are as coercive as verbal ones and therefore should also be criminal. One example he discusses involves four men who surrounded a woman unknown to them. The men demanded that the woman submit to intercourse with all of them, but actual physical dangers were not verbalized. The presence of multiple strange men was enough for a crime in this case—and this some forty plus years ago (73). Another case involved a man who "carried off an isolated woman who was virtually half his size" (77; see also 268–269). Physical danger is clear, if not palpable, in the "carrying off," not to mention the fact that this behavior might merit a charge of kidnapping. Even though actual physical force might not be plain and coercive threats were not verbalized, there was peril. Failure to express nonagreement was tied to threats of harm for not submitting. Coercion is inherent in these scenarios; implicit danger should take the place of implicit consent in such contexts. Implicit threats, if demonstrated, would establish coercion, and silence under coercion should be considered irrelevant or nonprobative of consent. If the victim feels endangered should she not submit, silence cannot mean willful agreement. The courts could easily use such a standard, despite the fact they do not regularly or currently do so (as was the case of the smaller women being carried off into the woods; see 76, 268).

Examining other legal definitions is useful in trying to close the door on silence as an automatic determinant of voluntariness, agreement. *Black's* definition of fraud provides a springboard. This example shows how far existing law already extends in defining what can be taken as evidence of crime. The law on fraud could be adapted to define involuntary submission in the face of silence. *Black's* (1991) fraud definition includes "anything calculated to deceive, ... by direct falsehood or innuendo, by speech or silence, word of mouth or look or gesture" (455). So, silence, looks, gestures, and words can be relied on to evince the crimes of deceit/fraud. Here we can see how victims are held to a much higher bar in sexual assaults, where expression of nonconsent must be behavioral, as in resisting, or verbal, as in saying the words "no," "stop," and so forth but where silence, or a look, or simple gestures don't convince juries and judges. In fact, of course, even the verbalization of no and/or victim resistance quite frequently don't cut it, either. The fraud definition is useful in pinpointing how far-reaching criminal law can be and delineating the broad range that could be accepted in law, practice, and public attitude as evidence of involuntariness, nonagreement when silence is the condition attending the crime of rape. Looks, gestures, and silence can all be taken to evince nonagreement by victims of rape and sexual assault (just as they can be relied on to evince crimes of fraud by offenders).

But silence can be indicative of agreement as well. And it is important to deal with the fact that silence can mean yes or no in different settings. The failure to give verbal approval or to say yes may be considered normal, as it characterizes routine sexual activities involving willingness. A lack of verbal expression commonly occurs in the course of consensual sexual activities. On the other hand, silence might be related to ambivalence or unsureness about sex act(s) or due to discomfort, tentativeness, and so on. If acquiescence or submission is not in any way coerced, silence can mean consent. But let me emphasize, consent or voluntariness, agreement is only tenable with the absence of force, coercion, aggravation, duress, and fraud (see chap. 12 on duress and fraud).

Because silence can mean yes or no, future changes, such as those being built into a model of future reforms here, incorporate further measures to get at the veracity of interpretations to ensure that, if there is no force, no intimidation, no threats, no weapons, no deceptive pretenses, and so on and the victim does nothing and is in a silent and passive state (even throughout all the sex acts), the volitional, willing nature of the participation in the sex act(s) can be proven. Consent, while tenable, would need to be shown under the circumstance of filed legal charges of rape. In other words, some affirmative indication that the silence meant consent would need to be demonstrated. A positive demonstration of agreement is necessary in order to offset the greater likelihood that silence characterizes nonagreement when rape has been charged by a woman. Put differently, silence can be indicative of agreement; however, if this is the case, the consent must be shown by other gesture(s) or conduct in the absence of words indicating agreement to the sex act(s) in an encounter charged as rape. It is only in the absence of all coercive, intimidating conditions *and* in the presence of other words, looks, gestures, or behaviors that indicate yes, or voluntary willingness to participate in the sex acts, that silence can reasonably be taken to mean voluntariness, agreement to sexual behavior.

This is justified on more than logical and reasonable grounds. Estrich points out how silence interpreted as consent is unique to rape. She compares how "in robbery, claims that the victim cooperated with the taking of the money or eased the way, and thus consented, have been generally unsuccessful. Only where the owner of the property actively participates in planning and committing the theft will consent be found; mere 'passive submission' or 'passive assent' does not amount to consent—except in the law of rape" (1987: 40). Construing silence as nonagreement in rape is both politically and legally viable. Schulhofer contends that "facts that will often be quite clear—verbal protests, ambivalence, passivity, or silence—are by themselves sufficient to establish an unambiguous offense" (1998: 271). In addition to facts of ambivalence, passivity, and silence being "quite clear," force, coercion, threats, and so forth also may be abundantly clear. And recall my argument that if coercive conditions of any nature are established, it is redundant to have to prove indications of unwillingness as well. The law needs to spell out that silence does not mean consent.[12]

A REASONABLE WOMAN'S POINT OF VIEW FOR A CHANGE

Statutes define rape with regard to force or consent (Baker 1999: 50–51; Gauthier 1999: 71–72; MacKinnon 2001: 852; Kadish and Schulhofer 2001: 343; Katz 1989:

43,47–48; Temkin 2002: 90, 98,168, 176, 177). There are obvious problems concomitant with either approach. Relying on force or even force/coercion rest on male notions of what constitutes violence—which involves physicality. This excludes constraints and compulsions, pressures, intimidations, and the like that women's, and even many men's, points of view would understand as perilous. It relies on male mental states or "awareness" of force/coercion, which is problematic as men often "discount" the force they use (MacKinnon 2001: 852) or dismiss it as no big deal, when such phenomena can simultaneously be terrifying to women.

Reliance on nonconsent in rape law, on the other hand, fares no better. Again, male definitions prevail, making what passes as reasonably perceived consent ludicrous. And, as I will discuss, mistakes of consent have all too often, and for all too many years, been successfully argued to be honest and reasonable, when, in fact, they pass not even the lowest measure of logic, sense, or coherent thought, for example, she struggled, kicked, spit, bit, and screamed, but he thought she liked sex that way. In addition, the focus on victims that is corollary to a focus on consent carries with it the historic problem of discriminatory burden by way of belief and requirement, as seen in rape resistance and corroboration standards.

The question boils down to whose definitions count. Which definitions of force, coercion, consent, unwillingness, duress, intimidation, pressure, voluntary, free, and so on are reasonable? The answer is simple. What counts as nonconsent, as a sufficient expression of no, as force, as coercion, intimidation, and fear, as reasonable, as honest, genuine, or sincere has always been determined by a male point of view. Definitions of terms and standards are not neutral and impartial, as the law is alleged to be. (Recall MacKinnon's principle that the law is most male when it is at the height of "aperspectivity," or allegedly most neutral [1983: 658]). Terms and standards reflect the vested interests of the group that has the powerful ability to define such phenomena. This is why just saying no has not been enough, why no is taken to mean yes, why silence is seen as consent, why the doctrine of implied consent permeates rape decision making throughout the legal system, why both force and nonconsent have to be demonstrated—along with corroborative evidence and resistance—to win a case, why nonforceful but nonconsensual sexual assault (a redundancy in terminology) is rarely recognized, why even unreasonable mistakes can exculpate, and why only the most heinous, atypical rapes are seen as real enough to sustain convictions.

A woman's point of view is what is required to counteract definitions that privilege males. A woman's point of view is useful in denoting up front that sex given into is different from sex agreed to. This improves the understanding of how compliance under compulsion is involuntary.[13]

Male-driven understanding about consensual and nonconsensual sex is, simply put, sexist. Schulhofer observes that what is seen as reasonable in rape "simply invites the worst abuses of cultural stereotyping and ingrained sex bias that rape reformers have tried for so long to escape (1998: 259). Catherine MacKinnon summarizes how the crime of rape has been defined from a male point of view: "the injury of rape lies in the meaning of the act to its victim, but the standard for its criminality lies in the meaning of the act to the assailant" (1989: 245). Henderson adds to this, elucidating how "both heterosexuality and rape are defined in male, rather than female, terms, including the terms of the morality of heterosexuality and assertions about what women want or are as sexual beings. The morality of heterosexuality ... creates a presumption of moral innocence for men and a presumption of moral guilt for women in sexual interactions. In cases of rape, then, men are presumed innocent and women guilty at the outset" (1993: 42). She goes on to note that the "cultural belief is that female submission to male sexual dominance or aggression is natural, romantic, and erotic" (42). Kinports puts it only a little differently: "Because both men and women are socialized to accept coercive sexuality as the norm in sexual behavior, men often see extreme forms of this aggressive behavior as seduction, rather than rape. A great many incidents women consider rape are, in effect, considered 'normal' by both male perpetrators and the male-dominated legal system.... Thus, what is 'normal' according to male social norms and 'reasonable' according to male communication patterns and expectations does not accord with what women believe to be reasonable" (2001: 766). This is quite similar to MacKinnon's assertion quoted earlier that false accusations are false to men, since they describe what men perceive to be normal sex.

A woman's point of view would define all manner of things differently. A woman's point of view would define which indications of nonconsent reasonably signal nonagreement or involuntariness (Estrich 1987). A woman's point of view would dictate that saying "please don't," "stop," or "I don't want to," or pulling away or pushing the assailant away, or crying and pleading "don't do that" all indicate unwillingness and lack of desire. A woman's point of view dictates quite simply that a verbal no is clear (contrary to Kinports's "normal" "male communication patterns" of convenient interpretation) and should be all that is socially and legally required to express nonagreement; that no means no, not yes or maybe. A woman's point of view would dictate that a woman says what she means and means what she says and that simple rape, when men ignore women's noes, is still really rape. And a woman's point of view would recognize that overpowering a woman is not seductive, erotic, or normal (see Henderson 1993: 42; Kinports 2001: 766; Schulhofer 1998: 257) and that resistance to a man's aggressive or violent sexual overtures is not feigned. A woman's point of view would see that the typical—and so more reasonable and safer—assumption that frames encounters does not entitle men to take sex from women. A woman's point of view would understand that bringing charges of rape or sexual assault forward to the criminal justice system is really difficult and that there is little to gain and lots to lose, so false accusations are a rarity.

A woman's point of view would mean simply that assessment would pivot around what a reasonable woman would judge, experience, perceive, interpret, or do about the presence of force, threats of harm, implicit threats (as opposed to implicit consent), the ability to express nonconsent (and hence the meaning of silence under conditions of "frozen fright" or fear-induced paralysis), and the belief about the ability of a man to carry through on threats. This standard needs to be written into law, and judges and juries need to be so instructed. (Along these lines, the prosecution could explain to jurors how the traditionally accepted male standards have operated as anything but generic, sex-blind definitions and how this has undermined the state's ability to go after those who rape and sexually assault women and girls.)

It is perhaps important to point out that I am using what might be referred to as an objective woman's point of view as the standard, in contrast to a subjective woman's point of view. By this, I mean that the gauge by which to measure the existence of consent, force, and so on is taken from what a (generic) reasonable woman would interpret in the situation. This can be contrasted to a more subjective approach, where what the individual woman involved in the case believed or interpreted would constitute the standard used to assess the absence/presence of a given condition such as force or willingness. Michigan's reform provides a relevant example. It states that "consent is to be determined from the victim's subjective state of mind, not the defendant's reasonable belief that the victim consented. *People v Hale*, 142 Mich App 451, 453 (1985)" (Michigan Judicial Institute 2002: 221; see chap. 11 on reasonable belief about victim consent). I would advance that using an objective reasonable woman's point of view to revise law is preferable to using a victim's subjective state of mind (as Michigan did). Relying on an objective woman standard repositions the reasonable belief in consent defense from being so readily available (as is the case now with reliance on just "reasonable"—which is to say male—point of view), while being more politically and/or popularly acceptable because it (a generic woman's point of view) is likely to be seen as less radical (than relying on a victim's subjective understanding). Using an objective reasonable woman's point of view as a standard is also likely to be more acceptable as it fits with extant legal logic and categorizations about objective standards and reasonableness (see the next chapter on mens rea for elaboration).

Schulhofer rings in on the woman's point of view argument. He contends that a woman's point of view should be the basis for judging, for example, fear or the believability of "I will hurt you," as well as the reasonableness of fears of injury and the presence of intimidation (1998: 78). Kinports also chimes in. As she puts it, "whether a reasonable person would have thought the defendant was using force—the question would arise as to whose perspective controls. Given '(t)he reality of our existence . . . that it takes less force to overcome most women than most men,' '(t)he question of whose definition of "force" should apply, of whose understanding should govern, is critical' " (Kinports 2001: 790, citing Estrich 1987: 22, 60). "That issue is particularly critical today given the 'gender gap'—perhaps more accurately termed the 'gender chasm'" in understanding (Kinports 2001: 790, citing R. Weiner 1983: 143, 147). And whose definition of force counts means a great deal for criminal responsibility and conviction or acquittal.

Some criticize that substituting a female for male point of view will lead to unfairness, that is, false accusations and convictions. Substantive and procedural law, rules of evidence, and constitutional rights of the accused protect all persons accused of crimes, however, not all persons excluding those accused of rape, and these safeguards will ferret out the small number of cases where falsity may exist. Pineau adds significant insight along this line in her contention that "the patriarchal point of view is unfair to women. The feminist point of view, however, is not unfair to men. . . . If . . . forceful seduction is actually a reflection of what men want, a desire that is then projected onto women, then it is clear that it serves men's interests while it frustrates and victimizes women." She goes on to make the analogous argument that "protecting the rights of those few people whose pleasure consists in being robbed cannot be justified if it is at the expense of a failure to protect the vast majority whose pleasure does not consists in being robbed" (1996b: 85–86).

Utilizing a woman's point of view, then, protects the "vulnerable" from criminal activity, imbuing the "right to consent to sexual activity" (Pineau 1996b: 91), while simultaneously—it should be noted—not stepping on the rights of parties who may be accused of its violation.

SUMMARY

There should be for all rapes/sexual assaults, whether involving "just" involuntariness or involving force, coercion, or aggravating characteristics:

1. The removal of the redundancy of requiring both force, coercion, or aggravating conditions and involuntariness, nonagreement.
2. The specification in law that nonagreement is presumptive under the conditions of force, coercion, or aggravating conditions.
3. The specification in law that nonagreement is presumptive even if the victim knows or has had previous contact with the offender.
4. The specification in law that either proof of nonagreement or proof of the crime-defining circumstances is sufficient for conviction.
5. The specification in law that the expression of no is adequate to establish the crime, as well as the specification that no means no.
6. The specification in law that silence cannot be equated with voluntariness, agreement.
7. The specification in law that a reasonable woman's point of view is to be used to judge rape charges or to assess the circumstances surrounding the crime, for example, the presence of weapon(s), force/coercion, the indication of no (see chap. 10).

Not only are the changes discussed in this chapter and delineated directly above recommended for inclusion in the model being built for reforming rape reforms in de jure legal definitions, they would form the second part of juror instructions that judges would be required to read and explain to jurors before deliberations.

That nonagreement exists when no is indicated is one thing. That it is reasonable to interpret nonagreement when voiced or when force and its ilk are displayed is another. That the law should state that voluntariness, agreement should not and cannot be assumed or implied is yet another matter.

Whether or not a man intends to perceive, or intends to interpret, or intends to ignore nonagreement when it is apparent, expressed, or legally stipulated as presumptive is a whole separate matter. And this is the matter of mens rea, or criminal intent.

THE ROLE OF MENS REA:
IGNORED, USED, OR REDUNDANT AND UNNECESSARY?

There are conflicting viewpoints about the role of mens rea in the crime of rape. Estrich, for example (as noted earlier), describes how intent in rape is disregarded in favor of resistance and consent requirements. She cites statements from specific cases to document her conclusion that "in completed rapes, questions of intent or mistake are rarely even mentioned" (1987: 94). The court cases she quotes supporting this are from Maine, Pennsylvania, and Massachusetts. These cases show how intent and mistakes, reasonable or unreasonable, were treated by the courts as irrelevant (94–95).

Interpretations of other scholars about intent in the crime of rape support Estrich's readings about how rape law skirts intent. Kinports, for example, states that "adhering to traditional formulations of the crime, the overwhelming majority of contemporary rape statutes contain no explicit *mens rea* requirement" (2001: 757). The rather obvious facts that force/coercion and resistance have had to be proven in order to demonstrate nonconsent and that this formulaic demand has presented such inordinate obstacles for rape convictions obviously buttress the notion that mens rea/intent is a less potent factor in defenses against rape prosecution. In other words, the role of mens rea or intent is ignored because it is easier to rebut a rape accusation with a requirement of proof of force/coercion, proof of resistance, and proof of nonconsent.

Some, however, have implied that scholars like Estrich have overgeneralized from the cases they examine. Henderson, for instance, specifically criticizes that Estrich is wrong in "her assertion that American courts ignore the issue of mens rea as to consent" (1988: 211). MacKinnon shares this opinion. Contrary to Estrich, MacKinnon contends that rape law "often contains a mental element, mens rea" (2001: 831). Pineau's characterization is useful to reiterate here. She notes that men's reasonable or honest belief in consent is the way mens rea has been used—and "defeated in many jurisdictions" (Harris and Pineau 1996: 116).

Kinports's discussion can be used to reconcile the two points of view regarding the reliance on mens rea. She clarifies that "instead of analyzing whether the defendant purposely or knowingly used force, or should have known that he was using force, the courts have disposed of such cases by evaluating the sufficiency of evidence offered to prove either the *actus reus* of force with the defendants *mens rea* vis-à-vis nonconsent. The absence of any real discussion of *mens rea* with respect to force points up the redundancy of the force requirement, once absence of consent has been proven" (2001: 767).

As Kinports explains elsewhere, "In rape cases involving physical violence or express threats to physical harm, proof of the *actus reus* obviously does establish *mens rea* with respect to force as well as nonconsent. A defendant who beat or threatened to kill his victim could hardly raise a plausible argument that he did not know he was using force" (2001: 757). Kinports continues that "it would seem pedestrian for a court to address separately the issue of *mens rea* in a case involving an obvious show a force…. A defendant who beat his victim into submission or expressly threatens her with a weapon is obviously using force knowingly, if not purposefully.... The defendant could not be 'accidentally or innocently' using force, and therefore the proof of the *actus reus*—the use of force—necessarily implies an intent or knowledge" (765–766).

Estrich actually makes a comparable point. She observes, "the man who jumps out from the bushes could hardly be expected to persuade anyone that he thought the woman was consenting; and in more 'appropriate' circumstance, the doctrines of consent and force provide far more comprehensive protection against any mistake as to consent" (1987: 94). Her reference to the Maine Supreme Court makes the point most succinctly: the "Court has stated that there is no requirement of a culpable mental state for rape: 'The legislature, by carefully defining sex offenses in the criminal code, and by making no reference to a culpable state of mind for rape, clearly indicated that rape compelled by force or threat requires no culpable state of mind'" (ibid.).

Although it is clear that men's intent is implicitly involved in rape adjudications, the relative ease of protecting men from rape accusations by depending on consent and resistance barriers renders proof of the intent to use force repetitive (with proof of nonconsent—as shown through the existence of force and resistance), and so it has been neglected. And as Estrich summarizes, "In virtually every case cited as rejecting an intent requirement for rape, the only reason the defendant was even arguing intent seems to be because his case would have been utterly hopeless on the issues of actual consent or resistance or force. It is not that American courts have been more willing to expose foolish and mistaken men to conviction than their English counterparts [recall the British *Morgan* decision allowing unreasonable mistakes to exculpate]. Rather it is that they have provided protection for men who find themselves in these potentially ambiguous situations through the doctrines of consent, defined as resistance, and force, measured by resistance" (1987: 95).

In any event, even Kinports, who devotes such careful consideration to the issue of the overlap between intent in force and nonconsent, interprets that "even in rare cases where the issue is discussed, there is no evidence that the courts' choice of *mens rea* has any real impact on the outcome of the case. In fact, the few courts that mentioned *mens rea* in discussing the force requirement typically go on to ignore completely that issue in disposing of the case" (2001: 757).

NEGLIGENCE

Estrich reasoned that relying on proof of resistance and force and so "refusing to inquire into intent leaves two possibilities: turning rape into a strict liability offense, where the man may be guilty of rape regardless of whether he (or anyone) would have recognized nonconsent in the circumstances; or defining the crime in a fashion so limited that it effectively excludes all simple rapes which present any risk that the man could have been unaware or mistaken as to nonconsent" (1987: 95). There are obvious problems with either alternative. I revisit the first option, defining rape as a strict liability crime, later in this chapter. The problem with the second option—defining rape so narrowly that any possibility of confusion over consent would be precluded—is that this would take a good deal of serious criminal conduct off the books based on men's interpretations. Estrich had a different idea back in 1987. This third option—one that by now is widely recognized, if debated—has to do with criminal negligence.

Just as the law has evaded considering mens rea in rape, it has evaded the issue of negligence or negligent liability in rape. Recall Estrich's claim that "intent or mistake are rarely even mentioned" and are hardly ever recognized by courts (1987: 94). This is because if men's state of mind (mens rea, men's intent to use force) is neither requisite nor focal because of the preference for focusing on victim consent/resistance and/or because of the redundancy with the existence (*actus reus*) of force, then negligence or disregard of that state of mind, mens rea, or intent to force (to overcome nonconsent) will not be focal or considered. If the intent to use force to overcome nonconsent is not focused upon, then states of mind pertaining to intent, like negligence or disregard, will not be considered.

Estrich conveys that criminal negligence has not been considered for rapists who unreasonably mistake or carelessly eschew their victims' nonagreement.[1] Kinports's intricate analysis (2001) along this dimension criticizes Estrich on the count that courts ignore intent (and hence negligence). Schulhofer is the other scholar who addresses this issue. He is ambiguous about whether the courts use a negligence standard.[2]

Irrespective of the criticisms by Kinports, Schulhofer, and others that Estrich is wrong in "her assertion that American courts ignore the issues of *mens rea* as to consent" (Henderson 1988: 211), Estrich is not entirely wrong, even after the reforms of the 1970s and 1980s. The fine distinction concerning the viability of all these authors' observations can be found in a remark by Kinports, quoted earlier. She elucidates that "adhering to traditional formulations of the crime, the overwhelming majority of contemporary rape statutes contain no explicit *mens rea* requirement" (2001: 757). Where law is silent, reliance goes to common law (755). And common law recognizes negligent culpability—in homicide and, by extension then, in rape (Kadish and Schulhofer 2001: 359; Schulhofer 1998: 258) and sexual assault (which would include contact crimes short of penetration).

Regardless of exactly how many of U.S. courts accept negligent liability or how the scholars paint it, it is important to point out that without directly defining negligence in statute, the determination of how far criminal negligent culpability actually extends is left up to the court in criminal matters (through verdicts in bench trials and through directed verdicts and jury instructions in jury trials). This is to say that recognition of criminal negligence is largely for the judicial branch to determine. This means that the court determines what constitutes knowledge of nonconsent or "injury," as Schulhofer terms it vis-à-vis homicide, mens rea, or intent to force/overcome nonconsent, as well as what constitutes "awareness of substantial risk," carelessness, unreasonable mistake, or disregard of nonconsent, on a case-by-case basis for rapes and sexual assaults. The problem is that the variety of terms/requirements potentially to be applied and the meaning of each are all left open—and ambiguous. This means differential application of differential standards, yielding differential justice, which is to say injustice.

ESTRICH AND THE LOGIC OF NEGLIGENT CULPABILITY

Recall Estrich's approach to criminal negligence, described in chapter 5. She contends that negligent liability should extend to instances where the defense claims that consent was present, in the form of a mistaken belief by the assailant. The defense argument is that the belief in consent, although mistaken, was an honest mistake or reasonable belief and hence should absolve the defendant of criminal culpability. Estrich's approach would attach criminal negligence to mistakes of consent that she deems unreasonable because of the use of force, coercion, and the like. This strategy is designed to eliminate the ability to use the defense of mistaken consent and/or to render the definition of such mistakes to be unreasonable and therefore no longer tenable as a defense to criminal responsibility.

Estrich moves on to say that unreasonableness or negligence (or negligent liability) can be found in other crimes, such as manslaughter, where a man's unreasonable action leads to loss of life (1987: 97). She contends that culpability should be present in rape crimes when a man "heard her refusal or saw her tears, but decided to ignore them. The man who has the inherent capacity to act reasonably but fails to has, through that failure, made a blameworthy choice for which he can justly be punished" (ibid.). "Unreasonable mistakes will not exculpate" (98) with killing, so why should rape be different? Unreasonable belief and action can lead to harm in rape as they do in manslaughter and so should be criminal.[3]

Estrich justifies negligence in rape as in manslaughter in her comparison that "the law has long punished unreasonable action which leads to loss of human life as manslaughter—a lesser crime, but a crime nonetheless. By holding out the prospect of punishment for negligence, the Model Penal Code commentators in 1980 pointed out, the law provides an additional motive to men to 'take care before acting, to use their faculties and draw on their experience in gauging the potentialities of contemplated conduct'" (1987: 97, though Estrich acknowledges in footnote 19 that the Model Penal Code commentators of 1980 did not include rape among the crimes for which they considered negligent liability). Estrich continues that "the injury of sexual violation is sufficiently great, the need to provide that additional incentive pressing enough, to justify negligence liability for rape as for killing" (97–98).

I would elaborate the comparison, or justification, for similar versus differential culpability in rape and other crimes. Criminal responsibility is conferred with manslaughter for harm (death) that results from "the commission of a lawful act without due caution and circumspection" (Black 1991: 664, defining involuntary manslaughter). Many rapes, quite analogously, entail the commission of acts "without due caution and circumspection," with resultant harm suffered. Therefore these acts are deserving of the law's protection.

The bottom line is that there is no solid justification for the differential treatment of rape when contemplating reason, care, prudence, caution, and circumspection of beliefs, actions, and harms. Men who unreasonably mistake consent and act to harm another person should not be exempt from culpability for rape. The reason this issue has not been salient in the past in this country, or in other similar countries like Britain, is that the victim's resistance has been relied on for prosecution and conviction, rather than the man's state of mind about the woman's agreement. The demonstration of resistance to prove nonconsent was a formidable and engaging task for the prosecution. Yet, in the wake of reforms that diminish the need to prove resistance, new defense possibilities relating to beliefs about consent or voluntariness, agreement open up. They also open up potential pitfalls that must be guarded against. Now that reforms draw more attention to the accused, the courts—and legislatures, for that matter—need to confront the issues relating to the honesty and reasonableness of beliefs or mistakes as to agreement. It is therefore of paramount importance to lay out alternative routes that can better address the issues surrounding belief about consent in more enlightened ways than so far have been contemplated or put forward. Estrich's negligence model provides one incisive model that begins to carve out a path in such a direction.

PITFALLS WITH NEGLIGENCE

Estrich's 1987 position (and, with less specificity, Adler's 1987 position, too) that mistakes about consent should confer negligent responsibility in rape are compelling, but they do not go far enough. There are several problems that, if recognized and rectified, would extend progress yet further with this line of reasoning.

A potential danger with the negligence approach is that, like the earlier reform approaches, attention to the accused's state of mind and belief about consent and its reasonableness, or to his mis-TAKING consent, actually reraises issues about victims' consent. Even though Estrich is advancing the position that such mistakes, or unreasonable belief in consent, is negligent and therefore criminal, attention to the defendant's belief as to the victim's nonagreement bespeaks attention to the victim's behavior as well. While it is in one way positive to cast attention on offenders and in this way hold defendants criminally responsible for unreasonable mistakes, there are drawbacks. As Goldberg-Ambrose points out, allowing reasonable mistakes of consent to absolve guilt, as England "practically invented" and apparently does quite "routinely " (1989: 951), means greater reliance on resistance or greater focus on victim consent, not less. Michigan's experience, where defendant beliefs about victim consent arise under even the most serious of conditions, bears this out, showing that considering defendant belief about consent means reconsidering victim consent. Henderson, too, says that Estrich is "mistaken in thinking that shifting attention to the man's mental state about consent and reducing the *mens rea* requirement to negligence will relieve the victim of the burden of physical resistance and having to prove she was raped" (1988: 211). And as Berliner observes, the defense of reasonable belief has grown, not diminished, in the wake of repealing resistance requirements (1991: 2696 n. 61).

MacKinnon raises several related concerns through a series of questions. She asks, "Should rape be defined in a man's mind rather than a woman's body? Should it be defined by what an accused thinks rather than, or more than, by what he does?" (2001: 831–832). She goes on to query whether defining rape with focus on the intent of the accused promotes or inhibits sex equality and finally poses the questions, "Does defining the injury of rape in terms of perpetrator perspective undermine or promote findings of culpability? How many accused rapists do you think believe their victims genuinely desired the sex acts in question?" (832). In addition to the problems indicated in MacKinnon's questions stands the problem that a negligence approach foregrounds male-driven definitions of the crime, when rape is "only an injury from the woman's point of view" (Kinports 2001: 767, quoting MacKinnon 1989).

A further problematic feature of a negligence model is that the defense can and does still argue that mistaken consent was reasonable, and this is accepted under all the old-fashioned, sexist rationalizations. In the short version, even more than suspect or questionable mistakes have successfully been argued to be honest and/or reasonable and hence to vitiate criminal responsibility. This is to say that, even if the net of criminal responsibility to capture men who are negligent about consent is expanded, allowing for reasonable mistakes (about consent to exculpate), *without additional safeguards*, leaves the door wide open for age-old excuses that exonerate men from criminal rape and sexual assault charges.

But at the same time, there is much to commend Estrich's approach and attribution of criminal culpability on the basis of negligence, as is done in other crimes. First, it makes the legal handling of rape more similar to the treatment of other criminal harms. Second, it shifts the focus of trial to the man versus the women, making the issue whether a man is a rapist instead of whether the woman was raped, even though all too often it ultimately causes attention to refocus on the victim. Third, it also replaces the ridiculous formula "resistance to show force to show nonconsent to show against her will," in order to meet the consent and resistance requirement, with an intent doctrine that would promote prosecution and conviction.

There is, then, much to commend and much to condemn, or at least be cautious about, with the negligence approach. The approach leaves loopholes that render it ineffective as a standalone measure. But if it could somehow be adapted in some other context or nestled within some greater set of measures that would operate as a firewall against the problems just discussed, it would be a model worth pursuing.

It is important to recognize this and to conceptualize yet further ways of progressing against rape victimization. It is important to confront and correct (rather than abandon) the features of law that can be used to promote the interests of victims and justice. We need to fix the negligence model so that it is not a singular measure and so reap the benefits of extended criminal responsibility, offender focus, and so on that would make rape more comparable to other crime. The model this book advances can embed negligent culpability to make it more effective.

Much of the problematic nature of Estrich's proposal on negligence is that common law traditions, translated to mean male law traditions, determine what consent, involuntariness, and reasonableness of mistakes mean. Although Estrich recommends using a woman's point of view elsewhere, she does not consider it in this context of negligent culpability (although she does say that reasonable should defy the male "no means yes" construction). What is lacking here is what the model in this book has begun to develop, namely: (1) a de jure definition of consent or voluntariness, agreement; (2) a de jure definition of nonconsent or involuntariness, nonagreement, wherein statutes specify that no is sufficient for defining rape and sexual assault offenses and that no means no; (3) a specification that nonagreement is concurrent and/or redundant with any force/coercion exercised and is therefore to be stipulated in de jure law to be presumptive under such circumstances; and (4) a de jure specification that a reasonable woman's point of view is to be used to judge the indication of nonagreement and the presence of force or coercive threats. These measures go a good way toward closing the loopholes surrounding negligent culpability as just described.

The rest of model described in the subsequent chapters builds on these components, develops these premises further, and adds new components and eventual complements. The model links the changes together in a way that buttresses each of the measures individually to make them all more likely to be applied and implemented in practice and ultimately to be cumulatively more effective.

BORROWING FROM HOMICIDE:
PREMEDITATION, RECKLESSNESS, NEGLIGENCE, AND RAPE

A permutation on the negligence approach can serve to correct some of the problems described and simultaneously widen the net to enmesh more perpetrators who dismiss their victims' nonagreement ("willy nilly," as in *Morgan*; see chap. 5). The culpability of the accused can most productively be determined by standards that not only are already on the books but also enjoy wide acceptance in criminal law governing other homicide offenses. Drawing on the definitions of culpable states of mind to define the crime of rape is a more exacting, and more expansive, approach and one that is more easily applied to sexual assault offenses than Estrich's focusing on negligence in unreasonable mistake of consent defenses (especially given the failure to define negligence, reasonableness, and/or consent).

As may already be clear, the crimes of homicide vary in name and in severity. Degrees of homicide are called different things in different states, but everyone understands that there are different levels. What are typically referred to as first-degree murders, for instance, are crimes where there is premeditation and malice aforethought. A second degree of murder, such as manslaughter, is often defined where the death is the result of recklessness or wanton, careless disdain for the risk or the consequences of one's actions. (Manslaughter is commonly divided into voluntary and involuntary, where voluntary manslaughter is generally provoked or committed in the so-called heat of passion and involuntary—"sometimes called unintentional" manslaughter—is when "extreme negligence or wanton or reckless conduct by the defendant brings about an unintended or accidental death" [Gardner and Anderson 1996:309]). A further type of homicide offense is often defined as negligent homicide, where an actor has failed to perceive the risk or likely consequences of his or her actions (namely, death) where a reasonable person would or should have perceived such risk.

Defining crimes through specification of the level of intent or mens rea attending the offenses is common in criminal definitions. In other words, predicating the severity of crime on type/level of criminal intent, such as malice aforethought versus failure to perceive risk, is not unique to crimes of homicide; it obtains in many instances throughout criminal law. Assault law provides equally familiar examples. It is readily known that assault with intent to murder is a more serious crime, carrying harsher penalties, than, say, assault with intent to do great bodily harm, or assault with intent to maim, or felonious assault, or aggravated assault, or assault and battery, or simple assault. Although many of these examples of assault are defined in different ways in different jurisdictions,[4] the logic underpinning inclusion of intent in crime definitions can easily be applied to force, to coercion, and to involuntariness, nonagreement in rape offenses, and this can be done with tremendous potential benefit.

The intent of premeditation and malice aforethought can be seen in rape cases in several alternative ways. First, malice aforethought could be seen in the intent, thought, or aim to rape. It could also be seen in the subsequent thought where the assailant devises his plan to carry out the rape. "The second thought would be the pre-meditation where the defendant was thinking about how best to carry out that formed intent (this can be done in seconds—extent of reflection, not duration" is what matters) (Kristine Mullendore, personal communication, 1998). Planning to rape a woman is a clear fit with the premise here, given that so many rapes are planned, with the rapist simply searching or waiting for the most vulnerable-looking target. The South Hills, California, serial rapist who stalked the area looking for women who were alone or the better-known case of Ted Bundy, who preyed on college co-eds, provide examples. Planning is present when an assailant thinks about how he will rape, or how he will pick someone vulnerable, or how he will take a victim, or how he will overcome a victim's involuntariness (hence how he will use force). This is surely evidence of "malice" (akin to the way it applies in first-degree murder) or a malevolent or hostile thought by the assailant. Intent to rape, to inflict sexual violence, to overpower a woman into sexual submission is malicious intent. Yet another way to apply intent to rape pertains to the accused's state of mind about consent. The premeditation and malice here would revolve around planning for or anticipating a targeted victim's potential involuntariness, nonagreement and formulating how to overcome it.[5]

A second level of intent is recklessness or careless disregard of risk. This intent involves the risk of nonagreement and the consequence of committing the harms of sexual violation. The accused would be blameworthy—negligent—for failing to act reasonably and perceive nonagreement, as in Estrich, or, put differently, the perpetrator would be criminally liable for carelessly dismissing or tossing aside victim involuntariness, nonagreement. The wanton dismissal of the indication of nonagreement on the part of the victim (or even the whole notion of nonagreement itself) would make the accused criminally liable.

Schulhofer's "Model Criminal Statute" for rape characterizes criminal recklessness in this vein. He defines recklessness as "the requirement of knowledge [that] can be met by proof that, at the time of his conduct, the actor was consciously aware of a substantial and unjustifiable risk that the fact in question existed" (1998: 284). "The fact in question" refers, of course, to nonagreement. The culpability attaches to his demarcation of first-degree "aggravated" sexual assault (force or compulsion, weapons, and additional injuries), second-degree sexual assault (victims under thirteen or use of force), and third-degree sexual abuse (e.g., the actor uses threats, invokes his authority, or "violate[s] any other right of the victim or inflict[s] any other harm" (283–284). (Schulhofer defines these degrees of crime as depending on crime circumstance, although he does not define the meaning of degrees in terms of sentencing or other considerations, as previously mentioned.)

Third, the failure to perceive the risk of nonconsent when a reasonable person would have perceived this risk would likewise be criminal in my scheme. Recall in this context Alston's claimed right to "take sex" one more time (with his ex-girlfriend) or Evans's veiled threat that, for all the victim knew, he was a killer or a rapist. A reasonable person would have figured out that nonagreement would have been the rational expectation (reasonable knowledge) under conditions like those in these cases. A reasonable person would have figured out that threatening to "fix her face" if he didn't get sex (Alston) or observing menacingly that the victim was a stranger in a strange and isolated place with a potential killer or rapist in (Evans) was something a reasonable person would see as indicative of involuntariness, nonagreement, that is, a reasonable person would have understood the risk that involuntariness or nonagreement was the case. This could form the basis for criminal conviction.

Schuhofer defines criminal negligence as a less serious offense in this regard. In his model, first- and second-degree crimes would become third degree, and his third-degree abuse crimes would be downgraded to fourth-degree offenses

if negligence (rather than knowing or reckless disregard) about nonconsent obtained. Schulhofer defines negligent offenses as either third- (if they involve force,
victims under thirteen, weapons, or injuries) or fourth-degree (if they involve
threats, any other violations or harms, etc.) felonies (although, again, he doesn't
stipulate what these degrees mean in his proposed model statute). Schulhofer's
definition provides that negligent sexual assault or sexual abuse felonies would
cover cases where "the prosecution proves that [the accused's] failure to appreciate that risk involved a gross deviation from the standard of care that a reasonable
person would observe in the actor's situation" (1998: 284). Rape offenses would,
then, include offenders who sexually penetrate others by gross deviation (from a
reasonable standard of care) (see 284) or negligence when there is failure to perceive nonagreement when reasonable people would interpret or see it. This is the
same as the failure to perceive risk just laid out.

It is instructive to look at another treatment of negligence here. *Black's* definition is that "negligence is the failure to use such care as a reasonably prudent
and careful person would use under similar circumstances; ... conduct which
falls below the standard established by law for the protection of others against
unreasonable risk of harm" (1991: 716). That rape is harmful cannot be gainsaid;
that reasonable prudence and care would dictate understanding a woman's no as
nonagreement cannot be gainsaid, either. Again, negligence in rape is unreasonable neglect or failure to understand involuntariness, nonagreement.

Applying such definitions to rape offenses would lead to distinctions regarding premeditated (comparable to first-degree murder) versus reckless
disregard (comparable to manslaughter) versus failure to perceive risk (comparable to negligent homicide) as mental states of intent that all go to define
levels of planning or overlooking or oblivion about nonagreement and hence
can establish culpability for rape. It is important to state that I am not espous-
ing that there be three different crimes of sexual assault predicated on intent
(premeditation/malice, reckless disregard of risk, and negligence in the failure
to perceive risk) but instead that criminal liability simply be extended to encompass the acts of rape/sexual assault when any of these unacceptable or "unreasonable" states of mind accompanies the commission of (differing severity
levels of) sexual assault offenses.

Again, I am not advocating graduating offenses further on the basis of intent. Parsimony, efficacy, charge bargaining, juror instructions, and other considerations all argue against a classification system that is too layered or too intricate. My recommendation for including recklessness and negligence in rape
is to use the most familiar and straightforward formulation in an effort to maximize clarity and the possibility for actual change.[6]

Although one could easily conceive of a scheme whereby the degrees of criminal culpability (or intent) would correspond with degrees of rape, this would be cumbersome; more significantly, it is not called for. Reforms like Michigan's differentiate rapes predicated not on intent but instead on "injuries" (extent of offensive sexual behaviors from less to more invasive touching to penetration) and "vulnerabilities" (victim age, victim-offender relationship, and incapacitation) (Kristine Mullendore, personal communication, 1998). But, again, the problem with this state's statute is its silence on consent, which let in the consent defense regardless of the vulnerabilities or injury levels charged. This identifies a need to take further steps in a model for rape and sexual assault. The model proposed here initially addresses the problem of consent coming in so easily by stipulating that nonagreement is presumptive and that recklessness and negligence make for culpability, that is, they do not make for reasonable mistakes in perceiving involuntariness, nonagreement. In other words, mistakes are unreasonable if nonagreement is carelessly disregarded or should have reasonably been interpreted, especially given the legal notice served by the presumptive involuntariness whenever force, coercion, or aggravating conditions are present (see the next chapter for further steps in the model).

Delineating crime circumstances that determine the level of severity (e.g., first- and second-degree rape where there are aggravating circumstances like young victims and weapons and simple rapes where there is "only" force or coercion), as many reforms do, is a preferable way of defining crime seriousness in rape, rather than differentiating new degrees of rape predicated on the magnitude of intent/indifference to nonconsent. Applying extant definitions of criminal liability to sexual assault offenses to encompass a legally established range in criminal intent should help the lay public and legal communities to accept such change, as well as restrict defense arguments of implicit consent and reasonable mistakes. This is because what is reasonable is spelled out to include rash dismissal and lax, derelict indifference or inattention, as is incorporated in other law. My attempt here is not to make rapes more serious offenses by escalating the consideration of intentional, malicious rape where assailants make plans to overcome victims' registered or observed nonconsent. Rape is already seen and treated as quite serious when it is "real" (e.g., Michigan's life sentence possibility for first-degree CSC). Recall that defining rape more seriously also suffers from the side effect of making judges and juries more reluctant to convict, given the harshness of criminal penalties (although, as will be explained later, it simultaneously gives the prosecution an advantage in plea negotiations). My objective is instead to move law to encompass more broadly what is really rape but may not be seen as such and/or may be excused with claims that offenders simply made mistakes. My attempt is show how rapes other than those where the victim is brutally beaten into submission—"other," "lesser," "simpler" rapes—are really rape, too, and should be prosecuted according to extant legal logic and principles. Simple negligent rape where the offender did not heed the forceful/coercive conditions attending his acts (see the next chapter) or the verbal or behavioral cues that indicated nonagreement is still serious and is still rape. The intimidation, overpowering, or ignoring of a victim occurs, the most personal sexual violation is committed, and the lifelong harm is done. Whether offenders recklessly or carelessly dismiss, or fail to think about, or neglect to pick up on nonagreement when reasonable people would and should have, especially when the law so announces this (through the presumptive involuntariness, nonagreement provision), the crime of forcing sex on another person has occurred. And it bears repeating that submission under such criminal circumstances is no more indicative of consent, voluntariness, or agreement than is the lack of physical resistance to the utmost.

What I am arguing here differs from what was argued in the *Morgan* case and what Estrich discusses in regard to reasonable standards. *Morgan* was about unreasonable mistake of consent or about looking at how the accused might be criminally responsible for being wrong but honest in thinking that consent was present. Estrich (1987), along with Adler (1987), goes to great lengths to show all that is wrong with this formulation. Estrich goes forward from identifying the problems in cases like *Morgan* to argue for a negligence standard that would include negligent liability for "ignoring a woman's words" (103) indicating nonagreement. My premise extends further to encompass not just men who intend to overtake victims and those who ignore a woman's words (or gestures or behavioral indications) of nonagreement but also those men who fail to understand the involuntariness, nonagreement that is reasonable to understand and statutorily privileged—when force, coercion, and so on is present.[7] In other words, my model extends negligent culpability to men who fail to appreciate, notice, observe, think about, or inquire into or feign ignorance about this reasonable belief of nonagreement to which the law gives notice in de jure statute whenever force, coercion, or aggravating conditions are in evidence.

The model here also differs in how it details the specifics of any aggravating, forceful, or coercive conditions that make involuntariness, nonagreement the legally presumptive premise (see the next chapter). A further step beyond Estrich's model is that a reasonable woman's point of view is the measuring rod to be used to make judgments about the indication of involuntariness, nonagreement (or the presence of forceful or coercive conditions, including implicitly intimidating threats and duress or fraud used to perpetrate the crimes, as laid out in subsequent chapters).[8]

It is worth emphasizing that unreasonableness exists independent from the belief in voluntariness, agreement or regardless of how genuine or earnest or honest that belief might be. A defendant might be truthful in stating that he thought that she meant yes, although she said no, that she came around to wanting it, that she asked for it or secretly wanted it, or that her resistance was just for show. But these beliefs are all "fanciful," à la *Morgan*; they are myths as opposed to sound, rational, realistic, or reasonable ways of interpreting such reactions. A reasonable person would know that voluntary assent was not present under these conditions As Berliner puts it so well, "reckless or negligent mistakes are not bases for acquittal from a charge of rape, and they should not be allowed to become so through manipulation of the standard of reasonableness" (1991: 2702). This is to say that careless disregard or failure to perceive involuntariness, nonagreement is criminal and will not be excused because it is argued that it was honestly misperceived.

Summarily, specifying culpability to attach when nonagreement is carelessly disdained or a matter of convenient, self-indulgent ignorance about the risks of forceful intimidation in order to exact involuntary compliance to sexual desires turns beliefs in consent into unreasonable beliefs. This makes the behavior of the accused more than just indifferent risk-taking behavior; it is behavior that is irresponsible and culpable because it is heedless of either the observable coercive or aggravating circumstance(s) or the victim's verbal or physical indications of nonagreement, for example, her saying "no," "stop," "please don't," "I don't want this," "you're hurting me," and the like or crying, withdrawing, trying to flee, fighting back, and so on. In total, my model looks for the criminal responsibility in the defendant's (unreasonably) overcoming or overlooking nonagreement, either expressed or when it is statutorily presumed to be reasonable (when any kind of force or threat or serious criminal condition attends the sex act[s] alleged to be criminal). (See the next chapter.)

SUMMARY

For all rapes/sexual assaults, the law should state in de jure fashion and instructions should be read to jurors that:

1. Once again (see the summary of the last chapter), proof of force/coercion/aggravating conditions is redundant with proof of involuntariness, nonagreement, and

so proof of both (force/coercion/aggravation and nonagreement) is unnecessary in law.

2. Mens rea is redundant with regard to force/coercion/aggravation or nonconsent with the *actus reus* of force/coercion/aggravation, and so both are not required de jure in law.

3. Negligence (vis-à-vis mens rea) is a standard used with other criminal offenses and so should be explicitly delineated with rape/sexual assault crimes.

4. Premeditation, recklessness, and negligence—that is, planning, carelessly disregarding, or failing to appreciate the involuntariness, nonagreement of a victim or the use/threat of force/coercion/aggravation—make for criminal culpability in rape/sexual assault when a reasonable woman would so appreciate.

5. Consequently, mistakes are legally deemed *un*reasonable if (a) force/coercion/aggravation is used or (b) involuntariness, nonagreement is intentionally overcome, or carelessly dismissed, or should have reasonably been interpreted, especially when the legal notice served by presumptive involuntariness is specified de jure whenever force/coercion/aggravating conditions are present (see the next chapter).

VOLUNTARINESS, AGREEMENT; PRESUMPTIVE NONAGREEMENT; RECKLESS/NEGLIGENT MISTAKES

Criminal recklessness and negligence can be applied in another way. This chapter looks at how mens rea can be juxtaposed with presumptive nonagreement. How would a provision for presumptive nonagreement (as spelled out in chapter 8) and criminal negligence (spelled out in chapter 9) work together? My model would not be as extreme as strict liability (e.g., Pineau's aggravated versus misdemeanor rape with no regard for belief, intent, or consequence), or as rigid as proving the lack of affirmative indications of consent in every case, or, especially, as demanding as Schulhofer's sexual autonomy model. My model is based on an extension of Estrich's logic of negligence and on Schulhofer's conception of recklessness and negligence. It goes further than Estrich's and Schulhofer's models, however, in ways that I will elaborate throughout the remaining chapters. At issue in this chapter is the positing of criminal responsibility when defendants fail to heed—intentionally, recklessly, or negligently—the nonagreement or involuntariness that would be statutorily presumptive under circumstances where reasonable women would appreciate force, threats, intimidations, or aggravating crime conditions to be present.

Here is what, first, presuming nonagreement and, second, applying reckless and negligent responsibility to mistakes (or to discarding or ignoring involuntariness) means. The real question is not "Did she consent?" but "Should he (as a reasonable person) have known nonagreement or involuntariness defined the encounter?" Did he know? Should he have known? A reasonable person would pick up on the nonagreement that the law gives notice to assume whenever someone uses or threatens harm, uses or threatens with a weapon, and so forth. (Third, as will be described later in this chapter, a reasonable person/woman would pick up on/understand the force, etc., when existent, which gives rise to the presumptive nonagreement just mentioned.)

This is both similar to and different from Estrich's negligent liability, discussed in the last chapter. It is similar insofar as it involves attributing criminal responsibility when the accused acts unreasonably. It is different insofar as Estrich focuses on defendants' negligence in mistakes in believing consent. I put forward the flip side, namely, that a reasonable person should/would have known that to which the law gives notice, which is that aggravating, violent, threatening, deceptive, or fraudulent conditions equate with the legal presumption of nonagreement. This is stronger than Estrich's posture that negligence in picking up on or disregarding nonagreement should make for guilt. I focus on the accused's failure to see or heed the willful nonagreement that it is reasonable to presume in the presence of aggravating circumstances or force, coercion, duress, or fraud. This makes it more difficult to get away with mis-TAKING consent, since its opposite is a priori the fact of the matter. The law would spell out that the reasonable expectation is nonagreement, that is, that a reasonable person would know that in the particular situation there was involuntariness or the submission/acquiescence to the sex act(s) would be unwilling or not freely given. Bear in mind in terms of the consent defense and the (un)reasonable mistake of consent defenses (which I elaborate later in this and subsequent chapters) that the model I am recommending includes the de jure provisions that expression of no is sufficient to establish involuntariness and that no means no. To defend on the basis of consent, or reasonableness of error in attributing consent, will be tougher to establish, not only because of the legal presumption of involuntariness, nonagreement where there is force/coercion/aggravation but because the law defines the meaning of nonagreement itself in the first place.

Again, my recommendation is to raise nonagreement to a reasonable legal assumption and specify this de jure when sexual assault involving coercive conditions is charged (so as to eradicate implied consent and the belief in false accusations by rape victims). So doing would state in law what is intrinsically already the case with other crimes. Spelling out the presumption that underlies rape, as other crimes, should make the unique forgiveness of mistakes about consent in rape more obvious for its atypicality, more readily recognized as unreasonable, and thus make the conferring of criminal responsibility more comparable to the way it is done with other offenses. A competent, reasonable individual would recognize that involuntariness is present under the conditions of ignoring a no or having to use force, weapons, threats, or the like to overcome the nonagreement of a woman.

Presumptive nonagreement, then, represents a way to set up what constitutes reasonable belief and hence negligence. A reasonable person would recognize involuntariness or nonagreement. This is to say that a reasonable, or competent, person would have the state of mind (mens rea) of being aware of the risks involved in intentionally, recklessly, or negligently not listening to, not caring about, being indifferent to, not bothering with, or not being aware of a woman's lack of volitional agreement or her no that is deemed legally sufficient up front in law. A reasonable person would see that to force, threaten, or otherwise overpower, intimidate, or put a woman in fear so as to exact submission to sex acts is wrong and criminal.

As noted earlier, few cases are so clouded with ambiguity that the accused doesn't have some sense of the victim's fear and/or aversion to having sex with him. Instead, offenders often rationalize, "she'd resist more if she didn't really want me," "she was asking for this, "she wants me but doesn't know it yet," and on and on. Schulhofer gives a fine example of how rape is rarely ambiguous in these ways by commenting on women who are drunk, where offenders commonly justify rape as consensual. He pointedly comments that it's a real stretch to believe that lack of resistance or even silence actually means desire when a woman can't stand up or even sit up on her own (1998: 270). I might add that for the minority of cases that would remain ambiguous, the convictions of a few men who conveniently interpret consent or rationalize away their use of power, threats, or violence with myths like "she was drinking and didn't mean no" would serve public notice that nonagreement is to be interpreted when a woman may be less than clear, or even silent, but where any kind of physical force or threats, incapacitation on the victim's part, deceptive tactics, and so on are used to impel involuntary acquiescence or submission to sex acts. A few notable convictions could go far to reduce unreasonable judgments where men might want unreasonably but opportunistically to mis-take consent.

This may seem radical at first blush to some, but really it is not. It is based on extant criminal law logic and principle, and the extension is not anything resembling a stretch. An analogy might be useful here. Presumptive sentencing provides the opportunistic example. Presumptive sentencing guidelines, which have grown so popular in this country over recent decades, give a presumed middle-ground sentence in years for particular crimes under particular conditions, as well as an upper and lower limit that may be meted out for exacerbating or mitigating circumstances. So a presumptive sentence for, say, an armed robbery might be twenty years, with bounds of fifteen- and twenty-five-year sentences for extenuating and aggravating circumstances, respectively. Presumptive nonagreement, like presumptive sentencing, invokes legislatively set terms to pursue the ends of justice. So, again, legally stipulating a presumption to be made under proscribed circumstances/behaviors is not very far afield from what already exists in the legal sphere. With presumptive sentencing, the law sets up the operative premise (the middle-range number of years) if the prosecution proves the criminal conditions equating to the elements of a crime. With presumptive nonagreement, the law sets up the operative premise (the existence of involuntariness, nonagreement) if the prosecution proves the criminal conditions equating to the coercive or aggravating elements (but not the nonagreement standing alone; see chap. 8) of the (sexual assault) crimes.

Presumptive nonagreement switches the emphasis from the woman's burden to indicate no (when there are coercive circumstances of any kind) to the reasonableness of the man's interpretation of the situation. (The man must recognize the coercive and injurious nature of his threats or harms, too; see the next section.) The woman must indicate nonagreement if there are no forceful or like conditions involved, but the man must consider, look for, and listen to no or the woman's protestations or indications of nonagreement. It is fair to burden the person accused of rape with the responsibility to show that he was not derelict in understanding the victim's unwillingness about engaging in sex acts or in understanding the law's definition of presumptive belief as to what is reasonable to expect in given coercive situations (and, remember, ignorance of the law is no excuse). A man has the personal and legal (not to mention civil and social) responsibility to know what is acceptable and reasonable in law and to listen, pay attention to, and respect what the law, as well as what a woman, says.

Intent, recklessness, and the negligence involved in failing to recognize the nonagreement that the law specifies to prevail under certain circumstances—the same circumstances where reasonable people would expect or interpret involuntariness to exist—should all confer criminal culpability. Intentionally or purposely ignoring, or callously disregarding, or failing to understand what a reasonable person/woman would understand as no or involuntariness, nonagreement, especially as the law has stipulated this to be the reasonable belief (if there is force, etc.), is what is to be specified as criminal in my model. Mistakes as to nonagreement are what would be unreasonable and criminal. Alternatively put, it is only equitable that the defendant be responsible for his intimidating, dangerous, or otherwise injurious behaviors (see the next section), as well as responsible for establishing how he was somehow reasonable in failing to heed what the victim complains was injurious, forceful, nonconsensual sexual assault. That mistakes are unreasonable when men don't watch or notice or check for a yes or a no must be more than merely recognized; it must be written into law and implemented in practice. What has been described in this chapter constitutes a beginning step toward these ends. Focusing on a man's behavior and what a reasonable person should have perceived takes the unfair onus and discriminatory focus off of victims, who do not choose, want, or ask for sexual violence or violation.

Specifying that involuntariness or nonagreement coexist with any exercise of force/coercion (and so involuntariness is redundant with force/coercion) is one way to fight the acceptance of alleged reasonableness in mistaking consent. Making nonagreement presumptive goes a good way toward closing the reasonable mistake loophole.

A few jurisdictions have taken yet a step further in this direction by stipulating that not only is unreasonably mistaking consent not a defense, even reasonably mistaking consent is not a defense (Berliner 1991:2696 n. 61, citing *People v. Hale*, 142 Mich. App 451, 453–54, 370 N.W.2d 382,383 [1985]; Kadish and Schulhofer 2001: 358).[1] Kadish and Schulhofer (2001) note the Ascolillo ruling in Massachusetts (*Commonwealth v. Ascolillo*, 405 Mass. 456, 541 N.E.2d 570 [1989]) as an example of disallowing reasonable mistakes or, as they call it, "strict liability" on mistakes. Here, even honest and reasonable mistakes of consent would not exculpate. In a subsequent case in this state, the court went so far as to introduce a jury instruction to this effect. The judge told the jurors that "a belief that the victim consented would not be a defense even if reasonable" (2001: 358, citing *Commonwealth v. Simcock*, 31 Mass. App. 184, 575 N.E.2d 1137, 1142–1143 [1991]). Kadish and Schulhofer conclude that "the weight of American authority now runs strongly against the Ascolillo view, but a few states appear to have joined Massachusetts and Pennsylvania in opting for strict liability on the consent issue" (2001: 358, see, e.g., *State v. Reed*, 479 A.2d 1291 [Me. 1984]).

It would appear that strict liability on all mistakes is too radical to be very realistic or likely to apply in any further jurisdictions. My recommendations are more modest than strict liability because of my model's attempt to emphasize practicality, implementability, and the underlying corollary concerns that can be raised about the rights of accused men (with strict liability on mistakes of consent).

Not only does the "weight of American authority" (Kadish and Schulhofer 2001: 358) support allowing reasonable mistakes to exonerate defendants, some have commented that there has been an increasing popularity of the reasonable mistake defense over the past decade or two (Berliner 1991). Berliner proclaims that this has happened in the wake of the repeal of resistance requirements. The two get intertwined in the views of some significant people, including some courts. For example, "most California cases in which the court allowed a reasonable belief defense involved insufficient or ambiguous victim resistance" (Berliner 1991: 2687 n. 70). What this means is that where victims do not resist, defendants are allowed reasonably to perceive agreement. Berliner notes that "none of the jurisdictions which allow a reasonable belief defense have retained a statutory requirement of resistance" (2699 n. 83). The problem is that reasonable belief in consent or agreement has grown as the requirement of victim resistance is removed (2696 n. 61).

Berliner suggests one way to counter this regressive tendency. She recommends a rebuttable presumption of unreasonableness wherever victims cry, argue, or physically struggle in assaults (1991: 2688). This, too, is problematic, however. The first problem is that it reintroduces or refocuses on victim resistance (evident possibly in victim arguing but definitely in victim physical struggle in assault) to prove nonagreement. It is ironic that Berliner critiques the reasonable mistake of consent defense for replacing repealed resistance requirements for much the same tendency from which her recommendation suffers. Berliner's solution is problematic as well in asserting that crying is tantamount to involuntariness, nonagreement. Do tears always signal nonagreement? Under what circumstances are tears to be equated with involuntariness? Also problematic is that Berliner is unclear on the meaning of victims' "arguing" with offenders, and this is to be a basis for attributing unreasonableness about mistakes about consent. Finally problematic is that these indicators of nonagreement pivot around not only victim behaviors rather than offenders' forceful conduct or objective crime circumstances but a nonexhaustive list of victim behaviors at that.

A better way to counter this regressive propensity is found in my recommendation to make nonagreement the de jure legal presumption whenever force, coercion, or aggravating conditions accompany the crime.[2] This can be seen as a more effective route for reforms insofar as the presumption of nonagreement cannot be rebutted; instead, a criminal defense must be established where voluntariness of agreement (consent) or the reasonableness of mistake would have to be demonstrated to a degree that overcomes the presumption (see next chapter).[3]

A statutory presumption of nonagreement, along with the reasonableness standard, is not a one-way street protecting the victim in a criminal proceeding. In "he said, she said" rapes of any sort where victims state they expressed nonagreement but there are no coercive elements present, the defense of agreement and of mistake of agreement are tenable under many conditions (see chap. 11 on unavailable defenses), with the latter argued by the defense to be a mistake that is reasonable in nature. Unreasonable mistakes would not exculpate (while mistakes that are proven to be reasonable could). In either case, considerations would encompass negligence and recklessness in carelessly choosing to ignore or failing to appreciate involuntariness, nonagreement when assessing the reasonableness of beliefs.

What I am recommending holds the potential to avoid the reemergence of focus on victim consent and resistance as previously described to be problematic. This is because the notion of criminal responsibility here is not a singular new measure but one juxtaposed with the repeal of resistance requirement, along with a statutory (de jure) presumption of nonagreement that makes nonagreement the reasonable belief under a large range of crime circumstances.

The bottom line is simply this: Men who mean to overcome, who disregard, or who are indifferent to or ignorant about the nonagreement that a reasonable person would appreciate (under the various conditions of sexual assault law) are men who force sex; men who force sex are rapists. Men who ignore no, when the law sees this as sufficient, and men who think no means yes, maybe, later, or even more, when the law declares that no means no, are criminally responsible—period. And men who are inattentive to nonagreement include those who may callously or intentionally overpower recognized lack of agreement and also include those who refuse to heed it, those who dismiss it, those who scorn it, and those who are too careless even to think about it. The fault is criminal, and it is the man's, whether he plans the rape, whether he hears and ignores the no, whether he is reckless, or whether he just doesn't grasp or doesn't even consider for a moment the involuntary acquiescence or submission he compels.

A FURTHER APPLICATION OF RECKLESS AND NEGLIGENT CULPABILITY: TAKING ADVANTAGE OF THE REDUNDANCY IN PROOF OF MENS REA IN NONAGREEMENT AND FORCE/COERCION

Thus far, I have focused on mens rea and extending negligent/reckless liability to the issue of nonagreement (and the alleged reasonableness of mistakes as to agreement). Yet consideration of negligence vis-à-vis the element of force/coercion (versus consent) is provocative, too. Kinports's 2001 attention to the redundancy in the proof of intent in nonconsent and the proof of intent in force/

coercion raises the specter of this tactic (of considering negligence and force/coercion) for the prosecution of rape. Demonstrating mens rea in the use of force could be an alternative way to prove criminal culpability relating to mens rea. While Kinports notes the possible redundancy of proving intent vis-à-vis force and the *actus reus* of force, she details that "a few courts have suggested that the strictest *mens rea* requirement attaches to the element of force in rape cases—that is, the prosecution must prove that the defendant purposefully or intentionally used force" (2001: 755). New reforms can usefully take into account mens rea and hence negligence/recklessness in the use of force.

What Kinports's observations bring up is that if intent is relevant to proof of force, then recklessness and negligence can and do exist in relation to force as well, and I would add in relation to coercion, too. Recklessness and negligence, then, are relevant to establishing the element of force/coercion and hence criminal liability for the crime of rape.

There are obviously purposeful, calculated, intentional force and/or threats of force to overcome a victim's articulated or actual nonagreement. It is this type of intent that is analogous to homicide that is premeditated with malice aforethought. There is, as well, carelessness or audacious inattention or negligent failure to recognize that force, physical danger, and intimidation were involved or threatened in the commission of the sex acts. If there can be recklessness and negligence about involuntariness/nonagreement, there can be recklessness and negligence about force/coercion. It is in these instances that criminal responsibility can reasonably be found. Alternatively put, reasonable people would have consciousness of guilt, a guilty mind, or criminal intent when cavalierly disregarding victims' fear of harm as well as victims' involuntary submission. Kinports sees the issue here to be one of whether or not a reasonable person would have known that the defendant was using force. She states, "the applicable state of mind requirement was negligence—so that the issue became whether a reasonable person [like the defendant if competent] would have thought the defendant was using force" (2001: 766).

The question becomes, Is it not possible that the state of mind of the defendant was such that he recklessly engaged in overcoming victim nonagreement, not caring whether he scared her witless, or pounded her into submission by causing a concussion or internal bleeding, or dismissed with abandon how extensively he tore her vagina or physically injured her in some other way? Is it not possible that a defendant, rather than decidedly, meaningfully executing his sexual assault with violence, force, or coercion, didn't pay any reasonable attention to how violent, forceful, or threatening he let himself become? Kinports puts it well: "But in other circumstances, the defendant's *mens rea* vis-à-vis force may be less clear, and it may therefore make a difference whether a rape conviction requires proof that the defendant purposely intended to use force, or whether it is enough that he knew he was exercising force, that the woman thought he was using force, or that a reasonable person viewing the situation would have thought so" (2001: 757). These are the circumstances where negligence and recklessness as to the use of force/coercion can productively be applied to assign criminal responsibility.[4]

Kinports brings up other examples involving interpretations that are worth review. She notes the *Evans* case as debatable because "the court found the meaning of the defendant's comments about killing and raping the victim to be ambiguous" (2001: 766), although what is ambiguous about such threats would escape most reasonable people, in my way of thinking. Kinports also references the "lightly choking" versus "heavy caress" terms that arose in the *Rusk* case, for the different slants given to the defendant's hands around the victim's neck, and she suggests that men who play up victims' fears based on histories of past abuse should not be "open to question" about the use of force (2001: 766). These are just some types of the situations where proof of force has been problematic in the courts but could beneficially be encompassed by reckless/negligent considerations. Reckless and negligent liability could reasonably attach to such behaviors, and resolve the alleged "ambiguities," so as to demonstrate that force/coercion were in evidence. Careless disdain or failure to appreciate force/coercion when reasonable people would see it, could stand in place of the difficulty of establishing force or coercion, as was the case with the assailants and their coercive threats and actions in these above instances.

Advantages of Using Recklessness and Negligence with Nongreement and Force/Coercion

Several things are accomplished by applying intent, as, for example, carved out in homicide law, to sexual assault offenses. First, to reiterate, these notions are not only well established in the legal community, they are easily understood in lay circles, too. This makes change along these dimensions more likely to be accepted. The approach also provides a range of criminal culpability, from the intent to overcome, to the reckless disregard, to the careless failure to perceive the risk of nonagreement or the exercise of force or threats—in other words, the commission of rape. In this way, these terms, and the logic underlying them, are mutually reinforcing and can operate to expand the concept of what might more realistically constitute negligence in rape. This method of defining criminal responsibility can help reduce the all too pervasive and persuasive defense of consent in rape or sexual assault cases. Change to incorporate reckless and negligent responsibility in relation to consent and force/coercion facilitates the prosecutorial burden to prove the crime by broadening what can be shown to be—beyond a reasonable doubt—criminal (negligence, recklessness, or intentional). As important, the approach focuses on the criminal responsibilities of the perpetrator rather than the (noncriminal) responsibilities of the victim (and/ or the discrediting of her claims). It places at least some of the burden on the assailant, instead of fostering the same old second-guessing of the victim. The approach burdens the male to contemplate nonagreement, to understand it or suffer the consequences of his behavior, as is the case with other criminal actions and actors. Again, homicides are just one instance of judging crime by mental states; this obtains throughout criminal law. What my model would accomplish is focusing on the offender's mistake or failure to heed, regard, or perceive involuntariness, nonagreement, which is presumed to exist in law when dangerous conditions exist and therefore is the only reasonable belief, one that a defendant is responsible to see and observe. Focus on a defendant's culpability, that is, his negligent/reckless or intentional disregard of nonagreement, would replace focus on the reasonableness of his mistakes about what the victim's behavior, demeanor, and so on might have conveyed regarding her alleged consent. In addition, the model of change discussed here can focus attention on the offender's negligent failure to perceive his (reckless) disdain or intentional use of force or coercion to exact submission to sexual demands or "consent to rape" (as was the coined vocabulary used by the defense in the Kobe Bryant case) in the same way his negligent failure, (reckless) disdain, or intentional ignoring of nonagreement would assign criminal responsibility.

It is important to reiterate that the model advanced here makes the treatment of sexual assault offenses more consistent with that of other crimes, not different or unique from them. And standardized rules that apply to all cases are an ideal of criminal law. Clarity and standardization in laws that proscribe behaviors is mandatory if law is to serve fair notice to men—and women. Clarity and consistency in prohibitions or prescriptions and even-handed application of rules are not designed only for due notice and compliance purposes; they are also indispensable to accomplishing justice—for men as well as women.

A WOMAN'S POINT OF VIEW FOR A CHANGE

Recall the recommendation in my model for a woman's point of view on nonagreement and force/coercion (see chap. 8). I hold that there needs to be a more balanced, as opposed to male, perspective on what is reckless, negligent, and reasonable as well.

The Appellate Court in Michigan provides an example of how this can be handled. As previously described, this court recognized the problem when it declared that "consent is to be determined from the victim's subjective state of mind, not the defendant's reasonable belief that the victim consented" (Michigan Judicial Institute 2002: 221, citing *People v. Hale*, 142 Mich. App. 451, 453 [1985]).

The problem of the differences between male and female points of view has been recognized elsewhere. Estrich points out that the Model Penal Code commentators acknowledged that legally recognizing negligent liability in rape held open the potential to "provide an additional motive to men to 'take care before acting, to use their faculties and draw on their experience in gauging potentialities of contemplated conduct'" (1987: 97–98). While these commentators open the door to recklessness/negligence in criminal responsibility, they miss that a man's point of view of negligence, given his "experience in gauging" women and his sensibilities and perceived responsibilities in sex activities, would generally be different from what a reasonable woman's "experiences in gauging," or a woman's perceptions and experiences, would judge sensible, responsible, or negligent. Estrich goes on to raise an important caveat about how to recommend models of negligent liability in relation to the issue of nonconsent. She warns that

> the real significance of saying that negligence is enough—or that unreasonable mistakes will not exculpate—will depend on how we define what is reasonable. If the "reasonable" attitude to which a male defendant is held is defined according to a "no means yes" philosophy that celebrates male aggressiveness and female passivity and limits the "tools of coercion" to physical violence, little is accomplished for women by expanding liability to negligence and requiring that mistakes be reasonable. Simple rapes would still be easy to exclude from the prohibitions of the law. On the other hand, if the reasonable man is the one who in the 1980s understands that "no means no" and that extortion for sex is not more justifiable than extortion for money, a great deal may be accomplished.
>
> (1987: 98)

The reasonable man in the twenty-first century should by now understand that no means no, but the reality is, sadly, that we are still far, if not further (because of conservative, sexist backlash), from such an understanding. MacKinnon recognized the same problem, as witnessed in her comment that "rapists typically believe that the woman loved it…. To them [men] the accusations are false because, to them, the facts describe sex…. To attempt to solve this by adopting the standard of reasonable belief without asking,... to whom the belief is reasonable...is one-sided: male-sided" (1989: 363). This brings us full circle to the male-constructed reality of sex, heterosexuality, and rape that I described in tracing the historical sequence in chapter 5.

The first part of MacKinnon's insight, which I have mentioned several times already, is repeated here because it integrates many of the concerns at issue. She advances that the law reaches a zenith in its maleness when it is most rational and most characterized by aperspectivity (1983: 658). What is most rational is what we think is most reasonable, and because rationality is male centered and law is rational, what is reasonable is male defined, which results in reflections and protections of male vested interests. These definitions are not in the interests of fairness and justice in any society, much less one characterized by pervasive gender inequality.

Using a woman's experience and viewpoint is therefore necessary and justifiable—and not terribly far-fetched or radical. After all, the standard of a "reasonable man" has been relied on for centuries. And should there be a question about how unreasonable male definitions of what is reasonable are, recall how excuses, justifications, and rationalizations asserting, for example, that women love being raped, love rough sex, and think that even injuries sustained from rape are only "loveplay" (Adler 1987: 53) have been accepted in both the legal and social realms for many centuries. It seems quite reasonable, given all this, to take the other side for a change and to define nonagreement, force, threat, fear, submission, what is reasonable, and what is fair from the point of view of the sex that suffers the injuries of rape and sexual assault. This is more than warranted, it is of paramount importance, since it is her understanding of force, coercion, threat, and so on and/or her involuntariness, unwillingness, or nonagreement that define the crime of rape in the first place.

DUE NOTICE ON UNREASONABLENESS OF MISTAKES OF NONAGREEMENT: NO UNTIL PROVEN YES

Schulhofer summarizes that "unfortunately, the negligence standard does little to solve the enforcement problems that anti-rape reformers are concerned about. When a man claims 'mistake,' he may be insincere or sincere but exceptionally insensitive. More often the difficulty is that his beliefs about the woman's consent are perfectly consistent with widely held attitudes. A successful criminal prosecution therefore remains difficult even in courts that accept the reformers' recommendation to punish men who make 'unreasonable mistakes'" (1998: 259). Because reasonable mistakes have exculpated, because unreasonable mistakes that were honestly or earnestly believed have exculpated, because even unreasonable mistakes that were not proved to be honest have exculpated, and because beliefs about reasonableness and consent "all but guarantee at least a reasonable doubt about whether the man made a mistake" (257), something new needs to be devised to thwart the facile intrusion of erroneous attitudes about involuntariness, nonagreement and reasonable belief and reasonable doubt in rape adjudications, most especially in simple, date, and acquaintance rapes where there are no aggravating circumstances. Specifying in law that there is no doctrine of implied consent and that people who report rape cannot be assumed to be lying (are innocent), changing the term "consent" to "voluntariness, agreement," specifying that an indication of agreement (or just no) is legally sufficient, declaring that no always means no, making the legal presumption one of nonagreement with any kind of coercion, extending liability to cover recklessness and negligence, and incorporating a woman's point of view of force/coercion and nonagreement (and hence what might be [un]reasonable in the recognition of these) constitute some synergistic measures in such an endeavor. These changes all need to be made in substantive and procedural laws (chaps. 13 and 14 discuss this). Denoting this series of recommendations in de jure law would give men—and women—notice about legal requirements and expectations.

If rape is charged and nonagreement is the definition of the reasonable assumption when any kind of violence, force, or threats are involved, then mistakes about what the law serves notice about (presumptive nonagreement) and so about what is reasonable to believe about taking sex under this circumstance (just like taking money) are what is unreasonable. And unreasonable mistakes cannot exculpate. Recall Krumholz's example of trespass as a rare instance where nonconsent needs to be noted a priori (personal communication, 1998). Posting "no trespass" gives due notice and makes any trespass illegal. The law's de jure specification that no is adequate, that no means no, that even silence under conditions of danger is involuntariness, nonagreement, that nonagreement is to be assumed wherever there is force, coercion, or the like certainly serves notice, and any sex taken, stolen, or inflicted is thereafter criminal. And it should go without saying that using violence, force, coercion, duress, or deception to take sex (in spite of the no) is always criminal.

Given history and the tenacity of male-centered prejudicial protections, it seems necessary to reiterate this in yet one more way. This is that unreasonable mistakes (e.g., ignoring no) make for criminal culpability, no matter how genuine, honest, earnest, or sincere. Still another way to think about this is to see that criminal intent, recklessness, or negligence in rape/sexual assault on the issue of nonagreement and/or force and coercion make the accused responsible for his faults of mistake, not the female for her alleged failure in not giving clear enough signals to preclude his making mistakes. Only a male point of view could deem such mistakes to be reasonable. Only male vested interest could conceivably be served. And only a male-slanted system would exculpate an offender on this basis.

What I recommend here is another de jure legal specification to proclaim, and to make ever so clear, that criminal liability is to be placed on unreasonable mistakes of consent, in place of the virtual carte blanche accorded (assuming, implying, or arguing) mis-taken consent or voluntariness, agreement as acceptable or reasonable in order to vitiate guilt. Criminal liability on mistakes is not to say that consent cannot be argued or that mistakes can never be reasonable (and reasonable enough to outweigh the presumption of involuntariness embedded in the model) but instead that it is typically unreasonable and criminal to make mistakes about consent under conditions where force/coercion or duress/fraud (see chap. 12) are present, where the victim is a minor, where both parties live in the same household, where the accused holds a position of authority over the victim, where victim and assailant are blood relatives, where the victim is incapacitated, when the alleged rape occurs in conjunction with simultaneous other felonies, where weapons are present, and where date rape drugs have been administered. Moreover, an allegedly reasonable mistake must be demonstrated with evidence in order to be proven to be reasonable in nature (the next chapter delineates just how this might be done). One last time, the operative principle should be that mistakes are not typically acceptable or reasonable, no matter how honestly made; that mistakes about voluntariness, agreement are generally unreasonable and therefore will not excuse responsibility for the crimes of rape and sexual assault. The bottom line is the de jure presumption of unreasonableness of mistakes about consent. It is important to state at the outset, however, that, as I am describing this, the legal presumption is a "rebuttable presumption" (see Berliner 1991) that can be successfully challenged in court. It is to this that the next chapter turns.

SUMMARY

For all rapes/sexual assaults, the law should state in de jure fashion and instructions should be read to jurors that, because the law specifies that nonagreement is presumptive wherever there is force/coercion/aggravation (or duress or fraud;

see chap. 12; see also the summary of chap. 8), and because premeditation, reck-lessness, and negligence confer criminal responsibility in relation to mistakes about involuntariness (nonagreement) and a reasonable person (a reasonable woman—see below) should/would have appreciated the involuntariness to which the law gives presumption whenever force/coercion/aggravation are established, intentional, planned, callous, or indiscriminate mistakes under these conditions are unreasonable and thus do not mitigate criminal responsibility. Or, because premeditation, recklessness, and negligence confer criminal responsibility in re-lation to mistakes about force/coercion/ aggravation and because a reasonable person (a reasonable woman—see below) should/would have appreciated the involuntariness to which the law gives presumption whenever force/coercion/ aggravation are established, intentional, planned, callous, or indiscriminate mis-takes under these conditions are unreasonable and thus do not mitigate criminal responsibility. A reasonable woman's point of view is to constitute the standard for what is intentional, recklessness, negligent, and therefore reasonable vis-à-vis involuntariness, nonagreement and/or conditions of force/coercion/aggrava-tion. The law serves due notice to men—and women—about legal obligations and expectations by de jure specification that involuntariness, nonagreement is presumptive whenever force/coercion/aggravation (or duress/fraud) are present, which makes intentional (or unintentional, for that matter) reckless or negligent mis-takes of nonagreement (or force/coercion/aggravation) unreasonable (mis-taking of sex from a female) and criminal.

Tchen quotes one of the drafters of the Michigan legislation: "When the victim is threatened with a dangerous weapon, or is beaten, robbed or kidnapped, the possibility of her willingly consenting to sexual intercourse is so *unlikely* that it ought to be raised as an alternative theory for the defense rather than have to be shown from the outset" (1983: 1549; italics mine). The next two segments of my model attempt to move toward an alternative theory of consent. The prevailing presumptive non-agreement should be born in mind as the frame for characterizing encounters involving force, coercion, or aggravating crime circumstances (and duress and fraud; see the next chapter) as we proceed to zero in on such an alternative theory.

While my model preserves a defense of voluntariness, agreement and a defense of reasonable mistake of voluntariness, agreement, it dramatically changes how these can be used. It is, naturally, important to preserve both defenses in order to exonerate those accused of rape who might not be guilty of the crimes. This is probably most germane to the "he said, she said" (or again, better put, "she said, he heard; he said, she heard") cases, where ambiguity may reside in the determination of whether coercion was present, whether she was too intoxicated/incapacitated to be able to give voluntariness, agreement, and so on. It is important to consider these types of cases as they are most often left behind by reform implementation. The defenses of voluntariness, agreement would be less tenable, one would think, in cases with less ambiguity or with more force or more evidence. The defenses described herein, however, would still obtain.

If the defense decides to use a voluntariness, agreement defense against a rape accusation, the burden of proof should switch from the prosecution to the defense, which would then need to demonstrate that voluntariness, agreement was in evidence during the acts alleged to be criminal. I advocate removing the burden of proof from the prosecution, which now has to demonstrate the aggravating, forceful, or coercive situations and/or victim expression of nonagreement, and placing it instead on the defense, which would have to demonstrate that agreement was freely given, despite the crime circumstances that make the acts criminal and/or make nonagreement the reasonable assumption. This move entails three different but interrelated changes: (1) the institution of an affirmative defense, involving a shift in the burden of production; (2) a shift in the burden of proof; and (3) the creation of an affirmative consent defense.[1]

AFFIRMATIVE DEFENSE: SHIFTING THE BURDEN OF PRODUCTION

An affirmative defense means that the defense must introduce some evidence to make its case (Michigan Judicial Institute 2002: 221).[2] It places on the defense the burden of production, alternatively referred to as the burden of going forward (MacKinnon 2001: 484) with evidence or the burden of proceeding, that is, the burden of introducing some evidence to support whatever kind of defense issue is being argued (Kadish and Schulhofer 2001: 45). Kadish and Schulhofer summarily state that "when the defendant bears the burden of production on an issue, the issue is commonly referred to as an affirmative defense" (45). This is to say, an affirmative defense shifts to the defense the burden of producing evidence to the defense to demonstrate its claim, requiring that the defense put forward substantiation that would refute defendant culpability on the criminal charges. This can be contrasted to the defense's merely introducing doubt or demonstrating that the prosecutor's case is inadequately established. If the defendant argues that the victim voluntarily agreed to sex acts or that there was a reasonable basis for mistaking that she did, the affirmative defense requirement would obtain. What I am specifically proposing is a shift in the burden of introducing evidence, such that the defense would shoulder the burden to produce additional facts or evidence to prove the reasonable basis for thinking there was willing agreement to the sex acts at the time and that the victim is lying about rape.[3]

SHIFTING THE BURDEN OF PROOF

I assert not only that the defense must shoulder the burden of production (must introduce evidence) but further that the defense must shoulder the burden of proof: the proof burden would attach to the defense, instead of the prosecution, to show that voluntariness, agreement (consent) was present, to substantiate the defense argument of consent, thus negating the charge(s) of rape/sexual assault. So, in place of the traditional job of simply introducing doubt that would rise to the level of reasonable in order to undermine the prosecutor's burden of proof beyond a reasonable doubt, the defense would have to demonstrate its claim by producing additional facts that would refute the defendant's culpability on the criminal charges by proving victim voluntariness, agreement. This would mean that if the defendant argues that the victim voluntarily agreed to sex acts, the defense would have to shoulder the burden of introducing evidence, as well as of proof or persuasion as to that evidence, in order to convince the judge or jury of the defense's premise that the victim willingly agreed to the sex act(s).

It is noteworthy that this is not an unusual feature in criminal case processing. Berliner reports precedent for shifting the burden of proof in rape statute in her comments about Washington's rape law. Here the burden is placed on the defense if/when attempts are made to argue consent (1991: 2693 n. 43). In addition to shifting the burden of proof, as Kadish and Schulhofer also point out, "in some instances state law may require the defense to bear both burdens" of production and proof (2001: 45). Tchen (1983) describes a similar requirement in court decisions. The Supreme Court in Illinois upheld a statute that required "the defendant to prove the existence of the exculpating factor beyond a reasonable doubt" (1552, citing *People v. Smith* 71 Ill. 2nd 95, 105, 374 N.E. 2nd 472, 476 [1978], n. 195). Tchen cites other examples of the legality of shifting the burden to the defense. She notes, for instance, that "a common law affirmative defense has existed in Michigan for nearly ten years" (1552).

Other examples of shift in the burden of proof are easily found. One is seen with self-defense. Here the defense has the burden to prove that force was necessary for protection against imminent harm (Black 1991: 947). Another example is found when the defense wants to argue discriminatory prosecution, where the burden of proof shifts to the defense to show that harm resulted from the selective prosecution of a criminal statute not typically enforced. In a similar vein, if the defense wants to argue that the defendant's right to a speedy trial was violated, the burden of proof once again shifts to the defense to show prejudice was caused because of this violation. "Defendant bears the burden of showing prejudice. The moving party has the burden of proof" (Michigan Judicial Institute 2001: 109;

also see Michigan Judicial Institute 2002: 287). The defense is the moving party in counsel substitution or withdrawal and so bears the burden of proof in Michigan (Michigan Judicial Institute 2001: 104). The list could go on; the point is there is precedence for shifting the burden of proof.

Preponderance of Evidence

Given my attempt to draw on extant legal principles in order to garner political and public support and minimize resistance, I would recommend adopting the preponderance of evidence standard for the burden of proof when attached to the defense. This is not as high a standard of proof as "beyond a reasonable doubt," which normally adheres to the prosecution.[4] It nonetheless is reasonable, insofar as it requires the defense to establish that voluntariness, agreement was more likely than not. I recommend preponderance of evidence in my model because of precedent (see below) but more because it would be more palatable and thus more likely to be enacted, along with the rest of the changes in the model I have developed. For reasons of political feasibility, my model does not go as far as shifting to the defense the proof standard of beyond a reasonable doubt in situations where agreement or mistake is argued as the accused's defense, though I might note that there is some precedence for going this far, too.

It is useful to examine definitions of the preponderance of evidence standard at this juncture. In *Black's* definition, "as standard proof in civil cases, [it] is evidence which is of greater weight or more convincing than the evidence which is offered in opposition to it; that is, evidence which as a whole shows that the fact sought to be proved is more probable than not.... Evidence which is more credible and convincing to the mind. That which accords with reason and probability. The word preponderance means something more than 'weight'; it denotes a superiority of weight or outweighing ... more probable than not" (1991: 819). Preponderance of evidence is "a standard under which the plaintiff wins who establishes that their facts are more likely than not" to be the case (Kadish and Schulhofer 2001: 48). So the test here would be whether the evidence proves it more likely, or more probable than not, that voluntariness, agreement framed the sex act(s) at issue. In other words, voluntariness, agreement is established as more likely than not to have been indicated (to the extent that it outweighs the assumption that nonagreement framed the sex acts if under the conditions of aggravating, forceful, or coercive conditions).

As intimated above, the preponderance of evidence standard is justifiable because it is a part of our legal system and practice in other instances. One parallel is found with the defense of insanity, which is an affirmative defense under federal and many state laws. Defendants must prove their insanity claims by the proof standard of preponderance of the evidence. In other words, just saying/ claiming "I'm insane" ("she consented," in the case of rape) is not enough; there must evidence supporting the premise as a "more likely than not conclusion for jurors to be able to use it to 'excuse' the behavior" (Kristine Mullendore, personal communication, 1998). Further instances of law requiring a preponderance of evidence standard corollary with a defense burden of proof can also be found. Michigan law details that in insanity cases the standard required shifts to a preponderance of evidence (Kristine Mullendore, personal communication, 2007 citing MCLA 7682a, enacted in 1986) where a "defendant must prove incompetency" to stand trial (Michigan Judicial Institute 2001: 103; also see Michigan Judicial Institute 2002: 227). Similarly, in arguing entrapment to exculpate defendants in Michigan, "the defendant must prove a claim of entrapment by a preponderance of the evidence" (Michigan Judicial Institute 2001: 205). In a related vein, MacKinnon analyzes a Supreme Court discrimination case (*Price Waterhouse v. Hopkins* 490 U.S. 228 [1989]). She reports that a preponderance of evidence was the standard the Supreme Court ruled applicable in overturning a lower court ruling requiring "clear and convincing evidence" by an employer in a discrimination suit (2001: 509).[5]

Other factors justify the changes I assert. A criminal defense burden to offer proof of agreement is surely not that unreasonable given the prevalent attitudes about rape, about females who claim rape, and/or simply the gross attrition in rape cases into which these attitudes translate. Judges and juries persist in favoring a belief in agreement or a disbelief in a victim's allegations, making my recommended shift in the (legal) burden to demonstrate voluntariness, agreement a balancing measure of fair-minded change.

Moreover, I am not recommending a shift in the prosecutor's burden (to establish the elements of the crime, such as defendant identity, penetration, weapons, force, or victim nonagreement). The defendant is still protected by the state's being encumbered to prove these things beyond a reasonable doubt. It is only when the defense wants to argue voluntariness, agreement or the reasonableness of a mistake of voluntariness, agreement that it must provide evidence to sustain that voluntariness was more likely than not the case or was strong enough to overpower the presumptive victim nonagreement that is reasonable to assume where there are aggravating, forceful, or coercive conditions. I'm only suggesting that the defense have the burden to demonstrate the existence of agreement (rather than letting it continue to be presumed) when the defendant claims that the victim agreed to the sex and/or is lying in her accusation or when he claims there were reasonable grounds to mistake agreement. To summarize, the defense would need to demonstrate the existence of the voluntariness, agreement to the sex acts claimed that would negate the rape charges leveled, rather than being able simply to introduce a doubt about consent in whatever (even misleading) way it chooses. The tactic of simply alluding to consent or simply alluding to victims' lying has been all that has been necessary in the past to introduce sufficient doubt to disable the "beyond a reasonable doubt" standard and thus prejudicially protect defendants. What I am calling for is not tipping the scales so far as to introduce similar unfairness on the other side. Rather, what I propose would contribute to evening out, or more evenly weighting, the scales so that justice can begin to be approximated.

What this does in my model is recognize that agreement can be a defense to a rape accusation, but in a way much less prejudicial than in the past. My recommendation replaces the focus on the reasonability of his mis-TAKING consent (as with Estrich's negligence approach) with a focus on nonagreement as the reasonable belief, while at the same time allowing the defense the option of proving that volitional, positive assent was present instead. The crux of the matter here is which beliefs are convincing and who—prosecution or defense—has to shoulder the burdens of introducing the evidence and proof for the case.

To review the steps in defense thus far, a voluntariness, agreement defense should be an affirmative defense, where the defense shoulders the burden of the production of evidence, as well as the burden of proof to show, with a preponderance of evidence, that the victim willfully agreed to participate in the acts alleged as crime. Changing the terminology from the old-fashioned "consent" defense to the "voluntariness, agreement" defense is a part of the strategy to emphasize that agreement must be volitional, willing, or freely given in order to constitute genuine agreeing, acceding, or conceding. Again, the seeming redundancy in the term "voluntariness, agreement" is intentional. Accentuating this is yet another way to ward off the historic, biased, damning connotations attending consent in rape.

SHIFTING TO "AFFIRMATIVE CONSENT" LEGAL REFORM: "SHE'S A LIAR" AND "I'M A BLUNDERER" DEFENSES

Referring to the voluntariness, agreement defense as the "she's a liar" defense is a way to make clear the nature of the constructions about consent in rape. Most of the time when the defendant and his defense attorney argue that the victim consented, they are claiming that the victim is lying in her charges that the defendant raped her, insisting instead that she agreed to the sex act(s). Associating the terminology "she's a liar" with the defense of voluntariness, agreement is simply calling it what it is, in virtually all instances.[6] Substituting the "I'm a blunderer" terminology for the mistake of voluntariness, agreement defense is to be used for the same reasons, that is, the old vocabulary is associated with historic problems, while the new calls the defense what it is in order to help fact finders determine the (non)guilt of the accused (while simultaneously removing the focus on the "guilt" of rape victims).

Victim Indication of Voluntariness, agreement

In order for the defense to establish that "she's a liar" or that "he's a blunderer," the defense must establish that the victim expressed voluntariness, agreement in some fashion. In order for the defense to make its case for the presence of consent, which is the factor that is generally unlikely to accompany rape/sexual assault allegations, it would need to establish that the case is aberrant or atypical. This would be perhaps the best way to show that agreement to sex acts was present under conditions of expressed protest or under conditions of violence, force, or coercion (or duress/fraud). Agreement to engage in sex with simultaneous partners, sadomasochistic sex, acts of bondage and discipline, so-called rough sex (this was claimed to be the nature of the activities, including partial asphyxiation, in the high-profile Judith Levine "preppy murder case"), and the like provide good examples to illustrate the point. Victim willingness would have to be shown, with verification, to convince triers of fact to the proof level of more likely than not, or more probable than the nonagreement that usually and reasonably accompanies charges of rape (especially where there is injury, violence, threats, etc.), because of the exceptional character of voluntariness, agreement being involved in such encounters. Establishing that volitional agreement was present is mandatory in order to prove that the involuntariness that usually frames such sexual contexts and rape allegations was absent. In other words, to argue successfully that "she's a liar" because voluntariness, agreement expressly accompanied sex—even sex involving, for instance, sadism, masochism, bondage, or discipline—the defense must bring forth evidence, indeed, a preponderance of evidence, to prove that the alleged victim expressed willingness, or voluntariness, agreement, to participate in the sex act(s) in question. Similarly, to defend successfully against a rape accusation by arguing that the defendant made a mistake ("he's a blunderer"), the defense must put forward that the defendant was reasonable in mistaking that and/or reasonably mistook that the alleged victim expressed willingness to participate voluntarily in the sex act(s) at issue.

Recall that with the policy of affirmative consent, what the prosecution must demonstrate is that the victim did not give any indications that she voluntarily agreed to, chose to, or willingly gave in to the sex acts claimed to be sexual assault. In other words, with affirmative consent legal reform, proof of affirmative consent requires that the prosecution show that the person alleging sexual assault did not, through words or conduct, clearly express freely given permission (in order to establish that consent was not openly in existence). As Kadish and Schulhofer report, in some few states, the prosecution must show nonconsent by lack of "verbal permission"; in two states—Wisconsin and New Jersey—anything short of this, even passivity or silence without force or even where nothing is overtly indicated one way or another, can make for nonconsent under affirmative consent reform laws (2001: 343–344). This is seen in the *M.T.S.* ruling, as well as in the jury instructions in the Glen Ridge case. Another definition useful to consider is a proposal in Texas that defined consent "in positive terms," specifically, as "voluntary indulgence in sexual intercourse in no way induced by fraud, threat, or force." In negative terms, it provided that "the absence of specific words or actions indicating … voluntary indulgence in sexual intercourse will constitute the absence of consent" (Weddington 1975–1976: 5).

In my model, the "liar" or "blunderer" defenses would fail (and the charges of rape would stand) when consent defenses are argued but no clear expression of agreement is proven (with a preponderance of evidence) by the defense (regardless of the existence of any sort of force, coercion, etc.). Conversely, consent defenses would succeed in exculpating defendants when the defense proves (with a preponderance of evidence) the clear expression of voluntariness, agreement by the victim (irrespective of force, coercion, etc.). What this means in light of the previous discussion on the shift in the burden of proof is that the prosecution would no longer have to prove that there were *not* indications of agreement or that there was a lack of victim agreement, or "verbal permission," or "the absence of specific words or action indicating … voluntary indulgence in sexual intercourse"; instead, the defense must prove (with a preponderance of evidence) that the victim *did* give (through words or conduct) indications of voluntary, free, or willful agreement to or permission for the sex act(s) (assuming conscious and competent victims with the ability to render such volition).

Defendant Took Reasonable Steps to Ascertain Agreement

It is worth calling attention to the fact that in order for defendants to pick up on indications of yes, or voluntariness, agreement, or no, or involuntariness, nonagreement, to their sexual overtures, they must be paying attention. This is eminently reasonable. The point is that attention has been paid to the signs—words or conduct, in Wisconsin's statute—of affirmative consent. Boyle, in talking about Canadian law, states the requirement well. She specifies that "an honest mistake as to consent is not a defense where 'the accused did not take reasonable steps, in the circumstances known to the accused at the time, to ascertain that the victim was consenting'" (2000: 502). The CLRC's proposal puts it in like framework, stating that "the jury should … have regard to whether the defendant availed himself any opportunity to ascertain whether the victim consented" (Criminal Law Revision Committee 2000: 77). Indeed, the defendant would have to be looking for a yes (not working out a yes, as in Reeves Sanday's fraternity gang rape characterization) in order to pick up on indications of voluntariness, agreement. And my model recognizes this. The Canadian Criminal Code states it summarily well: "It is not a defence for the accused to say that he believed the complainant consented, if the accused did not take reasonable steps, in the circumstances known to be accused at the time, to ascertain that the complainant was consenting" (section 273.2[b]).

Voluntariness, Agreement Not Withdrawn

The Canadian law goes in a further direction. It specifies that "there is no consent where the complainant, having consented to engage in sexual activity, expresses, by words or conduct, a lack of agreement to continue to engage in the activity" (section 273.1[e]). Colorado law is essentially the same and was brought to national attention in the Kobe Bryant case. That case led to publicity about this provision in Colorado's rape statute, which pertained to Bryant's protestations that consent framed the acts and therefore there was no rape. Colorado law is clear that should the victim, at any time, withdraw her consent, for example, say "no," "stop," "I don't want to do this," or the like, the sex acts, if not ceased, become rape or sexual assault. And it is this that the victim argued. Many were astonished that withdrawal of consent to initial sex acts was a valid basis for defining rape.

Recall that I am arguing that failure to perceive no when a reasonable person should or would have interpreted no is criminal negligence. Examining whether the defendant took steps to ascertain the agreement he must prove is another route to addressing the how the accused did or did not pay attention. Picking up on a victim's words, gestures, and/or conduct indicating no requires being attuned to a woman, just as does discerning indications of yes, as just discussed. It is only logical and reasonable that this does not mean such agreement need be present only initially, at the outset of an encounter. It is applicable throughout all the sex acts, so if involuntariness is ever—at any point in the encounter—expressed, the defendant must notice and heed it, or the acts become criminal offenses of rape/sexual assault.

Recapitulation and Justification

What this all means is that a shift in the burden of proof to the defense would entail that the defense establish, with a preponderance of evidence, that it was more likely than not that the woman alleging the rape did give clear indications of freely chosen agreement to engage in the sex acts. Affirmative consent constitutes the kind of consent that would be (theoretically, logically, politically, and sociologically) necessary to overcome the presumptive or implied nonagreement in the law (under the conditions specified in the model). Otherwise, how could you outweigh the nonconsent presupposing victim veracity instead of deception that the law reasonably assumes when rape/sexual assault is charged (under forcible, etc., conditions)? What the defense would be required to do would be to introduce adequate evidence to show that the alleged victim did openly and affirmatively express a yes of her own free accord.

It is useful to contrast the defense burden to prove affirmative consent that I am putting forward here with what Kadish and Schulhofer refer to as "strict liability on consent." Strict liability means even honest and reasonable mistakes do not exculpate (this still leaves the "liar" defense of actual consent tenable). Only "a few states" (Massachusetts, Pennsylvania, Maine) disallow mistakes altogether (Kadish and Schulhofer 2001: 358); most allow reasonable mistakes to exculpate. Strict liability on consent in rape is untenable, given its likely unpopularity because of perceived extremism. The advantage of my model is that it specifically delineates that a voluntariness, agreement defense and a mistake of voluntariness, agreement defense are tenable, but there are obstacles to using either, namely, overcoming the reasonable presumption of victim involuntariness, nonagreement and victim truth telling in place of (implied) consent, an affirmative defense requirement, a shift in the burdens of production and proof, and an affirmative consent standard in order to use the defense successfully. What I am arguing is that the defense can raise consent as a defense but must overcome the legal presumption of nonagreement with established proof of consent that is strong enough (preponderance of evidence) to dismantle the legal presumption (in cases of force, etc.) and meet the higher bar of affirmative consent.

Some might see this as a high standard and one that might be limited in application. Nonetheless, a preponderance of evidence is not as high a bar as "beyond a reasonable doubt." Showing consent or the reasonableness of mistake to be more probable than not is less of a burden than showing "clear and convincing evidence," as MacKinnon analyzes in the Supreme Court discrimination case of *Price Waterhouse v. Hopkins* (490 U.S. 228 [1989]). Recall here that MacKinnon is reporting that the Court reversed a lower court for using this higher standard of clear and convincing evidence, deciding that a preponderance of evidence was a more suitable standard (for the employer) (2001: 509).

A further benefit to my model is that the defenses remain available, in contrast to strict liability crimes where they would be unavailable. The defenses, however, will likely be useful only for extreme or unusual cases, for example, where females had agreed to be bound and tied, whipped, penetrated by several men, degraded, and/or hurt, as in sadomasochistic sex. My model allows for the voluntariness, agreement to such experiences, that is, of voluntariness, agreement to injury and pain. As Pineau herself says, not all women want "communicative sex" (1996a: 25). Allowing for behavior ranging from, for instance, an impassioned "zipless fuck" (Jong 1973: 86) to rough sex, bondage and discipline, and sadomasochism needs to be accommodated, but the law needs to be set up to recognize its atypicality.

I would anticipate that many would criticize that there wouldn't be many successful consent defense cases. This is the point. The small number would be more reflective of the reality of cases where voluntariness, agreement to sex exists under aggravating, forceful, coercive conditions or where women may express no but mean yes where voluntariness, agreement is demonstrable in some other way(s). This would go a long way in trying to balance the scales and minimize the damage of stereotypes about women and rape.

It is fair as well to shift the burden and call for the defense to demonstrate with a preponderance of evidence the victim's expressed willingness to engage in sex activities alleged as rape or sexual assault. First, this is no departure from the criminal law with other defenses. Second, there is precedent, as previously discussed. Moreover, such a change is justified because the consent defense is not foreclosed for cases where agreement may actually have been involved, but, simultaneously, the defense would no longer be allowed to have only to introduce doubt to establish this. The changes put forward for modifying the old-fashioned consent and mistake defenses are not only more fair for trials, they ultimately are more fair as they bear upon the plea bargaining that occurs in 95 percent or more of the criminal caseload. The changes advanced for defense stay within the parameters of other criminal defense law and standards, while simultaneously realigning the scales of justice by redressing historic prejudice while at the same timing potentially enhancing prosecutorial plea-bargaining leverage. The defense would have to show something by way of voluntariness, agreement, instead of relying on historic prejudice to sully the victim and poison her allegations and hence hinder the prosecution and conviction of the assailant.

DEFENSES UNAVAILABLE AND DUE NOTICE

There are several conditions that can be thought of as strict liability conditions, where the defense of "she's a liar" (voluntariness, agreement) or "I'm a blunderer" (reasonable mistake of voluntariness, agreement) are unavailable. Put differently, there are several scenarios under which voluntariness, agreement defenses should be specified in de jure codes as unreasonable and so not rebuttable premises. Specifying this in de jure law serves due notice that defenses are unavailable and will not mitigate criminal culpability under said conditions. Voluntariness, agreement defenses should be unavailable where victims are of minor age. Just as with statutory rape law, where persons under the age of majority are legally deemed incapable of forming or giving consent, unconscious or incapacitated victims likewise cannot give consent, and so the defenses of "liar" and "blunderer" would be disallowed. Those related or in the same household as offenders, who are under the authority or supervision or trust of others in superordinate positions, are not free or able to give unfettered compliance because of their subordinate position; this makes the situation inherently coercive, so the defenses would likewise be untenable. Similarly, when offenders brandish weapons, fear and intimidation characterize responses. This is to say, the scenario is inherently threatening, precluding the possibility of free agreement. Voluntariness, agreement is not possible with the presence (not even necessarily the use) of aggressive and potentially lethal types of force. The simultaneous commission of other serious crimes, such as aggravated assault, robbery, kidnapping, or breaking and entering, is hard to imagine as anything but forceful, or at the least implicitly terrorizing, which once again bars the possibility of freely chosen agreement and thus the use of the "liar" and "blunderer" defenses.

There is one further area that should be dealt with thusly. The growing problem of surreptitiously slipping date rape drugs to women to render them incapacitated in order to facilitate the commission of rape should be singled out from the more general category of incapacitation/unconsciousness for its new popularity as a rape tactic and its particularly heinous nature. Whether victims are drugged knowingly or unknowingly into subconscious or unconscious states ought never to matter in rape.[7] Administering drugs to incapacitate (to facilitate rape) and to impair later memory and potential later testimony about being raped should automatically preclude any sort of consent defenses. Women and girls so drugged cannot give knowing agreement, don't even know that they are drugged, and may not recall that they have been raped. Moreover, the substances being used, like flunitrazepam (Rophypnol, or roofies), gamma-hydroxybutyric acid (GHB), ketamine hydrochloride (Special K), Ecstasy, and so on, can be life threatening. This should be—and increasingly is—in and of itself a sufficient basis for (serious) criminal culpability.[8]

This leaves the voluntariness, agreement defenses of "she's a liar" and "I'm a blunderer" available under the conditions of multiple offenders, injuries, force/coercion alone, or the expression of nonagreement. These are serious conditions, but it is possible to conceive voluntariness, agreement to be present. For example, orgies involve multiple parties, while dare games and rough sex can result in injuries like bruising or spraining or even breaking limbs. All this can entail sex acts that are consensual. Sadomasochism, bondage and discipline, and kinky sex can be consensual and account for the presence of multiple parties and injuries as well. Allowing voluntariness, agreement defenses both recognizes and preserves a woman's agency—to depart from (male-defined) normative sex or sexual practices—and protects a man's right to challenge the involuntariness embedded in a rape accusation under non-normative, forceful circumstances. Allowing the defenses under such conditions also protects the defendant's Sixth Amendment right to "confront his accusers." (Temkin reports the conclusion of one official group that summarizes my point nicely. She notes that the British Sex Offences Review concluded that "the law should protect sexual autonomy by seeking to ensure that individuals are protected from sexual relations to which they do not freely agree and, by the same token, do not suffer interference if they engage in sexual relations to which they do freely agree" [2002: 355–356]). Again, the reasonable a priori presumption would still be involuntariness, nonagreement, as force, coercion, and so on are inherent in these situations; however, voluntariness, agreement could be argued by the defense to show how the victim lied about unwillingness or that the defendant's mistake of willingness was justifiable as a reasonable error in interpretation. To put it succinctly, the rationale for permitting for the "liar" and "blunderer" defenses under coercive conditions is to allow for sexual deviance and difference. This means that while voluntariness, agreement is not probable, it is possible under even such circumstances. This protects the rights of the accused to challenge alleged bogus accusations so as to preserve due process rights and equal protection under the law. It also promotes the sexual agency of women who have desires and engage in activities that stray from the societally defined norms of sexual behavior and pleasures.

A NOTE ON PAST SEXUAL HISTORY EVIDENCE
AND THE "LIAR" AND "BLUNDERER" DEFENSES

The admissibility of and reliance on past sexual history evidence to establish consent or the defense of voluntariness, agreement or reasonable mistake of voluntariness, agreement is ridiculous. Mistaking agreement to the offense(s) because the victim agreed to sex with the accused or other men in the past is far from reasonable. Because agreement to any man in the past has nothing whatsoever to do with present or future agreement, let alone to acts charged as rape, the role of past sex/character evidence must be securely limited and its irrelevance defined in law. This can be brought about in a comparable fashion to the manner in which consent was redefined earlier in the model. Specifically, the presumptive irrelevance of past sexual activity/character evidence needs to be delineated in de jure law (and jury instructions; see chap. 13). The law needs to state that past sexual activity has nothing to do with a victim's character or truthfulness.[9] The law needs to state that past agreement does not portend anything for agreement in the future; for that matter, future consent doesn't portend past consent. Kobe Bryant's victim brings the latter point to light. In that case, the victim may have had consensual sex after the alleged rape, but that doesn't make her unwillingness to be penetrated forcefully and involuntarily by Bryant somehow consensual, as the defense posited.

With all the states now recognizing marital rape—where there is clearly past agreement—and thus with the criminalization of involuntariness at any time regardless of past agreement with a spouse, one would think that this point has already been driven home. But we only need witness rape adjudications to know that this is far from the case. To help preclude excusing rape on the basis of belief, or even knowledge, of past volitional sex, the voluntariness, agreement defenses can never be argued on the basis of past consensual sex or (future) consensual sex that occurs after a rape. Voluntariness, agreement to sex acts cannot be evidenced from past or future sexual activity. Furthermore, *mistakes of voluntariness, agreement made on the basis of past or future sex acts are never reasonable*. Because of the insidiousness and prevalence of the association to the contrary, de jure law needs to state that mistaking agreement on the basis of past sexual activity is always unreasonable. The only relevance of past or subsequent sex is to determine the origin of semen, pregnancy, or disease (as in Michigan's model law).

SUMMARY

For all rapes/sexual assaults, the law should state in de jure fashion and instructions should be read to jurors that:

1. When the defense argues *voluntariness, agreement* as a defense to criminal charges, an affirmative defense must be mounted where the burden of production and burden of proof shift from the prosecution to the defense.
2. The standard becomes a preponderance of evidence in these circumstances.
3. The defense of consent is to be called the *voluntariness, agreement*: "she's a liar" defense, and the defense of (reasonable) mistake of consent is to be called the defense of *voluntariness, agreement*: "I'm a blunderer."
4. The defense must show that (a) the defendant took reasonable steps to ascertain voluntariness, agreement and (b) the voluntariness, agreement to the sex acts was not withdrawn by the alleged victim.
5. (a) The affirmative defenses of voluntariness, agreement: "she's a liar" and voluntariness, agreement: "I'm a blunderer" are unavailable (there is strict liability) where victim is a minor or in the same household (minors) as or blood relatives (any age) of the accused, or when the accused is in an authority or power position over the minor victim, or when the victim is incapacitated or unconscious, or when the offender has a weapon, commits a concurrent felony, or administers any known date rape drug. (b). That defenses are unavailable serves due notice to defendants that under such conditions the voluntariness, agreement: "she's a liar" and the voluntariness, agreement: "I'm a blunderer" defenses are unreasonable and will not mitigate criminal responsibility.
6. Past sexual history/character evidence is never a reasonable basis for believing or mistaking voluntariness, agreement.

Sexual Assault Under Duress and Fraud   **TWELVE**

Some authors analyze the comparability of rape and other crimes through the investigation of sexual assault in relation to property offenses. Estrich (1987), Pineau (1996b), Schulhofer (1998), and Fairstein (1993) examine other types of offensive sexual encounters that constitute criminal offenses in a few jurisdictions but are not codified as sexual assault offenses in almost all other jurisdictions. The authors consider acts where threats or deceptions to induce someone to do something they would not otherwise do make the acts criminal in other areas of law but not when sex is involved. The behaviors interrogated in this chapter are those where women acquiesce to sex acts under conditions of nonviolent, nonphysical threats and/or under false pretenses. The range of considerations moves from nonbodily coercion or threats of duress that are recognized in other areas of law (including extortion, blackmail, and harassment) to deceiving, lying, and/or economically defrauding a woman to exact sex.[1] Again, these acts are recognized as crimes in economic or property areas of law but not when sex is involved. What should differentiate volitional acquiescence to sex from rape/sexual assault are the nonphysical factors that are considered sufficiently harmful/damaging to be unlawful elsewhere in the criminal codes. I am not suggesting that simply trying to persuade someone to have sex or begging or pleading for sex become criminal offenses. This is no different from begging or pleading with someone for money. What I am proposing is that threats or deception recognized in property/economic/nonsexual law be applied to definitions of sexual assault.

Estrich was the first to make the argument that sex taken by even nonbodily threats or any kind of deception should by criminal. Her work draws analogies to property crimes in contentions that sex procured by nonviolent threat or deception ought to be criminal. Estrich puts the argument succinctly when she asserts that if a woman "submits only in response to lies or threats which would be prohibited were money sought instead" (1987: 103) of sex, the law should recognize the crime of rape.

Schulhofer also states the analogy well:

These distinctions are familiar when interests other than sexuality are at stake. A person may take $100 from me by physical force, or he may take it by coercive but non-physical threats, for example he threatens to spread false rumors that will ruin my business. A person may also get control over my property illegally without forcing me at all. He may take my $100 by stealth, when I'm not looking, or he may persuade me to give it to him by falsely promising something in return. In these cases, his actions are illegal but not coercive. If our law of theft punished only "coercive" takings, we might try to say that takings by stealth and deception were "in effect" coercive. But we would know that the language was strained, and a lot of theft requires no such verbal contortions. It simply punishes takings by force (robbery), by coercive threats (extortion), by stealth (larceny), by breach of trust (embezzlement), and by deception (fraud and false pretenses).

(2001: 100)

Larson summarizes that "when a person consents to sex, however, the law permits a far broader range of coercive practices to distort and manipulate her choices, including all the psychological and emotional tactics of deception. To put it plainly, a man may do things to get a woman's agreement to sex that would be illegal were he to take her money in the same way" (1993: 412).

Based on this same kind of logic, legal scholars such as Schulhofer and Estrich call for the criminalization of what might be called the theft of sex, though I shall refer to it as sexual assault under duress. Duress encompasses nonviolent, nonphysical coercion (as opposed to the aggravating circumstances, physical force, or coercion as threats of physical harm) used or threatened so that the victim gives in to sexual demands.

SEXUAL ASSAULT UNDER NONVIOLENT DURESS

The controversy around compliance to sex acts under a variety of threats or pre-varications revolves around just what should define or constitute coercion. Clear to all, coercion includes threats to kill. Similarly clear, threats to commit bodily harm constitute coercion. Less clear are threats that are nonphysical.

Another extension is found in defining as rape sex gained by means of ex-tortion. This is a rather unambiguous example of coercion that has been taken from the property crime realm and can be applied to rape. Extortion occurs when force or threats of physical harm are used to get money, property, or some other financial gain from another person. The property crime of extortion is an easy extension to the personal crime of rape because the threats in both are of physical harm. As Schulhofer makes the extension (of extortion to sexual as-sault), "a wrongful threat intended to induce sexual compliance is coercive in itself, just as a wrongful threat intended to obtain money is sufficient in itself to constitute the criminal offense of extortion" (1998: 131). I add that what is wrongful here is physical threat as recognized by law, hence the easy extension to rape. The point is that nonsexual assault law provides a basis for broadening considerations in sexual assault law. (When the threat in extortion is physical harm, though, offenses would fall under coercion and hence sexual assault law as discussed throughout previous chapters.) [2]

Burgess-Jackson makes another expansion on this. He sees it this way: "Therefore, since battery (nonconsensual touching), trespass, and larceny are crimes, a threat to inflict *any* sort of bodily injury (not just 'severe' injury) or *any* pain (not just 'extreme' pain) or even damage to property suffices" (1999: 106) to define coercion and hence rape and sexual assault. In other words, he is articu-lating that rape definitions include, first, every sort of threat of physical harm or pain but, second, threats of property damage, a concern not usually encountered in sexual assault law (and discussed later in this chapter).

Duress Definitions

After threat to life and violence to person or property, though, coercive threats and duress likened to threats involved in economic, rather than violent, offenses become less clear. This fuzziness crops up when threats are not about physical harm or are "only" about duress as I am starting to use the term. It is in this particular vein that Estrich originally reasoned that compliance to sex should be recognized as involuntariness, nonagreement, to use her terminology, "were money sought instead" (1987: 103). She thinks that this should be the case not only for (physical) extortionist threats but for all nonphysical threats intended to induce compliance to sex. In other words, she argues for creating rape offenses in law irrespective of whether the threats are physical or economic or involve misleading lies (see the next section) of any kind. Estrich specifically claims that threats to ruin someone's reputation or affect their livelihood (or lies or deceptions; see next section) to obtain sex should all be included in sexual assault offenses. She concludes that "the crime I have described may be a lesser offense than the aggravated rape in which life is threatened or bodily injury inflicted … but it is a serious offense that should be called 'rape'" (1987: 103). Schulhofer's view is similar to Estrich's insofar as he advocates that "an illegitimate sexual proposal should be considered coercive" (1998: 162), just as it would be in business. His example is of an official who offers business referrals to someone in return for kickbacks.

Black's definition makes explicit what might be interpreted as implicit in Estrich's and Schulhofer's work. *Black's* definition of duress qualifies threats or coercion to include only those that would be "unlawful." Estrich's phraseology of "were money sought instead" refers to criminal behavior in economic/property offenses. Schulhofer asserts that an "illegitimate sexual proposal should be considered coercive" (1998: 162) the same way an illegitimate proposal is coercive in business. All three point to the dimension of illegality with coercion. Estrich never talks directly about the legal standing of threats, leaving vague what might be included under "extortionist threats" and "material misrepresentations of fact" (1987: 103). She insinuates illegality with the phrase "were money sought instead" (Schulhofer criticizes that her vagueness leaves the door so wide open as to include pettier threats [1998: 84]). Schulhofer would himself go further than extant law to include threats that deprive women of anything to which they are entitled (anything that violates legal rights) (1998: 144) or that they should have a right to expect, like the right to sexual autonomy. His more specific example includes the right to a continuing relationship despite not giving in to "morally unjustified sexual demand" (123).

I would include only those threats where criminal designations would apply if the matter were monetary as opposed to sexual. Conversely, threats like those I earlier termed psychological pressures, for example, "I'll break up with you," "I'll love you," or "I'll marry you," are not criminal coercion, at least in my recommendations for defining new offenses of sexual assault under duress. For the purposes of my model, I see these instead as volitional acquiescence, albeit possibly reluctant.

Use of the word "consent" in arguments to criminalize nonphysical threats that beget acquiescence to sex is problematic, just as it was vis-à-vis rape and sexual assault involving physical threats and force. Consent should be understood as "an act unclouded by fraud, duress, or sometimes even mistake" (Black 1991: 177). This definition shows how, even in the past, voluntariness, agreement should have been seen or defined to be absent in the presence of nonphysical threats, which is how I characterize duress in the context of sexual assault. *Black's* definition also shows how far afield legal constructions have been over time, including our own, since what has been taken as consent is a far stretch from being "unclouded by fraud, duress, or sometimes even mistake." So, again, the words "(in)voluntary" and "(non)agreement" are better descriptors of the type of compliance under nonphysical threats (as was the case under aggravating, forceful, or physical threat conditions).

Under duress, the victim would not have engaged in the sex absent the unlawful threats or duress. Recognizing that compliance is exacted by the nonphysical perils held over a woman's head with duress, as is found with extant law relating to other crimes, facilitates the recognition of involuntariness and hence sexual assault crimes.[3]

Recognizing nonphysical jeopardy as duress diminishes the problem of these (lesser) crimes being confused with truly consensual acts. Just as the aggravating conditions, like weapons, injuries, or the like, all negate the possibility of true consent; compliance under the conditions of nonviolent duress negates the possibility of true consent, that is, the compliance cannot be construed as knowing, genuine, voluntariness, agreement. Duress is tantamount to involuntariness, nonagreement, and the compliance that may follow should not be confused with "unclouded," unfettered consent.

Black's definition of duress can be used to describe the basic nonviolent factors that would demarcate involuntariness and sexual assault crimes. Specifically, duress is "any unlawful threat or coercion used by a person to induce another to act (or refrain from acting) in a manner he or she otherwise would not (or would). Subjecting person [*sic*] to improper pressure which overcomes his [*sic*] will and coerces him [*sic*] to comply with demands to which he [*sic*] would not yield if acting as a free agent" (1991: 348).

Duress means that nonviolent threats or similar compelling forces are applied to procure compliance, wherein the sex acts are recognized by the victim as have been given in to, not wanted or desired, and under threat. The victim knows that granting sex is the condition of the offender's following (or not following) through on whatever (nonphysical, illegally coercive) threat is held over her head. In other words, the victim expects that the party imposing the threat will (or will not) carry through with it on the condition of sexual performance. This is akin to the physical coercion discussed throughout this book, where compliance is not voluntary, willingly, or freely given agreement; it is acquiescence given only under threat. But let me underscore that the threat, though not physical, is recognized as coercive or harmful enough to be illegal in nonrape law.

I agree with Estrich, and with aspects of others such as Schulhofer and Pineau, who later developed similar models, that nonviolent threats should be recognized as some sort of coercive factor in law. In order to make change more likely and in order for these offenses to be defined differently from acceptable, volitional sex (as well as from "simple" date/acquaintance, nonaggravated rape), they need to be conceptually distinct from rape and sexual assault but simultaneously a part of sexual assault offenses. In order for these lesser offenses involving duress to be conceptually distinct, I suggest the term "sexual assault under duress" be used in reference to these crimes. The problem I am attempting to evade is diluting the already minimized or trivialized "simple" (date, acquaintance, nonaggravated) rapes where overt force or coercion (but no aggravating circumstances) are present with sexual assault under duress where violent, physical force or coercion are not present. I think a new crime that maintains the sexual assault designation and adds the connotation of duress is strategic insofar as it draws on familiar crime categories. Further, it is a good tactic as the term itself can serve educative functions about how certain kinds of menacing pressures (and lies; see the next section) to induce sexual compliance are criminal, just as is the case for other crimes.

It is advisable to use some unique word, like duress, to distinguish nonphysical threats from violent or coercive threats in sexual assault in order to impart meanings with clarity. The differentiation is from psychological or emotional pressures that cause personal discomfort but not the harm that the law is allegedly devised to protect (and does at least recognize in property crime definitions). It is also advisable to replace the word "coercion" with "duress" in the specific context of nonphysical threats so as to maintain the strong tie of coercion to notions of physical violence, physical force, or physical threat in the more severe instances of sexual assault of real and simple rape, in comparison to the less serious kinds of sexual assault under duress. Using the word "duress" in place of "coercion" diminishes confusion of sexual assault crimes that entail nonphysical but criminal threats with the other crimes of rape or sexual assault that entail physical violence or threats of bodily harm. It simultaneously, however, keeps the offenses within the purview of sexual assault crimes, which, at core, they are.

Revisiting the perspective on a continuum laid out at the beginning of chapter 7 is instructive for delimiting meaning. Agreeing, or "giving permission" (Schulhofer 1998), to sexual initiatives can be done freely and willingly, in the absence of any sort of threats or pressures. Then there is acquiescence, which was discussed in terms of both voluntariness and "unwanted sex" (Lewin 1985). Giving in to sex that is not desired or wanted because of psychological or emotional pressures or appeals is still yielding without physical endangerment or threats to well-being (or false pretenses) and, because of this, still voluntary, knowing, or informed agreement. The agreement is a calculation of what is worth it in the absence of jeopardy or fear about safety and harm. Kadish and Schulhofer impart how it has been taken perhaps a step further in places. They note that "seduction has been made a criminal offense by statute in some jurisdictions," "seduction" being where "the consent of the woman, implied or explicit, has been procured, by artifice, deception, flattery, fraud or promise" (2001: 347). What I suggest is that where mere promises and flattery are concerned, knowing, voluntariness, agreement can still be given, and criminal designation ought not to go that far. What I am discussing in terms of duress is situated a step further along the continuum: past voluntariness, agreement and past knowing acquiescence under psychological appeals or ploys, like flattery and promises, to submission under certain types of nonbodily threat or coercion (as discussed below) that nonsexual assault or property law legally sanctions. These instances fall plainly on the side of nonvolitional, unwilling, or involuntary, nonagreement, as the following examples of types of sexual assault under duress or nonphysical threat illustrate.

To recapitulate, sexual assault under duress would include nonforceful threats or those of a nonphysical or nonviolent nature that are used to induce compliance to sex and recognized as criminal in nonrape/property law. The acts are crimes because such threats menace some tangible negative consequence, albeit not imminent bodily harm, that other law acknowledges. Stated somewhat differently, because the nature of threat is foreboding or intimidating, the threat can rightfully be deemed to create an involuntary condition. It is this that makes actual knowing consent or "permission" (as in Schulhofer) implausible. And, it is this that should make the behavior at issue a criminal offense.[4]

Offenses of Sexual Assault Under Duress

Threats to "injure property" (Black 1991: 116, in reference to blackmail—see below—and to damage property as earlier mentioned by Burgess-Jackson 1999) can first be considered in a schemata of sexual assault under duress. The threat of violence toward someone's property is unlawful elsewhere in law, therefore precedent exists to establish how unlawful threats to property to coerce sex are a form of intimidation that can create fear and negate the capacity to give meaningful agreement. Hence duress would be adjudged when threats to injure property are used to coerce sex. The "injury to property" type of threat might be the threat to burn down a house or room, smash in windows, pummel stereo equipment, slash furniture, or the like if a woman won't give in to sexual demands. In such scenarios, violence is being threatened, albeit to property rather than person. Regardless, the offender is positioning to engage in physical acts to cause harm. This may not be a likely threat case scenario; however, it would be violent behavior that would be menacing. Moreover, threats to destroy property physically could easily be taken as indicative of the willingness and capacity to inflict violence on a person. Implicit physical force would surely encompass what is afoot when such physicality is threatened, albeit not to the person. It would be reasonable to fear bodily injury when violence, even toward objects rather than persons, is threatened. For these reasons, the category of threats of destruction of or "injury to" property should be seen as a type of duress and included in the classification of nonbodily threats and sexual assault under duress.

Threats to take or steal property, as opposed to "injuring" property, can also be conceived of as duress. An example here might be a threat to take a woman's stereo, DVD player, jewelry, or car if she refuses sex. This may be an unlikely situation in the sense of either the threat or compliance to sex, that is, such a threat may be unlikely to be made or unlikely to beget acquiescence to sex. The circumstance, however, should be considered to fall fully under the categorization of sexual assault under duress.

The threat of criminal behavior, even if it involves stealing property rather than hurting a person, is harassing and can be intimidating in ways that can put a person in fear, which undermines the ability to give genuine or voluntariness, agreement willingly. This makes such threat a valid criterion for inclusion under the crimes of sexual assault under duress. The duress may be the fear of losing something of importance or value or may be fear that one's home would be broken into in the course of stealing the stereo, jewelry, or whatever. Duress could also be seen in the threat to security and/or mobility when the threat is to steal a woman's car. Recall the case of *Rusk* where the defendant took the victim's car keys away from her to force her up to his residence. This shows how fear can be generated from nonphysical injury acts because of the underlying nature of threat.

The threat to steal property would be criminal if the threat were carried out. This makes it obviously more than the "trivial" "Comply or I'll drink your soda" that Schulhofer talks about (1998: 131). The fact that the means to induce submission would be criminal if carried out makes for another reason to include such threats as criminal duress in my model.

A further justification for the inclusion of threats to steal property as sexual assault under duress lies in a comment by Schulhofer quoted earlier. In light of extending property crime law to sexual assault law (and creating greater parity by that extension), he states that wrongful threats should apply in sexual assault definitions as they do in nonsexual assault offenses. He asserts that "a wrongful threat intended to induce sexual compliance is coercive in itself, just as a wrongful threat intended to obtain money is sufficient in itself to constitute the criminal offense of extortion" (1998: 131). A threat to steal property to coerce sex is surely wrongful, again making such acts sexual assault under duress offenses in the model I am proposing.

Another instance of nonviolent duress can be found in the example of blackmail. Blackmail is commonly understood as seeking victim acquiescence under a threat to expose something negative or harmful (truthful or not) about the person who is being threatened.[5] The something the exposure of which is threatened usually concerns wrongdoing or criminal activity on the part of the threatened party or, in the case of sexual assault, often concerns past sexual conduct, which can be a source of anguish for the victim. The exposure that is threatened can be damaging to a victim in any number of ways, ranging from ruining her reputation, friendships, or marital or other partnered relationships to ruining her career or livelihood. Although not directly or immediately physically harmful, the threats are surely meant to destroy or cause suffering and are used in order to exact compliance when voluntariness, agreement or "freely given permission" to sex acts (Schulhofer 1998) is not present or forthcoming. Threats of blackmail are usually property crimes, where the law recognizes that the victim did not willingly give, hand over, or agree to share money with the threatening party. Threats of blackmail should similarly be seen to negate the victim's willingly giving, handing over, or agreeing to share or participate in sex acts with the threatening party and thus should be criminal. In other words, blackmail threats make duress the condition that forces sexual compliance and so should serve as a sufficient basis for sexual assault under duress charges.

Threats to fire a woman or ruin her livelihood or career if she does not yield to sexual advances pose special instances of blackmail. Schulhofer posits that such instances could be covered by sexual harassment law. This would be in reference to quid pro quo sexual harassment (and not hostile environment). Here power or authority is abused by gatekeepers in their decision-making capacity to affect outcomes for subordinates. The duress does not threaten physical harm, at least in the traditional sense of bodily harm (although bodily harm could be a long-term result of unemployment), but it nonetheless threatens something as serious, if not more serious, than exposing something harmful about a person as in threats of blackmail. Sexual assault under duress should encompass threats to fire a woman or ruin her job possibilities, because, as Schulhofer notes, sexual harassment law is too limiting to cover the abuse here. A major drawback to sexual harassment laws is that sexual harassment is handled in civil, as opposed to criminal, courts, where victims can only sue for pain and suffering or damages. Moreover, as Schulhofer points out, "the offender himself isn't personally liable for damages; sexual harassment remedies apply only against the university or business firm as an entity" (1998: 12). This avenue should, of course, be left open, but it needs to be broadened. Sexual assault law could easily encompass and sanction these behaviors, where livelihood or career are at risk, under a coercive rubric such as duress, when others have power, control, or supervisory or disciplinary authority over the person being threatened. Kadish and Schulhofer's description of *State v. Thompson* is illustrative of the kinds of cases falling within this purview. They report that the "defendant, a high school principal, allegedly forced one of his students to submit to sexual intercourse by threatening to prevent her from graduating from high school" (2001: 333). Offenses of this nature involve persons who are in power over their victims and threaten career-related harm. These offenses could be seen as a particularized case of sexual assault by blackmail and fit under the sexual assault under duress category.

In broadening definitions, it is useful to highlight that what some actors have in common is that they occupy positions of power, authority, and/or trust. What the crimes of sexual assault have in common, I am contending here, is the condition of duress (as opposed to physical or bodily force/coercion) where "improper pressures" (as in Black 1991: 348) are applied to procure sexual compliance. These improper pressures are more than psychological, emotional pressures or attempts at persuasion, like "I'll break up with you unless we have sex." They are pressures that would be criminal if occurring in other realms. As Estrich and Schulhofer define, the behaviors would be criminal if they were directed at taking money instead of taking sex. These two scholars draw support from comments on how the property crime of embezzlement is deemed criminal when money instead of sex constitutes what is stolen (through the conduit of victim gullibility or manipulability) owing to an offender's position imbued with trust, power, or authority. What I am positing here is that when persons in power, control, or supervisory or disciplinary positions make threats of economic/career consequence (or physical or mental well-being; see below), duress is involved and sex cannot be willfully agreed to and/or is sexual assault under duress.

In point of fact, though, such behaviors are not commonly seen as criminal by the law or much of the public. Schulhofer astutely observes that in addition to employers, current law gives "psychologists, doctors, lawyers, and teachers almost unlimited freedom to have 'consensual' sexual relationships with women whom they hold in their power" (1998: 167). This free rein is limited narrowly by ethical and professional standards and associations in some cases, but these are clearly inadequate (as the recent widespread scandals with priests, ministers, and other spiritual leaders show). Schulhofer defines these acts as "breaches of trust" that should be deemed criminal.[6]

Schulhofer's contribution about "breaches of trust" involving psychologists, doctors, lawyers, and teachers cannot be gainsaid. The law needs to define sexual assault under duress to cover at least nonbodily threats like harm to income or career by employers or superordinates in the workplace, threats to medical well-being by doctors, and threats to psychological health by therapists and counselors. I am not suggesting that the law go so far as to criminalize all sex with any person in a position of authority, power, or trust. Instead, I am proposing that sexual assault under duress cover sex where persons in power, authority, or trust exert "improper pressures" or make threats against financial, physical, or psychological well-being that operate to negate meaningful consent by menacing some harm that other (nonsexual assault) law would recognize.

I think it is useful to draw one further, and different, analogy about sex crimes under duress. Borrowing from assault law can serve to prop up arguments that superordinates' threats of extortion, blackmail, job security, physical health, mental health, and so on rightfully make for duress and so define new crimes. Assaults are crimes of threat where the offender puts the victim in fear or belief of impending battery/injury. In the case of more traditional rape (as compared to sexual assault under duress), this would be putting the victim in fear of having the sex violently or physically forced on her with greater physical violence and potential injuries than would be anticipated should she submit. The Canadian case of *R. v. Ewanchuk* (1999) provides a solid example. The victim specifically claimed here that, although she repeatedly said no, she did allow the assailant to touch, massage, and grind against her because of her terror at the prospect that denying him would make him violent (MacKinnon 2001: 853–854). In the same way, putting the victim in fear of nonbodily injuries is also menacing and should be criminal. There is a wide array of ways to give women the impression that some malady will befall them if they don't give in to sex. And, not coincidentally, there is a wide array of ways to reinforce women's belief that there is nothing that she can do about the ability of the threatening male to make good on his threats. The myriad ways to put a woman in fear and instill a sense of helplessness clearly exist outside the realm of physical force/coercion. The threats may not be of violent, forced sex but of character assassination, loss of income, ruination of livelihood, loss of economic security, or crippling of mental sanity or other wellness. Regardless of the type of threat, it is the threat that makes the woman in a subordinate position give in to sex. Such threats should rightly be included as duress that makes the sex involuntary, which, to be terribly redundant, is to say criminal. As Schulhofer points out, threats that are "intended to induce submission" (1998: 131) whether to gain money or sex, should be taken seriously, which is to say, legally defined and sanctioned.

SEXUAL ASSAULT BY FRAUD, GUILE, OR DECEIT

The final consideration in this series relating to property offense analogies pertains to lies, deceptions, frauds, misrepresentations, and the like that are used to exact sex from a woman. The difference between fraud and duress is that the victim has the illusion of choice about engaging in sex under fraudulent premises, that is, the victim does not necessarily think the sex acts are coerced by prevarications. Stated a bit differently, the victim thinks that participation in the sex act(s) is not against her will or involuntarily, unknowingly, or unwittingly induced, whereas in sexual assault under nonviolent duress she knows the act(s) are not freely chosen but feels impelled to yield to the offender given the threats or "improper pressures" as these have been delineated. Succinctly then, duress involves nonviolent threats or improper orders or demands of a sexual nature, while fraud misleads a woman into sexual activities that she does not know are being stealthily manipulated.

It is useful to revisit *Black's Law Dictionary*, this time on informed consent as it relates to fraudulent premises and deception. The definition of informed consent is "a person's agreement to allow something to happen ... that is based on a full disclosure of facts needed to make the decision intelligently" (1991: 537). Obviously, lies and misrepresentations to take sex, just like such means used to take money, would fit squarely within the purview of informed consent; that is, lack of the full disclosure of facts needed to make a decision intelligently should be criminal. Yet "the prevailing view in this country is that there can be no rape achieved by fraud, or trick, or stratagem ... no matter how despicable the fraud" (Kadish and Schulhofer 2001: 347).

There is an astounding variety of swindles, tricks, frauds, lies, and/or deceptions used to bilk people out of their money. People tend to be aware of many but not nearly all such schemes. People also tend to be aware that vulnerable populations, like the elderly, shut-ins, and children, are especially targeted with such tactics. What is probably less commonly recognized is how wide spanning are the deceptions that men use fraudulently to trick vulnerable women into sex that they are induced to think is normal or appropriate or necessary or required.

Estrich contends that just as it would be criminal to deceive to get money, it should be a "serious" (1987: 103) crime of rape to deceive to get sex. This means that lies, misrepresentations, and deceptions would constitute a type of coercion. Fraud and misrepresentations are considered property offenses, and using prevarication to procure sex rather than money should be a crime, too. The alleged agreement that many would read into the sex acts procured by false pretenses is not true consent or freely given, voluntariness, agreement; it is, again, compliance induced by deceptions. The acquiescence is misguided, and of a type that would not have been given had the falsities been known.

Larson (1993) argues that deception to take sex should be criminal, using the shorthand "sex exception to fraud" to refer to the problem of not defining rape in this way. She proposes a model dealing with fraud and rape where intentional misrepresentation (412) would form the basis for criminal responsibility in rape and sexual assault. She notes that "careless failures by another party to disclose useful facts" and negligent fraud and misrepresentation are sanctioned in "commercial transactions" (ibid.). This means that "in the marketplace protections against dishonesty have gone far beyond" what she proposes for fraudulent rape (ibid.), giving a sound basis for criminalization of sex by fraud.

That deception should be a part of rape law has precedent and acceptability, even in traditional law. Even the sexist Model Penal Code of 1962, which required prompt complaints and corroborative evidence, allowed promiscuity to mitigate, and so on, defines "ineffective consent" to be that "induced by force, duress or deception of a kind sought to be prevented by the law defining the offense" (Kadish and Schulhofer 2001: 1047). And recall that at least in a few jurisdictions "seduction" where "consent of the woman, implied or explicit, has been procured, by artifice, deception, flattery, fraud or promise" has been criminalized (347). Extending the law on sexual assault to be akin to nonrape law by including artifice, deception, fraud, and guile should thus be quite doable.

Fairstein's 1993 discussion of "sexual scams" (chapter 16) provides a model approach. She agrees that fraud employed to procure acquiescence to sex should be criminal but describes cases that show how such behaviors are not "sex crimes" in the state of New York. Fairstein outlines one case where a theater teacher had students imagine they were on a beach and asked them to shed layers of clothing, encouraging them to go as far as to mimic nude sunbathing in the exercise. The teacher engaged in private sessions with the girls he deemed promising, during which he helped them get over their inhibitions by having sex with them—waiving his normal $100 fee for private acting lessons (186–187).

A second example Fairstein discusses relates to auditions of theater students at New York University and area colleges for a part in a film supposedly shooting in the Caribbean. Women who tried out were spanked and told to scream while being spanked during filming. (Interestingly, it turned out that the so-called director was an IRS agent who rented the space for his "auditions" every day—on taxpayer's time and money. Incidentally, the prosecutor was able to get the offender on fraud because property—a video—happened to be involved in the case, there still was deemed to be no "sex crime" [196]). Fairstein's third example involves a holistic therapist (who labeled himself an "N.D.," for "doctor of nature") who claimed he needed to check the (saltiness of) his female patients' fluid levels for alleged therapeutic purposes. This meant he had to lick the secretions from first the breasts and then the vaginas of his clients/patients. (He was prosecuted for licensing fraud—practicing medicine without license—but again no sex crime was charged) (191–193).

If teachers and therapists were defined as persons who occupy positions of authority and/or trust and they pressure someone into sex, this would be a crime of sexual assault under (nonviolent) duress as previously described. The examples above, however, pertain more to fraud, lies, and misrepresentations or, in Fairstein's words, "scams." The difference is that the victim in fraud does not know she doesn't freely consent to the sex acts, though she may feel pressured nonetheless; the victim of the scams thinks the sexual behavior is somehow appropriate and that she agrees, albeit at times reluctantly, to engage in it. In the classic example, these two forces come together on the couch of the psychiatrist, where he tells his patient that the only way she will ever get over her hysteria, or psychosis, or other hang-ups is to have intercourse with him. Improper pressure from a trusted professional conjoin lies in a nasty way here. But there are many, many others, like those who pose as modeling agents, film directors, media photographers, rock star agents, sports managers, and personal trainers, who are not in a position of authority or trust but are in a position of advantage, who lie and set women up for any variety of sexual encounters. For this reason, further specificity in the model for change needs to be contemplated.

In the cases being discussed, the lies are what lead women to concede to the sex acts. Fairstein explains that when women comply or go along with the sexual requests or demands, there is no "sex crime" to prosecute (only frauds, if money or property is involved or, in the case just cited, medicine is being practiced without a license). Fairstein continues that the deceit to procure sex leaves nothing to prosecute because the element of "lack of consent" is missing (as is, I might add, the woman's no or any of the aggravating or forceful or coercive circumstances previously discussed to make involuntariness, nonagreement the reasonable belief). But the alleged consent is disingenuous. This is because the false premises incurring this alleged consent are fraudulent, precluding the possibility of informed consent (the victim lacks the "full disclosure of facts needed to make the decision intelligently" [Black 1991: 537]) or willing, knowing, voluntariness, agreement.

My recommendation to handle the problem is to criminalize these behaviors by drawing on premises that are not only existent but also generally accepted. Just as we have larceny by trickery or deceit, we could have exacting sex by trickery (although this terminology should be avoided, given the association with prostitutes' turning tricks), or sex by deceit, or sex by lies, or sex by fraud, or sex by fraudulent premises, or sex by misrepresentation. As an alternative to delineating each separate crime category for each type of scam or false pretense, we might simply criminalize these behaviors under one heading by making all these types of acts crimes of sexual assault under fraud. The acts are obvious in meeting the concept of fraud, for example, false representation, cheating, concealment, false allegation, guile, and/or dishonesty that causes harm, legal injury, loss of something valuable to the victim (Black 1991: 455), such as loss of bodily integrity, dignity, and exposure to pregnancy and disease. They are equally obviously sexual, that is, the ruse is designed specifically to take sex.

I agree with Estrich and Fairstein that there is clear sexual abuse in cases like those just mentioned that goes begging for legal recognition. Just as with sexual assault under duress, the nonphysical factor of deceit here would be recognized as crime in nonsexual assault law. It should be plausible to legislate a more accurate definition that would allow prosecution of at least some of these offenses under the rubric of sexual fraud. Arguing for a separate category of sexual assault fraud (or for sexual assault by guile, deceit, misrepresentation, and so forth) would take into account the sexual nature of the victimization, along with the fraud that is so clearly existent.

CRIMINALIZATION OF SEXUAL ASSAULT BY DURESS AND FRAUD: A REASONABLE WOMAN'S POINT OF VIEW

Basing the designation of new sexual assault duress and fraud crimes on extant legal principles and definitions from property law is consistent with my endeavor to mold new wave reforms, such as the model I am building throughout this book, after existing law in order to facilitate change. Defining crimes to involve fear, intimidation, peril, and fraudulent premises in the wake of nonphysical jeopardy and lies—but threats, jeopardy, or deceptions nonetheless as other law recognizes—ought to promote acceptance of such conceptualization and reform. After all, this is simply a call for greater parity with nonsexual assault law. And judging nonviolent threats, scams, and swindles from a comparative base that would explore the existence of duress and deception from a reasonable woman's point of view should have wide appeal—at least to most women, many of whom have experienced such offenses, as well as to the men close to such women (who have experienced tricks, scams, and cons of their own). This should bolster the effort to eradicate the notion that women's consent to sexual overtures is omnipresent, implicit, or everlasting.

In terms of my model array recommendations, new definitions would demarcate the crimes of sexual assault by duress and by fraud, more specifically, involving nonphysical threats, threats of destruction or theft of property, extortionist threats, and threats of blackmail; nonphysical threats and improper pressures affecting financial, physical, or psychological well-being by those in positions of power, authority, and trust; and sex scams involving lies, deceptions, misrepresentation, fraudulent premises, or fraudulent exploitation of positions of advantage for sexual purposes. These would be specified de jure. Likewise, a reasonable woman's point of view would be used to assess the presence of duress or deceit. These changes, again, would be specified in statute and read by a judge when charging jurors before deliberations (see the next chapter).

A CAVEAT: MAKING THE CHANGES TENABLE

In order to anticipate the charge that this approach is overly ambitious, it is important to delineate what the approach does not encompass or include. Succinctly, the model would not cover so-called unwanted or uncomfortable sex or sex begotten by psychological or emotional pressures or ploys. It is useful to examine the assessments some scholars have made in critically appraising one another's approaches to flesh out the types of concerns that might occur along this dimension.

One problem the research literature raises is that some reform advocates are vague about how broadly "coercion" should extend, while others go so far as to contend that any kind of pressure or persuasion should constitute menacing behavior, hence negating the possibility of voluntariness, agreement. Schulhofer critiques Estrich, for example, for leaving open the meaning of "extortion threats" and "misrepresentations" such that they "extend to insincerely professing love" (1998: 84). Others, like Paglia (1994)and Roiphe (1993), have criticized that even mild persuasions, like "he said he'd break up with me" or "he'd just do it with somebody else," are among the threats that some feminist work has been alleged to include as sexual assault (some allegations go so far as to say that even consensual sex is rape under the structural inequality of patriarchy).[7]

My corrective to these problematic aspects of arguments relating to the use of nonphysical and/or fraudulent premises to exact compliance to sex acts is to deem them instances of duress and fraud only to the extent that criminal law and case processing already allow for other, nonsexual crimes. In other words, I do not believe that some sort of sex fraud category of crime should be developed beyond what is encompassed in extant property law. Therefore I am not talking about threats that are not deemed criminal under other circumstances, such as the psychological or emotional pressures to do with dates, love, and relationships that accompany many attempts to get a woman into bed. The only coercive threats that should be encompassed under duress are the types that are already criminal in other realms of the law. Threats of extortion, blackmail, injury to career, and physical damage to property define the sexual assaults of duress I have spelled out. Fraudulent premises are widely recognized in property law on criminal offenses, and they should be similarly recognized in sexual assault law as lies or abuse of power, trust, and other misrepresentation employed to make women yield their bodies to men. Aren't these women being duped into handing over something at least as if not more valuable than the money or property given up in other crimes of concealment, guise, and guile? Again, keeping changes parallel with extant law should make for a more acceptable political strategy that will meet less public resistance while still extending the arm of legal protection to many victims previously neglected in sexual assault law.

This is not to say that there is no discretion or difficulty in drawing a line between sexual assault crimes of duress and fraud in contrast to sexual interactions and behaviors that would and should remain noncriminal or between duress or "improper pressure" (as in *Black's* definition) and acceptable pressures. But using *Black's* definition of duress as that which "induce[s] behavior that she otherwise would not" engage in, using Estrich's "were money sought instead" (1987: 103), and using extant law defining the circumstances that make deceit to take money illegal can all go a long way toward clarifying ambiguity and/or drawing lines. [8]

And yet we still need to recognize that relying on the law for problem resolution, like ameliorating the exploitation of women, is not without its drawbacks. Using the law is limiting, as many scholars have justifiably warned. Relying on the law is problematic, since the law is often intentionally ambiguous in order to capture a wide range of behaviors under its rubric and since it cannot spell out every context and action. The point is that, as it stands, using law is, in my estimation, one of the best possible compromises of interests that is likely to work toward greater parity and justice for all sexual assault victims (other means of change are discussed in chaps. 16 and 17, especially).

As previously stated, pursuing crime categories for these offenses could easily be derived from the property crimes to which they are similar, such as extortion sexual assault, blackmail sexual assault, and sexual assault by fraud, guile, and/or deceit; or they could be carved out as two generic categories: sexual assault under duress and sexual assault under fraud. These crimes would be lesser in severity than other rapes and sexual assaults that entail any of the aggravating conditions previously discussed and other rapes or sexual assaults that involve physical force or physical coercion/threat. The compromise strategy of staying within the confines of existing law to develop the two new crime categories should diminish political, legal, and lay resistance to the changes, particularly in light of the fact that some jurisdictions already designate some of these behaviors criminal.

An analogy with marital rape reforms is instructive along these lines. The nation was slow to eliminate the marital exemption to rape offenses. And even now, with all the states recognizing some type of marital rape, the number of prosecutions is minuscule, and the cases that do get adjudicated are the most flagrant and heinous of the host of marital rapes. The same lot might be anticipated for sexual assaults under nonviolent duress and sexual assault by fraud. Attitude change and criminalization may be slow, and only the most horrid cases will be brought forward, but some measure of redress would exist for some few victims, with slow but growing increments of change in conceptualization and legal practice occurring over time.

The significance of the reciprocal nature of legal and attitudinal change, as later chapters will explore further, cannot be overlooked. Declaring in law that nonviolent techniques designed to make women surrender to sex acts are wrong and that they should be legally treated as wrong, just like other offenses unrelated to sex, can serve logical, symbolic and educative functions. Defining new offenses would serve as a catalyst to change the nature of conceptualization about sexual wrongs. Showing the parallel between theft of money and theft of sex may help people understand why these acts deserve to be treated as crimes. For instance, sex, like money, is something most people want. Taking sex, like taking money, is wrong and should be criminal. Educating the public and professionals about the similarities so as to support new definitions would eventually result in the prosecution of some of these acts, thus expanding the scope of the legal protections for women.

Drawing parallels with other crimes is important in a different context. It facilitates broadening not only criminal responsibility but also the view of sexual assault offenses themselves. First, broadening the spectrum of sexual assault offenses might lead people to see the "lesser" or "simpler" rapes and sexual assaults as "real" rape/sexual assault (because there would be an even lesser tier of offenses), which would improve the views and treatment of simple, acquaintance, and date rape. Second, drawing parallels with other crimes can show that not only force, threat, and violence are part of sexual assaults, just as they are with other assaults, but also that power, manipulation, and exploitation, too, are part of sexual assault crimes, just as they are in other crimes of deceit and theft. This will help fight the myths about rape and sexual assault and its victims—like that notion that the victim really wanted the sex or agreed and later lied about it— because we don't think this way about the other crimes to which I am drawing rather exacting parallels.

Criminalizing sex fraud might meet more resistance than criminalizing sexual assault by duress (but, then again, it might not, given the multitude of fraud victims in this age of identity theft), since no threats of any kind are involved. Some thinking goes to the contrary, however, as the move to treat sexual assault by fraud as a criminal offense has gained so much momentum that at least one scholar concludes that "it would not be an overstatement to assert that the crucial question is no longer whether to criminalize rape by fraud and rape by coercion but rather when (or under what circumstances) to do so.... These cases ... currently provide an opportunity to recalibrate the outer boundaries of acceptable sexual conduct" (Falk 1998: 91–92). And "recalibrating the outer boundaries of acceptable sexual conduct" is part of what reforms must do next.

SUMMARY

For all rapes/sexual assaults, the law should state in de jure fashion and instructions should be read to jurors that:

1. For sexual assault under duress, offenses include but are not limited to nonviolent threats, for example, threats to damage or steal property, blackmail, and threats to career potential or financial, physical, or mental well-being by those in power, authority, or trust positions.
2. For sexual assault under fraud, offenses include but are not limited to deception, guile, or deceitful lies or premises to take sex or commit sex acts.
3. A reasonable woman's point of view is to constitute the standard by which to adjudge nonviolent threats (duress) and/or fraud (scams, deceptions, lies, etc.).

MAKING THE CHANGES: DE JURE LAW,
RULES OF EVIDENCE, AND JURY INSTRUCTION

Although some view change in rape law as largely symbolic and/or co-optive of the reform movement, the importance of statutory change cannot be overstated. Statutory law defines crimes, and procedural law defines how these are to be adjudicated. The state is exalted and hegemonically taken as a neutral, objective body that defines wrongs, protects interests, and promotes justice equally for all. The law holds the uniquely influential power to change conceptualizations about what we hold to be decent, acceptable, and good as opposed to bad, unacceptable, and criminal. Hence the law stands as the moral posture for a culture. Members of the culture internalize its values or accept the dominant ideology it embodies—largely unquestioningly. This is one way to elucidate the commanding educative force of law. Lay citizens must be educated about rape, and this matters greatly. Because citizens sit as jurors in criminal cases, their values, what they see as right and wrong, matter greatly. Given this, it is ironic that reforms have so overlooked educating jurors. The law's ability to educate citizens and by extension jurors and criminal justice officials like judges, prosecutors, defense attorneys, and police should be harnessed instead of neglected. These are the actors who so decisively affect the treatment of victims and cases that dictates whether reform objectives will be achieved. As I quoted at the end of the last chapter, the law has the ability to "recalibrate the boundaries of acceptable conduct" (Falk 1998: 91–92) and in this way to educate society and all its constituent members, including jurors, judges, and attorneys.

The reforms delineated in the array set out in this and the next chapter address changing statutory and procedural law. My vision is that the comprehensive set of changes could be modeled at the federal level, which could then serve as the exemplar for state jurisdictions to follow. This actually occurs quite frequently in law. For example, the federal system promulgates Federal Rules of Evidence to be used in federal courts and serve as a model for the states to emulate (although the states may individualize rules through their own statutes or court decisions). Other examples are Federal Rules of Criminal Procedure and Federal Sentencing Guidelines. The Model Penal Code (penned by the American Law Institute) serves as another example of the federal exemplar or ideal held out to states. Many states looked to, and adopted, the Model Penal Code in whole or in part as a guide to their own criminal codes, including the code's provisions. The 1962 Federal Code provisions on rape were what this book calls sexist, traditional rape legislation, with corroboration and prompt complaint requirements, concerns about victim precipitation, and the like. In the 1980 Federal Model Penal Code and Commentaries, much of this was retained, although, on the progressive side, sex-neutral, graduated offenses were demarcated (Estrich 1987: 46, 54–55; Field and Bienen 1980: 155; Kadish and Schulhofer 2001: 1082–1083). Unfortunately, this influenced rape reforms across the states in a way that maintained chauvinistic laws that continue to require corroboration and prompt complaints, provide for character evidence admissibility, and so on. Murthy points out how the federal court treatment of rape influences state court patterns, citing the substantive law on rape in general and rape shield legislation in particular (1991: 550).

All the premises described in the model array are envisaged as changes to be stipulated de jure in legal statutes and in rules of evidence. Rules of evidence pertain to what judges and juries can rightfully consider. They circumscribe what these fact finders are legally allowed to see, hear, and assess. Specifically, they prescribe and proscribe what is proper to consider, or what is relevant, material and competent evidence. Relevance is defined as "tending to prove or disprove an alleged fact. Evidence having any tendency to make the existence of any fact that is of consequence to the determination of the action more probable or less probable than it would be without the evidence" (Black 1991: 894). Material is defined as evidence that tends to prove or disprove facts because it "tends to influence … because of its logical connection with the issue" (674). "Competent" is defined as what will "assist … in determining questions of fact" (195) or, stated differently, as confirming that the evidence is what purports to be. Evidence that does not meet these standards is inadmissible in court. The court proceedings circumscribed by these rules include judicial determinations, the voir dire questioning of potential jurors, the jury deliberation instructions, and the opening through closing arguments (including witness questioning and so forth) by the attorneys for the prosecution and defense.

I believe that the most efficacious way to establish new standards for adjudicating rape cases is to delineate a specific array of changes that could be enacted legislatively through model statutory change and simultaneously to reflect the change as an array of model jury instructions. Jury instructions are defined as "a direction given by the judge to the jury concerning the law of the case; … an exposition of the rules or principles of law applicable to the case or some branch or phase of it, which the jury are bound to accept and apply" (Black 1991: 597). *Black's* definition goes on to note that "model" or "pattern" jury instructions, like those being proposed here, exist in "many states and federal courts" and that these "are required to be used, or substantially followed, by the trial judge" (ibid.).[1]

The following is designed as an array of changes that can simultaneously model legislative stipulations, rules of evidence, and jury instructions (at federal or state levels). To emphasize, the changes are designed as dimensions of de jure law, to be contained in state and federal statutes and read and provided to jurors as part of their instructions for deliberations. The advantage of the simultaneity in changes as put forward here is simplicity and consistency, as well as reinforcement: one set of changes (in law) can reciprocally bolster the other (in rules of evidence and jury instructions) in the model.

Before laying out the entire schemata, it is worth reiterating that much, if not all, that my model seeks to accomplish already has legal precedent in some form or fashion. In fact, many changes were established long ago. This is nowhere more clear than in the first provision, regarding continuing reforms on discriminatory requirements and standards. In the 1960s, all states had corroboration requirements, prompt reporting requirements, and cautionary jury instructions in place (Schulhofer 1998: 28). They also had resistance requirements and provisions for the admissibility of past sexual history and character/reputation evidence. The statutory changes to these that were enacted from the 1970s through the 1980s in many jurisdictions need to be enacted across all the remaining jurisdictions where such reforms are still wanting. The extant law pertaining to other changes in the array has been and will continue to be denoted throughout the chapters.

I have already described most of the changes delineated in the following array. It can be thought of as a kind of summary of the reforms advanced throughout this book. Some additional features, however, have been added in the model. All such changes in the array will be discussed in the next chapter, which explains the model array outlined here.

CRIME CONSIDERATIONS

Continuing Reforms on Discriminatory Requirements and Standards

1. Corroboration is not required. Victim testimony is sufficient to sustain conviction.[2]
2. Resistance is not required for adjudication or conviction.
3. Past sexual history is strictly limited (an in-camera hearing is required to determine the admissibility of such evidence, which is relevant only to determine the origin of semen, pregnancy, or disease, as in Michigan's model).
4. Prompt report by the victim is not required for adjudication or conviction.
5. Cautionary jury instructions, in the manner of Chief Justice Hale's, are unjustified and disallowed.[3]

Establishing the Crime in Statute

There are four concerns:

1. Aggravating conditions (borrowing from the Michigan model)

   Penetration (v. contact)
   Minor-age victims
   Offender power/authority/trust position, same household, blood affiliation.[4]
   Commission of another felony
   Weapons
   Multiple offenders
   Additional victim injuries
   Victim incapacitation[5]

2. Force/coercion (borrowing from the Michigan model)

Force or coercion are defined as "including, but not limited to the application or threat
of physical force/violence, threat of retaliation against victim or others, medical
treatment/examination in a manner recognized as unethical/unacceptable, overcoming through concealment/element of surprise" (Michigan PA 328 1974).

Force/coercion includes both explicit and implicit threats.[6]

3. Involuntariness, Nongreement: "she said, he heard"

Verbal expression of no is sufficient to establish involuntariness, nonagreement,
even without force/coercion.[7]
Gestures and other conduct may also indicate involuntariness, nonagreement.
No always means no. Women say what they mean and mean what they say.[8]
Silence cannot be equated with voluntariness, agreement. Submission or compliance under any sort of aggravating, forceful, or coercive conditions is never
voluntariness, agreement, irrespective of victim silence.[9]

Voluntariness, agreement is not implicit.

4. Nonviolent duress and fraud

Sexual assault under duress: offenses include but are not limited to nonviolent
threats, for example, threats to damage or steal property, blackmail, and
threats to career potential or financial, physical, or mental well-being by those
in power, authority, or trust positions.
Sexual assault under fraud: offenses include but are not limited to deception,
guile, or deceitful lies or premises in order to take sex or commit sex acts.

Reliance on a Reasonable Woman's Point of View

A reasonable woman's point of view is to be used to assess the presence of circumstances surrounding the crime, for example, the presence of weapons, force,
coercion, the indication of no, duress, or fraud. Put interrogatively, would reasonable women interpret that threats were made, that violence was in evidence,
that there was a gun in his pocket, that nonphysical threats or deceptions compelled compliance?[10]

Presumptive Nonagreement

Nonagreement is redundant with the existence of aggravating, forceful, coercive, or fraudulent conditions or duress. Involuntariness, nonagreement is therefore to be presumed in the presence of aggravating conditions, or force or coercion, or duress or fraud. This means nonagreement is the reasonable, probable condition under these circumstances. The single exception is in "he said, she said" cases where victim nonagreement is the sole basis for the criminal charge.

VICTIM CONSIDERATIONS

Victim Reporting

1. It is unreasonable to presume that women who come forward with allegations of rape and sexual assault are filing false police reports and/or falsely accusing men of rape.[11] The reasonable assumption is that women who report rape to authorities are sincere and being truthful, not lying to police when reporting that they have been raped (i.e., they are innocent of the crime of filing a false police report).
2. Past reports of rape by those reporting rape victimization, whether deemed to be fabricated or not, are irrelevant to the current determination of rape. Past reports of rape are therefore presumptively irrelevant to a rape accusation.
3. The promptness of reporting rape is irrelevant to the determination by police, prosecutor, judge, or jury of nonagreement to sex acts alleged as rape. The promptness of a report is therefore presumptively irrelevant to a rape accusation.[12]

Victim's Past Sex: Presumptive Irrelevance

1. Victim agreement to sex in the past with persons other than the accused has nothing to do with agreement in the present instance. Past sex conduct with others (i.e., not the accused) is presumptively irrelevant to rape victimization.
2. Victim agreement to sex in the past with the accused has nothing to do with agreement in the present instance. Past sex conduct with the accused is presumptively irrelevant to rape victimization.
3. Past sexual history or reputation in relation to the accused or others cannot be used to establish a voluntariness, agreement or reasonable mistake of voluntariness, agreement defense.

4. Evidence as to past sex is admissible only to show the origin of semen, pregnancy, or disease. A written motion and "offer of proof" (MI PA 328, sec. 520[j]) must be filed. If a judge is satisfied, an in-camera hearing shall take place to determine the relevance of such evidence before it may be introduced in court (as in the Michigan model).[13]

Victim Behaviors: Presumptive Irrelevance

1. Voluntary drinking and/or drug use by the victim is irrelevant to the issue of involuntariness, nonagreement to the sex act(s). Both are therefore presumptively irrelevant.
2. The victim's style of dress is irrelevant to the issue of involuntariness, nonagreement to the sex act(s). It is therefore presumptively irrelevant.
3. Victim demeanor, for example, informal, touchy-feely, warm, sexy, flirtatious, and so on, is irrelevant to the issue of involuntariness, nonagreement to the sex act(s). It is therefore presumptively irrelevant.
4. The victim's being acquainted with or having dated the accused is irrelevant to the issue of involuntariness, nonagreement to the sex act(s). Both are therefore presumptively irrelevant.

Summary

Victim characteristics, such as past reports of rape, promptness of reporting, past sexual involvements or sexual reputation, drinking, dancing, dress, demeanor, and/or being acquainted with/dating the accused are not indicative of voluntariness, agreement and do not make mistakes of voluntariness, agreement reasonable. These victim dimensions must be understood as immaterial (i.e., not tending to prove matters related to the outcome of the case), and/or irrelevant (not proving or disproving facts of the case), and/or incompetent (what they purport to be). Introducing them into evidence would cause unfair prejudice that would outweigh their probative value. These facts would also contribute to "confusion of the issues or unwarranted invasion of the complainant's privacy or undue delay, waste of time, or needless presentation of cumulative evidence" (Berger 1977: 98) or "misleading the jury (Kadish and Schulhofer 2001: 96). They are therefore inadmissible in court or, in my terms, presumptively irrelevant.

To be proven (vs. presumed) relevant, any of these factors must be ruled by a judge to be material, competent, and relevant and not causing unfair prejudice that would outweigh the probative value of the fact, confusion of the issues, unwarranted invasion of the complainant's privacy, undue delay, waste of time, or needless presentation of cumulative evidence.[14]

OFFENDER CONSIDERATIONS

Criminal Culpability

The defendant is criminally culpable if any one of the following applies:

1. The accused knowingly or purposely intended to ignore, recklessly disregarded, or negligently failed to appreciate the expression of involuntariness or nonagreement by the victim, which a reasonable woman would know or understand to be present.
2. The accused knowingly or purposely intended, recklessly disregarded, or negligently failed to appreciate the aggravating conditions or use of force/coercion or use of duress/fraud, which a reasonable woman would know or understand to be present.
3. The accused knowingly or purposely intended to overcome, recklessly disregarded, or negligently failed to appreciate the victim involuntariness or nonagreement that is the statutorily reasonable or ascendant legal presumption under conditions of aggravation, force, or coercion, or duress or fraud.

DEFENSE CONSIDERATIONS

The Voluntariness, Agreement: "She's a Liar" and Reasonable Mistake of Voluntariness, Agreement: "He's a Blunderer" Defenses

1. Changing the words: The "consent defense" is changed to the voluntariness, agreement: "she's a liar" defense; the "mistake of consent" defense is changed to the reasonable mistake of voluntariness, agreement: "I'm a blunderer" defense.
2. The defense of voluntariness, agreement: "she's a liar" and the defense of reasonable mistake of voluntariness, agreement: "I'm a blunderer" can be argued (are available) only under the argued circumstances of indication of involuntariness, nonagreement, additional victim injuries, and/or multiple offenders, force or

coercion, or duress or fraud. Conversely, the defenses are not available with minor-age victims, minor-age victims in the same household as the accused, or victims of any age who are blood relatives of the accused or when the accused is in an authority or power position over a minor-age victim, victims are unconscious or incapacitated, or when an offender has a weapon, commits a concurrent felony, or administers any known date rape drug.

Establishing the Defenses

1. The defense of voluntariness, agreement: "she's a liar" and the defense of reasonable mistake of voluntariness, agreement: "I'm a blunderer" are affirmative defenses, wherein the burden of production goes to the defense to provide evidence of voluntariness, agreement to the sex act(s) alleged as rape.

2. The defense needs to demonstrate voluntariness, agreement by the definition provided in affirmative consent law. Affirmative consent law and the model here both rely on the definition of consent or voluntariness, agreement as "words or overt actions by a person who is competent to give informed consent indicating a freely given agreement to have sexual intercourse or sexual contact" (Wisconsin's statute, cited in Tchen 1983: 1544).[15]

3. In order to show evidence of voluntariness, agreement, the defense must show the judge/jury that the accused took "reasonable steps, in the circumstances known to the accused at the time, to ascertain that the victim was consenting" (Boyle 2000:502, citing *An Act to Amend the Criminal Code (Sexual Assault) in Canada*, chap. 38, 1992 S.C. 273.2[b] [Can.]).

4. "There is no consent where 'the complainant, having consented to engage in sexual activity, expresses, by words or conduct, a lack of agreement to continue to engage in the activity'" (Boyle 2000: 502, citing *An Act to Amend the Criminal Code [Sexual Assault] in Canada*, chap. 38, 1992 S.C. 273.2[e] [Can.]).

5. The burden of proof shifts to the defense when the voluntariness, agreement: "she's a liar" defense or the reasonable mistake of voluntariness, agreement: "I'm a blunderer" defense is mounted against a rape accusation. Normally, the defense must establish enough doubt to undermine the prosecution's case as to the elements of the crime beyond a reasonable doubt. But here the defense shoulders the burden of proving the affirmative consent expressed by the victim.

6. The proof requirement is satisfied with a preponderance of evidence. The preponderance of evidence standard applies only when the voluntariness, agreement: "she's a liar" or reasonable mistake of voluntariness, agreement: "I'm a blunderer" defenses are being argued. The defense must show evidence that voluntariness,

agreement was expressed by the victim or reasonably mis-taken to the extent that it was more likely than not, more probative than not (in cases where no aggravating, forceful, coercive, duress, or fraud circumstances are argued; i.e., where there is only the expression of no), and more likely or probative than the presumptive nonagreement the law stipulates (as the reasonable assumption) when aggravating, forceful or coercive, duress, or fraud conditions are present.

7. Voluntariness, agreement: "she's a liar" and reasonable mistake of voluntariness, agreement: "I'm a blunderer" defenses are always unreasonable and so unavailable when the victim is a minor, a minor in the same household, or a blood relative of the accused of any age or when the accused is in an authority or power position over the minor-age victim, when the victim was unconscious or incapacitated, or when the offender had a weapon, was committing a concurrent felony, or administered any known date rape drug.

8. Due notice is herein served to men that the voluntariness, agreement: "she's a liar" and the reasonable mistake of voluntariness, agreement: "I'm a blunderer" defenses are unreasonable, making for criminal culpability, under the conditions listed in item 7, above.

SUMMARY

This chapter outlines the key reforms in requirements and standards that I'm proposing. I have set these up as a model array of changes both to be made in de jure law and to be read as juror instructions at trial. The next chapter describes the changes through a joint reiteration and elaboration of the meaning, rationale, and justification for the set of reforms advanced in the array.

Discussion of the Model Array | **FOURTEEN**

While the model array pertains to all rape and sexual assault crimes, it is significant to underscore that it is designed especially to target the difficulties of adjudicating simple, nonaggravated, date, and/or acquaintance rape. The recommendations are strategies devised to break the loggerhead of "he said, she said" rapes, which the criminal justice system has not taken seriously despite even the best reform laws of the past. These directions should assist in the prosecution of aggravated, stranger, "real" rape as well, but given the continuing neglect, minimization, and dismissal of simple rape, something must move us beyond earlier efforts and visions to handle properly the mass of rape that may be simple but is still real in its impact, not to mention prevalence.

The changes would be implemented via de jure statute changes and jury instructions, for which the judiciary would be responsible: to know, to use themselves in bench (as opposed to jury) trials, and to communicate to jurors. Some of the items require little comment—they have been discussed at length and summarized in previous chapters—others benefit from extended consideration of rationale, justification, additional context, potential added benefits, and so forth.

CRIME CONSIDERATIONS

The first group of dimensions consists of measures designed to be incorporated into de jure legal definitions of rape and sexual assault. They are also the first part of the jury instructions to be read before deliberations.

Continuing the Removal of Discriminatory Requirements

For those jurisdictions that instituted only nominal reforms, passing legislation to remove unique corroboration, resistance, and prompt report requirements is essential. Similarly, removing cautionary jury instructions and strictly limiting the questioning of victims about their sexual involvements in open court must be dramatically restrained. The specification of the removal of requirements is designed to get states that are lagging behind in rape reform up to speed, so to speak.

Establishing the Crime

The objective in this group of considerations is to specify that any sort of aggravating conditions, or force/coercion, or indication of unwillingness (involuntariness, nonagreement), or other threats or deceptions (nonviolent duress and fraud) makes the sex acts rape (penetration) or sexual assault (sex acts of contact, short of vaginal, oral, or anal penetration) offenses. Any of these conditions makes for the presence of involuntariness, nonagreement. This is to say that aggravating conditions, force/coercion, or duress/fraud are redundant with involuntariness, nonagreement and so do not also—in addition to involuntariness, nonagreement—have to be proven by the prosecution. Proof of either aggravating conditions, force/coercion, or duress/fraud or involuntariness, nonagreement would be a sufficient basis for criminal conviction. This is likewise to say that victim submission or compliance under any of these circumstances is not typically voluntariness, agreement or consent. (If, however, the defense contests the involuntariness, nonagreement by means of a consent defense, the burden and standards change; see "Defenses," below).

Reasonable Woman's Point of View

A reasonable woman's point of view is to be relied on to assess the presence of criminal conditions. In place of male-driven definitions of what constitutes expression of involuntariness, nonagreement, or aggravating conditions such as the presence of weapons, or explicit or implicit force or coercive threats, or non-physical (coercion) threats (duress) or fraudulent deception, what a reasonable woman would interpret to exist along any of these dimensions constitutes the standard to be employed. In other words, a reasonable woman's take on the indication of voluntariness, agreement, the presence of peril, the presence of non-violent menace, tricks, or deceit, and so forth trumps what the accused claims about such circumstances (any claimed consent or mistake of these factors must be proven by the defense in particular ways specified further on in the model). Any uncertainty about the force, nonagreement, penetration, weapon, duress, and so on would have to shown by the defense at a level sufficient to raise reasonable doubt (to undercut the prosecution's burden here to prove these elements beyond a reasonable doubt. But this changes if consent is argued; again, see "Defenses," below).

Presumptive Nonagreement

Aggravating conditions, or the presence of force, or threats, or duress or fraud each automatically establish presumptive nonagreement to the sex acts. This is warranted and is elevated to a legal presumption in law. The presumption of nonagreement includes the condition of silence when there are any coercive conditions. Any sort of coercion makes involuntary, fear-driven submission the operative principle that is to be assumed.

Remember that presumptive nonagreement is not applicable to instances where victims indicate nonagreement but there are no weapons, additional injuries, violent or nonviolent threats, and so forth. This presumption is not warranted when designating the acts as sex or rape rests solely on who is believed in a "he said, she said" scenario. It is up to the prosecution to demonstrate that the victim did not voluntarily agree or that the acquiescence was coerced by some outside factor, in order to prove that what "she said" was nonconsensual, involuntariness, nonagreement and therefore rape. When the only element of the crime to be proven by the prosecution is nonagreement (the penetration and identity would be uncontested if they both said that they had sex), the law cannot in all fairness establish a legal presumption of nonagreement. This is because agreement is a possibility in reality, and the defense should have the opportunity to make this case (see "Defenses," below). This upholds the right of accused parties to be "innocent until proven guilty" of crimes.

The goal in changing language and laying out presumptive victim involuntariness is to eliminate the implied consent that permeates de facto practices by specifying the nonexistence of an implied consent doctrine. Further, involuntariness is the reasonable presumption if criminal circumstances spelled out in law exist, and the model directly states this. This is particularly called for since juries have always been instructed on the consent defense, or honest and/or reasonable mistakes when consent is claimed, and on how allegedly easy it is to make a rape accusation and allegedly difficult it is to defend against it (as in Chief Justice Hale's cautionary jury instructions). Historic prejudice illuminates the dire need to level the playing field to compensate for the serious disadvantages that confront victims and the prosecution of crimes of sexual assault and rape.

Nonagreement in rape should be the implicit assumption in the same way it is presumed in other criminal cases. For instance, the absence of free agreement to give away money or property or to have property destroyed is an implicit assumption or presumed to be the likely or reasonable state of the matter in other crimes. Stating this for rape is just making explicit what is implicit with other crimes. The difference between how rape and other crimes are viewed becomes more obvious if we imagine having to change a law to state that it is wrong to assume that people who report robbery or burglary actually wanted to give away their money or property. The idea that such agreement could exist in robbery or burglary would be laughable to most, and the absence of free agreement should be presumed in the same fashion in cases of rape. If criminal elements like force or threats to harm or blackmail make it unreasonable to believe that consent was present with other crimes, then it is not asking a lot to use the law simply to notify or educate that it is not likely or presumptively reasonable to think that rape victims wanted to give away their bodies when the same forces are present. Alternatively put, willing agreement is not likely or presumptively reasonable when danger is the alternative. Mistaking voluntary sharing with concurrence when it has been gained by means of power, force, and so on should be seen as rather ridiculous, or at least as foolish, at best an error in judgment for which there should be no exoneration in criminal matters. Specifying presumptive nonagreement should reduce discrimination in case processing by making the adjudication of rape and sexual assault more like other criminal adjudications. Moreover, specifying that nonagreement prevails can educate and guide the decisions of judges and juries to facilitate rape conviction.

In sum, what prosecutors must establish is the existence of the delimited conditions or the expression of no, and they must do so under the burden of proof of the state to show culpability beyond a reasonable doubt. In other words, the prosecution must prove the guilt of the accused on the charges levied by demonstrating the elements of the crime, namely, the identity of the accused, along with the sexual penetration or contact/offensive touching and the aggravating condition (like additional injuries or weapons), and/or the force/

coercion/duress/fraud (that make presumptive nonagreement automatic), and/ or the involuntariness, nonagreement or "no" itself (though if the defense wants to introduce voluntariness, agreement or consent as a defense under certain conditions, this would be allowable, though then the burden of proof shifts to the defense; see "Defenses," below).[1]

VICTIM CONSIDERATIONS

The fight against myths about rape and rape victims must be undertaken on many fronts. The dimensions discussed below are an innovative way to combat the ubiquitous misperceptions about rape victimization. What is new is putting into de jure law and jury instructions what is and is not true about women who report rape and what is not at all indicative of the veracity of their charges.

Victim Reporting

Three aspects of victim reports of rape require direct remedial attention. First, the myth that women frequently cry rape after consensual sex because of ulterior motives like regret, a desire to protect their reputations, a need to cover up infidelity, or the hope of hiding the source of pregnancy or disease begs for correction. The law can simply state that this is a myth, by declaring in legal terms that it is unreasonable to think that women are liars when they report rape. In other words, the law needs to state that allegations of rape cannot be presumed to be false (just as is the case with reports of other crimes), and juries need to be so instructed.

Second, whether or not a woman has been raped has nothing to do with whether or not officials disbelieved past charges of rape and so declared them to be fabricated. The law needs to redress this through a provision that specifies that past reports determined to be fabricated are not relevant to the determination of rape in the present instance and through instructions guiding juries to this effect. This is necessary because, just as defense attorneys have squirmed their way around shield legislation and interrogated victim witnesses about their past sexual experiences and had these exceptions accepted as relevant, defense attorneys will likewise bring up past accusations of rape—founded or not (see below)—to make it look like a woman has a propensity to cry rape to cast doubt on her credibility and the veracity of the charges in the present instance. As for arguments that the present (as opposed to past) charges are fabricated, the model recommends quite another route for arguing that current charges of rape are lies or fabrications (see below, "Offender Considerations" and "Defense Considerations," for details).

Allegations of rape that were allegedly fabricated in the past have been legally recognized as relevant to (undermine) current charges or rape. Gardner and Anderson (1996: 427) report that the U.S. Supreme Court, in *Olden v. Kentucky* (488 U.S. 227 109 S.Ct. 480 [1988]) overturned a conviction on the basis that shield legislation unconstitutionally barred the defense from cross-examination that would have tried to show that the victim had fabricated the charges against the accused. The authors continue that this same principle (exception of evidence pertaining to the falsity of the accusation as a result of shield provisions) was upheld in Florida (*Lewis v. State* 50 CrL 1303; see ibid.). The Supreme Court of Nevada also allowed prior fabrication of an accusation of rape into the proceedings as relevant evidence (in *Miller v. State* 779 P.2d 87 [1989]; see ibid.). Given the prejudice against women who report rape and particularly the myths about false accusations and crying rape, the exception to shield legislation alleging unfounded charges or fabrications as relevant evidence bearing on a victim's present claims is most disturbing.

Currently, a victim's past experiences and reports of rape are allowed as relevant to determine credibility regarding the charges at hand, irrespective of any charges of falsification. Many states allow evidence of past accusations of rape to go to the issue of the credibility of the victim's charges or accusations, which is to say, as evidence of a false accusation in the present instance.[2] What a victim has said or done in the past and how the criminal justice system responded to this cannot rightfully be taken to mean that the current charges are false. The standard in law is that when prejudice outweighs probative value, evidence ought to be disallowed. Past rape accusations are not probative and certainly not probative enough not to be outweighed by the prejudice they would lend in the present instance. Yet states still make an exception to shield laws for just such information. This is so unfair that some judges won't allow such past rape report evidence in their courtrooms, despite the statutory exceptions to shield legislation that would allow it (Carnell 2002: 1; Gardner and Anderson 1996: 427; Gibeaut 1997: 36; Temkin 2002: 225).

The rules of evidence must declare, then, that past rape or sexual assault charges by victims—founded or not, alleged to be fabricated or not—are inadmissible as they are irrelevant, immaterial, and incompetent evidence vis-à-vis the charges at hand. Even if the complaining witness/victim has been charged with or prosecuted or convicted for filing a false police report for a rape or found guilty on some other charge like contempt of court for filing a false police report (a very rare occurrence by the way), her past record should be irrelevant. It is not the victim who is supposed to be on trial. It is not the victim whose guilt is supposed to be determined. If the accused is supposed to be presumed innocent until proven guilty, isn't it only fair, logical, and reasonable that the victim should be presumed innocent, too? This—that women who report rape are innocent—is the basis for the reporting provision in the section on the presumptive irrelevance of victim's past report history in the model. The law needs to redress the problem of bringing in past experiences—believed or not, or claimed to be lies or not, criminally prosecuted fabrications that happen once in blue moon or not—by clearly asserting that past accusations of rape, fabricated/false or not, are not relevant to determination of rape in the present instance. In addition to the law specifying this, jurors must be so informed by judges through jury instructions.

The third myth relates to the promptness of reporting. The false notion here is that women who do not run immediately to the police to report their victimization are lying when they accuse men of rape. The promptness of reporting rape has nothing to do with being raped, and the law obviously needs to specify this in order to eliminate not only the historic legal requirement but the concomitant belief underlying it. This needs to be put in statute and in the instructions that judges would be required to read to jurors before their deliberations.

Past Sex: Presumptive Irrelevance

The next dimension of my model applies to rape shield reform measures themselves. Past sexual activity and character evidence have been disallowed under the rationale that they not only "completely lack probative value" (Kadish and Schulhofer 2001: 377) but further because the prejudicial value eclipses probative value. Past sexual history evidence needs to be declared to be prejudicial and disallowed as evidence of victim character or credibility.

Although many shield statutes prohibit past sexual activity evidence from being used to show that consent in the past indicates a proclivity toward consent in the instance at hand, such evidence still comes in the back door. This is to say that the defendant's mistaken belief that the victim consented in the present instance has been deemed to be reasonable because he presumed consent in the instance at hand based on his knowledge that the victim had consented to sex in the past (even with a different man/men). This was the ruling in the federal case of *Doe v. United States* (666 F2d 43, 4th Cir. [1981]; Harris and Pineau 1996: 123).

Many states long ago passed a statutory presumption of the irrelevance of past sexual conduct as evidence of consent (Field and Bienen 1980: 171–172). Field and Bienen note that Colorado and Georgia passed this even before 1980 (199). What needs to be done now is to delineate explicitly that consent in the past has nothing to do with consent in the present, whether to try to show consent in the present instance or to disparage the victim's character, malign her reputation, and/or characterize her as a whore or slut and so not credible or believable because she is an illegitimate victim, that is, rapable without repercussions or sanctions, because she consented so much in the past. The defense uses such tactics to try to show the victim to be a liar, or to show the element of consent, or to show the alleged reasonableness in a defendant's mistake about consent. Past sexual character evidence is as irrelevant to determination of consent as it is to assessing the reasonableness of mistaking consent or to assessing the truthfulness or believability of an alleged victim. Hence it is summarily unreasonable to use it to exculpate defendants. My recommendation therefore is to specify this by stating that past sexual activity and/or reputation evidence is irrelevant, immaterial, and incompetent as evidence of voluntariness, agreement and cannot be used to establish victim credibility, or present consent, or reasonableness as to mistakes of consent. This might be seen only to duplicate the shield restrictions that prohibit such evidence (even if the defendant is the person involved in the consensual sex with the victim in the past), but apparently it is necessary to reiterate this in some other way than shield legislation has already done. Proclaiming the irrelevance of past sex reinforces shield provisions and has the added benefit of serving due notice to men that assuming consent because of past sex is unacceptable and can be used to confer criminal responsibility.

I am recommending that legislatures enact a de jure change to improve shield provisions by stating in statute (as well as in jury instructions) that triers of fact (judges or juries) may not consider claims that a defendant thought the victim consented to the sex act(s) alleged as rape or that he made a (reasonable and acceptable) mistake as to her consent because of her past sexual activities with the defendant or with others. Past sex, no matter what, is not a reasonable basis for establishing voluntariness, agreement or the reasonableness of mistaking it in the case at hand. It is similarly not a reasonable criterion for adjudging character credibility. Murthy explains the "chain of inferences: 'The victim was reputed to be sexually experienced; the defendant knew of this reputation; sexually experienced women are widely seen as being more likely to consent in a given situation; thus, the defendant thought the victim was sexually available although she did not explicitly indicate consent' " (1991: 549–550). Murthy describes how even though reforms have limited the use of sexual history and reputation evidence, the mistake of fact defense allows in past sexual history and character through this chain of evidence or backdoor manner (543). In other words, Murthy illuminates how even though reforms disallow sexual history evidence to go to the issue of victim consent, it comes back in to establish the reasonableness of a defendant's belief about consent (voluntariness, agreement) because of past consent, character, and credibility.

Because of how past sex, character, and reputation evidence have slithered back in despite shield prohibitions, I recommend closing this door with the admonition that past sex and/or character evidence can never be used to assess the issue of victim character or credibility (as in the Michigan model) or of victim agreement to the sex act(s) alleged as rape in the crime(s) charged in the present instance. The provision of "never" can be thought of as a kind of strict liability on the consent defense ("she's a liar") and on the honest or reasonable mistake of consent ("I'm a blunderer") when past sexual history evidence is the basis for the belief in victim consent.[3]

It is worth pointing out that if the defense introduces the victim's past non-criminal sexual activities (and/or past reports, experiences, or supposed fabrications of rape), the prosecution ought, at a minimum, to be able to introduce the defendant's past criminal activities, including his past criminal sexual activities. The past record of the accused has generally been disallowed as evidence of guilt in the crime charged (although it can be used for other purposes, such as to indicate motive).[4] Some changes, however, allow such evidence in, conditionally. Bryden and Lengnick note that "urged by feminists, Congress has amended the Federal Rules of Evidence to enlarge the circumstances in which evidence of the accused's alleged prior sexual assaults is admissible" (1997: 1353). Kadish and Schulhofer provide the most detail. They note that Federal Rule of Evidence 413, which the Violent Crime Control and Law Enforcement Act of 1994 amended, now allows in past criminal sexual offenses by the accused as evidence in criminal proceedings (2001: 30). The rule states that "in a criminal case in which the defendant is accused of an offense of sexual assault, evidence of the defendant's commission of another offense or offenses is admissible, and may be considered for its bearing on any matter to which it is relevant" (ibid.; see also Editorial staff of LexisNexis 2003: 997). Kadish and Schulhofer go on to note, though, that this is the case only if it complies with rule 403, which specifies that if the prejudicial outweighs the probative value of the evidence, the evidence is disallowed.[5] This determination is up to the court.

So evidence of defendant's past crimes can be allowed, or it can be disallowed for the prejudice it might introduce. Whether or not a defendant's past record is allowed depends on the court and the jurisdiction. It varies by individual court determination under Federal Rule 403, as Kadish and Schulhofer point out, and it varies in courts on a state-by-state basis, as states are only guided by Federal

Guidelines. My points here are that past record of the accused, including past rapes and sexual assaults, can be excluded as evidence; further, the law recognizes that such evidence can be more prejudicial than probative. Simultaneously, however, past noncriminal sex by the victim can be and is still introduced. The victim's past sexual activity can go to issues of victim consent (in two states) or to victim credibility (in two states) (Herman 2004). I contend that with victims past sexual history evidence, the prejudicial far outweighs the probative value. This buttresses the premise that there should be a legally stated presumption that past sexual history/character evidence is irrelevant to voluntariness, agreement and mistake herein.

Yet, while the criminal past of the accused can be disallowed, the victim's sex that is not criminal, that, in fact, may be quite normal or typical, can be relied on to judge her credibility and character, and it comes in frequently, and in more than the four states noted above. Temkin expressed it well. She says that the "imbalance" is unfair, when the "character of complainants is routinely trashed, while the past behaviour of defendants remains obscured from view" (2002: 356).

And there is more. Recall that if the victim has reported rape in the past and the accusation was deemed false (by a demonstrably sexist criminal justice system), this can be used against a victim's present allegations. Again, the manner by which justice officials judge past allegations of rape is about as relevant to establishing whether a woman has been raped in the present instance as her past consensual sex is to the present consent in the case alleged as rape—which is to say, not at all relevant, material, competent, or probative.

Putting these facts together is indicative of the magnitude of disfavor and imbalance in the scales of justice as these are tilted against victims. Past criminal, even rape, offenses by the accused can be disallowed as evidence of his credibility, while the past noncriminal sexual behavior of the victim can be allowed to go to both her credibility and the issue of consent. Add to this that past allegations of rape can be allowed in as evidence of victim character and veracity, and the discrimination simply has to be more than obvious to all.

The injustice of questioning the woman's character by examining her non-criminal, volitional sexual behavior and her past reports that were considered to be fabricated—or to be true for that matter—while simultaneously disallowing the examination of the defendant's past forceful, sexually assaultive, criminal behavior—even including past aggression against the present victim—cannot be overstressed. I am arguing that the shield legislation should stipulate the presumptive irrelevance of the victim's sexual past, so that her past becomes moot, irrelevant, immaterial, and incompetent to the issue of credibility or to agreement to the act(s) involved in the criminal charges at hand. Her past is unrelated to judgments about voluntariness, agreement and only makes for errors as to its existence that would legally be deemed unreasonable. Its prejudicial value clearly overshadows its probative value, at the very least to a degree similar to how the defendant's past record would prejudice more than prove facts bearing on current culpability.

In addition, the statutory specification of the irrelevance of past consensual sex with the accused in the model is especially formulated to permit for the prosecution of marital rape, rape among cohabiting partners, rape of prostitutes, rape by estranged lovers, and rape by old boyfriends, current dating partners, and so on, by disallowing the discrimination introduced in those cases by the reliance on past sexual conduct and character evidence. Again, it is the circumstances attending the acts, like weapons, force, coercion, and/or saying no, and not past agreement to sex that determines involuntariness, nonagreement and hence the criminal status of the acts.

Victim Behaviors: Presumptive Irrelevance

The changes described in the model are to accrue regardless of victim behaviors or characteristics, like drinking or dancing, or victim demeanor or style of dress at/around the time of the crime. In other words, these changes would be in effect irrespective of victims' knowing offenders in any way, dating offenders, drinking with offender(s) (or any others), dancing with offender(s) (or any others), or dressing in a manner that some adjudge to be provocative. It must simply be repeated at every turn that these behaviors do not make for voluntariness, agreement. The final component of the victim segment in the model array (Victim Considerations) is to state this irrelevance specifically in de jure law and juror instructions.

My model's conditions would pronounce victim dress, demeanor, and so on legally irrelevant to the determination of voluntariness, agreement or mistakes about voluntariness, agreement. These factors are to be presumptively irrelevant, that is, the operating assumption is that they are not indicative of voluntariness, agreement. Illinois provides an example of a jurisdiction that has legally specified terms of this nature, providing an exacting precedent for the provision I am talking about. Illinois law stipulates that the way a woman dresses is irrelevant to rape. Reeves Sanday provides detail for the example. She points out that the Illinois law states that "the manner of dress of the victim at the time of offense is also mentioned as not constituting consent" (1996: 282). My model specifies that dress, demeanor, and so forth are presumed to be irrelevant to determining voluntariness, agreement and so presumptively irrelevant to the reasonableness of making mistakes about voluntariness, agreement as well.[6]

It is important to elaborate that, by association, other victim-blaming tactics like claiming "she asked for it," "she had it coming to her," "she wanted it," and so on are all correspondingly irrelevant, incompetent, and immaterial to the issue of consent. These are myths that can no longer be allowed to imply that women and girls willingly and freely agree to, or desire or deserve, the sex acts they charge as rape and other offensive sexual assault crimes. This is a reasonable point of view, and not just from a woman's point of view, as judged by women's experiences and women's interpretations and thought. And the statutes need to delineate, and judges and juries need to be guided by, the specification of reasonable perception and presumption about nonagreement and defendant culpability in the cases involving such victim characteristics as those listed along the dimension relating to the presumptive irrelevance of victim behavior in the array, namely, victim drinking, dating, dress, demeanor, or acquaintance with the accused. At the very least, the law needs to define that drinking, dress, and so on are not, in any way, indicators of consent and that such factors will not vitiate offender culpability. To parallel what was said about presumptive irrelevance and past sex/character evidence, I add that the presumptive irrelevance of victim behaviors can also be thought about as a type of strict liability on the voluntariness, agreement and reasonable mistakes of voluntariness, agreement defenses when any of these behaviors is the sole basis of the defense of "consent" or alleged reasonableness herein.

OFFENDER CONSIDERATIONS

The following dimension of change with regard to those accused of rape and sexual assault offenses pivots around legal responsibility. This is where I extrapolate to rape offenses the criteria embodied in other criminal law, particularly that relating to homicide. What I borrow centers on considerations of mens rea.

Culpability

Another major group of statute definitions and instructions for jurors in the array relates to the specification of criminal responsibility. The model draws from Estrich's recommendation about negligent liability and from Schulhofer's notions of reckless and negligent liability. The model here adds further definitional detail that would apply extant legal principles upheld in homicide charges to cover not only intentional rapes (likened to murder) but also rapes where men recklessly disregard a victim involuntariness or their engagement in aggravating conditions, force/coercion, or duress/fraud (likened to manslaughter), as well as rapes that are committed by men who do not watch, listen, pay attention to, pick up on, or attend to victim nonagreement or fail to appreciate their engagement in aggravating conditions, force/coercion, or duress/fraud that a reasonable woman's point of view would dictate to be in existence (likened to negligent homicide). This is to say that men who intend to rape, or intend to overcome nonagreement (or to employ any sort of coercive conditions), or recklessly dismiss nonagreement (or the coercive conditions they employ), or fail to understand involuntariness, nonagreement (or the coercive conditions they employ) when it would have been understood to exist from a reasonable woman's point of view would be held, in any of these instances, to be criminally liable. Men who conveniently rationalize that a woman "wanted it," "loved it," "asked for it," "deserved it," and the like would be recklessly culpable when there are aggravating circumstances or, as Schulhofer puts it, "substantial and unjustifiable risk" to a woman (1998: 284) or negligently culpable, as Schulhofer puts it, for "gross deviation from the standard of care that a reasonable person would observe in the actor's situation" (ibid.).

Criminal responsibility obtains because involuntariness, nonagreement is defined by aggravating criminal circumstances, force/coercion, or duress/fraud and constitutes the reasonable, if not obvious, belief. Failing to get it, dismissing lack of agreement, and/or conquering involuntariness, nonagreement with power, violence, force, or threat of any sort is not only unreasonable, it is criminal. The law serves notice that the presumed state is nonagreement, that a reasonable person would have cared or heeded (versus disregarded) this (presumptive) nonagreement articulated in law or not acted to overcome the involuntariness and compel the offensive and injurious—and criminal—sex acts.

Presumptive nonagreement is to be the assumption under all said conditions, namely, aggravation, force/coercion, or duress/fraud. The accused, then, should know that the law presumes nonagreement (when aggravation, force/coercion, or duress/fraud would be understood to be present from reasonable woman's point of view) and that carelessly disregarding or failing to appreciate what the law states (the presumptive nonagreement)—or ignoring the law—is no excuse for the criminal conduct. This is just another way of talking about how recklessness and negligence apply not only to the appreciation of aggravating conditions, force/coercion, or fraud/duress but also to the law's stipulation on presumptive nonagreement where any of these conditions exist.

In nonaggravated, nonforceful/coercive, or nonduress/fraud cases, where presumptive nonagreement does not apply, recklessness and negligence still adhere to the offender for not heeding or regarding (reckless) or picking up on (negligent) the involuntariness, nonagreement expressed by the victim. The difference is that, in the absence of aggravating, forceful/coercive, duress or fraudulent conditions, nonagreement is not *assumed* to exist but must instead be expressed. The accused hence does not have to defend with a level of proof to overcome the presumption of nonagreement in such cases but instead must only defend to show the expression of agreement.[7]

DEFENSE CONSIDERATIONS

The final set of factors around which new de jure specifications and juror instructions revolve pertains to offenders defending themselves against rape accusations on the basis of voluntariness, agreement, or what has historically been called "consent," and mistakes herein. I emphasize that this is the only defense to which the following considerations pertain. In other words, these directions are not being advanced for the defense of wrong identity (where the prosecution would still bear the burden to prove identity), or the defense that no sex took place (where the prosecution would still bear the burden of proving penetration or contact), or other criminal defenses such as insanity. The routes to be taken for defending against rape accusations while admitting to sex acts (because the accuser allegedly voluntarily agreed to those acts) are delineated below.

The Voluntariness, Agreement: "She's a Liar" Defense and the Reasonable Mistake of Voluntariness, Agreement: "I'm a Blunderer" Defense

Just as the word "consent" must be eschewed, the defense of consent and the defense of mistake of consent must be linguistically avoided. Substituting the defense of voluntariness, agreement and mistake of voluntariness, agreement is one route to take. But I take it a step further, since the consent defenses are so often used, so prejudicial, and so lethal to rape case prosecution. The wording of the defenses I would substitute for consent defenses is merely descriptive. To claim "she consented" is to claim that she is lying in her charge of rape; therefore, the defense should be called "she's a liar." This is bluntly stating it as it is, so as to be direct and up-front about what the defense is trying to claim about the case/victim. The defense needs to convince the fact finders that "she's a liar," and the judge and/or jury should know—clearly and straightforwardly—what they are deciding. Making such a decision might take a little more gumption on the part of fact finders, but this clarity certainly should breed a little more honesty when defendants are excused from criminal responsibility.

The same goes for the defense of mistake of consent. What the defense is trying to show with this defense is that the defendant blew it, that she did not voluntarily agree to the sex but he didn't get it or understand this (when a reasonable woman would have understood it). He made a mistake, honestly, or true in fact (not fraudulently conjectured), and reasonably—meaning where other regular (reasonable women) also would have missed the fact or interpretation that the victim was not voluntarily agreeing to the sex acts. He blundered, he erred, but this was understandable, as he was judged to have a rational or reasonable basis for the error and thus made an excusable mistake.

Agreement would be untenable in cases where victims did not have the wherewithal or requisite ability to give meaningful consent or where the acts are inexcusable because they were so heinous or coercive that consent could not be meaningfully conceived or given. Agreement defenses would thus be unavailable under conditions where consent or voluntariness, agreement is untenable or unjustifiable. The specific conditions are victim minor age; relationship to offender (relative, same household, or authority position); incapacitation, especially where the offender administered date rape drugs (either voluntarily or unknowingly ingested by the victim); the presence of weapons; and commission of other felonies.

In terms of defendants' rights, I might note that the right to due notice is served by the specification that any/all mistakes about voluntariness, agreement are unreasonable under certain circumstances. These can be thought of as strict liability crimes, where mistakes—no matter how earnestly, genuinely, or honestly believed—will never be reasonable and so will not exculpate.

Conversely stated, the defenses *are* available in the "he said, she heard" or "she said, he heard" cases of what Estrich calls "simple" rape and sexual assault where victims say they expressed nonagreement or where there were conditions of force or coercion, or additional victim injuries, or aiders and abettors, or duress, or deception. The defenses are allowable because it is conceivable that while such sexual involvements may not typically entail volitional agreement, it is conceivable that voluntariness could attend such contexts of sexual activities.

Defenses

The final section of the array deals with the voluntariness, agreement defenses. To be effective, actual voluntariness, agreement has to be proven to defend against a rape accusation. For the reasonable mistake of voluntariness, agreement, errors or misperceptions about consent would have to be demonstrated to be reasonable because indications that could be taken as agreement were shown. If the defense provides evidence to establish the existence of voluntariness, agreement to the sex acts, defendants are exonerated, whether the agreement was real or mistakenly but reasonably interpreted. The defense would likely bring up statements like "she never said no," "I used no illegal deceptions," "I made no threats," or "I used no physicality/force," "she agreed freely, on her own," "she agreed but regretted it later," "she falsely accused me," "she's lying," "she came around to agreeing once we got into it," "she would have resisted me more if she didn't really want it," "anybody would have thought that look meant yes," "she didn't say anything like she didn't want to," and so forth. (Other defenses—claiming mistaken identity, that no sex took place, or that the accused is sick, incompetent, and not responsible—would all be available).[8] To have any impact, the defense has to supply evidence to prove that there was positive, demonstrable expression of yes, irrespective of any of these above beliefs (under the allowable conditions delimited).

Since consent comes up so frequently, especially in the cases where there are no aggravating or coercive conditions in addition to the alleged indication of involuntariness, nonagreement and in the "he said, she said," "simple" rapes, where women are the most notoriously disbelieved, the law needs to confront the consent issues in an extraordinarily direct and up-front manner. My model does this by encumbering the defense to prove that consent actually existed. And the defense must show this consent as more likely than the presumptive nonagreement that the law lays out when aggravating, forceful/coercive, duress, or fraudulent circumstances are shown to be in existence. In order for an acquittal/dismissal to occur on the basis of alleged voluntariness, agreement to the sex acts or on the basis of a mistake that is honest and reasonable, several things must happen.[9]

As the array delineates, first, an affirmative defense must be mounted, wherein the defense attorney shoulders the burden of production. This is to say that the defense has to provide evidence that the victim willfully or voluntarily agreed to the sex acts under the affirmative consent standard: by "words or overt actions by a person who is competent to give informed consent indicating a freely give agreement to have sexual intercourse or sexual contact" (Wisconsin statute). The defense must show that the victim indicated this voluntary choice and that the defendant assessed its existence. The defense must also show that the victim continued this voluntariness, agreement throughout the sex acts (if the prosecution claims it did not continue because the victim indicated nonagreement at some point during the sexual activities).

Next, the burden of proof becomes the defense attorney's, not, as present law would state, only the burden to introduce doubt as to consent, but instead to demonstrate how the expression of voluntariness, agreement would be more probable or weighty or reasonable to believe than the belief that the victim had not expressed voluntariness, agreement. Recall that the shift in the burden of proof borrows from extant (insanity and other) law that relies on the preponderance of evidence standard. Recall also that preponderance of evidence means "evidence which is more credible and convincing to the mind.... Preponderance ... denotes a superiority of weight or outweighing ... more probable than not" (Black 1991: 819). Under the proposed model, what the defense must establish is that a woman expressed voluntariness, agreement to the sex acts and that this is more probable, more likely, more weighty than not, when there are no aggravating conditions, force/coercion, or duress/fraud ("he said, she said" cases where the expression of no is in contest), and significantly more likely, probable, or weighty than the involuntariness that the crime circumstances (aggravation, force, coercion, duress, fraud) establish to be presumed. This may not be a beyond a reasonable doubt standard, but overcoming the legal presumption of nonagreement as reasonable (when force, coercion, aggravating conditions, duress, or deception are present), as well as the prosecutor's demonstration of the criminal circumstances (force, coercion, aggravation, duress, deception), will not be a walk in the park, either. The defense will need to overcome the reasonable expectation—the agreement that is salient and legally presumed to characterize the alleged crime of rape under specified aggravating conditions—and the prosecutor's proof of force, coercion, aggravating conditions, duress, or deception. This means that the defense will need to prove indications of the expression of free and voluntariness, agreement to the sex acts to be more believable than the prosecutor's established grounds that the woman submitted involuntarily, especially when under force/coercion, multiple assailants, injuries and so on, nonphysical threats, or fraud.

Consent defenses of any sort cannot even be argued under certain conditions. Voluntariness, agreement: "she's a liar" and reasonable mistake of voluntariness, agreement: "I'm a blunderer" defenses are untenable and hence cannot be used when there are conditions that make free, unfettered, willing, knowing, voluntariness, agreement unfeasible, for example, with unconscious and underage victims who cannot form consent. The legal stipulation that the voluntariness, agreement: "she's a liar" and reasonable mistake of voluntariness, agreement: "I'm a blunderer" defenses are unavailable serves notice to men ahead of time that sex acts under these conditions will not be exonerated on the basis of alleged agreement to said sex acts. Again, making the defenses unavailable can be thought of as a kind of strict liability on offenses where date rape drugs are administered, blood relatives are involved, and so on.

It is beneficial to elaborate on this listing of defense considerations. An affirmative consent standard must be met by the defense by showing (with a preponderance of the evidence) that the victim offered positive, notable indications of consent or that the victim's indications of willingness were sufficient to make the defendant's mistake of her consent reasonable or more credible than the belief that she did not express free and uncoerced volition. This is important for more than ambiguous cases where there may have been mixed signals. It is applicable to cases where the defense wants to convince judges/juries that what "he said" about her overt agreement is more believable than what "she said" was involuntary and rape under conditions that are typically (but not always) imbued with involuntariness. It is to say that when introducing consent the defense must show much more than doubt about what "he said, she said." The defense must prove that she acted, indicated, did something in some way that would allow a reasonable woman to understand consent or accept that a mistake was reasonable (or more weighty than the expression of nonagreement). The defense would have to prove that acceptable indication of voluntariness throughout the sexual assault, under conditions typically imbued with unwillingness, for example, multiple accused parties, injuries, or other force or duress, characterized the encounter (or at least where the victim claims she expressed involuntariness, nonagreement).

It is useful to remember that this model is different from affirmative consent reform laws in the few jurisdictions where it exists, because the burden of production and proof in my model is moved to the door of the defense, which must show (with a preponderance of evidence as opposed to beyond a reasonable doubt) that the victim did express voluntariness, agreement and must convince a judge/jury that the defendant took steps to check whether there *were* indications of yes by the victim, which were not withdrawn at any point. This stands in opposition to the affirmative consent law reforms requiring the prosecutor to prove that there were no indications of voluntariness to engage in the sex acts or, alternatively put, that there were indications of involuntariness, nonagreement.[10]

It is also important to rearticulate that if the defense were to try to introduce doubt as to the existence of consent or voluntariness, this would constitute a consent or voluntariness, agreement (or reasonable mistake of voluntariness, agreement) defense and hence trigger the changes delineated in the model, for example, the shift in the burdens of production and proof. While some might see this as too large a change because it is a disincentive to argue consent (and instead try to introduce doubt as to force, weapons, the victim's indication of involuntariness, etc.), the (lower) standard of a preponderance of evidence makes the change more tenable. Furthermore, the defense quite often does not enjoy such a choice; for example, it is untenable now (in a few states) to introduce sufficient doubt when force or coercion are shown in a case and themselves stand as a sufficient basis (without nonconsent also having to be proved) for the defining of the crimes of rape/sexual assault. Moreover, making consent or agreement to sex acts that the criminal legal system charged as involuntary acquiescence or submission more difficult to sustain is precisely the objective of the changes described here. On top of that, the changes might at least slightly realign, for the vast majority of cases where defendants' pleas are leveraged for leniency to settle dispositions (see chap. 16), the imbalance that has carried through the times and pages of history. Balance levels in plea bargaining would adjust because rather than simply relying on the bias surrounding consent and counting on judges' and juries' acceptance of statements such as "she's lying," "she agreed to it," "she wanted it," and so forth, the defense would know that it had to prove something to demonstrate voluntariness, agreement or reasonable mistake of it in order to go forward. This diminishes the strength of the defense's starting hand to a more equitable level.

A final note on the premise on which this model is predicated: It is important to understand that I am proposing this paradigm not in order to provide more protection for women than men; instead, I am seeking consistency in the treatment of serious crime and equal protection under the law. The goal is progress toward justice in place of protection for the "just us" of men. I have taken care not to override the rights of the accused. For instance, past sexual activity evidence, if deemed relevant in an in-camera hearing, is still admissible. In addition, legal definitions through de jure changes and legal presumptions written into law operate to give adequate notice to men and women about legal expectations and obligations. And, as Pineau remarks, fairness is ensured by due notice (1996b: 85). The concern to avoid trampling the rights of the accused and the endeavor to infuse more balance should ultimately bring greater parity and fairness to the legal processing of rape.

CASE EXAMPLES: APPLICATION OF THE MODEL ARRAY

Two rather prominent cases of rape neatly exemplify ways in which the changes embodied in the model array could remedy problems in defining, interpreting, and adjudicating acquaintance and possibly nonaggravated, nonforceful, "simple" rape cases.

The Jansson Case

Susan Estrich describes a case of "simple" rape where the Michigan courts up-held a conviction although nothing inherent in the law ensured that this would be the result. She observes that the conviction, given Michigan law, could have just as easily been overturned. In fact, she says that this was precisely what happened in a very similar case in Maryland around the same time. Her description of this case points to the potential pitfalls that Michigan's model reform law leaves open. My model is directed at closing the kinds of holes that Estrich's comments in this case bring to light.

In *People v. Jansson* (323 N.W.2d 508 Mich. App. [1982]), the Michigan Court of Appeals upheld the conviction of a man who raped a newly made acquaintance. The accused met the woman through a friend at restaurant. He asked the victim if she were looking for a job, which she was. She drove with him to the alleged job site, where he showed her around, explaining things to her about the supposed job. He took her to a private office, where he said wanted to have sex with "someone." She cried and said she didn't "do things like that," whereupon he "grabbed her, pulled her to the floor," took her clothes off, and penetrated her (Estrich 1987: 91).

Estrich explains that the court recognized that the defense of consent to the force/coercion was available but "reasoned that if the prosecution proves that the defendant used force or coercion to 'overcome' the victim, that 'necessarily tends to establish that the act was nonconsensual'" (1987: 91, citing from the appellate case). "As to the defense's further argument that there was insufficient proof of her nonconsent and his intent to overcome her, the court was unpersuaded" (ibid.). Basically, the court wouldn't require the victim to resist. Estrich says that "the court could have required a greater showing of force to make penetration criminal" but did not (ibid.). The court could have required that "more evidence was needed to establish that the defendant knew the intercourse was without consent" (ibid.) but did not. Estrich concludes that the conviction was just a quirk of a court interpretation, the result of discretion as it happened to fall out in this case and not due to the way the reform law was written (ibid.), since the law's ambiguity and failure to address consent could have driven an interpretation either way.

My model would improve the probability that the law (rather than some fluke chance) would facilitate convictions in cases like this. The following lists how and why this would be the case:

1. Force such as grabbing the victim, pulling her to the floor, and pulling her clothes off could easily go to showing force/coercion. The force/coercion would be clear

from any reasonable woman's point of view. It might also be easier to demonstrate force/coercion because of the inclusion of implicit threats—evident in the grabbing, pulling, and disrobing of the victim—in force/coercion delineations.

2. Because the victim cried and said she didn't "do things like that," "no" can be seen to be in evidence. And, because "no" is sufficient to establish involuntariness, even without the force he used, nonagreement would be given credence.

3. Reasonable people, not just reasonable women, would see crying and rather obvious negative statements like "I don't do things like that" as nonagreement.

4. The woman's nonconsent to "things like that" would need to be indicated or the force would need to be shown, but the presence of either would suffice. This is all the prosecution would have to demonstrate (beyond a reasonable doubt). Yet in this case there was both involuntariness and force, making the case stronger.

5. The prosecution doesn't have to prove that the defendant used force/coercion to overcome the victim in order to establish nonconsent. This would be superfluous or redundant with nonagreement (shown in item 2, above).

6. The defense stated there was insufficient proof of the victim's nonconsent and the accused's intent to overcome her, but this, once again, would be unnecessary or irrelevant for prosecutors to establish. This is because nonagreement is privileged in a de jure fashion since force was used.

7. Involuntariness, nonagreement is a statutory presumption with the proof of force. This is what the defense would have to overcome with proofs of consent. Alternatively put, this presumption is what the defense would have to overcome in order to show that the nonconsent was insufficient in measure.

8. It appears that the job was a ruse. Telling the victim there was a job opening and driving her to the site of the supposed job were fraudulent, deceptive tactics to get the victim alone. This also supports a reasonable or presumed belief in involuntariness, nonagreement.

9. The presumptive irrelevance of being acquainted with the defendant would help to buttress the fact of her nonagreement. In other words, the legal statement that having prior acquaintance with someone is irrelevant to involuntariness, nonagreement helps dispel the notion that prior acquaintance has anything to do with involuntariness, nonagreement, which helps to frame an interpretation of her words of unwillingness.

10. The defense argued that the prosecution showed insufficient proof of the accused's intent to overcome the victim, but this is wrong according to Estrich's and Kinports's legal scholarship about intent, consent, and force (whether in regard to her nonagreement or his use of force) and would be unnecessary under my model. His disregard of her statement that she "didn't do things like that" would have been sufficient to establish "no" (his knowledge of involuntariness,

nonagreement) and hence, in this case, his reckless culpability for disregarding "I don't do things like that" as involuntariness, nonagreement. This is because a reasonable woman would have known her statement meant nonagreement. A reasonable woman would not think that she actually meant yes or was freely choosing to participate in intercourse with the man (and so was lying when she reported being raped). A reasonable person would also see the exercise of force/coercion to overcome the nonagreement expressed. He certainly didn't have to intend or mean to overcome her, and his behavior made the exercise of force redundant with the intent to use force to overcome her. Moreover, the story about the job and the defendant's taking the victim to a private office suggests that he might have planned ahead of time. Interrogating him or his statements to the police might lend support to this, showing his intent at a higher level of premeditation or malice aforethought, which would capture criminal responsibility. A prosecutor might share in front of the judge, jury, and/or defense attorney at trial (or pretrial for plea-bargaining negotiations) that the suspect's saying that he wanted to have sex with "someone" lends an "air of reality" (169 D.L.R.4th at 214, citing *R. v. Esau* [1977] 2 S.C.R. 777 [Can.]) to the interpretation that he had concocted the job story ahead of time. He had the location picked out and simply went out looking for "someone" to bring back to an isolated room allegedly for a job interview but in actuality for sex, which he took with force and against her protests. This is indicative of a stronger degree of planning and malice than the chronicling report would lead one to see.

11. The defense was arguing actual consent, or the voluntariness, agreement: "she's a liar" defense, not for any reasonableness of a mistake about nonagreement. While voluntariness, agreement under force/coercion is arguable in my model (she voluntarily agreed to the sex act(s) even though there was force/coercion), it is the defendant's burden to produce evidence (the burden of production under an affirmative defense) to prove (burden of proof) that volitional assent to the behaviors was expressed and strong enough to outweigh the presumptive status of nonagreement that would be ascendant because of the force, coercion, fraud, and indication of "no" (any one of which would do, though the prosecution would likely establish them all). The defense must introduce some type of evidence to show the alleged consent, which is hard to imagine in this case, and then demonstrate (with a preponderance of evidence) what the alleged victim did to indicate that permission to the defendant or how she acted to show agreement to the penetration and what reasonable steps he took to ascertain her words or actions indicating freely given agreement, which was not withdrawn at any point, so as to outweigh the presumption that it was involuntary, because force was shown.

The Alston Case

Kadish and Schulhofer discuss a case that can be assessed the same way. They describe the case of *Alston* where abuse had caused the victim to move out of the dwelling she had shared with the defendant. The defendant encountered the victim a month later and made her accompany him to a friend's place to exercise his "right to have sex one more time," threatening that he was going to "'fix' her face to show he 'was not playing'" (2001: 332). The victim objected and refused to go with the defendant, but he blocked her way and grabbed her arm, insisting she had to go with him. She clearly said no to the sex and stated that she wanted to leave. The defendant "pulled her up from a chair, took off her clothes, pushed legs apart and penetrated her" (ibid.). The lower court conviction was reversed on appeal. Kadish and Schulhofer comment that "the court conceded that the evidence of nonconsent was 'unequivocal,' but it held that the evidence was insufficient to establish the element of 'force'" (ibid.). This, of course, exemplifies the problems of requiring high levels of force and requiring evidence of both force and nonconsent, both of which my model redresses.

Estrich illustrates the thinking of the court by quoting that "although (the victim's) general fear of the defendant may have been justified by his conduct on prior occasions, absent evidence that the defendant used force or threats to overcome the will of the victim to resist the sexual intercourse alleged to have been rape, such general fear was not sufficient to show that the defendant used force required to support conviction of rape" (1987: 61–62). To this, Estrich responds "the undressing and the pushing of her legs apart—presumably the 'incidental' force—were not even mentioned. *Alston* reflects the adoption of the most traditional male notions of a fight as the working definition of force. In a fight you hit your assailant with your fists or your elbows or your knees. In a fight the person attacked fights back. In these terms there was no fight in *Alston*. Therefore, there was no force" (62).

Estrich highlights that the victim said no, pulled away from the ex-boyfriend, and made it clear she didn't want sex, didn't want to be confronted with his "right" to take sex, and did not want him to grab her, pull her legs apart, and penetrate her. She sums up with this: "To say that there is no 'force' in this situation, as the North Carolina court did, is to create a gulf between power and force and to define the latter strictly in schoolboy terms. Alston did not beat his victim—at least with fists. He didn't have to. She had been beaten, physically, emotionally, long before" (1987: 62). Think about this finding in light of *Black's* definition of force as "power, violence, compulsion or constraint exerted upon or against a person" (1991: 444), and it is difficult not to see manifest force.

Pursuing the case with my model would enhance rape prosecution in several different regards. First, remember that resistance by the victim would not be required. Next, force/coercion or nonagreement, not to mention both, makes this a case of rape. The model facilitates the recognition of this, even in this "simple," nonaggravated, acquaintance situation of rape.

The fact that the court recognized nonconsent "unequivocally" would have made the case rape and nothing further would be necessary under the model law drawn up in these chapters. The presumed nonagreement under force/coercion would have been buttressed instead of turned around by the focus and findings of the case. The law would state, and judges and juries would be guided by the principle, that when a woman indicates nonagreement, it means that no consent has been freely given, and nonagreement is always to be understood to be in existence when "no" is uttered. "No" is to be accepted and taken as the answer and sexual behaviors halted. When the defendant did not heed the nonagreement, the behavior became rape. No meant no, and no was expressed; in addition, the victim refused the sex, and her involuntariness, nonagreement was indicated when she refused to go with the defendant, such that he had to block her way and grab her arm (force/coercion) in order to get her to go with him. Nonagreement was also evident when she stated that she did not want to go to or be in the friend's apartment. It was again expressed when she said she wanted to leave. Wide indications of nonagreement therefore were present. This should have been sufficient. The force demonstrated by physically subduing the victim and the coercion by threatening physical harm both make the victim's submission clearly involuntary and render the case for nonagreement obvious.

The force that was said to be lacking can easily be found to exist, even using traditional connotations. Force, in addition to involuntariness, was indicated by the facts that the defendant "took off her clothes, pushed her legs apart," as Estrich observes. Additionally, he "pulled her up from a chair." Still further, coercive threats were made, for example, he threatened that he was going to "fix her face" to show he "was not playing," and she had every reason to believe that he could and would do so, given the past abuse. He additionally had blocked her path when she was walking, thus I would interpret, restricting her freedom of movement and potential route for escape, and then he forcefully grabbed her arm, stating that she must accompany him (1987: 60–61).

A male understanding of what constitutes force/coercion was responsible for overturning the conviction in this case. As Estrich articulates it, "the 'reasonable' woman under [this] view ... is not a woman at all. [This] version of a reasonable person is one who does not scare easily, one who does not feel vulnerable, one who is not passive, one who fights back, not cries. The reasonable woman, it seems, is not a schoolboy 'sissy'; she is a real man" (1987: 65). Using a woman's point of view to judge what would be reasonable would lead to the appreciation that the victim experienced physical force and clearly perceived threats to injure her, and she knew all too well the defendant's ability to make good on these threats, that is, "to fix her face," because of past abuse. It would also be reasonable, from a woman's point of view, to take the facts that she said she didn't want to have sex and said she wanted to leave as evidence of involuntariness, nonagreement. That she said no, not to mention that the defendant used physical force and coercive threats and pulled and pushed her around, constitutes the crime of rape—fairly clearly and simply.

The next step in the model would be helpful in prosecuting this rape because, again, judges and juries would be explicitly guided (de jure law and rules of evidence) by the principle that the past sexual relationship is irrelevant to the present alleged rape, which means, in this instance, that the defendant is not entitled or imbued with any "right to have sex one more time." This, along with the provision stating that voluntariness, agreement is not implicit, would highlight the error of the entitlement to sex the defendant thought he had. The significance of a provision of this nature is that it can educate to correct myths about rape for fact finders (as well as other criminal justice and public audiences). The past behavior of relevance here would be the victim's experience of prior violence by the accused. As just stated, the victim knew all too well the defendant's ability to follow through on his threats because of past beatings. This would contribute to implicit coercive circumstances.

The subsequent step in the model ("Offender Considerations") addresses the egregious nature of the crime, allegedly "only" a "simple" rape between excohabitants. There was allegedly little additional force (previously discussed by Schulhofer in light of the *M.T.S.* case as force in addition to what is involved to accomplish consensual penetration [1998: 95–96] and in Estrich as male-defined "schoolboy" or "fighting" type of force [1987: 61–69]) and no apparent additional injuries beyond the rape itself. Still, the defendant clearly planned to rape his ex-girlfriend, which constitutes criminal intent. He had planned ahead of time to carry out the rape (premeditation), as he took the victim to his friend's house, strong-armed her off a chair, separated her legs, and penetrated her. He announced that he was going to "fix her face" to show her he "was not playing" and impose penetration, which he opportunistically claimed was his due. These malicious statements are all coercive threats that are indicative of violence and of the plan to take sex with force (as was in evidence) and without consent, which in each instance constitutes rape.

The defendant's statements are indicative that he didn't expect the victim would agree to his plan or, at the very least, that he couldn't have cared less about her willingness. This means that if there were an issue about intent or about the woman's voluntariness, agreement to the sexual penetration, criminal culpability would not easily be negated. This is because under the proposed model, reckless or negligent liability would apply even if the defense could have established doubt as to the defendant's plans. In other words, the utter disregard for the ex-girlfriend's refusal of his "right to sex" makes for criminal responsibility, even had there been no obvious intent, premeditation, or forethought. There was at least recklessness or negligence about her nonagreement, his force, and/or the presumptive nonagreement his force would entail. The defense here would either have to establish a sufficient amount of doubt to undercut the state's case (of force/coercion) or have to prove voluntariness, agreement (consent) itself (with a preponderance of evidence).

The final step of the model, while not directly observable in the *Alston* case, can be considered for heuristic purposes. While the defense of consent was not argued, and so shifting the burden to show voluntariness, agreement in the face of presumed involuntariness, nonagreement would not be germane here, it is useful to explore it for defense purposes. In cases like *Alston*, the defense would rely on introducing doubt as to the existence of force or coercion in place of directly arguing consent (Kadish and Schulhofer 2001: 322). Establishing a doubt in fact finders' minds about whether the alleged crime entailed force/coercion is a tactic that actually endeavors to establish consent through the back door. If doubt can be created about force/coercion, then consent to the sex acts is implied. Under the proposed model, however, consent cannot be implied; it must be proven. Attempts to argue consent as a defense implicitly like this, through the back door, would not work. In order for consent to work in the interest of the defense/defendant, voluntariness, agreement must be explicitly argued, along certain lines. Putting consent forward as an issue would trigger a shift in the burden of introducing evidence and proving the crime of rape. This, juxtaposed with altering the standard to affirmative consent, not only renders the defense attempt to demonstrate consent less insidious, it also makes the demonstration more onerous. Imagine trying to find the positive, overt signs of yes, not to mention the continuing yes to the penetration in the *Alston* case. This is fair since the crime circumstances demonstrate the presumption of involuntariness, nonagreement to be reasonably grounded, if not easily shown beyond a reasonable doubt. Therefore, the reasonable and probable existence of nonagreement (not to mention force/coercion) is the most reasonable and probable condition and what the defense would have to overshadow or outweigh with evidence to prove the opposing side of voluntariness, agreement: "she's a liar." The only way to overcome this eminently reasonable assumption turned legally presumptive premise (because of his outward force and coercion), which should have been understood by the defendant, would be to show that it was more likely than not (preponderance of evidence) that she gave outward signs that positively expressed voluntariness, agreement to the sexual penetration.

Advantages of a Paradigm Shift | **FIFTEEN**

RENEWING EFFORTS

One advantage of positing a new paradigm, or way of thinking, about rape reform law is that it holds the promise of changing the nature of the discourse
about rape. This is to say that it offers the possibility of altering the conceptualization and dialogue that frame the issues surrounding rape victimization.
Such a discourse could illuminate unrecognized hegemonic assumptions about
causes, criminal justice treatment of cases, and cures for the problems of rape.
This holds the potential of breaking through the loggerhead of dammed-up clichés, stereotypes, and archaic conceptualizations about the nature of the crimes,
victims, and offenders and about what constitutes justice in rape cases.

The model I put forward should change what is brought to the table of discussion about rape and sexual assault in ways that are both expanding and limiting with regard to what might be considered relevant. For example, expanded
considerations invite discourse about strict liability, presumptive nonagreement,
and model law, while narrowing discourse would shut down considerations
about present consent that is concocted from past sexual relations, victim lies,
and victim blame. The model I advance can be thought of in terms of discourse

or alternatively simply as a frame that circumscribes the parameters of what is and is not important and germane when addressing rape victimization.

We stand at a time when feminist-inspired rape reform tenets, laws, and ideology are facing some searing conservative backlash. It is my hope that this book will reengage dialogue, critique, and response among constituent parties, which should stand as a catalyst for future change. We need a jump-start, and regardless of how my recommendations are received, they can certainly serve as a fulcrum around which new discourse and debate can be generated about how we can best direct our energies to change the law, the attitudes, and the institutional structures these embody, which all continue to revictimize rape victims. As Deborah Rhode concludes, striving for equality under law

> requires fundamental restructuring of social priorities and the ideologies underlying them.... These objectives require a richer appreciation of both the capacities and limitation of law as an instrument of public policy.... Reforms ... lay the foundations for more fundamental changes. Law can be a focal point for political organization and popular education; it can validate injuries and in some instances deter or redress them. It can also help redistribute power and increase the number of voices that are heard in distributive decisions. By reshaping legal policy, we can in some measure reshape social experience. By broadening our aspirations to justice, we may come closer to attaining it.
>
> (1989: 321)

The directions drawn in the previous chapters can serve as a catalyst to change awareness, choices, and the pace, direction, and power underlying change.

A new wave of change in law is necessary now to continue to improve legal and social stances against rape. The successes realized thus far can easily be played up to make further inroads toward more equitable victim and case treatment in rape. That the rape reform movement did not end in achievement of all its goals is just one more reason to reinvigorate the struggle for justice, to pick up where we left off and try to complete the project successfully. As Pineau sees it, even if a movement falls into disfavor, as manifested in the backlash of the recent era, that is no reason to give up on it; instead it is "all the more reason, then, to argue for a different point of view" (1996b: 81). We need to understand that reforms cannot be maximally effective if they are thought about as a one-shot panacea. Instead, they are a part of a solution that works in combination with other rape prevention and control measures in cumulative ways over time and jurisdiction. With the recent backlash movement's criticisms of feminism and feminists and the potential backsliding of gains for rape victims, the need for reenergized struggle for justice for rape victims is all the more pressing.

We need to continue to improve substantive and procedural laws governing rape and sexual assault for other reasons. The modifications of the past have improved the lot of many victims, and further refinement can boost the numbers and levels further. As well, legal change is indicated because some states changed rape codes only slightly, for example, merely changing the term "rape" to "sexual assault" with nothing more forthcoming. Moreover, additional legislative reform is in order to remedy areas, like the resistance requirement, where many, if not most, jurisdictions have failed truly to move forward in practice. Further, legal reforms need to close loopholes (like the mistake of agreement defense) that thwart reform effectiveness. We must begin to put checks on discretionary decision making (see the next chapter) that has foreclosed progress along all these dimensions for so long.

Change in thinking is further needed to confront developments that were not anticipated by reformers. One example here lies in the increased use of DNA evidence. The greater reliability of DNA evidence means that persons convicted of rape who were mistakenly identified can be freed and that some unsolved (serial) rape cases (cold cases) might then be reopened for investigation. The greater reliance on DNA evidence also means that mistaken identity cannot be used as a defense as often and simultaneously that consent to sex act(s) may be argued more often. Legal change must respond to such developments. One approach that has been successfully utilized to challenge defense claims of agreement is evidence of rape trauma syndrome (RTS) evidence, discussed at chapters 8 and 14. Developments like this that are subsequent to the early rape reform movement need to be constantly assessed for their effects on justice and for what they portend for the next round of legal changes that might be warranted.

Changes in law, in public attitudes, and in legal practices influence one another. Laws change to reflect the values and beliefs of the public, and the public's beliefs are changed by the legal definitions and practices enacted and implemented in laws. Stated somewhat differently, the impetus for change in law is the citizenry, and the impetus for change in citizens' beliefs about crime is change in law. Changing laws to change attitudes has been effective. The parameters of the discourse about rape and sexual assault have been widened immensely, and significant inroads have been made. This is why the symbolic, educative function of reforms is the perhaps the most salient point of agreement about reform successes. We should learn from our successes and let these inspire optimism, the better to eradicate ignorance about sexual assault crimes, victims, laws, and practices. As Schulhofer puts it, "legal reform can play a crucial part in the effort to raise public awareness and alter social assumptions" (1998: 258), which feed into criminal justice attitudes and rape case treatment. As Falk concludes, "the law on rape has not ceased and in all likelihood will not cease to evolve. Nor, arguably, should it, for the law of rape, like any body of law—reflects changing social attitudes and conditions, normative as well as material" (1998: 91). Berger concludes, "the law converts as well as mirrors cultural norms and expectation" (1977: 100). We can capitalize on all this if we would only raise our awareness of such possibilities.

Part of working with attitudes means working with the men and women who sit in judgment on rape/sexual assault cases as judges and jurors. These fact finders must receive the means to base their decisions on accurate information rather than erroneous, prejudicial beliefs. As Pineau sees it, "it is *practical* both to contribute to the production of a more progressive judiciary and to provide it with resources" (1996b: 81; emphasis in the original), –resources such as the language, tools, and rules the model here proposes to guide the judiciary in general terms and the jury more specifically, in juror instructions.

Maximal effectiveness in dispelling myths and informing fact finders about the actual nature of the crime and victimization of rape and sexual assault also requires parsimony. By parsimony I mean succinct and simple explanation. This dictates that definitions, rules, standards, and instructions be as clear and concise as possible. Research has shown, for example, that jurors can understand instructions that are simple and straightforward and that they use those instructions more effectively when they understand them. I have attempted to realize such parsimony in the model array outlined and discussed in the two preceding chapters.

Earlier features of reform failure and reform success, as well as the ways they have been applied both on the books and in practice, inform the model laid out in this book. It also responds to recommendations by other scholars and what both commends and condemns these. Building the model in this way endeavors to pave a new direction in enacted law, as well as a means to begin to address the practice of law that circumscribes the implementation processes. The breadth and depth of changes embodied in the model foster the possibility for one change to back up others, so that there is a greater chance that the law on the books matches the law in action. The reform model thus provides for the measures to be mutually reinforcing, which affords a way to forestall officials' side-stepping or short-circuiting of the changes. In other words, the interlinked nature of the changes serves as a kind failsafe against failure to implement any particular measure.[1]

Implementation is where reforms fell down the most. The changes I advocate are a prescription for combating failure by keeping an eye on implementation in order to ensure that practices meet reform objectives. Recall cases like *Morgan*, where a husband's having given permission to friends to "have sex with"—we should say, to rape—his wife stood as an exculpating mistake, even though she struggled against the sex. Recall *People v. Hearn*, where a gun- and knife-wielding stranger who raped a woman and attacked her boyfriend successfully employed the consent defense under model law in Michigan. These cases are indicative of how the courts can determine almost anything to count as consent, just as almost anything can be interpreted by the courts to be an "honest," "good faith," or "reasonable" mistake. This means that negligent culpability for rape doesn't hold much weight by itself, since careless disdain of nonagreement can so easily be construed as "reasonable" mistake. Further legal change must thus close the back door that allows nearly any mistake of consent to exculpate offenders. Raising (non)consent to an explicit, legally defined standard is one way to close the back door of reasonableness that lets assailants slip through with consent arguments that translate into victim blame and fault. The premises that reports of rape made to police cannot automatically be assumed to be false ("innocent accusation") and that there is no "implied consent" in my model combine with presumptive involuntariness, nonagreement as well as reckless and negligent responsibility to make reasonableness less arbitrarily, indeed, more reasonably, established. These changes, taken individually and together, also serve due notice to men that they are responsible for their judgments and actions and that they must pay attention to assessing the presence of voluntariness, agreement as reasonable women would see it and not mistake voluntariness, agreement conveniently, as self-serving men might mistake it, or mistake it "willy nilly" as in *Morgan*. The systematic set of changes should preclude men from displacing blame and responsibility onto the victims they terrorize. As Estrich puts it, law that confers responsibility for mistakes "provides an additional motive to men to take care before acting, to use their faculties and draw on their experiences in gauging potentialities of contemplated conduct" (1987: 97–98). The model changes also draw the spotlight to men's irresponsible behaviors instead of to victims' alleged errors. Disallowing unreasonable mistakes is what is reasonable, as well as consistent with other criminal law and practice. If there is any error in this, it should be on the side of physical safety from rape for women, not on the side of sexual gratification for men. This is what should clearly be the ascendant, and reasonable, legal quest.

The focus on the conditions attending crimes, the behavior of the accused, and the reasonableness of the accused's expectations and interpretations, in place of the scrutiny on victim consent, leaves us with many lessons. First, it teaches males responsibility, the need for them to be looking for "no" in place of not looking and/or assuming "yes." This fosters greater carefulness and affords more protection for women. Further, it offers the potential of enhanced relationships between men and women. And this should not be taken as an inconsequential aside or segue; it is a significant point. Second, and this is inspiring, men seem to be able to learn such lessons—for example, what courts are willing to accept as reasonable—pretty darn well; witness "jail bait" fears about statutory rape. As Estrich comments, it won't take a mountain of cases to get the word out that "no" is to be heard—more, looked for more—and respected.

Finally, a conceptualization that may be useful to disseminate is that it doesn't seem to be so much to ask for women to have the right *not* to have to have sex. All that is being sought here is a right to be left alone, not a right to do something or have something done to another. What women desire is not to have suffer the imposition of anybody unwillingly. This should prevail over men's right to have or (mis)take sex and actively impose what they want on someone else's body. Along this line, I again question why it is that "just say no" is considered weapon enough in this country's drug wars, sufficient to stop adults and children from using and dealing drugs, yet just saying no is clearly not enough when men force sex. What reforms are asking is really no big deal: just ask! just hear no when women say it! Learning this simple lesson could make leaps and bounds of progress, and the law can be both stimulus and response to the learning of the lesson as attitudes evolve over time and over court cases.

THE MODEL FOR REFORMING RAPE REFORMS

Overall Middle-Ground Strategy

Some rape reform advocates warn against going too far and "enfeebling" or "cheapening" (Kadish and Schulhofer 2001: 333, citing Berger 1988) women's sexuality or sexual agency when considering sexual assault law. My framework on the continuum of (non)consent respects rights of women to sexual desire, passion, variation, and gratification. It also permits for the reality of different sexual preferences by maintaining a consent defense, where it is recognized that females can voluntarily participate in sex activities that are not typical, for example, that are forced, or in sex activities where physical injuries are suffered, or in sex involving multiple men. This recognizes female's sexual agency, desire, and preferences that are not universal, indeed, that can be what mainstream society deems abnormal. As previously noted, this allows for consent or voluntariness, agreement to be proven to attach to behaviors ranging from a "zipless fuck" (Jong 1973), to willingness to be penetrated orally, vaginally, and anally by penises or other objects; to be dominated; to be hurt; to be spanked, whipped, or involved in other forms of so-called rough sex entailing beatings; or other forms of sadomasochistic sex activities. The key feature here is that because voluntariness, agreement is unusual in such scenarios, the defense has to prove that the atypical—voluntariness, agreement under forceful, injurious, atypical conditions—was the reality in the case at issue in order successfully to mount and prove the defense. The bonus of my formulation is that when the defense argues this nature of sex play as consensual or agreed to, such agreement is in the purview of deviant, atypical, non-normative behavior, rather than within the context of alleged normal or typical female desire, behavior, and sexual response. This serves definitional, border-differentiating, educative purposes that recognize these kinds of sex as separate from acceptable, consensual, or so-called normal sex. It construes consent to forced or injurious sex acts as abnormal but nonetheless allows for consent to such sex. As Tchen puts it, "a statutory consent defense will permit defendants to allege that the victim consented to physical force" (1983: 1548). My model allows this but also stipulates that the defense in these cases would be held to a high standard that would be limited in application. Nonetheless, the defense would be available for these extreme or unusual cases, for example, where females have agreed to be bound and tied, whipped, penetrated by objects, by more than one man, and so on. The model strives to balance sexual gratification both with the sexual agency of women who vary from the norm and with the right to be free from sexual assault victimization.[2]

The balanced or compromise part of the strategy is perhaps more pronounced in the voluntariness, agreement specifications. Specifying in law and rules of evidence that voluntariness, agreement (consent) can be a defense to rape is likely a more favorable framing of the issue, as well as a more acceptable legal position, than is strict liability on consent. It is not as radical as an overall affirmative consent law, like New Jersey's or Wisconsin's, or a strict liability on consent law, such as the *Ascolillo* ruling in Massachusetts represents. My model recommendations are, though, akin to saying that there is strict liability on unreasonable mistakes. Because my model lies somewhere between conventional and radical stances, it is more likely to be broadly accepted and therefore enacted into law. In addition to allowing for a consent defense even where there are aggravating circumstances, the shift of the legal burden to a preponderance of evidence can make the model more palatable to lay and legal audiences alike. A preponderance of evidence may be a less weighty standard than the typical burden of proof (the "beyond a reasonable doubt" burden that typically accrues to the state), but, again, it remains within the purview of legal practice that is found and accepted with other crimes. As well, when embedded in the rest of the model changes, it would be sufficiently weighty as the standard to which the defense must rise in order to demonstrate proof.

The model in this book is middle ground, in part because it is intended to be pragmatic, enforceable in such a way that practice meets objective. Because it is based on extant law and a compromise tactic, it ought to be more readily taken on and hence more likely to be put into law and practice. A further distinctive feature behind my effort to develop a balanced reform model is that the model is designed to be different from the more theoretical or philosophical models by being more practical in application. This is so that the changes will be sellable to politicians and the public. Politicians need to be able to sell the changes to the public, and popular support is needed to enable politicians to advocate the changes (and maintain/gain votes). And this means that there must be compromise in some areas. This in turn means that while I am sympathetic with some of the more extreme theoretical and philosophical logic and argumentation, I am not advancing an approach that would entail a greater degree of change than can realistically be anticipated to garner support.

The approach in this book is more balanced than some of the work that analyzes gender, law, and inequality as these define males and females in society and sexuality. MacKinnon and Dworkin, for instance, describe heterosexual sex as trapped by systemic patterns of domination and subordination, wherein full and willful consent to intercourse is problematized by inequality. My approach does not extend this far. Nor does it extend as far as Schulhofer's. His model is radical in seeking to define a new right: to sexual autonomy, to be free from unwanted sex, to have the law protect our sexual autonomy the same way it "protects our control over our labor, our vote, our right to receive honest services from professionals, and our privacy, including confidential information about ourselves" (1998: 100). The real problem here, of course, is that crafting a new right for people is rather extreme and not likely to have a great deal of practical impact, especially when extant rights are not respected but instead increasingly challenged and eroded by the courts and excessive executive privilege.[3]

Viability: Extant Law and Compromise

The model here attempts to move change beyond reforms previously enacted and even beyond earlier conceptualizations, drafts of legislation, and hopes. While the model moves beyond the status quo, I take care to build on extant principles of law in order to maximize the acceptability and hence actual change potential stemming from the recommendations. Abiding by historic legal standards and processes makes my model less radical than some others but enhances its practicality and hence potential impact. To put it bluntly, the more radical models simply will not fly in this conservative day and age. In fact, it is these models that have engendered so much exaggerated criticism. As witnessed in the case of Antioch, even if such notions make it into policy, they are not accepted, respected, or obeyed. To the contrary, they are laughed out of existence in many quarters. The model in this book works within accepted legal definitions and substantive legal principles and procedural standards in criminal law so as to make change more agreeable while still not compromising, indeed, while promoting, the rights of women without trampling on the rights of men.

I should comment that my focus on existing principles and practical change is not meant to forsake or downgrade theory. I agree with Goldberg-Ambrose that theoretical treatments can be a luxury indulged by academics and that scholars (like MacKinnon and Estrich, according to Goldberg-Ambrose 1992) can overestimate the importance of definitional debates. Yet theory can still be used to move matters forward. Theoretical treatments of a topic like rape are necessary to inform and guide the next steps of change that can yield improvements in justice. It is when theory is developed for theory's sake, with no eye toward practical usage, that Goldberg-Ambrose's criticism holds true. The model I propose incorporates theory (feminist perspectives) and legal perspectives (like Estrich's and Schulhofer's) and tackles the next steps by drawing from laws, practices, and models (like Michigan's) to forge measures to improve the criminal legal processing of cases. The ultimate model (expanded upon in the last chapter) is informed with these aforementioned factors as a guiding framework, as well as by experiences with previous statutory and procedural reforms. The model in these ways targets de jure law and de facto practice, as well as the means to implement the recommended directions through principles of law, such as rules of evidence and juror instruction. I follow Michigan's tactic of ridding de facto practices by specifying requirements (or lack thereof) in de jure law. I recommend de jure legal change to define things such as reasonableness of belief (about, for example, victim drinking or expression of nonagreement), about responsibility (e.g., of victims to say no and of offenders to hear and heed it), and levels of proof (e.g., beyond a reasonable doubt for prosecutors; preponderance of evidence for consent—i.e., "she's a liar" and "I'm a blunderer" defenses). And I craft a series of instructions to educate jurors (e.g., on the irrelevance of drinking and dancing) and judges, who must learn, utilize (in bench trials), and pass such instructions on to jurors. Judges and jurors are some of the most important actors who need to be disabused of myths and instead equipped with accurate facts, since they are the people who have the power to determine case outcomes.

Fighting myths by providing accurate knowledge and legal definitions, as in jury instructions stating that past sexual activity is irrelevant to voluntariness, agreement in the case under dispute (and that if any sort of force attends the crime, this nonagreement is presumptive), gives teeth to correct misinformed views in a way that nothing other than law can do. Educating through law not only assists jurors to rely on fact over fiction in determining their verdicts; it also bolsters educational campaigns at every other level.

One further point in my approach of building from preexisting legal formats deserves mention. I envision my changes as an array of interrelated modifications that can serve as a new federal model, akin to a Model Penal Code (and/or model Federal Rules of Evidence) and/or model jury instructions, that can be adapted in whole or in part in different jurisdictions across the country. Adopting changes in this way would provide for a measure of coherence as states gradually undertake their own revisions. A national example, too, allows for the possibility of gradual, incremental, piecemeal, or wholesale change, which again makes change more likely to be undertaken.

In the effort to stay close to accepted law and practice, changes in the model are based on existing definitions, for example, of homicide offenses and reckless and negligent culpability; on notions of strict liability for unconscious victims as for young victims in statutory rape; on a preponderance of evidence test for consent defenses in rape, as is the case for insanity and other criminal offenses; and on making nonagreement explicit (consent or voluntariness, agreement cannot be assumed, accusers are not making false accusations, and presumptive involuntariness, nonagreement under certain circumstances) for sexual assault as it is (implicitly) assumed when all other crimes are charged. The change specifying presumptive nonagreement in law in order to eradicate the concept of implied consent deserves special comment. I think this change would lose some of its persuasiveness if I had used parallel terminology, that is, "implied nonconsent" (to parallel "implied consent") instead of "nonagreement." We need to replace "consent" in all the contexts of its usage and to change "implied consent" to "implied nonagreement" because changing words not only helps to bring about new types of understanding, it also helps to jettison the baggage that accompanies old terms.

Basing changes on standing law should make changes more probable, too, since this promotes familiarity, acceptability, passage, and enforceability in dialectic ways, where each phenomenon plays in to and back on the other. Appealing to extant doctrine is strategic because it also plays to hegemonic notions—implicitly accepted ideas about the way things should be—of the legal and lay communities, making changes more appeasing and once again, then, more likely to be passed.

One dimension of status quo law that deserves singular attention concerns the rights the law confers to (lay) citizens at large, as well as to those accused of crimes. My model seeks to preserve these protections. Although the model described in this book will likely have appeal not just to rape reform advocates but also to victims' rights and "law and order" affiliated movements, it is not attached to the punitive "get tough" movement (as the victim's rights movement often has been) in contemporary culture. Rather than catering to the popular punitive "get tough" movement by arguing, for instance, that we need longer sentences, the model described in these chapters strives for justice in greater balance, comparability, and equality for rape offenses and victims, in place of the discrimination against victims and for offenders historically true with rape. I agree with reform sentiments that stand against harsher sentences for rape, both because of the excessive punitiveness that means injustice and because of the greater reluctance to convict that attends excessively harsh penalties. A large part of my effort here seeks improvement in the legal system's handling of rape cases by bringing rape case processing in line with standards and practices that are concomitant with other crimes, not by enhancing types and lengths of punishment.[4]

Along a related line, striving for comparability means standards and practices must accord with constitutional guarantees for defendants. This is pertinent most especially to shield legislation, which my model and the courts are both to uphold and protect. Upon challenge, courts have ruled that shield legislation safeguards defendants' Sixth and Fourteenth Amendment rights to confront accusers, to due process, and to equal protection. This is because prior sexual history evidence remains admissible in extant law (and in my model) but is restricted based on its relevance to the issues in the case at hand. This provision for the introduction of said evidence, while simultaneously limited on the grounds of relevance, "strikes a better balance between the rights of the defendant, the sexual freedom of rape complainants and the integrity of the judicial quest for truth" (Anderson 2002: 51).

Contrary to what some would believe, not all feminists and not all rape reform advocates favor trampling on the rights of the accused. My model protects the rights of the accused in several additional ways. First, notice is served to men by the law's forthright dictate that consent or voluntariness, agreement cannot be assumed and that those who report rape will not be presumed to be criminal liars. Second, stipulating presumptive nonagreement for rape similarly serves notice. These measures merely render sexual assault offenses more like other crimes. In fact, implied nonagreement so surrounds other criminal offenses that it is unnecessary, indeed unthinkable, to specify that consent cannot or should not be assumed or presumed. Third, the aggravating conditions like the presence of weapons or injuries that make for the more severe crimes of rape (based on the Michigan model) directly parallel other criminal definitions, for example, the differences between armed and unarmed robbery and among assault with intent to do great bodily harm less than murder, aggravated assault, and simple assault.[5] Fourth, notice is served that not paying attention or forcing, threatening, or deceiving to overcome reticence, unwillingness, or involuntariness, nonagreement leads to criminal responsibility. Recklessness or negligence makes for culpability for raping, just as they do for killing. Stipulating that recklessness and negligence in the use of force or in the perception of agreement makes mistakes unreasonable and therefore makes for criminal culpability obviously stays in the mold cast by existing law.

Additionally, the jury instructions in the model are balanced. Summarily stating that victims are not to be blamed and are not liars is not prejudicial like the Justice Hale jury instructions that codified the prejudice about women falsely filing and innocent men having such a hard time defending against rape charges. Jury instructions in the model simply neutrally state facts, for example, that being acquainted with the defendant, and/or dating or drinking with him, and/or dressing in what is deemed a sexy fashion do not mean voluntariness, agreement to sex. Just as situations like dating or dancing don't mean voluntariness, agreement to share or give away money or property in nonsexual assault crimes, they don't mean agreement to share, have, participate in, or give way to sex in rape and sexual assault.

The model here can be justified as comparable to other law and fair even on the most radical component concerning affirmative consent. Showing affirmative consent, or outward signs of agreement, or the demonstration of willingness, or "yes" as to agreement in order to establish the voluntariness, agreement: "she's a liar" or the reasonable mistake of voluntariness, agreement: "I'm a blunderer" defenses can be seen as setting the bar higher for both victims and the accused/defense. This is true for victims by demanding that they express no, nonagreement, or involuntariness in some fashion (but only in the absence of any sort of force or coercive, aggravating, or otherwise threatening or fraudulent conditions). This is not demanded of victims of other crimes, where involuntariness is commonly just assumed. It is also setting the bar higher for the defense, but this, again, is to level the playing field to compensate for traditional sexist beliefs and prejudices such as the implied consent doctrine and the like. Leveling the filed is a move toward balance and greater equity, not unfair advantage or privileged position, for those who report rape. Balance or compromise can also be seen in the model's allowance for the tenable but unusual cases where women voluntarily concede to be injured, to be forced, or to have sex with simultaneous or consecutive partners through the consent or "liar/blunderer" defenses, which the defense must prove.

Comprehensive Change

Being cognizant of both de jure law and what has and can happen in de facto practices surrounding such law led me to mount safeguards in the model for reforming rape reforms. By safeguards I mean, for example, reifying facts to dislodge myths by stipulating presumptive involuntariness, nonagreement and the irrelevance of dating, drinking, past sex, and so forth in order to train judges and juries with straightforward premises and the repetition of tenets throughout the model array and especially the juror instructions. Addressing both substantive and procedural law in this way provides for one change to prop up another. Addressing the whole set of erroneous assumptions surrounding rape and criminal justice processes from the initial police investigation of culpability through prosecution and eventual defense strategies makes the model quite broad in scope. It is the details that provide the depth. Setting up a model akin to exemplary federal laws for states to follow in reforming their own rape and sexual assault legislation provides a means to implement the recommendations. These are the factors that make this model for reforming rape reforms inclusive and wide-ranging.

POLITICAL CLIMATE AND BACKLASH

Extreme or radical positions are especially problematic in the conservative era characterizing recent times. The reign of the right has taken such a hold that the backlash against liberals (not even radicals, just liberals) and against feminism has been reentrenched with dynamism in the most recent years. In the arena of rape, not only has this emerged in the exaggerated backlash critiques speared at rape reforms; it has also translated into backlash policies against rape. Roiphe, for example, characterized rape as nothing more than regrets "the morning after" (1993), while backlashers like Paglia (1994) blame women for rape for as little as walking around "like melted sticks of butter" and accuse them of inviting rape by just sitting there (70). Backlash policies are epitomized in the example of Harvard University, where a new sexual assault policy mandates that corroborating evidence or witnesses be provided before the school will even undertake investigation when rape is reported to police (Dusky 2003: 39). Other examples of backlash attitude and policy are easily found, glaringly so, for instance, in the extension of the exemption for spousal rape to unmarried cohabiting couples and even to "voluntary social companions" in a number of states (Finkelhor and Yllo 1985). In another example, when a proposal in the Illinois House defined consent as "freely given agreement ... the Illinois State Bar Association criticized the definition as 'practically requir[ing] a written document before engaging in sex.' The Illinois State Judiciary Committee staff commented that the 'specific acts' requirement seems a bit too constraining and businesslike for your average tryst " (Tchen 1983: 1553). In like fashion, and most recently, when Maine was contemplating a change in the spousal exemption for rape, one legislator said "any woman who claims she has been raped by her spouse has not been properly bedded" (National Center for Victims of Crime 2004b). The recent challenge of the constitutionality of the shield legislation in Colorado by Kobe Bryant's attorney on the basis of the Sixth and Fourteenth Amendment rights to confront accusers, to call witnesses on the accused's behalf, and to due process and equal protection provides another easy example of backlash (*People of the State of Colorado v. Kobe Bean Bryant*), even though the challenge was denied. And recall the recent New Jersey Supreme Court ruling mentioned earlier that prior interactions—not even sexual ones—between the victim and the defendant are relevant to the determination of consent (www.vpico.com/articlemanager/printerfriendly.aspx?article = 112620, accessed March 4, 2005). And this is just the barest listing of examples of regression in beliefs and policies about rape.

Backlash sentiments, challenges, and policy initiatives that roll back gains for women and minorities (affirmative action is a favorite backlash target) necessitate renewed efforts at change in rape law and practice. The backslide witnessed in the above examples revitalizes myths that reproach sexual assault victims for their plights and blame them for just "routine activities" (Cohen and Felson 1979). This regression must be confronted in order to ward off further degeneration, not to mention regain lost ground and turn the tide against the injustice heaped on rape victims by society and the law.

Backlash has renewed myths about rape with a vengeance. Women's gains are lost as rape victims are once again condemned, but with a new punch. Backlashers have leapfrogged on the feminist recognition of women's sexual agency, to reinvigorate myths about desire and provocation. Backlashers assert that a woman who dates, drinks, dances, dresses stylishly, and so on wants, precipitates, and implicitly agrees to sex, that is, she brings it on herself because of her sexual agency and enjoyment of sex. This reenfranchises male access and reentitles men to force sex, that is, to rape women. It gives men the right, once again, to indulge, impose, and privilege their whims, interests, and power to dominate women. The backlash movement effectively disenfranchised "no means no," reempowering men to disregard women's nonconsent. "No" is depicted, once again, as insincere, the normal response to sexual overtures, disingenuous because of women's allegedly newly discovered sexual agency. It is what women are supposed to say even though they are supposedly interested in sex because of their sexual agency. This "game" of saying no while meaning yes, wanting sex, is "sexy" to men, and to women as well (since apparently we do not mean no when we say it). Men can therefore force and coerce and in other ways threaten and deceive women in order to take sex, which is subsequently concocted—by men and women now—as consensual or at least precipitated by women's own faults and provocations.

The renewed popularity of backlash sentiments punctuates the need for reforms that are practical, as opposed to being strictly theoretical. It also shows the need for reforms to represent compromise and be situated within familiar and comfortable bounds. These are the reasons I opted to keep my model within the parameters that relevant communities, such as the public and the legal and political systems, already accepted as legitimate, rather than straying radically far afield. My strategy builds on yet stretches hegemonic legal categories and principles in order to institute real change that these various communities will more readily adopt.

POLITICAL WILL

The media do a horrific job sensationalizing crime, sex, and violence. They could and should instead play up the horrific nature of how we treat sexual violence and its victims. They could impart accurate information to dislodge tenacious myths about women, desire, sex, and rape. They could unfurl a social movement to end sexual violence through saturating coverage of how appalling the legal system's handling of rape in general or some case of rape in particular actually is. The media's sensationalizing abilities to create awareness of issues, problems, and injustices can be seen in the cases of, for example, John Hinckley, O. J. Simpson, or Bernard Goetz, the Clarence Thomas–Anita Hill hearings, and the Clinton–Monica Lewinsky scandal and impeachment proceedings. The awareness generated by the media can lead to actions both grassroots and legislative, as with the rape reform movement in the past. The power of the media can and should be harnessed.

The distorted views about rape and sexual assault contribute to the incidence of these crimes, because so many believe, "it can't happen to me." If we were to become aware that the next victim could be our daughter, our mother, our grandmother, our sister, or our brother, sexually assaulted and then revictimized by the justice system, we just might generate the popular support that would engender the political will to change both the laws and the attitudes that mutually reinforce one another to fuel or diminish the crimes of rape and the mythology surrounding rape (forces that also mutually reinforce one another).

Informing communities about the commonality of sexual assault, in those "simple," "mundane," but typical cases that affect the people we know and love, should open our eyes to how nonsimple and nonmundane rape and sexual assaults really are. This should capture everyone's attention. Showing that rape and sexual assault can and do happen to every single type of person, without exception, can go a long way toward generating political will for the changes in attitude and law so desperately needed.

The law's educative function is simply compelling. It sets an example, it serves notice, and it lays out the rules. But in order to move forward by changing rape and sexual assault laws to be more just, there must be political will. Political will is influenced by popular support (ideological as well as financial), and so any endeavor to galvanize political will to effect legal change will be more successful if it can be sold to the public sector(s). MADD provides a model of how social movements can be mounted to bring about legal change. Women's groups, victim advocacy groups, and other grassroots movements were behind the success in changing rape laws across all jurisdictions in recent history. A coordinated campaign involving groups like these, along with politicians and the media, could generate the political and popular support that would effect the changes in the legal system that so many understand to be so direly needed.

One of the lessons about the consequences of legal change, and perhaps the most significant one, has completely escaped us. This heretofore unrecognized lesson concerns a different kind of success stemming from the use of law for reform: The law is an incredibly effective tool to organize and gel a social movement. Legislative change brings together and then focuses a concerted effort like that to combat rape. There is nothing quite like law in modern society to mobilize advocacy. Alliances develop not only within existing groups, like political parties, along an issue-specific policy, or along racial/ethnic or sexual lines but also between groups over specific issues like rape as well. We increasingly turn to law to deal with virtually all problems that come into the public arena. And the lobby groups and political action committees (PACs) that have developed around legal change have grown in size, organization, and influence, fueled by concerns over, for example, drunk driving (MADD, SADD), drugs (DARE), guns (NRA), cigarettes, and even food and air and water. We need not only to recognize this function of law but to harness and exploit it. We can capitalize on how legal change unites and centers concerns by functioning to form and empower groups and subsequent movements for change.

It is important to highlight that part of the uniting is, often times, among disparate groups, which can make for broader and stronger coalitions. As in the past case of rape reform, law and order advocates joined feminist forces, practitioners joined academicians, and men joined women in the cause of legal change. This is why the legislative reform movement was so successful in effecting alterations in statutes in every jurisdiction. More legal reform in rape can be readily achieved given the conjoining of forces and especially given the tenacious popularity of the force of the "law and order" campaigns that were influential in getting the original rape reforms passed (Berger, Neuman, and Searles 1991). This can be played up to renew the political will to change law along the lines of the model this book posits to promote greater justice in rape.

New directions carved out in law are generally based on either statute change or precedent-setting court decisions (stare decisis) like the Canadian *Ewanchuk* decision that discarded implied consent or the opposite British decision in *Morgan* that allowed unreasonable mistake of consent. Statutory and case law fashion the parameters within which new laws and procedures are implemented and enforced, yet basing new reform on statutes and court decisions alone suffers by neglecting the daily decision making that dialectically or reciprocally determines the contours of the law in actual application. This is true regardless of the source of change. Innumerable processes and decisions in the administration of justice occur out of the public eye. Lack of visibility means lack of knowledge about what goes on, and this translates into lack of accountability for criminal justice actors for the manner in which they handle cases. This is a large part of the reason that implementation practices so often deviate from the changes hoped for in reforms. There is neither awareness of nor consequence for ignoring or differentially enforcing legal changes. The wide discretion that exists in criminal justice juxtaposes with decision making that is both informal and invisible to create an environment ripe for abuse and discrimination. The abuse in this instance is ignoring the goals of rape reforms and maintaining historic discriminatory practices and victim maltreatment.

On the one hand, the discretion that permeates criminal justice allows for justice to be tailored in each individual case; on the other, it allows for discrimination on any variety of bases, such as race, class, sex, or sexual preference, as criminal justice officials choose the cases to pursue at all, those to pursue most vigorously, those to pursue most punitively, and those to ignore and drop from the system altogether. That criminal justice officials engage in discriminatory decision making and practices at all levels is widely known. In the case of rape, it means that the targets for prosecution are only so-called real rapes; it means that only pristine victims are believed; it means that only chaste, traditional women have their claims legally processed. It also means that women who have what are considered to be illegitimate (nontraditional) gender role characteristics, such as being a single mother, drinking in a bar, dating more than one man, or being poor and/or a minority group member (not to mention women who share more than one of these characteristics; consider, for example, the plight of poor, minority women who don't fit middle class feminine stereotypes) are cavalierly disbelieved and dismissed by the criminal justice system.

It should be clear by now that only a small minority of cases fit rape stereotypes, though these few are the "real" rapes that the criminal legal system handles most seriously and most publicly. In fact, only a small minority of criminal cases overall fit another stereotype as well: that of the adversarial, open, speedy, public trial by a jury of one's peers, where the accused enjoys the right to counsel, to call witnesses on "his" (*sic*) behalf, and so on. The public trial is where citizens can witness the alleged normal or typical workings of the justice system as they have come to understand them. It is these relatively rare publicly adjudicated cases that are observable and hence more reviewable, in a way that could hold officials to some standard of accountability. And from what we've seen here the formal treatment of even real rape is less than inspiring. But the vast majority of the decisions are under no such scrutiny, as the vast majority of decisions are made out of the public view. Since most cases are handled in an informal and private way, abuses, discrimination, and differential enforcement and implementation of law in a fashion contrary to objectives all must be guarded against. These concerns inform the series of recommendations that follow.

VICTIMS' RIGHTS

Accountability is important because it can govern how victims are treated after reforms are instituted. In rape and sexual assault, as in other criminal cases, victims are often left in the dark about why their cases wind up dismissed, or processed on different (lesser) charges, or accorded short(er) sentences than they had originally expected. This is hard for victims to take: it is they who were raped or sexually assaulted, but they who have little role in the disposition of their cases. Victims are, historically speaking, nothing more than witnesses for the prosecution and have been treated thus. The crimes committed are committed against the state, not the individual person who is the actual victim: consider, for instance, that case names reflect an opposition between the accused and the prosecution acting on behalf of society as the "People" or the "State" for example, *People v. Jones* or *Smith v. State*. The victim's name is nowhere in sight. This is hard for victims because it compounds the theft of control they first experienced from rape victimization, leaving them, once again, without power or influence over what happens to them or their case. They have no say in the criminal matter that they, at their own cost, with their own set of risks and losses, brought forward to the state for justice.

What is needed here is trite but true. First, victims simply must be supplied with updated details about what goes on with their cases, and they must be provided these in a timely fashion, with specifics supplied on all decisional outcomes. Victim-witness units (in court or prosecutors' offices) have been helpful in routinizing the provision of this type of information to victims in many jurisdictions, but these are not priority services and so suffer from underfunding, understaffing, and overloading. Second, victims should be consulted, at the least, for their opinion about the number or level of charges levied or pled out (see below), the place and length of imprisonment if institutional sentences are to be recommended, and so forth. I am not advocating that victims should determine case outcomes; only that they be informed and that they be heard, not that they would be heeded, necessarily, but at least they would have an advisory vote or voice in all matters pertaining to the disposition of the case where they are the ones who suffered victimization.[1]

Adler ended *Rape on Trial* by proposing several "procedural innovations" (1987: 163) exactly along the lines of the suggestions just made. She states that "these suggestions for procedural reform are not intended to be exhaustive, but rather to point to areas where with relatively little effort and without detriment to the accused, the victim's ordeal in court could be lessened to a considerable degree" (165). She concludes that there are five areas for improvement that pertain to practice (her term is "procedure"). (Although she claims that she focuses on five areas, her recommendations concern strictly court proceedings). Her call is to inform victims of trial dates, provide separate space so that victims don't have be in such close proximity to the accused and his family and friends during proceedings, maintain victim anonymity (name and address, if not already known to the defendant), allow the victim the right to give her evidence in privacy, and allow the victim to draw support from family and friends while in court (163–165).

All states have by now passed victims' rights legislation that is supposed to guarantee rights of this nature. And, although the move to make victims' rights a constitutional amendment at the federal level was unsuccessful, thirty-one states have constitutional amendments on victims' bills of rights (National Center for Victims of Crime 2004a; Kilpatrick, Beatty, and Smith Howley 1998: 1). The specific rights vary but generally include the right to notification of proceedings, the right to be present at hearings, the right to be heard, for example, to make a victim impact statement about the criminal victimization—and the right to restitution. The effectiveness of these rights is questionable. Often they are not respected or exercised or are of merely symbolic value, making victims feel as though they have a say when their statements or presences actually influence very little (Kilpatrick, Beatty, and Smith Howley 1998; Miller and Meloy forthcoming). Here we see another—and prime—example of how implementation practices can annul instead of meet the goals of legislation. Walsh (1986) discusses this "placebo justice," whereby victims are placated with rights that are surface level only or not terribly meaningful (sugar pills).

I discuss victims' rights in light of criminal justice practices or procedural improvements à la Adler (1987) but—more important in the context of this section—as a concern about oversight of implementation practices. This is because victims' rights legislation provides something new: a concrete model of one way that implementation practices can be monitored. We can see this in the legislation introduced in Congress in April 2004 to exact compliance with victims' rights laws.

The legislation provided "procedures to promote compliance" with victims' rights, such as notice of proceedings and the right to be present at proceedings, to be heard at proceedings, and to confer with the state's attorney (S. 2329, 2004, *Scott Campbell, Stephanie Rope, Wendy Preston, Louarna Guillis, and Nila Lynn Crime Victims' Rights Act*, chap. 237, "Crime Victims' Rights," sec. 3771[a][2][3][4][5]). The legislation called for the attorney general to develop "regulations to enforce the rights of crime victims and to ensure compliance by responsible officials with the obligations described in law respecting crime victims" ([f][1]), as well as "a course of training for employees and offices" ([f][2][B]), the investigation of complaints by Department of Justice personnel, and "disciplinary sanctions, including suspension or termination from employment, for employees of the Department of Justice who willfully or wantonly fail to comply with provisions of Federal law pertaining to the treatment of crime victims" ([f][2][C]). It is novel, and high time, to write laws to enforce laws like this. Without overseeing how laws are implemented, anything can happen, including nothing at all, for example, victims remaining ignorant about their rights or when or how to express them. There have been few reviews of or consequences for how laws are implemented by criminal justice officials, and this is especially pronounced vis-à-vis the informal decision-making processes that determine implementation practices. Providing sanctions for compliance can go a long way toward ensuring that the laws in practice look a little more like the laws that are written or changed on the books.

The Clery Act (or the Jeanne Clery Disclosure of Campus Security Policy and Campus Crime Statistics Act) provides another example of a way to generate accountability in the handling of reforms. This federal-level act, originally known as the Crime Awareness and Campus Security Act of 1990, requires institutions of higher education to report rape to the government. Colleges and universities must report campus security policies, prevention programs, procedures, and statistics on reported rape on and around campuses. The act was amended in 1992 to afford rape victims rights and again in 2000 to require notification about where Megan's law information (sex offender registration lists) is available to students (Carter 2000: 1). Failure to comply with the Clery Act can result in fines (up to $25,000 per violation; see Epstein 2001: 6) or denial of U.S. Department of Education student financial aid. This holds true for any institution receiving such funds and so applies to both public and private colleges and universities. Sanctions may not guarantee compliance, but compliance in the absence of sanctions is certainly much less likely.

Harvard University's sexual assault policy of 2002 is shocking and warrants highlighting in relation to the Clery Act. This regressive policy is characteristic of backlash, as mentioned earlier, but, more to the point here, it shows precisely how and why it is so critical to oversee implementation practices. Recall that Harvard's new rape and sexual assault rules require corroborating evidence of a rape complaint before investigation and adjudication can take place. After being assailed for the promulgation of the new policy, the administration responded. "In mid-December 2002 [it] posted a new page to its website characterizing the 'sufficient independent corroboration' rule as a requirement of 'supporting information' that would 'corroborate' the student. Harvard wrote that such information might include an email sent by the victim to a friend, or a 'prompt' report of the incident to a university official or student" (www.securityoncampus.org/lawyers/murphy_titleix.html). While the response may placate some by appearing to accept low-level or easily obtained evidence as corroboration, it should be seen for what is really is: a return to a corroboration requirement and the necessity of a prompt complaint in university policy, when the criminal law has seen fit to repeal such requirements. This is simply outrageous. And it is certainly one way to diminish the numbers of students who report sexual assault and hence the number of rapes and sexual assaults that must be reported in accordance with the Clery Act. Obstacles like this cause less reporting, which, of course, makes the university look good. The university appears to be safer than it might actually be, and this attracts more students and more contributions from alumni. This is precisely why oversight of law, policy, and implementation must be mandatory if real change is to occur.

POLICE AND PROSECUTORS

The refusal to investigate a rape complaint, with or without eyewitnesses, other corroborative evidence, prompt report, and so on, is problematic beyond college campuses. Police attitudes, like the persistent belief, despite reforms, in myths about false accusations, victim precipitation, and the like (Campbell and Johnson 1997), lead to high rates of unfounding complaints and the failure to pursue arrest warrants.[2] Police are reluctant to go after rape suspects, even without new policies like Harvard's. The decisions to unfound cases, to investigate complaints, and to pursue arrests have low visibility. This is why practices need to be watched, reviewed, and made public: to make police accountable to the citizenry. Supervisors—sergeants, lieutenants, or those higher up in the ranks—or crime statistics divisions within a police department could be made responsible for keeping summaries of the number and type of rape/sexual assault complaints (acquaintance vs. stranger, aggravated vs. simple, etc.), the percentage unfounded, the manner of investigation, whether an arrest warrant was sought, and what level (of charges or counts) was authorized. This information could be made available to the public on a regular basis through local newspaper or television news summaries, public meetings held as a part of community policing sessions, published on a Website, or posted in the police department or courthouse, where citizens could go and read the reports. Prosecutors should similarly be held accountable by being required, for example, to record, tally, and post the warrant requests from police, the charges issued, and reasons for any changes in the number and level of counts or for outright denials (see next section). Oversight is vital, since the accused, the victim, and the public are not aware of or involved in the arrest decision; the Sixth Amendment right to "confront accusers" does not obtain when prosecutors decide which cases to take on or which targets the prosecution/state will pursue in the "interests of justice" when they authorize, alter, or deny police arrest warrants. Should there be any doubt as to public interest about these data on police decisions, just think about the popularity of reality TV shows such as *COPS, America's Most Wanted*, the programming on the Court TV channel, and the variety of television crime dramas. The visibility engendered by posting such statistics would breed at least some accountability.

PLEA BARGAINING

There are several other ways that the fairness and efficacy of legal reforms in action could be enhanced. Plea bargaining constitutes perhaps the most tremendous issue in terms of discretion, implementation, visibility, and accountability. The vast majority of cases in the criminal justice system are disposed via negotiation. Very few criminal cases make their way through the formal adjudication processes that attend trials. The estimates are commonly that upward of 90–95 percent of the criminal caseload is handled with plea bargaining.[3] This rather informal practice takes place typically among a prosecutor and a defense attorney, the defendant, and often a judge (although at the federal level "the court may not participate in these discussions" under the Federal Rules of Criminal Procedure for Federal Courts, rule 11[b][N][3][c][1]; see editorial staff of Lexis-Nexis 2003: 858–859). The defendant has a guilty plea to barter with; the prosecution generally has the number and level of charges/counts and/or a sentence recommendation with which to barter (depending on state legislation that can restrict sentence bargaining, for example, determinate sentencing or mandatory minimums). A plea bargain, or deal, occurs when a defendant offers to enter a plea of guilt (or nolo contendere) in exchange for some promised leniency if the defendant does not exercise the right to trial (by a jury of "his" peers, to confront "his" accusers, etc.). Because this process is neither formal nor public, abuse is not only possible; it runs wild. Package deals are made, decisions are reached arbitrarily in the matter of a few seconds, discrimination on the basis of class, race, ethnicity, (traditional) sex roles, and sex preferences is pervasive, and much, much more. Because of the multitude of such problems, plea bargaining absolutely needs to be made more visible and transformed into a more public and/or formal process.

This practice needs to be rooted out and put in front of the citizenry, which generally has no awareness that this is how the bulk of the routine work of criminal justice is executed in this country. Making the practice public is the first step toward accountability concerning the disposition of the criminal caseload. It should be mandatory to record in case files the charges that are altered and the sentences that are recommended, along with the reasons for the leniency/ plea deal. The reasons could at a minimum consist of a checklist (for the sake of economy of time and personnel) of common factors associated with pleas, for example, problems in the chain of evidence, no witnesses, victim recalcitrance, weapon not found, no rape kit/hospital exam, victim credibility problems. Just as court data are public record, plea deals should be public record.

Another dimension of plea bargaining and public record concerns victims. Victims have varying rights in plea bargaining across the states. These range from being informed of the plea deal to being consulted about plea arrangements. The meaning of "consulting" or "conferring" with prosecutors is ambiguous, how- ever (Office for Victims of Crime 2002: 2–3). Given the recognized importance of victim input (most states allow victims at least to express their views in plea agreements), records should be kept—and made public—as to victims' views of, or at least their objections to, negotiated deals. This would put a modicum of weight behind victims' words.

Perhaps summaries of plea negotiations, for example, monthly counts, could be posted outside courtrooms (where schedules of cases are often posted) or made available to newspapers and news reporters. Profiles of decision mak- ing (including victim recommendations regarding decisions and outcomes) in plea bargaining (as in police investigation and police/prosecutor arrest activi- ties) could serve the purpose of accountability and, what is more, help flesh out the reputation of prosecutor's offices, of defense attorneys/firms, and of judges sitting on the bench. This latter dimension could be useful in reelection cam- paigns or political appointments of chief prosecutors, bids for public defender contracts, and/or appointments/elections of judges. The public, not to mention victims, victim advocates, defendants and defenders, and other such parties, would likely have considerable interest in such profiles, as would those active in local politics and elections.

It is interesting to comment on plea bargaining in light of the issue of pub- licity. It is not the plea-bargained cases that grow into the sensationalized, high- profile cases with which the nation becomes intimately familiar. It is the New Bedford pool table gang rape, New York Central Park jogger, and Kobe Bryant cases that go through (or begin to go through) full trial processes that garner media and national attention. There are rarely widely known cases of routine "street" or conventional crime and criminality. This points up the invisibility and lack of accountability pertaining to plea-bargained cases. It is also empha- sizes how plea bargaining is an area in criminal justice that cannot be used, as jury instructions or alterations of substantive law can be used, to educate the public or criminal justice officials themselves as they do the work of justice, because it is so little known, so low visibility, so unwatched, and so unchecked. Bringing the invisible and informal processes and decisions out in public would provide criminal justice personnel within and across agencies and jurisdictions, as well as crime victims, offenders, and the public at large, a great deal of information about how justice is actually done, regardless of law, crime category, or reform legislation.

Making plea bargaining less informal and officials more accountable could also be accomplished by means of standardized procedures or guidelines, oversight like appellate review, and sanctions. These could work just as they do in other formal public proceedings (like trials). This is not to say that plea bargaining has to be turned into a costly, drawn-out, or lengthy process; indeed, resource allocation is an overwhelmingly serious issue given the percentage of cases affected. It is merely to say that there should be guidelines and oversight to provide another doable step toward curbing abuses and injustice.

The model I've laid out offers a critical bonus vis-à-vis plea bargaining. The substantive and procedural changes in law should change the plea-bargaining possibilities, such that the state's hand would no longer be so disadvantaged. In other words, the model changes should enhance (a victim's and) a prosecutor's leverage in plea negotiations in all rape/sexual assault offense categories. This is because the protections in law and procedure for those accused of rape would be diminished and the playing field leveled at least to a degree by the institution of de jure laws that would define presumptive nonagreement, a shift in burdens, and so on. Given the model specifications, a prosecutor's hand would be strengthened if a case were to go to trial, which should give the defense added incentive to want to plead it out. If the defense planned to argue consent or mistake, it would be more onerous to go to trial because of the shift in the burdens of production and proof, affirmative consent definitions and requirements, and preponderance of evidence standards. A stronger position for the prosecution at the outset means that reductions in charges and in recommended sentences would diminish (in numbers and in levels), making rapes—real and simple— more likely to result in conviction and more likely to sustain more realistic conviction charges and sentences, that is, higher-level charges and charges disposed as rape/sexual assault versus reductions to lower-level and/or non–rape/sexual assault crimes. And, if reforms were being implemented with integrity, that is, if acquaintance, nonaggravated rapes were yielding convictions and sentences comparable to other similar crimes (in terms of severity or compared to violence or assault), the public (and criminal justice officials) would be educated about what the law sees as crime—a redefinition—and about what types of injury the state sanctions under power of the law.

It is important to expound on a related dimension of practice that constitutes a further potential advantage of the scheme I am proposing. The overall model array delineated in chapter 13, as well as the way plea bargaining would actually operate within the changes this model array would institute, would provide more "truth in criminal labeling" (Loh 1981) in terms of the offenses for which offenders would be convicted and sentenced. The benefit is that the new and lesser sexual assault offenses, such as sexual assault under duress or sexual assault under fraud, would allow prosecutors to reduce the severity of charges in plea deals but still sustain convictions on crimes called sexual assault. As it stands now, without the duress and fraud sexual assault crime possibilities, bargained reductions to low-level charges in many jurisdictions wind up with convictions on nonsexual assault crimes. What is more, there is little latitude for negotiating in lower-level cases in general and in weaker cases where there is less evidence in particular, making conviction, not to mention conviction on sexual assault charges, more problematic. The more accurate designation of sexual assault crimes is important for assessments of recidivism, punishment, treatment, and protection (e.g., community notification).[4] This is a significant potential benefit, given that 90 percent or more of criminal cases are plea-bargained. The ability of judges and juries to find defendants guilty of lesser sexual assault charges in the minority of cases that go to trial would also be enhanced. For example, if fact finders think that there is insufficient evidence, or reasonable doubt, as to the physical force or coercion in a case, they could be satisfied that duress, or improper pressure, was in evidence and thus find guilt on a lesser sexual assault charge.[5]

JURORS

Reforms in rape law succeeded in changing some, although not nearly all, people's perspectives about the crime, the victims, the myths, the legal system, and the treatment of rape. Reforms need to continue to address educational issues (see below), but they must also be augmented with an allied objective that has not been contemplated seriously in the past: the goal of educating the specific jurors who sit in judgment on individual cases.[6] This is, after all, one of the most significant ways that attitudes about rape matter, since they translate into behaviors that so directly affect victim and case treatment. They also matter as they translate into altered or engrained attitudes post-trial, which in turn come to form part of public or cultural attitudes about rape and the treatment of its victims.

The host of juror instructions laid out in the model array in chapters 13 and 14 attack rape myths and stereotypes by educating jurors about the facts, in place of the fictions, about rape. The instructions are devised to eradicate detrimental views that make jurors scrutinize the behavior of the victim in place of focusing on the offender and his behaviors. They provide knowledge relevant to the facts of a particular case, at the time when this knowledge matters most, that is, during contemplations about guilt and sanctioning. This is critical since jurors have no training or background on rape, or the dynamics of rape, or rape law, or rape reform. As Goldberg-Ambrose concludes, "there are many obstacles to measuring and achieving rape reform, the most notable being the need to eliminate juror misconceptions about rape and its victims" (1992: 173).

Revamping jury instructions will also help retrain judges, who will have training on the legal reforms in general and on juror instruction in particular, since it is the bench that has to give the jurors the instructions (see below). Further, the training on legal reform will cause judges to revise their decision making in bench trials, where they will be guided by the same principles they would have read to a jury.

As a part of making fact finders accountable for the decisions they render and to make reforms more effective, we might consider having judges poll jurors or ask jury panels to formulate a statement about the rationale for arriving at the decision they report to the court. If jurors knew they would have to explain to the court the reason(s) they arrived at their verdict, they might be more careful to follow the instructions they receive. This is not to say that they could not fabricate reasons or hide the discriminatory premises on which they based their decisions; for example, they might not tell the court that they acquitted because they took consent as implicit because of past sex or promiscuity. Requiring an explanation, however, increases the likelihood that jurors will heed jury instructions and hence the likelihood that implementation will match reform objectives. We might also glean information about the impact of legal caveats, for example, whether the juror instructions that dating and drinking with the defendant are irrelevant to the determination of guilt had any effect on jurors' deliberations.

Bryden and Lengnick say that "it is critical, therefore, to understand jurors'—which is to say the public's—attitudes towards rape" (1997: 1255). Lawyers regularly use consultant groups that do research and/or focus groups that make mock trial decisions to help them read and pick jurors in different crime scenarios. They set up shadow juries to predict what tactics will work best during the course of a trial. They seek feedback from people who have served on juries. They turn to the myriad books that have been written on the subject. And so forth. All these sources of information could be mined to assess what form of jury instruction, or other method, might best assist the effort to eradicate the myths about rape stemming from perceptions about the unique roles of, for example, consent, acquaintanceship, partying, resistance, and so on.

The research on jury instructions suggests that clarity is important if instructions are to be followed (Kadish and Schulhofer 2001: 34). Jurors will be leery of using what they have a hard time understanding. This means that instructions should as far as possible avoid legal jargon and technical vocabulary (both of which abound). Instructions should be kept plain, written simply and comprehensibly. They should probably also be repeated at several points and written up as reference points for jurors to take into their deliberations

JUDGES

For purposes of visibility and accountability, judges in bench (rather than jury) trials, like police in arresting, prosecutors in charging and plea bargaining, and jurors in jury trials, should have to specify and make public their reasons for verdicts.[7] Although almost all states have instituted some form of determinate (a set amount of time to be served for given crimes) and/or mandatory (a minimum time to be served for given crimes/offenders) sentencing laws, judges still have some discretion. For example, they still have the latitude to increase or decrease sentence possibilities by aggravating or mitigating circumstances (presumptive sentencing) and to hand out indeterminate (specifying a range of time to serve) sentences under many laws. The public should therefore be entitled to know how/why judges exercise the discretion they do in sentencing decisions.[8]

CRIMINAL JUSTICE TRAINING

Because all criminal justice decision makers must know the laws and will have a decisive impact on whether improvements in case and victim treatment will be realized, training seminars, in-service sessions, and the like are another must. The need to educate officials is vast. Officials hold the greatest power to determine the ultimate effects of rape reforms. They also hold roles of influence and leadership with jurors and the citizenry. The training mandated needs to encompass education about such dimensions as the objectives inspiring legal changes, in addition to the legal changes themselves: both de jure changes in substantive law (e.g., force/coercion *or* involuntariness, nonagreement) and procedural changes in the rules of evidence about incompetent, immaterial, and irrelevant evidence (such as past sexual history, drinking, and dancing), as well as the sequence of juror instructions and changes in the voluntariness, agreement: "she's a liar" and reasonable mistake: "I'm a blunderer" defenses. Education will also need to cover the dynamics and myths about rape offenders and victims, investigation and evidence collection techniques, and interviewing strategies and sensitivity to victim needs and rights, as well as any new compliance measures, reports, and reviews (elaborated below) for use and dissemination by the agencies of criminal justice, as well as the public.

COMPLIANCE

The recommendation to require public reporting on the decisions made under new reforms in order to monitor implementation practices and promote accountability might most productively entail federal legislation. This could be modeled after other federal law requiring public reporting, like the Congressional Victims' Rights Compliance Act (2004), discussed earlier, or the Clery Act (1990), the Violence Against Women Act (I passed in 1994, II passed in 2000), and the Violent Crime Control and Law Enforcement Act (1994). All these federal laws could serve as exemplars for the states (just as the Model Penal Code or Federal Rules of Criminal Procedure or Federal Rules of Evidence were federal models for this book's model of de jure rape statute reforms). Model guidelines for monitoring reform practices across the various criminal justice agencies (through publicizing case characteristics, decisions, and outcomes of cases) could be developed (to go hand in hand with the model reform described throughout this book). The federal attorney general's office could be used as the conduit to guide the states in drafting their own compliance laws corollary to new rape reform statutes inspired by the federal model.

The sorts of requirements inherent in the Victims' Rights Compliance Act that calls for "regulations to enforce" new victim's rights could guide the development of procedures to ensure implementation true to reform objectives. Such a model could also inform the development of a federal template or model law on compliance (to go along with the federal model rape reforms laid out in this book). This in turn would guide state efforts in developing compliance laws that would mirror the federal compliance model yet tailor it to accommodate state-by-state variations and conditions.

To clarify, a federal model (guided by the Crime Victims' Rights Compliance Act)[9] would call for states to develop "regulations to enforce" compliance with reform law stipulations that are supposed to remove discriminatory requirements in practice, make irrelevant evidence inadmissible, provide for the more vigorous pursuit of simple rapes, and so forth. Training guidelines and procedures for the investigation and sanctioning of noncompliance could similarly be developed as a part of a federal exemplar for the states to follow.

I have already touched on the issue of training and education programs on features of rape reform law and case processing and on the dynamics of rape for criminal justice agents who enforce reforms. The Equal Justice for Women in the Courts Act in the Violent Crime Control and Law Enforcement Act of 1994 could be used as a model in this specific type of effort. This authorizes grants for the "purpose of developing, testing, presenting, and disseminating model programs to be used by states ... in training judges and court personnel in the laws of the States ... on rape, sexual assault, domestic violence" (title IV, subtitle D, chap. 1, sec. 40411, 108 Stat. 1942, October 28, 2000, PL 106-386, Div. B, title IV, sec. 1406 @ [2][d][1], 114 Stat. 1516, 1517). The training topics embedded in this subsection are broad, covering, for example, the nature of rape, the reasons for underreporting, "sex stereotyping," and "application of rape shield laws" (sec. 13992, "Training provided by grants" subtitle [42 USCS, secs. 13991 et seq.]) These are precisely the kinds of training and funding possibilities I am proposing here (see "Funding," below).

Sanctioning mechanisms could be positive as well as negative. For example, awards like the Women's Safety award given to model initiatives could be instituted, with publicity and stipends attached. Sanctions could also include such things as condemnation; unfavorable or unpopular assignments on specialized squads, units, and teams; promotion/demotion; financial (dis)incentives; and/or suspension or termination of employment. Consequences must attend assessment if accountability is to be achieved.

Process

A state model law on compliance or enforcement of regulations would steer municipalities to gather and report data on rape and sexual assault complaints, investigations, warrants sought and authorized, charges authorized versus charges adjudicated/pled out, the reasons for alterations in arrest warrant and plea-bargained charges, the percentage of convictions versus dismissals/acquittals, respectively, judges' and juries' reasons for these decisions, the sentences for the various types of rape and sexual assault cases, and the reasons for these sentences. By "types of cases," I refer to acquaintance, date, marital, and stranger rapes and also conditions such as aggravating circumstances, type of force, coercion, and duress and/or fraud involved. Data should also indicate whether the "liar" defense (consent and false accusation) or the "blunderer" defense (mistake of consent/implied consent) were attempted/successful, whether an attempt was made to introduce evidence of past sexual activity (and the nature of the evidence and ruling herein), and so forth for those cases that go far enough in the system for these dimensions to be pertinent. Where and how all this information was made publicly available in each jurisdiction should also be reported. Victims who had used the justice system might also be surveyed for their opinions about the law and treatment by the various branches of criminal justice. This population's experiences and recommendations could be incredibly constructive in assessing the impact of reforms.

The logical place from which to promulgate statewide regulations to enforce compliance under new rape reform measures would be the state-level attorney generals' offices (as opposed to the office of the federal attorney general, which would provide the federal example or prototype law for compliance to guide the state attorney generals' development of compliance law). The state attorney general's office could also serve as the clearinghouse for collection of the state-mandated data; that is, local agencies could send their data to the state attorney general. Alternatively, it would be quite feasible to use some other court administrative or legislative office for this purpose. Regardless of which agency serves as the clearinghouse, it would collate the information and send it on to the Bureau of Justice Statistics (BJS) in the Department of Justice for compilation and analysis, much as the states send crime data to the FBI for compilation and analysis for the *Uniform Crime Reports* every year.[10] The BJS would then construct state-level profiles from the locally based data in annual reports and make an implementation assessment that would be widely available. This is akin to what the BJS does with the volumes of other crime, victimization, criminal justice agency, and legal policy statistics. The advantage of having states send their statistics on rape case handling to a federal agency is that there would be greater consistency in statistical compilation techniques and output profiles, a broader database, wider availability, and wider dissemination possibilities for the information gathered. State-by-state comparisons could also be conducted to learn from the varying experiences with varying reforms both on the books and in practice in the different state jurisdictions.

Patterns of Action: Sanctions

Collecting data on implementation would permit examination of de jure changes in light of de facto practices, which would in turn offer insights about further reform and compliance measures to local, state, and federal agencies. Tracking records of decisions and case outcomes by agencies, and even by individuals within offices, would also serve accountability because it would feed into (re)elections and (re)appointments, as well as identify individual and/or agency patterns of decision making. Police departments or officers, prosecutor and defense offices or attorneys, and court systems and judges could be identified for their positive (e.g., arrests, authorizations at high levels, conviction rates) or negative (e.g., unfounding charges, plea bargaining down to misdemeanors, directed verdicts, mangled jury instructions, dismissals) actions in rape and sexual assault cases. Those higher up in the chain of command would more readily be able to include the patterns of decisions made by their officers/officials in performance reviews. Patterns would further show whether/how each objective and dimension of change had been met, for example, whether simple rapes continued to be discarded, whether sexual assaults under duress or fraud were being prosecuted or officials were only going forward with so-called real rape cases, which, again, are the minority. In addition, system actors' actions under rape reform laws will influence public support or critique, which in turn can impinge on funding contingencies for agencies, projects, facilities, and staff. The capacity to keep tabs on those actions is thus of vital importance for future funding.

Another form of sanction would involve the media, which could be used to honor or castigate individuals and/or agencies for practices or patterns of action. This could work to enhance performance, improve funding contingencies, and collect data for new rounds of policy reform recommendations grounded in the daily practices involved in handling rape and sexual assault cases.

Organizational Concerns: Using External Groups

The need to use resources and prioritize cases efficiently is especially pronounced in strained fiscal times. This can detract from attention to victims and their needs. Yancey Martin and Powell find that even "well-meaning staff in legal organizations are oriented to routinely treat victims unresponsively ... concerned with, for example, public approval, the avoidance of losing, and expediency" (1995: 853). They conclude that officials are in a good position to foster "positive changes in their organizations and communities, but those who do to [sic] want to change may have to pressured by external groups" (889). (The external groups they discuss are feminists and rape crisis workers.) They go on that "if these pressures are pervasive and unrelenting legal officials may decide giving in is easier than resisting" (890). The selling point they note is that "responsive processing can expedite organizational effectiveness and community cohesion. When staff treats victims responsibly, they waste less time and energy and they precipitate, and experience, less emotional distress. Prosecutors who file aggressively, establish specialized units, and produce high conviction rates can impress voters and show the police they value their work. Police officials view rape cases as less burdensome and work harder at their investigations when prosecutors file charges on more of their cases" (ibid.). These insights indicate how external groups can easily be used to pressure officials to implement the goals behind the reforms defined in the model array laid out in this book. (The publicized patterns of action just touched on would facilitate this subsequent effort.)

A multitude of other external groups could easily be brought in to raise the visibility of appointed and elected officials meting out justice in sexual assault cases. Citizen advocacy groups, neighborhood watch groups, city commissions, crime commissions, task forces, and even civilian review boards for law enforcement, for instance, all could promote publicity and accountability for local criminal justice system agencies and officials. Another route that could most productively be explored would be to tie in with the ever-increasingly popular community policing movement. Citizen involvement in criminal justice has proven amazingly effective, and given that community policing is already set up in so many jurisdictions, it would be the perfect route by which citizens could get involved in redressing rape and sexual assault. Citizens could observe and publicize how rape cases are handled in different locales, disseminating the data and statistics discussed in these sections and hence helping to hold police, lawyers, and judges accountable for the practices that hurt or help rape victims.

Funding

Funding needs to be allocated for collecting and disseminating the information on implementation practices. This could minimally be part of the Violence Against Women Act appropriations in STOP (Services, Training, Officers, Prosecutors) grants designed to provide training, enhance victim treatment, establish specialized units, and so on. These specific monies come under the general provision in the VAWA to provide "grants to combat violent crimes against women." There are also rape prevention and education monies earmarked (through the Department of Health and Human Services) for education and training for judges and court personnel through State Justice Institute grants, as well as other sources, for which VAWA II reauthorized money.

The problem here is that the veritable lion's share of VAWA monies have gone to domestic as opposed to sexual violence agencies and efforts; sexual assault has received only 7 percent of the monies under the VAWA (Miller and Meloy forth-coming: 266). This type of mandate and resource allocation for rape and sexual assault needs to be seriously increased. The underfunding of sexual assault was recognized in the VAWA II Reauthorization Act of 2000, which doubled pre-vention and education grant monies for rape (National Center for Victims of Crime 2004a). Yet the amount of money remains almost token in comparison to domestic assault allocations, let alone other federal expenditures.

The Equal Justice for Women in the Courts Act of the Violent Crime Control and Law Enforcement Act (1994), mentioned in the context of training, educa-tion, and model programs, is another perfectly suitable source of grant monies. It should be mined and augmented to develop national, state, and local assess-ment of the implementation of a new wave of rape reforms, like those advanced here, once they are enacted. And it would behoove the Department of Justice in obvious ways to allocate resources for such a purpose.

Sexual assault programs can supply advocacy for legal change and the as-sessment of it in practice, as they can and have served as watchdogs over the ad-ministration of justice at the local level so often in the past. But their diminished funding in these difficult fiscal times when social services are all so hard hit and the immense need their services deplete workers, who are largely volunteer to begin with. This resource thus needs most to be buoyed up by additional sources of funding. Because of the high need yet low resource allocation, funding for sexual assault programs needs to prioritized, at least to catch up with the fund-ing of domestic violence services and agencies (Burt et al. 2001: vii–xvii). The government would do well to step up the VAWA in this regard.

EQUAL PROTECTION?

Discretion allows differential case treatment that is not in the interests of fairness and justice for all. That rape cases are treated differently, and discriminatorily, in comparison to other criminal cases cannot be doubted and needs to be more widely understood. In addition to prejudicial requirements, standards, attitudes, and practices stands the tremendous attrition rates in rape. Attrition is so high that this deserves to be underscored yet again. The Senate Judiciary Committee reported that "98% of rape victims never see their attacker caught, tried, and imprisoned. Over half of all rape prosecutions are either dismissed before trial or result in acquittal. A rape prosecution is more than twice as likely as a murder to be dismissed and 30% more likely to be dismissed than a robbery. Forty-eight percent of cases are dismissed before trial" (Hunter, Burns-Smith, and Walsh

2000). Levine reports a striking comparison from some earlier research showing that "only two types of federal prosecutions resulted in lower conviction rates" than rape: "alleged violations of migratory bird statutes and antitrust laws. Only 38% of defendants in rape cases were convicted in contrast to an overall federal jury conviction rate of 70 percent during that same period" (1992: 110). Bryden and Lengnick (1997)report that "such figures have led advocates and scholars to conclude that the criminal justice system discriminates against rape victims" in a fashion that has been called "institutionalized sexism.... The Senate Judiciary Committee warned that low rates of reporting and processing of rape 'provide dramatic testimony of the power of our stereotypes of crime—how these stereotypes distort our understanding of violence against women and deprive individuals of the equal protection of our laws'" (1997: 1211, citing Staff of Senate Committee on the Judiciary 1993: 13)

Given that the Fourteenth Amendment guarantees equal protection under the law, can we accept such facts as representing equal protection of rape victims? Sex is not a "'suspect classification' requiring 'strict scrutiny and a compelling state interest'" (Kristine Mullendore, personal communication, 2004) in law, and so women are not a protected category like race or alienage.[11] This may be a part of understanding the status quo of structural inequality where women are not protected by law that supposedly protects against inequality and thus as a sex remain unequal to men. In parallel fashion, women who are victimized by rape are not afforded the same protections in treatment by the criminal justice system as other crime victims. This asymmetrical treatment should be conceptualized as unequal protection under the law, even though women are not specified as a protected category. Publicizing this would help stimulate support for renewing legal reform against rape victimization. Miller and Meloy indicate that "some federal legislation includes gender as a category needing protection," but this is only in relation to hate crime legislation, which is "narrow in application" (forthcoming: 249). Rape victims deserve support and protection, too. The restricted access to the criminal justice system should be seen as a form of unequal access and unequal protection dictating remedial action.

That rape is the most notoriously underreported offense in the country (Federal Bureau of Investigation 1975: 15), with reporting rates commonly put at about 5 percent (Brownmiller 1975; Curtis 1976; Koss, Gidycz, and Wisniewski 1987), speaks to the effect of the discriminatory double victimization wherein many victims say that the criminal processing experience is worse than the rape itself. This phenomenon is itself criminal. It can also be understood as restricted instead of equal access to the criminal justice system, as the majority of victims do not use the criminal legal system because to do so means to be traumatized anew. And if the double victimization of rape victims reflects one kind of inequality, another is found in how double victimization uniquely obstructs rape victims from the realistic availability of the criminal legal system for redress.[12]

A VICTIM'S ATTORNEY: LESSONS FROM ABROAD

The legal systems' handling of rape is unique enough to justify providing the victim with her own attorney, as some other countries clearly recognize. To recapitulate, rape is unique in putting the victim on trial and in the abysmal attrition, even for the few cases (5 percent) that do get reported. According to Temkin, rape is a unique crime because of the centrality of the issue of consent and because the victim is often the only witness for the prosecution (2002: 281–283). According to Bryden and Lengnick, it is unique because of proof problems and because the lack of corroborative evidence makes it necessary to prove the victim is not lying (1997: 1377). For these and many more reasons, rape victims suffer uniquely. And, as elucidated above, we can view rape victims as having unequal or restricted access to the legal system because of this uniqueness. Because of these dimensions, rape victims should be afforded legal services beyond the prosecutor's office, which needs and treats them merely as witnesses for the state. Victim-witness units have cropped up across the country to facilitate meeting victims' needs, but these are not yet sufficient in scope, resources, and so on to accommodate crime victims in general, let alone rape victims, who experience such prejudicial trauma and burden throughout the legal process. Because rape has been treated so differently from other crimes throughout history and across continents, there is a need for some approximate guarantee to guard the interests of victims, as there has been (at least in an approximate sense) a guarantee to guard the interests of defendants. Provision of counsel has been a pivotal route in many countries, the United States among them, to provide fundamental fairness and protection of law to defendants in order to guard their interests and the interests of justice. Victims deserve no less.

Denmark provides the example of a system providing rape victims with their own attorney. It is useful to examine how this came about, especially for what we can learn for institutionalizing changes like those discussed throughout this book. As Temkin describes, the seeds for Denmark's victim's attorney system were sown by a female lawyer who petitioned the court to be able to represent a victim, whereupon the court instructed her to find an existing law that allowed for this practice. She did, but it specified that victims could enjoy representation only in civil compensation-for-damage cases. Representing the victim in court, although tied to compensation claims, allowed a lawyer to depict the trauma or psychological, in addition to economic, damage a victim had suffered. Having found this precedent, the volunteering attorney was allowed to represent rape victims in this and several further cases. This garnered wide attention and eventual support by the Ministry of Justice and Parliament. What ultimately resulted is that the law now allows the court to appoint the victim an attorney to "explain to the victim the nature of the proceedings, to prepare her for the case, and to assist her in the police station and in court," as well as to inform and help provide "continuity of assistance," for example, counseling and medical assistance, from the community at large (2002: 283). The victim's attorney can further help the victim give her account in court. The victim's attorney does not, however, have the right to do anything in relationship to the determination of guilt, cannot object to questioning, and cannot question the defendant or witnesses (283–284).

A victim's right to a lawyer exists—in limited ways—in several other countries. The Republic of Ireland provides an interesting example of the right of a victim to counsel, as well as a limitation on it. There, the victim's right to an attorney applies only to the proceedings when the accused files an "application to introduce evidence" of past sex (303). In Scotland, representation is afforded during cross-examination (295). Temkin also notes that France and Germany permit victims of rape a more "active role" by allowing for representation of victims (ibid.). (As with other reforms, law on the book differs from law in action. Rape victims do not always get an attorney in practice, despite the legal provisions for an attorney [Temkin 2002]. Again, we see why monitoring reforms is so crucial). The United States needs to develop legal assistance for victims of rape, as other countries have done. The need and justification are more than clear.

Laws and policies already in place can be drawn upon to set up a system for victim representation. The Violence Against Women Act has a provision that could be extended beyond its present scope to meet the need of rape victims for their own legal representative. The provision is to "enable the Attorney General to award grants to increase the availability of legal assistance necessary to provide effective aid to victims of domestic violence, stalking, or sexual assault who are seeking relief in legal matters arising as a consequence of that abuse of violence, at minimal or no cost to the victims" (2000, sec. 1201[a]), where "legal assistance includes … immigration, administrative agency, or housing matters, protection or stay away order proceedings, and other similar matters" (2000, sec. 2001[2]). The extension would be to have resources for lawyers to work with victims to reduce the trauma of their ordeal by helping them anticipate, prepare, and cope with the processes and practices involved in pursuing their case and seeing it through to a successful conclusion. Victims need their own representative who has their interests at heart, not the organizational concerns, demands, and constraints of the criminal legal system. As in the European instances, a victim's attorney would not be active in any fact finding, determination of guilt, and the like. This would upset the laws, procedures, protections, balance, and so on in the legal system. The recommendation is simply for a representative to assist the victim through the legal ordeal so as to render it less traumatic and to help her be more effective as a witness for the prosecution. Finally, it is worth highlighting yet again that what is already in existence can be employed for implementation that meets the reform interests of promoting justice after rape.

Moving Forward | **SEVENTEEN**

Social Institutions, Structures, and Processes

Key social institutions can be drawn into the effort to renew reforms to address the issues revolving around rape victimization. The two most significant are the media and the educational system, given the powerful role they play in acculturation and socialization. They shape definitions about what is and is not considered rape, where blame should be sought and placed, and how we—as a society of laws and rules—should respond, treat, and govern citizens when they harm us through crimes like rape and sexual assault.

MEDIA

The media pulls overwhelming weight with the public when it comes to common understanding about crime. Print, audio, visual, and Web media—fiction, news, movies, and so on—all create profiles of crimes, victims, and offenders. And the media single out some crimes, victims, and offenders to such an extent that they become more familiar to us than our own neighbors. Unfortunately, the celebrated cases and causes on which the media focus and the portraits they construct tend to maintain myths and stereotypes about rape and sexual assault. Sensationalized cases are those like the gang rapes on the pool table at Big Dan's bar in New Bedford, Massachusetts, or the assault on the New York Central Park jogger or those involving high-profile people like William Kennedy Smith, Mike Tyson, or Kobe Bryant. Coverage, especially in this backlash era, reinforces uniquely unfair beliefs, like she asked for it, she's lying to cover up consensual sex, she was out after dark, she went to a bar or to his hotel room, she's an exotic dancer (as in the recent Duke University case): what did she expect, for Pete's sake? The media contribute enormously to the erosion of gains made by the feminist rape reform movement's education and legislative enactments (recall, for instance, the 1994 New Jersey Supreme Court decision declaring shield legislation unconstitutional and instead allowing in past interactions between the victim and assailant as relevant evidence). As noted earlier, however, the media could be used in a completely opposite fashion, namely, to light a fire under the feet of public to bring about change. If the media chose to focus their coverage on cases that pointed up the injustices and discrimination rape victims suffer, this would evoke critique, challenge, and change, instead of reinforcing the more typical victim blaming modalities characteristic of the status quo.

Social scientists, like criminologists, could facilitate this turn of events. The scientific communities should arm the media with facts about rape and sexual assault and perspectives on the particular issues in particular cases. This would offer the media more grounded research, theory, and perspective to balance coverage and counterbalance bias. Some criminologists actually have asserted that they have a responsibility to interject themselves in the media to provide factual information, as well as an alternative perspective to counter the state, government, criminal justice, and other official points of view (Barak 1998; Robinson 2002). Official viewpoints reflect organizational concerns and the vested interests of agencies and bureaucracies more than the full facts and real nature of the cases that come before them.

Robinson (2002) contends that criminologists need to get involved with media spokespeople not only to correct the misinformation spewed out for public consumption but also to stop the sensationalization of crime and the spread of fear and myths. We need to supply information that is accurate to displace sexist, unsafe, and unjust slants in coverage of rape and sexual assault crimes, victims, and offenders.

Perhaps the development and dissemination of new sound bites and jingles could be productive. People seem to remember things like the FBI's "Take a bite out of crime," Nancy Reagan's "Just say no" (to drugs), the get-tough movement's

"If you do the crime, you do the time." The term "jail bait" used in relation to statutory rape is another kind of example. Here are a few suggestions:

No means no, whatever I wear, wherever I go (Take Back the Night chant).
Listen to "no," or off you go.
"No" prevails, or you're off to jail.
She says what she means and means what she says.
Don't guess; get a yes.
Don't assume; jail could loom.
Drink is a kink not a link to good sex.

The media would be key to disseminating such slogans. The media help to frame notions about what is "cool," or "way cool," or "awesome," and so on, in other words, the acceptable or best way to approach and understand sexual interactions. And the media help frame what rocks, is "lame," "hip," and the like and the way the public understands rape: its causes, who is to be faulted, and how victims should be treated.

Naturally, the media can be mobilized against rape and sexual violence by more than criminologists. Grassroots campaigns to mobilize media coverage of rape issues and cases, for instance, could help make the media more responsive. Brooks reported along these lines that a good deal of popular support for VAWA legislation was, in fact, generated by media accounts (1997: 70, cited in Miller and Meloy forthcoming: 273). Grassroots organizing could work with political action committees (PACs) and other lobby groups, for example, the Feminist Majority, the National Organization of Women (NOW), and the League of Women Voters, to get the media to spread the word about the rationale and types of new wave legal reforms that this country so desperately needs. Since legislators are responsive to PACs because they contribute money and help bids for (re)election, rape reform legislation that builds on prior successes, corrects prior oversights, and addresses contemporary developments could begin progress anew.

A further recommendation stems from the fact that the media can, and sometimes does, police themselves. Miller and Meloy describe a group that does precisely this with sexual and domestic violence coverage. They report that the Dart Center for Journalism and Trauma promotes ethical guidelines that "include the need for reporters to educate themselves on the emotional devastation often associated with these acts of violence, how the media can assist in the creation and improvement of victim services and criminal justice reforms" (forthcoming: 275–276). Public notice and accolades to groups such as this could increase the popularity and strength of similar efforts.

EDUCATION

The powerful role of education cannot be underestimated. The educative function of the earlier waves of rape reform should be capitalized upon, not minimized as only symbolic or otherwise dismissed. Bryden and Lengnick put it well: "Even where law reforms are ineffective, attitudinal change … may achieve the desired result" (1997: 1381). They continue that "this is not to say that symbolic victories are meaningless.… A reform whose short-term impact is purely symbolic may affect attitudes that eventually change society in ways more subtle than we understand or can trace. On a cumulative, national basis, publicity about rape law reforms may already have helped" (1292).

Education of criminal justice workers, jurors, and other citizens about the true nature of rape and sexual assault and the injustices its victims suffer from misogynist and erroneous information has reduced or realigned such beliefs to some degree. There is still a long way to go, however, because the road was so long and so arduous to begin with. Reactions to sexual assault victimization do not begin or end with criminal justice personnel or jurors, who so frequently make ill-informed decisions. Many girls, boys, women, and men remain ignorant about rape and sexual assault dynamics, the lived effects of myths, legal definitions, requirements, processes, and outcomes. Rape myths persevere to misinform all groups—bar none—about any and all types of rape and sexual assault.

It is as unfortunate as it is evident that both attitudes and laws about sexual assault are still in grave need of change thirty years after the first wave of reforms began. General knowledge about the crime of rape and about reform laws is disheartingly flawed. On the one hand, some people hold on to the stereotypical view of the atypical stranger-out-of-the-bushes rape; on the other, some people go so far as to think that "if he is just bigger or older than she is," it is automatically defined as rape. Many think resistance to the utmost is still required, even at gunpoint, while others believe that almost any uncomfortable sex is rape. The need to inaugurate a new educational campaign, beginning at elementary school and continuing through high school and college, should be obvious. It is acute if girls/women and boys/men are to learn to act responsibly and with decency toward one another.

The most needed education about rape concerns what Estrich calls simple rape. Men and women alike do not understand that expressing involuntary non-agreement, "no," is enough to make further sexual activity criminal and that this is so even in the absence of any other circumstances. The law must be clearer on this fact, and men and women alike must learn this clear, precise, and concise legal definition. It would do wonders for prevention and reporting in the vast majority of rapes and sexual assaults, which occur among dating and acquainted men and women. Women give in because they fear force and greater injury if they don't acquiesce but also because they don't know that saying no constitutes legal grounds for rape or sexual assault charges. Teaching people that men have a legal obligation to get it and heed it when a woman says no and that they have a moral, social, and legal obligation to look for willing agreement would go far in mitigating this situation. A similar lesson would involve teaching people that drinking doesn't mean that a woman automatically concedes to sex or that she cannot say no or that a man is not responsible for hearing no. Perhaps more important, drinking can lead to incapacitation, where a woman cannot give meaningful, free agreement: men have to know that when a woman is so drunk or high that she is passed out or unable to walk, stand up straight, or comprehend her surroundings, they are not entitled to intercourse. Men must learn that any sexual activity with a female who is incapacitated by alcohol or drugs (or by other means), even if voluntarily ingested, is rape or sexual assault. It is truly amazing how many people do not know this.

We must renew campaigns for the prevention of and education about rape. Sayings like "Just say no," "Just hear no," "No means no," "She says what she means and means what she says" get the point across most broadly. Using the media, grassroots, and lobbying groups can help to launch new educational crusades to eradicate, instead of reify, erroneous beliefs, misogynistic attitudes, and discriminatory practices in the legal system that contribute to the double victimization of women and girls as rape victims. New research and programs on rape prevention can easily be integrated with the older models that spread the word about rape and reform in years past. New research about the effectiveness of resisting an attacker (the greater the number of strategies, the greater the effectiveness of the resistance, which means the greater the chances of avoiding rape), about the effectiveness of self-defense classes and men-only classes, the danger of acquaintances, and so forth all need to be publicized, as well as put into class contexts across the country (see Rozee and Koss 2001 for a review of these strategies).

And the educational segments need to be broadened in the next round. We need to educate about the laws and the reforms in both substantive and procedural terms. We need to teach how law on the books versus law in daily decision-making routines. We need to teach how the reforms are tenable, justifiable, and immediately necessary to fuel a new wave of change against rape victimization by society, the law, and the criminal justice system. And we need to educate about the structural causes of gender inequality, power and resource polarization, and the male supremacy, control, and domination that are inextricably tied to these (see conclusions below for elaboration). We need to teach how structural inequality leads to sexual violence, to the myths, laws, and attitudes that undermine reforms in practice. And we need to teach how a move toward more egalitarianism in place of gross levels of social and sexual inequality is beneficial for men and women, bringing about mutuality of satisfaction in sexual interactions as well as in other interactions and relationships. And we need to start all this education young; in fact, it is the young who are our real hope for improvements in terms of rape awareness, prevention, and control (Herman 2004; Miller and Meloy forthcoming).

It is important to highlight that jurors might be playing an increasingly influential role in deciding case outcomes in the immediate future.[1] They are now responsible for decisions about the death penalty (Judicial Committee on Model Jury Instructions in the Eighth Circuit 2006: 495–561 (sec. 12)), and it looks like the federal model may now specify that it is the jury, not the judge, who will interpret the aggravating and mitigating circumstances that extend sentences beyond determinate sentencing guidelines (*Blakely v. Washington* 111 Wash. App. 851, 47P. 3d 149, 2004; 124 S. Ct. 2531 [2004]). Educating the public therefore becomes a pressing need, as this is tantamount to educating jurors. And given the importance of educating jurors, the model array of juror instructions described in these chapters will grow more important than might have even been previously imagined.

Education needs, too, to be widened so that police, law students, and others making decisions in the present (and future) learn about more than just the law but also about the causes and actual dynamics of rape; the statistics on offenses, offenders, victims, and case outcomes; and some of the alternative recommended directions for ameliorating the problems surrounding these phenomena. Judges (like jurors), prosecutors (like defense attorneys), and not just students taking college courses should all be required to undergo training on gender issues in order to open their eyes to the discrimination women experience in society and within the law because of gender inequality and, relatedly, violent victimization by men.[2]

CONCLUSIONS

Social Structure: The Why of It

Recommendations and conclusions in books on rape usually wind up saying something about the dual prongs of legal change and attitude change—and there is good reason for this. As is clear by now, we increasingly turn to the law for problem resolution, and the law is far from perfect. Furthermore, as Temkin concludes, "for the foreseeable future, ... it will primarily be the criminal justice system which will bear the burden of regulating rape" (2002: 355). Attitudes influence the practices surrounding the implementation of all law, and, even if the law were perfect, attitudes about rape victimization are so far from it that they bombard rape victims with difficulties and trauma. Thus attitudes as well as laws must be targeted. Attitudes have an impact on law, but laws in turn play an influential role in changing attitudes. The reciprocal nature of attitude leading to law—both de jure and de facto—and law leading to attitude can be mutually reinforcing in a manner that institutes positive changes in both.

Calls for change in both law and attitude "will not abate" (Temkin 2002: 357), especially in light of the statistics on the incidence and prevalence of rape and sexual assault, the fear of rape, and the continued double victimization of rape victims by the apparatus of the legal system. Plans like the model in this book can go a long way toward further remedying the multifaceted problems surrounding rape victimization. But there is more.

We must not lose sight of the underlying structures that give rise to both laws and attitudes. Structures of inequality envelop U.S. and other modern-day societies. Sexual inequality, along with racial and class inequality, are systematically infused to form the culture in this country. Deep and widespread polarization of capital and nonmaterial resources, like money and power, divided along the lines of sex, race/ethnicity, and socioeconomic status/class, have everything to do with laws and attitudes. Inequality determines dominance and subordination, which is reflected in the laws, both substantive and procedural, that are—or are not, for that matter—enacted. Patterned domination/subordination is similarly reflected in the attitudes that affect the implementation practices that shape victim and case treatment and outcome. Calls for change should not lose sight of the bigger picture and long-term goals of reducing levels of inequality.[3]

Inequality itself is a significant cause of rape, as well as of unequal laws and biased attitudes against its female victims. The social system of patriarchy infuses sexism throughout social institutions, establishing male supremacy and female inferiority. This is interwoven with class and racial inequality in modern capitalist society in ways that are mutually reinforcing.[4] The social structure of patriarchy creates a hierarchy where all things male are superior, where male is dominance, where male is powerful. Violence is a central means to this male triumph, and rape is a part of this violence. The myths about rape and the recent conservative backlash against feminism, feminists and rape reform serve to sustain this type of ideological hegemony where these overarching rationalizations for inequality become taken-for-granted assumptions about the way things are and should be.

Gender roles corresponding to sex establish the concomitant cultural attributes that are socialized as superior and inferior, masculine and feminine. Masculinity is dominance, aggressiveness, independence, physical prowess, and strength, and these phenomena convert into the control, manipulation, and exploitation of women. Femininity is passivity, weakness, submissiveness, acquiescence, nurturance, and dependence. Rape is an outgrowth of these roles corresponding to the very culture of society.[5]

Sex is constructed in terms defined by male pleasure, and sexual relations are constructed in terms defined by male entitlement. In other words, women are for men, hence the doctrine of implicit consent, the relevance of past sex, the implied premise that women want men: any men, anytime, and any way it suits men. Women are constructed in terms of sexual objectification, reduced to body parts, not whole human beings, even inferior human beings. Reducing women to sex objects for men removes all compunction about the use and exploitation of women and the costs surrounding the assertion of power and control to dominate women and take sex, or rape.

Violence grows to be valued in its own right, intrinsically, as a part of masculinity, machismo. Violence is also instrumental in garnering power to dominate in order to make men's desires and vested interests ascendant. Violence is eroticized in culture as forcefulness, which is male, which is superior, which is used to exact and exert control. And violence is eroticized in men's beating, whipping, and raping women in the multibillion-dollar pornography industry. In these ways, dominance and violence in sex are normalized, and all three melded together.

The United Nations Declaration on the Elimination of Violence Against Women (1993) echoes how these forces are causes of rape and sexual assault, this time in a global context. Weldon summarizes the declaration to argue that

> violence against women is a manifestation of historically unequal power relations between men and women and that violence against women "is one of the crucial social mechanisms by which women are forced into a subordinate position compared with men." Indeed, cross-cultural studies of violence against women have found the economic inequality between women and men, cultural patterns of conflict resolution through violence, cultural norms of male dominance, toughness, and honor, and male economic and decision-making authority in the family are the best predictors of high levels of violence against women (Levinson 1989; Sanday 1981). As

research on this topic has progressed, the relationship between violence against women and male dominance has become increasingly well established.

(2002: 13)

We need to move forward by recognizing and teaching that inequality is a cause of sexual violence. Inequality leads to international, structural, institutional, and individual violence in general and to the violence of rape in particular (Schwendinger and Schwendinger 1983; Iadicola and Shupe 1998). We need to inform across audiences about the social disasters to which high levels of inequality lead and to develop policies aimed at redressing the gross levels of inequality that U.S. and similar cultures are not only tolerating but promoting. And education about sexual, class, and racial and ethnic inequality, about the intersectionality of these, and about their relationship to violence against women, as well as about more egalitarian gender roles and sexuality, needs to begin at an early age—in elementary school—and carry through the college years. It is worth reiterating that Susan Herman, past director of the NCVC, concludes, along with other experts and scholars, that our best chance of reducing rape and other violence directed at women is precisely to begin education at an early age. What is novel in the suggestion at hand concerns the content of that education.

Social Processes: The How of It

Another direction for the future is inspired by Weldon's 2002 research. Her international work across thirty-six countries is a fine example of creative research that reveals successful measures relating to the reduction of gender inequality and violence against women. She investigates the factors impinging on "strong" legislation to combat violence against women and gender inequality. The specific policies that Weldon examined were wife battering and sexual assault reform legislation; funding for emergency housing and crisis centers; training for police, social workers, and other service providers; public education programs; and a coordinating authority, for example, linking victim services to the police, a coordinating center, or an agency to coordinate policies on violence against women (13–17).[6] Her results show the power of an organized women's movement, independent from government, that tries to work with extant state/government institutions and "women's policy agencies," defined as "state institutions designed to promote the status of women" (5), that operates to reduce gender inequality, as the most significant dimension affecting strong violence against women legislation. In brief, she interprets the cross-cultural data to show that partnerships between women's political or policy machinery and an autonomous women's movement put violence against women on the national, public agenda (196) and maximize its impact.

Other scholars in the field have pointed out the importance of grassroots movements in effecting the political and legal change that Weldon notes. Schneider, in her book *Battered Women and Feminist Lawmaking* (2002), concludes that there would be no violence against women reforms without the feminist movement. Other books dedicated to researching the feminist domestic and sexual violence reform movements also underscore the powerful role of grassroots organizing and activities in getting changes passed (Matthews 1994; Miller and Meloy forthcoming).[7]

It is instructive to highlight briefly the influential activities of the women's movements that were instrumental in improving the lot of women in thirty-six countries. Fink's review of Weldon's work most succinctly chronicles the "three modes that women's movements use to influence civil society" (2003: 393). These are "first … everyday politics … changing attitudes … challenge discourse … second … books, movies, magazines, and theatre that make issues and perspectives visible. Third is organizing and promoting activities, such as letter writing, petitioning, and lobbying" (ibid.). Stated somewhat differently, the movement moves from consciousness raising to broad-based educational messages, to the creation of cultural products and the mobilization of political resources and agenda setting.[8]

Weldon (2002) also talks about directions for future improvement. She suggests five areas where yet stronger policy could be realized against sexual and domestic abuse. These involve the creation of:

1. "a women's bureau" (198), with a cabinet-level figure in government;
2. "an advisory council" (198) to facilitate communication and access to government for women and other marginalized groups;
3. "advocacy structures for other marginalized groups," similar to commissions for racial/ethnic groups and the disabled, that "may improve responsiveness to violence against women" (199);
4. "a government commission on women" nationally based to "review progress on women's status and to lay out specific policy recommendations" (199); and
5. "institutional reforms to provide public access to policymakers and accountability" that would furnish the public with information and data to monitor how the groups representing women and other marginalized groups are working, so as to guard against co-optation and practices that "do not speak for them" (199), or, in the terminology used in this book, to watch implementation practices.[9]

Weldon concludes that these "areas of government response to violence against women are consistent with the main recommendations for national action developed by the UN Convention on the Elimination of All Forms of Discrimination Against Women (CEDAW) at Beijing and updated in committee discussion in the reports of the UN Special Rapporteur on Violence Against Women" (2002: 17). Truly international support thus underpins the directions described in this section.

Weldon's research is most constructive in enumerating internationally based, concrete, and productive directions that can diminish sexual and domestic violence against women and the sexual inequality that is inextricably connected to such violence. The examination of what can and has been employed across the globe paves the way for future, and perhaps greater, progress in the struggle against the pervasive violence directed against women. The initiatives pursued in the future need to be informed by international, structural, institutional, and individual levels of analysis (as in Taylor, Walton, and Young 1973) in the examination of inequality, general violence, and sexual violence, as these feed off one another at all these levels.

What is clear in the model of change that Weldon lays out is similarly clear in the model of reform developed in this book. The directions carved out need to be broadly conceived, multifaceted, and interrelated in a way that is mutually reinforcing but also in a way that can set up firewalls against corruption of reforms. This is the way change can be maximally effective.

Relatedly, what should be clear by this juncture is that any new wave of reform measures simply must address practices. Accountability through monitoring implementation of policies must accompany changes to redress violence against women, whether these changes are in law or in training or in setting up new agencies. Institutional forces and interests, and individual beliefs, will taint how any policy is carried out. Oversight has to be a new key feature of reforms in the movement against violence against women. Implementation is where legal reforms of the past fell apart, and it is where provisions like victim attorneys, or educational programs, or cabinet level women's bureaus, or funding for crisis centers, or building women's coalitions across class, race, and religion can become hollow promises, too, if we neglect such things as monitoring, accountability structures, and implementation practices.

To move forward, we must learn from one another and learn from past theory, research, and practice. We must learn from both our successes and our failures in order to fashion pathways into the future. We must learn, too, that the way to a future of less violence and more justice for women will benefit women and men alike.

Notes

1. Introductory Overview

1. On Michigan as a model of rape reform law for the United States and beyond, see BenDor 1976, Dean and DeBruyn-Kops 1982, Estrich 1987, Field and Bienen 1980; Marsh, Geist, and Caplan 1982; National Institute on Law Enforcement and Criminal Justice 1978.

2. Rape and sexual assault can be distinguished but are often treated synonymously. Sexual assault is the term often used to describe offenses of sexual contact not involving penetration, whereas rape is generally viewed as crime involving, historically speaking, penetration of a vagina by a penis. Both terms have been used in rape reforms criminalizing oral and anal penetration and penetration with objects. Unless otherwise indicated, they will be used synonymously in this book.

3. Because females are so overwhelmingly, disproportionately victimized by males in crimes of rape and sexual assault, this book will refer to rape victims as women and accused rapists as men. I do this not only for economy's sake but also to portray the sex- and gender-based character of these criminal acts. "Women" is used inclusively to refer to adult females and young girls, "men" to refer to adult males and young boys, also for the purposes of linguistic parsimony.

4. Kalven and Zeisel's classic 1966 study on jurors used the terms "simple" and "aggravated" rape. Estrich follows this tradition but coins the term "real" rape for aggravated rape.

5. As DeKeseredy has pointed out, a feminist realism like that embraced by the model I describe corrects for the problem suffered by a feminist idealism that argues that "the state and the law, the legal mechanism and the police, are a part of a patriarchal structure, under which attempts at legal reform are only tinkerings within the overall system of control and regulation—so legal change serves only to perpetuate the basic conditions of patriarchy" (DeKeseredy, personal communication, 2007, citing Edwards 1989).

6. The polarization evident in these perspectives may account for part of the dwindling attention to rape reform, in that one sees reform as untenable and the other is unlikely to be accepted because of its excesses.

2. Legal Change Sweeps the Nation

1. The early and extensive Michigan law has been discussed for its influence on many jurisdictions, among them, New Jersey (Field and Bienen 1980), Washington (Estrich 1987), and Illinois (Spohn and Horney 1992).

The Model Penal Code (MPC) approved by the American Law Institute in 1962 was another influential model for state's rape reform legislation (Field and Bienen 1980: 155). This code, while supposedly improving on carnal knowledge statutes, reflected many of the same problems that those statutes were known to cause. I do not discuss the MPC at length here, because so much of it is at odds with the rape reform movement. For instance, while the MPC is sex neutral and graduates offenses along severity levels, its retention of Justice Hale–type notions about the difficulty of defending against rape charges, and about victim promiscuity, victim consent, victim lies, and victim precipitation are manifest in its requirements of corroboration and prompt complaints (ibid.; Estrich 1987: 46). I discuss these Hale-type cautionary jury instructions, victim promiscuity, and so forth further in this chapter.

"Forcible rape" is the term traditionally or conventionally used in law to describe rape. Yet the term is problematic since it conjures up the sexist, indeed misogynistic, interpretations associated with carnal knowledge statutes, in that "forcible rape" implies that some rape is not forced—and hence may not be rape. In other words, "forcible rape" is a term that is largely redundant. I use "sic" to call attention to this and make clear that "forcible rape" is not a term of my own choosing or crafting.

2. The Michigan CSC Code defines two assault offenses. Assault with intent to commit CSC involving sexual penetration (MCL 750.520g[1]) and assault with intent to commit CSC II involving contact (MCL 750.520g[2]). These are different from attempted CSC offenses that entail someone who "may commit an overt act beyond 'mere preparation' but never actually 'assault' the victim." Assault with intent to commit CSC offenses—penetration or contact—are "crimes of sexual violence" that do not "culminate in the actual sexual penetration or touching of a victims. In some cases, the perpetrator may be thwarted from carrying out a sexual penetration or contact despite having the intent to do so" (Michigan Judicial Institute 2002:43).

3. It is noteworthy that Michigan reforms did not originally repeal the exemption for husbands. This change wasn't enacted until more than a decade after the CSC Code went into place in 1988 (amendment 24, PA 138, in Michigan Judicial Institute 2002).

4. Just as there is a relatively little literature on the nature and outcomes of rape reforms in the United States, the literature on rape reforms in other countries, too, is scant. It is instructive to note that the accessible/published foreign research from nations deemed less developed or advanced frequently underscores different, and horrendous, problems for women. Some problems of note are, for example, bride capture, dowry deaths, and honor killings after rape. Many foreign scholars have pointed out that research from first-world nations is biased when it assumes that the issues surrounding violence against women (when studied in nation/state as opposed to global contexts) are universal. This is clearly a significant and valid criticism and should be drawn on as a corrective to essentializing the plight of women. These problems are not discussed here for the rather obvious reason that rape reform movements and reform legislation are so rare in such countries.

3. Failures and Successes

1. There is, however, one somewhat positive result in this regard: consideration of evidence of past sexual activity did not emerge as a factor influencing charging and plea-bargaining reductions in sexual as opposed to nonsexual assault case prosecutions in Michigan (Caringella-MacDonald 1988). I say "somewhat" because this does not mean that it did not arise in court (where it resulted in sustained objections by the prosecution) or in discussions about pleas. Nevertheless, the factor did not differentiate the types of assaults from one another.

2. Deborah Denno indicates the strength of this convention. She cites that "ninety to ninety-five percent of the media have non-disclosure policies on victims of rape, irrespective of the law of the particular state where they are based" (1993: 1130, citing Jones 1989: A18, which provides an estimate from Deni Elliott, the executive director of the Institute for the Study of Applied and Professional Ethics at Dartmouth College).

3. Misdemeanors are less serious than felonies, carrying only up to one year of jail, as contrasted to a year or more in state or federal prison. Arizona provides an example of a state where marital rape is a misdemeanor offense.

4. It is interesting to note that Temkin claims that "only in New Zealand the discretionary legislation appears to be operating with a certain degree of success" (1995: 308, citing Young 1983: 1:43–46).

5. They note that in Canada "the defense strategy is to elect Supreme Court [i.e., a trial by judge and jury] in those cases where the victim may be open to critical social judgment for her behaviours or lifestyle. This tactic, which maximizes public exposure and holds the victim accountable for the crime, is often successful even in the face of a strong case presented by the crown" (Yurchesyn, Keith, and Renner 1995: 73, cited in Du Mont and Myhr 2000: 1111).

4. Avenues for and Attitudes About Victims

1. Susan Hippensteele and Meda Chesney Lind presented an exceptional case on civil litigation and sexual harassment at the 1994 American Society of Criminology conference in Boston. They discussed how harm is determined to be less severe in instances where victims of sexual harassment are found to have been raped in the past. In civil

litigation, the university can hire a private investigator to dig up this kind of information. If the plaintiff has been raped, the view is that, while the present sexual harassment has caused some harm, harm had already occurred in the past, so the impact of the faculty member's illegal behavior is less damaging.

2. The total cost of the VAWA of 1994 is roughly between $1 and $1.5 to $2 billion. The lower estimate is from Frazee et al. 1995: $1.62 billion over the projected six-year period between 1994 and the twenty-first century. The higher estimates, by the Congressional Budget Office, are $1.896 and $2.056 billion, calculated to cover the years of 1994 through 1998 (U.S. Senate 1993: 68–72). The discrepancy is between "amounts Specified in the Bill" (the lower number) and "Net Additional Authorizations" which is "total Authorizations in S.11" "Less: Authorizations in Current Law Act" (70).

3. In *Brzonkala v. Morrison*, 935 F. Supp. 779 (WD VA, 1996), District Judge Kiser dismissed VAWA civil rights claims. The plaintiff appealed to the Fourth Circuit Court of Appeals, where a three-judge panel reversed the dismissal, with Circuit Judge Motz writing the majority opinion and Circuit Judge Luttig writing the dissent (at 132 F. 3d 949 [1997]). In a rehearing before an en banc panel of the Fourth Circuit Court of Appeals, with Circuit Judge Luttig now writing the majority opinion (169 F.3d 820 [1999]), the court reversed the three-judge appeals panel and affirmed District Judge Kiser. Certiorari was granted by the Supreme Court, which affirmed the en banc panel in *United States v. Morrison* (529 US 598 [2000]), with Justice Rehnquist writing for the majority (Mullendore, personal communication, 2007).

4. Battelle published an earlier study in 1977. The research inquired about prosecutorial charging decisions in rape. The researchers did not publish pre- to postreform comparisons and so is not featured here. Briefly though, the findings were that most factors deemed important to prosecutors related to legally relevant variables like age and injury; however, the two extralegal variables of circumstances of initial contact and the victim-offender relationship were also mentioned (Spohn and Horney 1992: 111).

5. For reviews of this body of research, see Allison and Wrightsman 1993; Lonsway and Fitzgerald 1994; and Ward 1995. A few of the most familiar and most widely used pieces of research on attitudes about rape are Burt's research on the Rape Myth Acceptance Scale in 1980, Field's "Attitudes Toward Rape" (1978), Williams and Holmes's 1981 research on sex, race, ethnicity, and attitudes toward rape, and Ward's extensive 1995 review of the research published in book form. Williams and Holmes's summary of the public's beliefs is useful for an overview of the general findings from the attitudinal investigations. They state that "the vast majority of respondents view rape as a behavior problem—primarily that of the rapist (mental illness) and secondarily that of the victim (inappropriate behavior and/or appearance). Few respondents of any group saw societal (macro-level) problems as causally related to rape, and fewer yet saw sex-role problems as causal.... A majority of respondents resorted to law-and-order clichés or admonitions for women to change their behavior as their best suggestion on how to reduce the rape problem" (1981: 123).

6. The research on the media and rape is rarely as specific as that addressing reform objectives relating to corroboration requirements and the like, as has been discussed in this chapter. Although there is no research directly comparing media treatment of rape in the pre- and postreform periods, the evidence of victim-blaming myths is indicative of the failure of reforms to achieve goals.

7. Although the rape charges against the three lacrosse team members were dropped, and District Attorney Mike Nifong was forced to resign (and sentenced to serve one day in jail for contempt charges stemming from making untruthful statements to a judge), the point is that before any of this and before the circus (e.g., the prosecutor was accused of essentially campaigning for reelection by filing charges for a black woman who accused three white, upper-class Duke University students of rape) ensued, the press, the public, and the students all repeated victim-, woman-, and black-blaming stereotypes and dismissed women and minority victimization as an unreal, unserious falsehood.

5. The Legal Landscape

1. Kristine Mullendore (personal communication, 1998), a former assistant prosecuting attorney, associate professor at the School of Criminal Justice at Grand Valley State University, observes that it should be noted that while statutory rape is a common lay example, it is not an accurate legal example of strict liability. This is because statutory rape is a general intent crime, where the act is the intent, and the consequence is irrelevant. *Black's Law Dictionary* states that general intent "in criminal law [is] the intent to do that which the law proscribes. It is not necessary for the prosecution to prove that the defendant intended the precise harm or the precise result which eventuated" (Black 1991: 560). It is only necessary to establish that the actor intended the act, in this case, sexual penetration (or sexual contact/offensive or invasive touching). This is different from a strict liability crime where one commits the act, and regardless of intent the actor is criminally responsible. With strict liability, intent does not have to be proven because it is irrelevant, whereas with general intent crimes it is the consequence, harm, injury, or result that does not have to be proven because of its irrelevance.

2. See Deborah Denno's 1997 work on rape and mental incompetence for a critique of the law here.

3. As Mullendore has observed, the problem in Michigan is that the CSC Code is a particularized case of battery/assault crimes, where injury is "particularized" to different categories of victims, for example, the young or the mentally incapacitated (personal communication, 1998). With assault law, the assault is putting the victim in fear; the fear is seen as the fear of battery—which is the actual injury. The violence, force, coercion, or threats put the victim in fear in sexual assault cases in much the same way. The fear would be the fear of battery or the physical harms associated with forced sex, should the victim refuse to submit to the assailant. The assailant here exploits the victim's fear that she cannot do anything about his intentions, his advances, his threats, or his actual use of force or violence and/or her fear/knowledge that she cannot defend herself against these. Because of the particularized injury or battery, the penalties are greater for rape (CSC) than for simple battery/assault offenses. The problem is that because the defense of consent is available to battery/assault crimes, for example, in the context of contact sports and other mutually agreed-upon physical fighting where consent precludes culpability for injuries, the defense of consent also pertains to rape (as a particularized case of battery/assault crime) (ibid.). In other words, the general notions of consent are allowable as a defense to simple battery and hence available as a defense to rape, regardless of degree/severity.

Mullendore elaborates that change in law is construed "narrowly," or in a limiting sense, whenever criminal responsibility would be created or enhanced by a legal change. Because penalties are greater for CSC offenses, the "narrow" interpretation would be that consent is available as a defense to any degree of rape, as it is available to other crimes of battery.

4. Defenses other than consent and mistake of consent are available in rape cases. Bohmer (1991) lists the following four defenses to rape charges: (1) "It wasn't me"; (2) "No sex took place" (3); "I'm not responsible"; and (4) "Sex was consensual" (319). Gardner and Anderson spell out some of the permutations on consent defenses in rape in their criminal law and procedure book. They delineate the following: "I honestly thought she consented, she never did say 'no' "; "she consented, then changed her mind during the sex"; "the manner in which the woman dressed was sexy and provocative and her conduct (such as placing her hand on the defendant's upper thigh) ... led him on"; "she consented, but later developed guilt feelings and regretted what she did" (1996: 424). Diana Scully's book on convicted rapists' "vocabulary of motives" explains in some detail how even convicted and incarcerated rapists rationalize away the assessment that what they did was rape by relying on myths such as victim precipitation, lack of resistance, fantasized desire, "coming around to liking it," and so on (1990).

5. It is interesting to note how a victim's postvictimization behavior gets used to infer consent to a prior act that is criminal. The same occurred in the Kobe Bryant case, where the victim's alleged activities with other men after the alleged rape were used as indicators that she was not raped by Bryant.

6. A final issue in a critical appraisal of Estrich's model is that she devotes very little space to explaining her analogy of rape and sexual assault to property crimes. What exactly would these offenses be? How would they vary? How would these types of sexual assault correspond to other crimes involving money or property? The statement "were money sought instead" is clear enough, but follow-through would have been most useful in identifying the new crimes she is trying to carve out. Furthermore, she states that such offenses might be lesser crimes but fails to pursue how this might work out in the law. Would they still be sexual assault offenses or some new category of fraud? Would these be lesser in the sense of being misdemeanor offenses or just carry lower sentence possibilities? (See chap. 12 for treatment of these issues.)

The commonality in problems with Estrich's model is that follow-through with these important conceptualizations and directions would have been most beneficial. It would inform the effort to develop a model to stimulate and guide further reform efforts.

6. Affirmative Consent Reform Models

1. The castigation of Antioch's code is largely due to the extremity of the staging measure requiring permission for each sexually oriented behavior as these progress. This should not be confused with other affirmative consent reforms that require only that there was an indication of consent on the part of the victim. Additional features of the Antioch policy are that it is gender neutral and explicitly recognizes same sex as well as group sex. It also recognizes that past consent does not portend future consent, so agreement must perpetually be communicated in any sex relationship (Antioch College Community 1995).

2. Affirmative consent reform law should not be confused with affirmative defenses to crimes. Affirmative defenses are rejoinders to criminal charges that attempt to negate criminal culpability. Affirmative defenses require the defense to produce evidence (the defense has the burden of production or going forward here; see chap. 11) to substantiate its defense claim (Kadish and Schulhofer 2001: 45). The consent defense to the criminal accusation of rape provides an example of an affirmative defense.

3. The New Jersey law (like Michigan's, although the CSC model is certainly not an affirmative consent law reform) is strongly influenced by that state's assault and battery law. The battery is the offensive or unauthorized touching, or criminal sexual assault, ranging from criminal sexual penetration to criminal sexual contact (Kadish and Schulhofer 2001: 341–342). Under affirmative consent statutes like that in New Jersey, rape or sexual assault exists when penetration occurs with no voluntary or willing (uncoerced) permission (Reeves Sanday 1996: 281).

4. Schulhofer says the same definition—of a man having intercourse while knowing he doesn't have a woman's consent, in his words "without having clear indication of consent"—is present in the laws in Pennsylvania and Utah as well (1998: 96).

5. The converse is explicitly recognized in, for instance, Antioch's affirmative consent policy, wherein females, too, need to ascertain male consent before acting in sexual ways. Given that the topic here is sexual assault, it makes more sense (and is more efficient) to talk about males ascertaining consent from females.

6. The same has/can be said of resistance, where because of fear victims are afraid or unable to resist just as they may be unable to speak.

7. In point of fact, in the two cases involving silence that Reeves Sanday discusses, aggravating circumstances were apparent (rendering consent or the possibility of a meaningful yes untenable). In the Glen Ridge gang rape case, the young woman who failed to say no was mentally impaired, and in the M.T.S. case, the young woman was asleep until awakened by the defendant's lying on top of her (1996: 278).

8. Although Antioch's affirmative consent policy specifically recognizes same-sex relations in part to avoid this.

9. Chamallas's approach is like Pineau's, only with a "broader range of motives" (Schulhofer 1998: 85).

10. I would go further to argue that willful participation should be examined for its connotation and differentiation from permission. I see mutual participation as yet farther out (from permission and from willful agreement) along some sort of continuum of meaning of accord, where sexual partners interact jointly in sexual encounters. It may be a matter of semantics, but again, semantics matter.

11. Schulhofer cites research indicating that "most women (at least 60 percent in most studies) say 'no' only when they mean it" (1998: 267), leaving 40 percent, or some percentage thereof, that either say no when they do not mean it—or when they mean yes—and/or another 40 percent or some percentage thereof saying yes when mean yes.

12. I also take exception to Schulhofer's view that sexual offenses of penetration committed on incapacitated victims or "physically helpless, mentally defective, or mentally incapacitated" victims (1998: 243, sec. 202[c][1]) should only be second-degree felonies. Rape of unconscious persons (like those unsuspecting victims who are given drugs like roofies, GHB, etc.) should be treated among the most heinous of crimes.

Further, Schulhofer's model makes no mention of gang rape or aiders and abettors in any degree of sexual offense. Clearly, such an oversight is also a problematic omission in a model statute.

7. Consent and Voluntariness, Agreement

1. This discussion of consent presumes the absence of aggravating, violent, forceful, and so on conditions. This absence is typically the condition that makes any kind/range of consent voluntary, meaningful, or genuine (although there are a few, comparatively rare exceptions; see chap. 11).

2. It should be mentioned that voluntary intoxication or impairment on the part of the defendant is not defense to criminal charges of rape (Criminal Law Revision Committee [CLRC] 2000: 67,72; Michigan Judicial Institute 2002: 244–246).

3. Lewin (1985) discusses how patriarchal norms about sexual initiative, entitlement, and pleasure and the nurturing and passive roles for women contribute to what I am defining as noncriminal acts or acquiescence of the kind just mentioned. Katz goes a little further in the comment that "men are socialized to desire women in such a way that the desired woman's own desire for the desirer is irrelevant" (1989: 56). These factors can also contribute to the ascendancy of male privilege, male entitlement to take sex—even "against her will"—and the rampant ease with which a man may rationalize that the woman wanted what he wanted, how he wanted it, when he wanted it, and so on in order to legitimize rape. These premises epitomize the perspectives arguing that patriarchy engenders rape, and ultimately they must be addressed for legal change to be fully effective (see chap. 17).

4. Chapter 11 details the exceptional cases—and the processes provided for these atypical cases—where the defense of consent (mutual, voluntary acquiescence or permission) can be used under some of what are normally considered involuntary or forceful conditions.

5. Mullendore (personal communication, 1998) makes an interesting note on a different type of law (not criminal law) that can be juxtaposed here. This is contract/civil law on adhesion contracts. *Black's Law Dictionary* defines these as a "standardized contract form offered to consumers of goods and services on essentially a 'take it or leave it' basis without affording the consumer realistic opportunity to bargain and under such conditions that consumer cannot obtain desired product or services except by acquiescing in form contract. Distinctive feature of adhesion contract is that weaker party has no realistic choice as to its terms"(1991: 25). The analogy is that the "take it" could be applied to agreeing to engage in sex, with the objective of getting something like a relationship/boyfriend. "Leaving it" would be not agreeing to the sex and not getting the relationship with the boy/man. It should be highlighted, though, that submission that is coerced with threats of harm is not freely yielded and is not consent as it is being discussed here in the sense of a real choice absent anything coercive accompanying demands or sexual requests. What is being suggested here is that the sexual overtures accompanied by merely psychological or emotional pressures not involving implicit or explicit threats, harms, deceptions, and so forth are not crimes.

6. The prosecution would continue to shoulder the burden to show nonconsent in the absence of force or coercion, but consent could not be taken to be implied or presumed under any circumstances (see chap. 8).

7. Or pressures, intimidation, and so on directed at those in proximity to her at the time. I add this consideration because threats to harm loved ones, roommates, and the like who are at hand at the time of the alleged crime can constitute a coercive force, notwithstanding the fact that the model reform in Michigan, for instance, excludes this consideration.

8. To emphasize, I do not include consideration of factors other than physical force or threats here; that is, I do not take into account emotional pleas or psychological tactics as forms of coercion in rape. Later, I will fit false pretenses, fraud, and so on into the model I propose.

9. Tchen notes that this definition is problematic because it uses the words "sex act" in reference to rape and sexual assault. On the flip side, she commends the Minnesota definition as it "clearly precludes the use of implied consent" (1983: 1542).

10. Past sexual history has been a vehicle used to impugn rape victims on the basis of the implied consent predicate, that is, the belief allowed is that consent to sex with one man at some point in time implicitly implies consent to sex with other men in future times. Chapter 10 discusses how this, too, can and must be altered because of consent arguments, implied or otherwise. The de jure specification in rape statutes that consent is not, and cannot, be implicitly assumed might go further than waiting for decisions on an individual case or jurisdictional basis.

11. The much to lose and little to gain for women lies in such phenomena as the horrendous stigma and loss of time, money, reputation, relationships, and career that are so often corollary to the mere reporting of rape. The much to lose and little to gain for women also lies in facing the public, the press, and the person she accuses time and again, in open court, while she is scrutinized, and often defiled, by questions about her credibility and character and past sexual friends, dates, and just contacts, often ultimately only to see the assailant acquitted.

12. The small percentage drops even lower for "cases without merit" (Estrich 1987: 16), or unfounded cases, when female as opposed to male officers take rape complaints. What is more, the laws and procedures of the criminal justice system will certainly ferret out the very few false claim cases, as attrition rates of up to 98 percent evince (CONNSACS 2000: 2), without additional discriminatory obstacles mounted for every person who might charge a man of rape. It might be helpful to note in this regard that cases are unfounded because of the belief in false accusation but also because of similar prejudicial factors such as late reporting of the incident, a victim's intoxication, a victim's reputation/occupation as prostitute (94: 1), or even a victim's prior relationship, or just prior acquaintance, with the accused (Hunter, Bentley Cewe, and Mills 1998).

13. MacKinnon puts it eloquently when she lays out a related problem: "The problem is this; man's perceptions of the woman's desires often determines whether she is deemed violated.... It (rape law) presumes a single underlying reality, not a reality split by divergent meanings, such as those inequality produces.... Men's pervasive belief that women fabricate rape charges after consenting to sex makes sense in this light. To them, the accusations *are* false because, to them, the facts describe sex" (1983: 652–653; emphasis in the original).

14. Other victim-centered concerns that are to be specified in de jure law and ju-ror instructions as unreasonable and therefore presumptively irrelevant fall along the dimensions of (a) past sexual history/character evidence and voluntary agreement and (b) victim-oriented behavior (and voluntary agreement), such as victim use of alcohol/drugs, victim style of dress, victim demeanor, and victim acquaintanceship with the ac-cused. These facets of victim-related concerns are dealt with in the array in chapter 13 and discussion in chapter 14.

8. Presumptive Nonagreement

1. I have just discussed explicit and implicit force and coercive threats, but enumer-ating the aggravating circumstances associated with different levels of sexual assault of-fenses will be useful here. The Michigan model reform statute illustrates the kinds of compounding factors that are considered in establishing the degree or severity of sexual assault crimes. Michigan's law, like many other state reform laws, delineates the following determinative variables: the age of victim (is she a minor?), the victim-offender rela-tionship (is there a blood affiliation or a shared household, or does the defendant hold a position of authority over the victim?), the commission of simultaneous other felony crime(s), the presence of weapons, additional injuries, aiders and abettors, victim inca-pacitation, and incapacitation and/or coercion (PA 328, 1974).

2. The only other author that directly speaks to how repetitive force and nonconsent definitions are is MacKinnon, who bluntly comments that "lack of consent is redundant and should not be a separate element of crime.... Rape should be defined as sex by com-pulsion, of which physical force is one form (1989: 245). Estrich recognizes but glosses over the redundancy when she observes that "the force or coercion that negates consent should be extended to extortionist threats and misrepresentation of material fact" (1987: 102–103). She doesn't go on to address the issue of proof of the force/coercion in relation to proof of nonconsent.

3. Exceptions to requiring proof of aggravation/force/coercion and proof of noncon-sent exist in the reform jurisdictions, like Michigan, that tried to do away with the need to prove nonconsent. Tchen comments here that eliminating "the lack of consent as an ele-ment of the crime" (1983: 1551) means that the prosecution does not have to prove noncon-sent, leaving it to prove the identity of the accused, the penetration or criminal contact, and the existence of aggravating conditions, or force, or coercion. Because proving ag-gravating crime circumstances and/or force/coercion is tantamount to proving nonagree-ment, proof of both force/coercion and involuntariness, nonagreement should be legally unnecessary under any type of force/coercion or aggravating conditions, such as multiple offenders or the presence of weapons. But again, even in Michigan, as mentioned earlier, the law on the books and the law in action are quite often two different phenomena.

4. It is instructive to comment on the degrees or severity of sexual assault offenses and presumptive nonagreement. Michigan, for instance, steps or graduates crime sever-ity by specifying objective crime circumstances in order to differentiate the offense (and punishment) level(s). The difference between the circumstances delimited in Michigan reforms and what I'm recommending here is that I would include all the conditions in law as serious enough to make involuntariness the ascendant assumption, whereas

Michigan's reforms do not include the conditions of incapacitation, gangs, or force/coercion alone as sufficiently weighty to make for the higher degrees of CSC in the first and second degrees. (I would argue that gangs or victim incapacitation should alone drive a definition of the higher aggravated levels of rape.) Gang rapes that do not occur in combination with force/coercion or with incapacitated victims and rapes involving additional victim injury without force/coercion or incapacitated victims are all lesser degrees of CSC in Michigan.

The presumption of involuntariness, nonagreement should hold under all severity levels, that is, all crimes accompanied by aggravating, or forceful, or coercive conditions, regardless of degree. This means that under the listed conditions, it should not be necessary for victims to express their involuntariness, nonagreement in order to elevate nonagreement to the reasonable assumption. What I am contending is that under some conditions, like "just" force or coercion, or "just" gangs, or "just" additional injuries, that pertain to the less serious and/or the "simple" rapes, the condition alone is sufficiently clear, and sufficiently serious, to lead to a presumption of involuntariness without the victim having to express nonagreement or the prosecution having to prove nonagreement. This stands despite the fact that such conditions are insufficient to make the crimes the "real" rape of, for example, CSC in the first degree. The presence of "simple" force or coercion or victim incapacitation should, like the other crime circumstances of youthful victims, weapons, and so on, tip the balance in favor of the presumption of involuntary submission on the part of the victim in the criminal acts alleged. This would help make simple rape part of what "really" is rape.

While I am commenting on broadening the Michigan model, let me add another consideration. Estrich addresses coercive threats and Michigan law and the problem of the person to whom these threats are directed. She points out that "the threat to use immediate force must be 'on the victim'; violence against her escort or her child are not enough" (1987: 86) under Michigan's model law. This is clearly a problem with this state's reforms, although, as Estrich notes, it is not true in many other states, including even some nonfeminist reform law jurisdictions. I concur with Estrich's point that threats to kill, maim, bludgeon, beat, or otherwise do bodily harm to the victim herself, or to her loved ones (like children or parents), or simply to those in proximity to her (like dates or roommates) all should be included under coercion. Submission under any such ominous/sinister conditions is never the same thing as voluntary compliance, not to mention consent. The presumption of involuntariness would apply identically, then, under conditions of threat bodily harm to loved ones or those in proximity. Nonagreement would not have to be proved if such physical coercive threats were established.

5. Just as the victim might be incapacitated by mental impairments or disabilities, she can be incapacitated and unable to indicate her involuntary nonagreement because of ingesting alcohol or drugs. In actuality, for victim intoxication to equate with involuntary nonagreement or count in the prosecution of rape, the intoxication has to be proven to be at such extreme levels that the victim is basically blacked out, completely unconscious, or near death. Moreover, while lesser levels of voluntary drunkenness do not automatically equate with incapacity (Estrich 1987: 97), a drunken woman can still indicate nonagreement, can still say no, and/or can still suffer under circumstances of force/coercion, and so on, all of which make for the crimes of rape and sexual assault.

6. Harris quotes a 1991 court case (*Ellison v. Brady* 924 F. 2d 872 [9th Cir. 1991]) that recognized this point. She reports that the court adapted the reasonable woman—over the reasonable person—standard because "a sex-blind reasonable person standard tends to be male-biased and tends to systematically ignore the experiences of women" (1996: 60).

7. A strong reform recommendation would be to have presumptive nonagreement stipulated whenever charges are brought forward. Charges brought forward show police and prosecutor concurrence with victims' reports, which intends a belief in nonconsent. Because consent does frame so much of sexual activity, however, and because the prosecution has the burden of proof with nonconsent as an element of the crime (or force, coercion, or aggravating circumstances), it therefore would not be fair to privilege agreement statutorily.

8. Although if the defense introduces a consent defense, this burden of proof would shift (see chap. 11).

9. To me, this should be viewed as unwanted sex that is not rape or sexual assault, because of the absence of compulsion; should there be any sort of coercive force that begets the less than heartfelt yes, however, it is rape or sexual assault.

10. I might point out that this stands in contradiction to the assertions of some self-declared feminists, most notably Naomi Wolf (1993), who believes that feminists need to teach women how to communicate their boundaries, since we allegedly don't know how to do this, in spite of the fact that many of us know our boundaries and desires, as well as how to express them out loud.

11. Instead of being debated as consent, the inability to indicate nonagreement physically or verbally (that Reeves Sanday calls "frozen fright") might be seen as a type of incapacitation. In Michigan law, the aggravating circumstance of incapacitation is defined as being "physically helpless—unable to communicate unwillingness to an act," (sec. 70.250[i]). Victims who are unconscious or sleeping are examples of victims incapable of expressing unwillingness. This could constitute a criminal circumstance my reform model could employ to dictate that a victim need not say no. Under this condition, then, silence could not rightfully be interpreted as consent. Silence as a type of aggravating condition would then define rape. The law would have to state this explicitly, because of the custom of treating silence as consent. In other words, the law would have to be altered to recognize frozen fright as a type of incapacitation to be demonstrated in order to prove rape. Alternatively, though, what I have been setting up in this (and previous) chapters for the model for reform is that the proof of aggravation/force/coercion that begot the frozen fright would be sufficient to prove crimes of rape and so the silence would not matter or have to be attended to as representing consent or nonconsent (as nonconsent would not have to be proven if force, aggravation, or coercion could be established).

12. A creative route to rectifying the problem of taking silence to mean consent is found in the post-traumatic stress disorder of "rape trauma syndrome" (RTS). RTS evidence could be used to rebut defense claims that silence meant consent. RTS evidence is provided by experts who give testimony about the nature and sequence of reactions to being raped, in order to demonstrate that victims' responses are consistent with someone who was raped.

It is in this way that RTS might be used to rebut consent defenses. Expert testimony can contribute to establishing that victim responses are of the same pattern that someone experiencing nonconsensual sexual attacks would exhibit. The pioneering work of Ann Wolbert Burgess identifies two stages in the "stress reaction to a life-threatening situation" (1995: 239). The syndrome consists of "somatic, cognitive, psychological, and behavioral symptoms" (ibid.), including fear, anxiety, depression, guilt, memory impairment, an inability to concentrate, intrusive imagery, nightmares, other "disturbances in sleep patterns", an "exaggerated startle response or hyper alertness", numbing of responsiveness to and decreased involvement with the environment and "avoidance of activities that might arouse recollection" of the rape incident (240–242). The stages are the acute or disruptive phase and the long-term process of adjustment phase (240).

RTS evidence can sensitize judges and jurors to the typical response patterns associated with rape victimization. As Goldberg-Ambrose indicates, prosecutors "have found such evidence invaluable in rebutting assertions that rape victims welcomed or reluctantly submitted to sex" (1989: 953, citing Rowland 1985). This can be invaluable in cases where victims were passive or silent, as such a response would be consistent with being victimized by rape. It is important to underscore that RTS is not used as evidence of rape; it is evidence of a characteristic trauma disorder in reaction to being raped.

13. This stands in contradiction to Catherine Wells's argument that "decency" ought to be the standard used to judge sexual assault. She criticizes using a women's experience or point of view because it suffers from the problem of casting women in universal, essentialist terms (cited in Davion 1999: 234). While I am sympathetic with this point, my fear is that unless male privilege is decentered, counterweighed, and corrected, male interests and points of view would define decency—much as they have defined reasonableness.

9. Mens Rea

1. Mistaken consent should be kept conceptually distinct from the defense of consent, which I will call the "liar defense" later (see chap. 11).

2. First he says that "the argument for expanding liability in rape cases from deliberate wrongdoing to carelessness remains controversial" (1998: 258). Next he states that most serious felonies, from murder to ordinary theft, require proof that the defendant knew he was causing injury or was aware of substantial risk. Yet extreme carelessness (criminal negligence) is sometimes accepted as the basis of criminal liability, for example, in homicide prosecutions based on drunk driving or on the use of unreasonable force in self-defense. A similar approach seems appropriate for sexual violations as well (ibid.). Then Schulhofer observes that "since the mid-1970's, this [negligence] view has largely prevailed with the American courts; the great majority now accept a negligence standard in rape cases" (ibid., citing Kadish and Schulhofer 1995: 326–328, on the resistance requirement vis-à-vis the *Hazel* case). As Kadish and Schulhofer summarize, "most of the recent American cases permit a mistake defense, but only when the defendant's error as to consent is honest and reasonable" (2001: 358). Berliner weighs in, noting that "the current standard is less reasonable" in rape than in other crimes (1991: 2704 n. 107).

3. Kristine Mullendore observes that the difference between manslaughter, defined by a mental state of recklessness, and rape, defined by nonconsent to often otherwise acceptable acts, is that, legally speaking, one cannot consent to being killed (or injured

with great bodily harm) but can consent to sex acts that become rape when consent is not present (personal communication, 1998). This is one reason for the historic difference in criminal liability as a result of negligence or recklessness in killing and in rape. But historic logic about the uniqueness of rape has been quieted by critiques showing the discriminatory nature of beliefs like these, the similarities between rapes and other crimes, and the prejudicial lack of protection such beliefs have led to. Because of the similarity and the discrimination in treatment of rape and other crimes, negligence and unreasonable mistakes should be recognized in law as criminal in rape as with other crimes.

4. For instance, the FBI classifies aggravated assault as one of the four serious violent offenses in the country (along with murder and non-negligent homicide, forcible [*sic*] rape, and robbery), while in the state of Michigan an offense such as aggravated assault is classified as a misdemeanor and defined as "assault; infliction of serious injury" (Michigan Penal Code, sec. 750.81a).

5. I am implicitly relying on the objective versus subjective mens rea standard for intent. Objective mens rea obtains where a reasonable person would have consciousness of guilt. The reasonable person is the yardstick employed to assess intent with the objective standard of rea, rather than an assessment of particular individual's state of mind for intent, as is the case with the subjective mens rea standard. (See also objective versus subjective reasonable woman's point of view, described in the previous chapter.)

6. In fact, even finer distinctions could be made. For example, a distinction between gross versus ordinary versus simple negligence could be made in a fashion akin to the differing kinds of intent levels being discussed here. The CLRC addresses subjective versus objective recklessness and negligence in precisely this context (Law Commission Report to the Home Office Sex Offenses Review, www.lawcom.gov.uk).

7. Recklessness and negligence would be the basis of assessing criminal culpability, as opposed to some "air of reality" test "which may be conferred by all the circumstances in which the alleged assault took place" (Harris and Pineau 1996: 65; also see Temkin 2002 on the "air of reality" criterion and the Canadian Supreme Court cases of *Papajohn*, *Osolin*, and *Park*, esp. 132–133). Simply put, this type of standard ("air of reality") requires some kind of factual basis, or corroboration, or support for the allegation that belief in consent was reasonable under the circumstances.

8. David Archard's (1999) examination of the "the *mens rea* of rape" discusses how the convenient substitution of "authoritative rule," sexist "convention," male voice, male view, and/or myth emanates from male vested interest, when the case is—or, I should say, when the case should be—determined from what I am referring to as a woman's point of view. Archard states, "in the case of rape,... the injured party is the authoritative source of knowledge about her consent" (223). A man may sincerely believe the victim agreed to the sex acts (or disregard her nonagreement, as Archard also recognizes in this context), but it remains the victim's knowledge—or, in my scheme, a reasonable woman's knowledge—about the existence and expression of involuntary nonagreement that matters.

10. Applying Recklessness and Negligence

1. It is unfortunate that although mistakes are disallowed in the model case of Michigan, the consent defense remains viable. Estrich says, "Michigan courts have consistently

construed these definitions as 'implicitly' preserving the consent defense" (1987: 86). As previously noted, the defense of consent has been successful under even serious aggravating conditions, for example, where the victim was kidnapped (*People v. Thompson* 117 Mich. App. 522, 526, 324 N.W. 2d 22, 23 [1982]) and where a gun was present but an accomplice rather than the assailant was holding it (*People v. Bernard* 360 N.W. 2d 204, 205 [Mich. App. 1984] 84, 90). See Estrich 1987: 84–85.

2. The flip side of stating that is nonagreement is the reasonable legal assumption is that mistaking (non)agreement by believing that consent was given is unreasonable. This is not a preferable way to articulate a provision, as it places the focus on getting away with a mistake (of agreement). Focus should be centered on the nonagreement as stated in law rather than on rebutting the nonagreement.

3. It might be reinforcing to specify both the presumptive nonagreement and the rebuttable presumption of unreasonableness of mistakes of agreement. This seems redundant, however. Moreover, to specify both would be cumbersome and possibly confusing in instructions for the jury.

4. The lesser level of negligent liability could tenably be treated as separate from recklessness in terms of force and coercion and crime definitions. Here the question would revolve around whether the defendant carelessly dismissed versus failed to appreciate the force or coercive power he was wielding over a victim, which a reasonable person would understand to be involved. But as with recklessness and negligence in relation to consent, my model simply incorporates both as culpable states, without making a finer differentiation as to levels or gradations of crime.

11. Defenses

1. Consent defenses would not be arguable in my model in cases where I would advance strict liability; that is, those involving minor-age victims, unconscious victims, the commission of other felonies, and the administration of date rape drugs.

2. An affirmative defense should not be conflated with affirmative consent, as in the Antioch staging policy that requires permission for each sex act.

3. Temkin comments that "arguably, the defense has no evidential burden to discharge in this situation, for, since the defence is seeking to do no more than deny the basic elements of the prosecution's case, any assertion of consent by the defence should be placed before the jury. This view has not, however, been taken by the courts, which have generally insisted upon some evidence or consent before a jury direction on consent is required" (2002: 172). Temkin's observation indicates that my recommendation is not seeking that much of an alteration from at least some current practices.

4. Reasonable doubt can be "difficult to define, some courts evade defining it to the jury" (Kadish and Schulhofer 2001: 38); however, "a traditionally accepted definition of reasonable doubt is … not a mere possible doubt; because everything relating to human affairs, and depending on moral evidence is open to some possible or imaginary doubt. It is that state of the case which, after the entire comparison and consideration of all the evidence, leaves the minds of the jurors in that condition that they cannot say they feel an abiding conviction, to a moral certainty, of the truth of the charge" (37).

5. Kristine Mullendore points out, however, that the federal standard is "clear and convincing" evidence for insanity defenses (personal communication, 2007, citing 18 USCA 17 [2007]) as a part of the Federal Crimes and Criminal Procedure Code.

6. It should be noted, however, that there are times when a defense of voluntary agreement might mean the victim was mistaken about, for example, having indicated her nonagreement or the presence of threats, fraud, or the like. This is not to say that she was lying when she charged rape but that in the eyes of judges or jurors she made an unreasonable—from a woman's point of view—error in judgment about the nature of the situation. This may exonerate a defendant, because, though the victim was not lying, she may yet be assessed to be wrong. The upshot is that with my model of change the woman accusing rape would not be susceptible to charges of perjury or filing a false police report (because she wasn't fabricating charges). This is noteworthy since some victims have been prosecuted for just such offenses in just such circumstances.

7. It does not matter how victims got into incapacitated states in all other rape circumstances, e.g., whether they were knowingly or volitionally or unknowingly drugged or intoxicated. The point is that such states preclude the rendering of agreement.

8. Burgess-Jackson gives the example that "the Model Penal Code adopts this approach by counting as rape cases in which a male 'has substantially impaired (a female's) power to appraise or control her conduct by administering or employing without her knowledge drugs, intoxicants or other means for the purpose of preventing resistance'" (1999: 104). In point of fact, in response to this growing problem, Congress passed the *Drug-Induced Rape Prevention and Punishment Act* in 1996, which criminalized "the use of any drug to commit sexual assault or other violent crimes, and stipulated a 20 year sentence as punishment" (Stap 1997: 2). This act also banned the import and export of flunitrazepam and made simple possession a criminal offense carrying up to a three-year term of imprisonment (ibid.). President Clinton signed a bill similar to the Rohypnol law that criminalized GHB in the year 2000 (National Institute of Justice 2000: 13).

9. In some jurisdictions, past sexual history evidence is limited as to consent; in others, it is limited as to credibility (see Snow 1999: 247–248).

12. Sexual Assault Under Duress and Fraud

1. Crimes of sexual assault under duress should not be confused with the criminal defense of duress.

2. Michigan CSC law includes extortion as a type of force/coercion under the condition of threats to retaliate in the future. The CSC Code states that "to retaliate" includes threats of physical punishment, kidnapping, or extortion (PA 328 1974). As Estrich points out, however, there have been no cases where "'force' was based on a threat to extort" in court cases (1987: 141 n. 37).

3. In my thinking, however, sexual assaults under duress would be lesser offenses, as in Estrich.

4. Needless to say, if a victim refuses, that is, says no, in the face of fraud or deceit (see the next section), subsequent sex acts would be coercive and criminal.

5. *Black's* defines blackmail as "unlawful demand of money or property under threat to do bodily harm, to injure property, to accuse of crime, or to expose disgraceful de-

fects" (1991: 116–117). The way I am using the term "duress" and hence blackmail is, however, exclusive of violent or physical threats to do bodily harm, in order to distinguish it from rape involving coercion.

6. Yet many of these kinds of positions are not recognized in law as inherently coercive or powerful or influential enough to negate the ability of victims truly to give agreement that is free and willing. Schulhofer's sexual autonomy approach to rape and sexual assault dictates that when "economic power or professional authority unjustifiably impairs the weaker party's freedom of sexual choice" (1998: 167), criminal conduct needs to be recognized. I do not go so far. Instead, I am arguing that the (nonphysical) economic/career threat as opposed to the position of power/authority creates the impairment to freedom of choice in this context.

7. MacKinnon is frequently accused of saying that all sex is rape; I point out here that she never went this far.

8. Remaining ambiguities are inevitable, and that is what fact finders like judges and juries are to decide.

13. Reforming Rape Reforms

1. Kadish and Schulhofer (2001: 33–34) offer that jury instructions can be an effective way to eliminate prejudice against a defendant; I would add, against a victim as well.

2. The Model Penal Code also persists in a corroboration requirement. Kadish and Schulhofer report that Texas is the only state to maintain a corroboration requirement. They note that this obtains, however, only when an adult takes over a year to report the incident (2001: 374). Bryden and Lengnick cite that Nebraska is an example as well (1997: 1197). Perhaps they note this additional state because of the way the law is written there. It specifies that corroboration of victim testimony is not required but is "is not rendered inadmissible" either (official Nebraska government Website, sec. 29-2028, "sexual assault; testimony; corroboration not required," uniweb.legislative.ne.gov/LegalDocs/view.php?page=S2920028000, accessed March 24, 2008).

3. About half of the states still admonished jurors in this fashion in 1988, according to Bryden and Lengnick (1997: 1198). An argument could be made that some sort of instruction opposite to the historical "rape is an accusation easily to be made, hard to be proved, and harder yet to be defended by the party accused, tho' never so innocent" (1971: 635) is justified, given the pervasiveness and persuasiveness of this instruction. Something like "rape is a crime hard to charge and harder to defend against by the victim, though never so innocent" stands as fact and could be used. I am not contending, however, that rape should enjoy any unique status that an instruction like this would raise; I am only arguing for comparability with other charges and procedures by removal of cautionary jury instructions in rape.

4. Both Michigan's and Schulhofer's reforms evince deep concerns about positions of authority and trust. These kinds of positions, where offenders prey on especially unguarded, accessible, naive, dependent, and/or defenseless girls—and women—are rampant and pernicious, as Schulhofer (1998) chronicles. These populations and crimes go neglected in the work of other scholars. Addressing these susceptible populations in laws and practices should figure into rape reform schemes.

5. The model places the last three conditions as aggravating factors on a stand-alone basis, in contrast to Michigan's required combinations of multiple offenders with incapacity or force/coercion or injury with incapacity or force/coercion in order to sustain the higher-level crimes in the first (criminal sexual penetration) and second (criminal sexual contact) degrees (as opposed to the lesser crimes of criminal sexual penetration in the third and criminal sexual contact in the fourth degrees).

6. Under Michigan law, the court must assess whether the victim believed in the ability of the assailant to carry out the threat in order to establish coercion. I advance that this is unnecessary. Like Estrich (1987: 86), I would also extend the law to cover threats against others like loved ones or roommates or friends in proximity at the time of the offense, not just threats to the victim.

7. A few states already specifically recognize rape with nonconsent in the absence of force (Kadish and Schulhofer 2001: 343).

8. Recall that Remick goes further than my provision here, remarking that we should state, "Always take 'no' for an answer. Always stop when asked to stop. Never assume 'no' means 'yes.' If her lips tell you 'no' but there's 'yes' in her eyes, keep in mind that her words, not her eyes, will appear in the court transcript" (1993: 1106).

9. Florida's statute provides the example for inclusion in statute and the respective instruction here. It states that consent "does not include coerced submission" (Kadish and Schulhofer 2001: 343).

10. Again, Michigan's CSC Code has a provision stating that the "victim's subjective state of mind, not the defendant's" constitutes the measuring standard for consent (Michigan Judicial Institute 2002: 221). To parallel existing law more, the objective reasonable woman is the standard to be used (not the subjective reasonableness of the woman or the subjective state of mind or belief of the individual victim—or offender, for that matter—in a case).

11. Although it is possible that a woman could be prosecuted and convicted on such a charge, this should not be the assumption at the outset.

12. In addition to the repeal of the prompt complaint requirement, the law needs to state the irrelevance of past reports, as I have done here.

13. Colorado law provides an alternative example of legal language to write out the relevance of past sex. The court's response to the constitutional challenge by Kobe Bryant's attorney was based on Colorado law and stated that "with certain exceptions, evidence of specific instances of an alleged sexual assault victim's sexual conduct 'shall be presumed irrelevant'" (*People of the State of Colorado v. Kobe Bean Bryant*, citing Colorado Revised Statutes sec. 18-3-407). Another, less strongly stated example is found in a jury instruction quoted in Berger: "There has been testimony about the sexual experience of the complainant in this case. You are to judge this testimony by the same standards of credibility which you apply to all other evidence. Even if you find it credible, you should not infer that, because a woman has consented on prior occasions to sexual intercourse, she necessarily consented with the defendant on the particular occasion at issue in this case." (1977: 96). Berger simultaneously notes, however, that the instruction can be problematic in refocusing attention on victims and their behavior instead of the accused and his conduct. I contend that the de jure specification and jury instruction on its irrelevance is worth the risk because past sex is frequently brought up in rape cases.

14. These considerations are not introduced as evidence in other criminal justice processing. This therefore bolsters the rationale, need, and justification for the recommended changes here. I do not go so far as to say that these factors are completely inadmissible, since some of them may be demonstrated (vs. presumed) to be relevant at times, for example, past sex and the origin of semen, lack of promptness of the report and the rape trauma syndrome, voluntary drinking and victim incapacitation. The point is that because of historical biases these considerations need to be legally declared to be irrelevant unless it is proven that they are material, competent, and relevant and do not introduce "unfair prejudice that would outweigh the probative value of the fact in question" or contribute to unwarranted invasion of privacy and so on.

15. Other state definitions of affirmative consent are similar. Illinois law defines affirmative consent as "words or overt action by a person indicating a freely given agreement to the specific acts of sexual penetration or sexual contact in question" (cited in Tchen 1983: 1549). Minnesota defines affirmative consent as "a voluntary uncoerced manifestation of a present agreement to perform a particular sex act" (cited on 1542). These definitions are of interest for their commonality in precluding implied consent, since indication of present, willful agreement is required.

14. Discussion of the Model Array

1. The evidence that goes to demonstrate the crime alleged can be tangible or testimonial (as is the case with all crimes). Tangible evidence would be physical evidence such as photographs, lab reports, rape kit findings, guns, knives, and so on. Testimonial evidence would be from the victim, who serves as a witness for the prosecution. The victim testifies as to the facts of the case: what happened, when, where, and how, along with details about the aggravating conditions—the force, the coercion, intimidation, fraud, and so on—and about her expression (or lack thereof) through words, gestures, or other conduct of the involuntariness of her submission, in other words, her expressions of nonagreement. The de jure specifications, the rules of evidence, and jury instructions—stating, for example, that corroboration of a victim's testimony is not required, that victim testimony is sufficient for conviction on rape charges, that no means no, that a reasonable woman's point of view is to be used to determine what is reasonable as an indication of involuntariness, and that a woman's point of view is to be used to determine the perception of force or threats/coercion/duress/fraud (in the absence of aggravating factors), or the involuntariness of submission—are all formulated to promote successful rape prosecution. This should help to make nonagreement more weighty, probable, credible, or reasonable than the historic discriminatory belief in implicit consent. Other witnesses who could testify to any of the alleged criminal acts or circumstances would be relevant and helpful, but these are rare in cases of rape. Attackers very often plan and/or carry out their crimes specifically to avoid onlookers, passersby (res gestae witnesses), or witnesses of any other kind, hence typically there is an absence of such corroborative evidence in rape. Because corroboration is explicitly unnecessary, additional witnesses are, legally speaking, unnecessary. It is important to bring in a further possibility regarding witnesses that should be figured into the potential evidence that can facilitate rape prosecutions. This is evidence from expert witnesses who can testify to the rape trauma

syndrome. As noted earlier, the existence of RTS has been used by prosecutors to counter consent claims by the defense by showing that a woman's responses are consistent with those of a person who has been raped. RTS evidence is useful to make sense out of victim reactions that seem inconsistent with rape, like being calm or obsessive or not coming forward right away. Prosecutors could use expert witnesses to show the RTS that would serve as another sort of testimonial evidence, especially useful to prosecutors to rebut voluntariness, agreement (consent) defenses. RTS evidence is useful as a type of (testimonial and) corroborative evidence that enhances conviction probability (Goldberg-Ambrose 1989: 953).

2. Susan Herman, director of the National Center for Victims of Crimes (NCVC) discussed this issue in a radio interview on March 10, 2004 (Herman, 2004).

3. As in the Michigan model, past sexual activity evidence would only be admissible for its relevance to determining "the origin of semen, pregnancy or disease" (sec. 520j[1][b]), not determining victim character/credibility, that is, to show that she is a "dishonest woman" (Harris and Pineau 1996: 121). I would change the Michigan model on the first allowed premise for past sexual evidence, though, and disallow "evidence of the victim's past sexual conduct with the actor" (sec. 520j[1][a]), which it allows, since past consent does not mean consent in the instance being adjudicated even if with the defendant. Like the Michigan model, though, the process and allowance for past sexual history evidence for the origin of semen, pregnancy, or disease would require the filing a written motion and "offer of proof" (sec. 520j[2]); then, if the judge were satisfied, he or she would order an in-camera hearing to be held before trial to determine the relevance/admissibility of such sexual history evidence (Michigan Judicial Institute 2002: 324–325) to be used to show the origin of semen, pregnancy, or disease (and not credibility or character).

4. While Federal Rule of Evidence 404 disallows evidence of a past criminal record to go to the character of the accused, and while "evidence of other crimes, wrongs, or acts is not admissible to prove the character of a person in order to show action in conformity therewith. It may, however, be admissible for other purposes, such as proof of motive, opportunity, intent, preparation, plan, knowledge, (identity), or absence of mistake or accident" (Kadish and Schulhofer 2001: 26). The defendant's record, of sexual assault or otherwise, can also be considered (in addition to motive, etc.) for enhancement at sentencing, as a part of presumptive, "three strikes," "habitual" or "career" criminal, or "patterned sex" offender guidelines that have been passed widely across the country.

5. Federal Rule 403 states that "although relevant, evidence may be excluded if its probative value is substantially outweighed by the danger of unfair prejudice, confusion of the issues, or misleading the jury, or by considerations of undue delay, waste of time, or needless presentation of cumulative evidence" (Kadish and Schulhofer 2001: 26).

6. The Criminal Law Revision Committee provides another example that could easily be adapted in this context. They recommend that the jury be given "additional directions. Those directions would be ... that, if his asserted belief in consent was caused solely by reason of his voluntarily intoxicated state, whether through drink or drugs, then his failure to appreciate that she might not consent is no defence" (2000: 77). The adaptation would be that if his asserted belief in consent was caused solely by reason of her voluntarily intoxicated state, whether through drink or drugs, then his failure to ap-

preciate her involuntariness, nonagreement or her inability to give voluntariness, agreement (consent) is no defense. Similarly, if his asserted belief in consent was caused solely by reason of her dancing, dress, demeanor, acquaintanceship, or history dating him, his failure to appreciate her involuntariness, nonagreement is no defense. But I think it more parsimonious just to stipulate legislatively the irrelevance of such factors as drinking, dancing, and so on to consent or voluntariness, agreement and mistakes herein.

7. A bonus from adapting mens rea from homicide offenses to sexual assault offenses by including reckless and negligent intent is that "a defendant obviously enjoys no constitutional right to present irrelevant evidence; to the extent that the legal issue is framed in terms of his intent, rather than hers, her reputation and her history which was unknown to him is far less relevant and thus far more easily excluded in a balance of probative value and prejudice" (Estrich 1987: 143, referencing Berger 1977). This point is well taken, but what I previously advanced in the model goes further. I contend that even when a defendant has knowledge of a victim's sexual history, it is irrelevant and would not legitimate mistaken consent as anything resembling reasonable belief.

8. The Kobe Bryant case showcased a new defense. The defense tried to argue that the victim was sick, and her clinical depression affected her ability to identify and perceive reality.

9. This is especially needed to buttress the unreasonableness of assuming voluntariness, agreement with the de jure specification of presumptive nonagreement that—I must emphasize—stands regardless of the victim's past sexual conduct, despite her drinking, dating, dancing, and so on (because of the presumptive irrelevance to consent of these victim behaviors).

10. It might be noted, too, that requiring the defendant to observe or notice the withdrawal of agreement, once indicated, is different from requiring the exacting of agreement with each sexual move as the Antioch Code further requires. The latter is a more demanding approach; the former is less demanding as it would target withdrawal of voluntariness, agreement rather than demand the securing of permission for each successive act.

15. Advantages of a Paradigm Shift

1. The increased likelihood that real change can come about as a result of the overlapping nature of the alterations set out in the model can be discussed in more specific terms. For instance, applying reckless and negligent liability to offenders' appreciation of aggravating conditions, force, coercion, duress, fraud, and the expression of nonagreement as these things are determined by what a reasonable woman would understand to be aggravating conditions, force, coercion, duress, fraud, or the expression of nonagreement—that is, an objective woman's point of view—replaces historic reliance on chauvinistic standards and rape myths to determine the presence of criminal conditions or nonconsent. Applying recklessness and negligence to understanding the presumptive nonagreement that the law stipulates when aggravating, forceful, or coercive conditions, duress, or fraud are present (but not when nonagreement is the sole basis of the crime) moves in this same direction. It does this by stating (and thus reinforcing) clearly and simply in de jure law what the reasonable belief should be (which would be non-

agreement when aggravation, force/coercion, and/or duress/fraud are what a reasonable woman would understand to be in existence). These changes are pivotal to defining that no means no, that women don't want rape or desire sex that is forced (by male "schoolboy" standards of force; see Estrich 1987), that women who don't resist "enough" (by male-defined standards, measures, and understandings) really want rape or coerced sex acts, or tricks, or scamming, or the like.

2. It should be recognized that sexual gratification originates, unfortunately, from a hegemonic, male-defined view. Changing this is beyond the scope of the present effort.

3. Schulhofer's affirmative consent and sexual autonomy model is unlikely to be widely adopted. As he notes, even legislating that a verbal no is sufficient to establish nonconsent has not been accepted in most jurisdictions (1998: 255). The low probability of enacting more radical change is reinforced by the fact that only a "handful" of states— three by his count (New Jersey, Wisconsin, and Washington)—have managed to get affirmative consent provisions through the legislatures (271). Given the relatively low level and narrow range of change along a tenet (affirmative consent reform law) so critical to his work, his claim for "affirmative" and "freely given" "permission" to protect a right yet to be recognized in law (sexual autonomy) seems outlandish. His articulately detailed argumentation is great for theory but bad for political and social change. As he says himself of radicalism (in reference to MacKinnon, Dworkin, and Rich), it is "well intentioned but stultifying" (57). Unfortunately, the same might be said of his own work on this count.

4. This is a first step toward justice. True justice will require more fundamental change than the confines of extant law allows, but such considerations (of alternative models of particularly social justice) are beyond the purview of the present discussion. My model and arguments are designed to move toward the ideals of law and justice but recognize that the reality of law as it is practiced is a far stretch from this ideal.

5. Again, the graduated step structure allowing for degrees of rape and sexual assault is not necessarily a move to be harsher on all those accused of these crimes.

16. Recommendations Complementing the Model Rape Law

1. While some worry that victims will be excessively punitive or even advocate vigilante justice, what really concerns many rape victims is that the defendant be prevented from doing it again, to them or anyone else. Many victims therefore want the assailant to be forced to get counseling through criminal sanctioning, not necessarily castrated or killed, as many tend to think. Not only this, but victims may not be aware of their rights to register their opinions or wishes (as in victim impact statements), or they simply may not exercise these rights even when legislated (Miller and Meloy forthcoming).

2. Arrest warrants should not be confused with search warrants. In the majority of jurisdictions in the United States, the police need to have a prosecutor authorize (and a judge sign/issue) a warrant for the arrest of suspected parties (either before or after an arrest is effected). Prosecutors enjoy nearly total free rein in this realm, where they have the power to authorize, change, or deny any charges the police request.

3. Even so, "the absolute number of jury trials is not so small: there are about 300,000 every year" (Levine 1992: 36), which explains in large part why court dockets are so backlogged. The number of cases potentially affected at trial, not to mention the hand

the changes in the model would deal out for plea negotiations, makes my recommendations all the more far-reaching. Furthermore, as previously mentioned, the enacted law contours the parameters of discretionary decision making that falls within its bounds, and hence enacted law sets the parameters for enforcement whether inside or outside of court/trial contexts.

4. While some might object that low-level charges for sexual assault offenses would be disadvantageous, because they would allow for more deals that excessively minimize the severity of sexual assault charges, the availability of lower-level sexual assault counts could lead to more convictions. Moreover, excessive reductions already occur routinely now, and to nonrape charges.

5. Prosecutors' decisions to authorize arrest warrants can be reconsidered in light of these plea-bargaining recommendations and potential advantages. To reiterate, because prosecutors can change the number and level of initial charges and counts and outright deny arrest warrants, just as they are empowered to alter offenses and sentence possibilities in plea bargaining (albeit limited by determinate sentencing; see below), accountability is at least as critical with warrant decisions as it is with plea bargaining, and it would likely carry the same benefits of publicity, enhanced leverage, and "truth in criminal labeling" (see Loh 1981).

6. The influential nature of jury instructions was reflected in a news commentator's recent observation that if the pictures of prisoner torment from Abu Ghraib prison in Iraq were released, the soldiers could maybe get a fair trial, but it would take mounds of jury instructions in order to effect this result (Paula Zahn, *CNN News*, May 13, 2004).

7. Just as a point of information, the conviction rates between bench and jury trials vary, but not tremendously. Spohn and Horney report conviction rates of 64 and 53 percent, respectively (1992: 72).

8. The discretion to determine aggravating and mitigating circumstances that would alter sentences beyond determinate statute ranges in federal and some state courts may be taken away from judges and conferred instead on juries because of the Supreme Court's 1994 decision in *Blakely v. Washington* (111 Wash. App. 851, 47P. 3d 149).

9. Additional models could also guide state development of compliance legislation. For example, the Clery Act requires regular reports on rape and sexual assault; a similar requirement might be useful in monitoring implementation practices. And the VAWA requires research on the impact of the legislation; this affords a further model.

10. Although the Tenth Amendment pertaining to the separation of powers between the federal and state governments precludes the feds from requiring states to report directly to them, most states have laws in place that require localities to report to the FBI or to report to the state police, who then forward compilations on to the FBI. Similar laws and procedures could be used to require reporting of the decisions and outcomes associated with rape reform laws in action, in order to monitor compliance so as to assess the effectiveness of reforms and make further improvements as suggested by the successes and failures of implementation. Alternatively, as stated above, federal compliance law could stand as the model guiding the states to develop their own mechanisms for the required data and assessment. I recommend municipalities sending data to the state attorney general and the state attorney general then sending compilations to the feds, rather than the localities being required to send data directly to the BJS, because of

potential separation-of-powers issues and because I am trying to base recommendations on existing models.

11. "The first case where sex was identified as a characteristic requiring more than a rational basis to justify a legislative act was Reed v. Reed, 404 U.S. 71 (1979) when the Supreme Court found that an Idaho statute giving preference to the appointment of fathers over mothers to act as administrators of their children's estates for administrative convenience was a violation of the 14th Amendment. The US Supreme Court case that most recently reaffirmed the idea that sex based characteristics are not suspect classes under the 14th Amendment is the VNI case, United States v. Virginia, 518 U.S. 515 (1996), where Justice Ginsburg noted that such a characteristic required 'an exceedingly persuasive justification'" (Kristine Mullendore, personal communication, 2007).

12. One salient factor contributing to the uniquely obstructed access to and protection by the system for rape victims that has to be emphasized is the release of the victim identity and background information. Broadcasting victims names—intentionally or allegedly accidentally (as in the Kobe Bryant case)—and/or allegations about previous sexual activities and sexual reputation, alleged ulterior motives, medical conditions, psychological difficulties, or psychiatric treatment or help-seeking behaviors combine to thwart the reporting and prosecution of offenders by those victimized by the crimes of sexual violence. The penchant for drawing out such details about sexual assault victims makes them prejudicially impugned in the media. Laws need to be enacted or, where enacted, enforced and/or strengthened so as strictly to prohibit violations of victims' privacy by spotlighting them, raising misgivings about them, and discrediting them in such a singular way. Many laws, customary habits, practices, and/or news etiquettes protect victims' names and circumstances, such as medical and counseling histories, from publication by the press and from release to the public. But as we recently saw in the Kobe Bryant case, leaks, mistakes, and intentional release of alleged facts are still commonplace. This is why we need reforms that will be monitored and sanctions that punish actors and agencies when violations occur. Not only does release of such information violate victims' right to privacy, it contaminates jury pools and weakens the district attorney's hand in plea negotiations. In this instance, victims' right to unrestricted, nondiscriminatory—equal—use of the criminal justice system outstrips the public's right to know, not to mention idle public curiosity and interest in gossip.

17. Moving Forward

1. For a discussion of sentencing changes vis-à-vis jurors and other legal actors, see Ball 2007.

2. There are a multitude of additional recommendations for improving the treatment of rape and its victims. While it is beyond the purview of this book to enumerate them all, it might be instructive to convey a sense of the range of measures. Such recommendations would cover a wide span of proposals, policies, and laws. Measures would range from the increased funding and use of standardized rape kits for HIV/AIDS testing and the collection of medical evidence and DNA samples for the identification of assailants to the development of training, education, and reporting policies and manuals, case management systems for criminal justice agencies, the development of task forces,

local councils, and commissions to study and make recommendations on rape, the prohibition of victim polygraphs, the filming of child victim testimony, and the use of rape and sexual assault offender notification and registration systems.

3. I would agree with critical criminologists that care needs to be taken that the site of struggle and change extend beyond the state and the law. Foucault states that "the law produces the subject it claims to protect or emancipate," while Brown avers that "the effort to seek legal redress for injuries also 'legitimizes law and the state as appropriate protectors against injury while obscuring the masculinist state's own power to injure' while creating 'dependent subjects' that reproduce inequality" (cited in Mardorossian 2002: 9–10). My recommendations attempt to encompass a bit more than the state to reach, for example, education, the media, grassroots organizations, and PACs, as well as pursue the goal of rectifying inequality in its many manifestations.

4. Socialist feminists point out, for example, that capitalist patriarchy relegates women to being the property of men, banishing them to the private (versus public) realm where they are unpaid labor in economic production and unpaid reproducers of the next generation of consumers for capitalist markets, as well as reproducers of the dominant ideology that perpetuates the patriarchal capitalist system. The avarice and lust of capitalist patriarchy contributes to rape when it celebrates men's ruthless competition to take money, property, and status from one another, and this includes the taking of sex, which is to say, the rape of women.

5. Rozee and Koss describe "dangerous men" as those who believe in or act on "sexual entitlement," score high on "power and control" and on beliefs and attitudes corresponding to "dominance," and are "overcompetitive" and "rigid" about traditional notions of gender roles (2001: 299, citing Malamuth et al. 1995 and Rozee, Batemen, and Gilmore 1991). They identify such characteristics as contributors to rape. Miriam Lewin's theory of "four societal norms" that cause "unwanted sex," or sex that is reluctantly given into, follows along the lines of male dominance and entitlement as contributors to one-sided sex, which I would contend ultimately contributes to sexual assault and rape. She advances that "a) current remnants of the ideology of male supremacy, b) the norm of male initiative, c) the lack of positive sexual experience norms for women, and d) the 'stroking norm' for women" (1985: 184) cause women to accede to sexual intercourse they really don't want.

6. Temkin's concluding call for a "one-stop shop" type of coordination where medical, forensic, and counseling services are contained under one roof, as in Manchester and London (2002: 35) is similar to this last dimension in Weldon's research.

7. The influence of grassroots and women's organizations was seen in Michigan's first and sweeping rape reform and then in women's grassroots efforts across the United States. A network of women worked long and hard to get the model law passed in Michigan. The resultant reforms were exemplary in most ways (the spousal exemption was not repealed until years later), and other states followed suit. NOW followed up the Michigan accomplishment by establishing a national-level task force designed to stimulate change in rape laws across the country (Schulhofer 1998). This example confirms Weldon's finding concerning the power and effectiveness of grassroots work.

8. Those few who study women's movements against sexual and domestic violence and follow them over time have disclosed problems. The first problem to guard against

is placation. Advocate groups get appeased because of all the changes that actually do get put into place. The second problem to watch for and resist is co-optation of the social movements, political institutions, agencies, and front-line workers. Feminist protest and critique get buried by social service bureaucracies and the policies and workings of a therapeutic state. We need to keep a watchful eye out for such potentialities and think about remedial actions to reduce placation and co-optation should they arise with a new round of changes.

9. Weldon continues with recommendations for "maintaining an autonomous women's movement": (1) government funding for women's movements and (2) a united women's coalition independent of government, separate nongovernmental organization or caucuses for women from marginalized subgroups (2002: 200).

References

Adler, Zsuzsanna. 1987. *Rape on Trial*. London: Routledge and Kegan Paul.

Allen, Judith A. 1990. *Sex and Secrets: Crimes Involving Australian Women since 1880*. Oxford: Oxford University Press.

Allison, Julie A. and Lawrence S. Wrightsman. 1993. *Rape: The Misunderstood Crime*. Newbury Park, Calif.: Sage.

Allred, Gloria and Margery Somers. 2004. "Rape Shield Laws." *Ms. Magazine* 14 (1): 63.

American Bar Association (ABA). 1996. "When the Law Says No." *American Bar Association Journal*, August, 87.

Anderson, Michelle. 2002. "From Chastity Requirement to Sexuality License: Sexual Consent and a New Rape Shield Law." *George Washington Law Review* 70 (1): 51–162.

———. 1998. "Reviving Resistance in Rape Law." *University of Illinois Law Review* 1998 (4): 953–1012.

Antioch College Community. 1995. "Antioch College: A Sexual Consent Policy." In *Rape on Campus*, ed. Bruno Leone, 10–12. San Diego: Greenhaven.

Archard, David. 1999. "The *Mens Rea* of Rape: Reasonableness and Culpable Mistakes." In *A Most Detestable Crime: New Philosophical Essays on Rape*, ed. Kenneth Burgess-Jackson, 213–229. New York: Oxford University Press.

Bachman, Ronet and Raymond Paternoster. 1993. "A Contemporary Look at the Effects of Rape Law Reform: How Far Have We Really Come?" *Journal of Criminal Law and Criminology* 84 (3): 554–574.

Bailey, F. Lee and Henry B. Rothblatt. 1973. *Crimes of Violence*. Rochester, N.Y.: Lawyers Co-operative Publishing.

Baker, Brenda M. 1999. "Understanding Consent in Sexual Assault." In *A Most Detestable Crime: New Philosophical Essays on Rape*, ed. Kenneth Burgess-Jackson, 49–70. New York: Oxford University Press.

Ball, Jeremy. "Sentencing and the Supreme Court: The Implications of *Apprendi*, *Blakely*, and *Booker*." In *Current Legal Issues in Criminal Justice: Readings*, ed. Craig Hemmens, 228–256. New York: Oxford University Press, 2007.

Barak, Gregg. 1998. *Integrating Criminologies*. Boston: Allyn and Bacon.

Battelle Memorial Institute Law and Social Policy Center. 1977. "Forcible Rape: A National Survey of the Response by Prosecutors. National Institute on Law Enforcement and Criminal Justice." Washington, D.C.: U.S. Government Printing Office.

BenDor, Jan. 1976. "Justice After Rape: Legal Reform in Michigan." In *Sexual Assault: The Victim and the Rapist*, ed. Marcia J. Walker and Stanley L. Brodsky, 149–160. Lexington, Mass.: Lexington.

Benedict, Helen. 1992. *Virgin or Vamp: How the Press Covers Sex Crimes*. New York: Oxford University Press.

Berger, Ronald J., Lawrence W. Neuman, and Patricia Searles. 1991. "The Social and Political Context of Rape Law Reform: An Aggregate Analysis." *Social Science Quarterly* 72 (2): 221–238.

Berger, Ronald J., Patricia Searles, and Lawrence W. Neuman. 1988. "The Dimensions of Rape Reform Legislation." *Law and Society Review* 22 (2): 329–358.

Berger, Vivian. 1988. "Not So Simple Rape." *Criminal Justice Ethics* 7 (1): 69–80.

——. 1977. "Man's Trial, Woman's Tribulation: Rape Cases in the Courtroom." *Columbia Law Review* 77 (1): 1–103.

Berliner, Dana. 1991. "Rethinking the Reasonable Belief Defense to Rape." *Yale Law Journal* 100 (8): 2687–2706

Biden, Joseph. 1993. *The Violence Against Women Act of 1993: Report*. Washington, D.C.: Senate Committee on the Judiciary, September.

Biden, Joseph R. 1995. "Rape Should Be a Civil Rights Offense." In *Rape on Campus*, ed. Bruno Leone, 101–104. San Diego: Greenhaven.

Bienen, Leigh. 1983. "Rape Reform Legislation in the United States: A Look at Some Practical Effects." *Victimology* 8 (1–2):139–151.

——. 1980. "Rape III—National Developments in Rape Reform Legislation." *Women's Rights Law Reporter* 6 (3): 170–213.

Black, Henry Campbell. 1991. *Black's Law Dictionary: Definitions of the Terms and Phrases of American and English Jurisprudence, Ancient and Modern*. 6th abridged ed. Ed. publisher's editorial staff, with coauthors Joseph R. Nolan and Jacqueline M. Nolan-Haley and contributing authors M. J. Connolly, Stephen C. Hicks, and Martina N. Alibrandi. St. Paul, Minn.: West.

Bohmer, Carol. 1991. "Acquaintance Rape and the Law." In *Acquaintance Rape: The Hidden Crime*, ed. Andrea Parrot and Laurie Bechhoffer, 317–333. New York: Wiley.

Bohmer, Carol and Andrea Parrot. 1993. *Sexual Assaults on Campus: The Problem and Solution*. New York: Lexington.

Boyle, Christine. 2000. "Symposium: The Model Penal Code Revisited. What Makes 'Model' Sexual Offenses? A Canadian Perspective." *Buffalo Criminal Law Review* 4 (1): 487–514.

Brooks, Rachelle. 1997. "Feminists Negotiate the Legislative Branch: The Violence Against Women Act." In *Feminist Negotiate the State: The Politics of Domestic Violence*, ed. Cynthia R. Daniels, 65–81. Lanham, Md.: University Press of America.

Brownmiller, Susan. 1975. *Against Our Will: Men, Women and Rape*. New York: Bantam.

Bryden, David P. and Sonja Lengnick. 1997. "Rape in the Criminal Justice System." *Journal of Criminal Law and Criminology* 87 (4): 1195–1384.

Burgess, Ann Wolbert. 1995. "Rape Trauma Syndrome." In *Rape and Society: Readings on the Problem of Sexual Assault*, ed. Patricia Searles and Ronald J. Berger, 239–245. Boulder, Colo.: Westview.

———. 1975. "The Victim Goes on Trial." In *Victimology: A New Focus*, ed. Israel Drapkin and Emile Viano, 3:21–30. Lexington, Mass.: Heath.

Burgess-Jackson, Kenneth. 1999. "A Theory of Rape." In *A Most Detestable Crime: New Philosophical Essays on Rape*, ed. Kenneth Burgess-Jackson, 92–117. New York: Oxford University Press.

Burt, Martha R. 1980. "Cultural Myths and Supports for Rape." *Journal of Personality and Social Psychology* 38 (2): 217–230.

Burt, Martha R., Janine M. Zweig, Cynthia Andrews, Ashley Van Ness, Neal Parikh, Brenda Uekert, and Adele V. Harrell. 2001. *2001 Report: Evaluation of the STOP Formula Grants to Combat Violence Against Women*. Washington, D.C.: Urban Institute.

Cahill, Ann J. 2001. *Rethinking Rape*. Ithaca, N.Y.: Cornell University Press.

Campbell, Bonnie J. 1996. "Message from Violence Against Women Office Director: Bonnie J. Campbell." *Violence Against Women Act NEWS* 1 (1).

Campbell, Rebecca and Camille R. Johnson. 1997. "Police Officers' Perceptions of Rape: Is There Consistency Between State Law and Individual Belief?" *Journal of Interpersonal Violence* 12 (2): 255–274.

Caringella-MacDonald, Susan. 1998. "The Relative Visibility of Rape Cases in National Popular Magazines." *Journal of Violence Against Women* 4 (1): 62–80.

———. 1991. "An Assessment of Rape Reform: Victim and Case Treatment Under the Michigan Model." *International Review of Victimology* 1 (4): 347–361.

———. 1988. "Marxist-Feminist Interpretations of the Aftermath of Rape Reforms." *Contemporary Crises: Law, Crime, and Social Policy* 12 (4): 125–144.

———. 1985. "The Comparability of Sexual and Non-sexual Assault Case Treatment: Did Statute Change Meet the Objective?" *Crime and Delinquency* 31 (April): 206–222.

———. 1984. "Sexual Assault Prosecution: An Examination of Model Rape Legislation in Michigan." In *Criminal Justice Politics and Women: The Aftermath of Legally Mandated Change*, ed. Claudine Schweber and Clarice Feinman, 65–82. New York: Haworth.

Carnell, Brian. 2002. "Do Rape Shield Laws Forbid Questions About False Allegations?" www.equityfeminism.com/print/archives/years/2002/000036.html. Accessed March 6, 2002.

Carrington, Frank and George Nicholson. 1984. "The Victim's Movement: An Idea Whose Time Has Come." *Pepperdine Law Review* 11 (1): 1–13.

Carter, Daniel S. 2000. "Covering Crime on College Campuses." www.securityoncampus
.org/reporters/coveringcrime.html. Accessed March 8, 2005. (Originally published
in *Quill Magazine: A Publication of the Society of Professional Journalists*, September 2000.)

Chamallas, Martha. 1988. "Consent, Equality, and the Legal Control of Sexual Conduct."
Southern California Law Review 61 (4): 777–862.

Chancer, Lynn. 1998. *Reconcilable Differences: Confronting Beauty, Pornography, and the
Future of Feminism*. Berkeley: University of California Press.

——. 1997. "Introduction: The Seens and Unseens of Popular Cultural Representation."
In *Feminism, Media and the Law*, ed. Martha A. Fineman and Martha T. McCluskey,
227–234. New York: Oxford University Press.

Chappell, Duncan. 1982. "The Impact of Rape Reform Legislation." Paper presented at
the American Society of Criminology, Toronto, Ontario, November.

Clark, Toni F. and Deborah Buchner. 1982. "Critical Issues in the Prosecution of Rape: A
Cross-Jurisdictional Study of 17 U.S. Cities." Paper presented at the American Society of Criminology, Toronto, Ontario, November.

Clark, Lorenne and Deborah Lewis. 1977. *Rape: The Price of Coercive Sexuality*. Toronto:
Women's Press.

Cobb, Kenneth A. and Nanct R. Schauer. 1977. "Michigan's Criminal Sexual Assault Law."
In *Forcible Rape: The Crime, the Victim and the Offender*, ed. Duncan Chappell, Rob-
ley Geis, and Gilbert Geis, 170–188. New York: Columbia University Press.

Cohen, Lawrence E. and Marcus Felson. 1979. "Social Change and Crime Rate Trends: A
Routine Activity Approach." *American Sociological Review* 44 (4): 588–608.

CONNSACS. 2000. *Connecticut Sexual Assault Crisis Services*. April 6. connsacs.org/li-
brary/justice.html:1–6. Accessed April 6, 2000.

Criminal Law Revision Committee (CLRC), Law Commission. 2000. "Consent in
Sex Offences: A Report to the Home Office Sex Offences Review." United King-
dom: Crown Copyright and Disclaimer. www.lawcom.gov.uk. Accessed July 15,
2007.

Cuklanz, Lisa M. 1996. *Rape on Trial: How the Mass Media Construct Legal Reform and
Social Change*. Philadelphia: University of Pennsylvania Press.

Currie, Elliot. 1985. *Confronting Crime: An American Challenge*. New York: Pantheon.

Curtis, Lynn A. 1976. "Present and Future Measures of Victimization in Forcible Rape."
In *Sexual Assault: The Victim and the Rapist*, ed, Marcia J. Walker and Stanley L.
Brodsky, 61–68. Lexington, Mass.: Lexington Books.

Davion, Victoria. 1999. "The Difference Debate: Rape and Moral Responsibility." In *A
Most Detestable Crime: New Philosophical Essays on Rape*, ed. Kenneth Burgess-
Jackson, 230–244. New York: Oxford University Press.

Davis, Noy S. and Jennifer Twombly. 2000. *Handbook for Statutory Rape Issues*. February.
www.vaw.umn.edu/documents/stateleg/stateleg.html. Accessed July 1, 2004.

Dean, Charles W. and Mary de Bruyn-Kops. 1982. *The Crime and the Consequences of
Rape*. Springfield, Ill.: Thomas.

DeKeseredy, Walter, Shahid Alvi, and Martin D. Schwartz. 2006. " An Economic Exclu-
sion/Peer Support Model Looks at 'Wedfare' and Woman Abuse." *Critical Crimi-
nologist* 14 (Spring): 23–41.

DeKeseredy, Walter, Martin D. Schwartz, and Shahid Alvi. 2006. "The Role of Profeminist Men in Dealing with Woman Abuse on the Canadian College Campus." *Violence Against Women* 6 (9): 918–935.

Delgado, Richard. 1996. "No: Selective Enforcement Targets Unpopular Men." *American Bar Association Journal* 82 (August): 87.

Denno, Deborah. 1997. "Sexuality, Rape and Mental Retardation." *University of Illinois Review*, no. 2: 315–399.

Denno, Deborah W. 1993. "Perspectives on Disclosing Rape Victims' Names from the Privacy Rights of Rape Victims in the Media and the Law." *Fordham Law Review* 61 (5): 1113–1145.

Department of Justice, Office of the Attorney General. 2005a. "Final Guidelines for the Jacob Wetterling Crimes Against Children and Sexually Violent Offender Registration Act." March 4, 2005. www.ojp.gov/vawo/laws/jwaguide.htm. Accessed March 4, 2005.

——. 2005b. "Final Guidelines for Megan's Law and the Jacob Wetterling Crimes Against Children and Sexually Violent Offender Registration Act." www.ojp.gov/vawo/laws/jwaguide.htm. Accessed March 4, 2005.

Dershowitz, Alan. 1984. "Letter to the Editor." *Boston Globe*, March 2, 10.

Dressler, Joshua. 1998. "Where Have We Been, and Where We Might Be Going: Some Cautionary Reflections on Rape Law Reform." *Cleveland State Law Review* 46 (3): 409–442.

Du Mont, Janet and Terri L. Myhr. 2000. "So Few Convictions: The Role of Client-Related Characteristics in the Legal Processing of Sexual Assaults." *Violence Against Women* 6 (10): 1109–1136.

Dusky, Lorraine. 2003. "Harvard Stumbles Over Rape Reporting." *Ms.*, Spring, 39–40.

——. 1996. *Still Unequal: The Shameful Truth About Women and Justice in America.* New York: Crown.

Dworkin, Andrea. 1997. *Life and Death: Unapologetic Writings on the Continuing War Against Women.* New York: Free Press.

Editorial staff of LexisNexis. 2003. *Federal Criminal Laws and Rules.* Charlottesville, Va.: Matthew Bender.

Edwards, Susan 1989. *Policing 'Domestic' Violence: Women, Law and the State.* London: Sage.

Eitzen, Stanley D. and Maxine Baca Zinn. 1997. *Social Problems.* 7th ed. Boston: Allyn and Bacon.

Epstein, Joel C. 2001. "Understanding the Jeanne Clergy Disclosure Act." *Catalyst* 6 (1–3): 31–32.

Estrich, Susan. 1987. *Real Rape.* Cambridge: Harvard University Press.

Fairstein, Linda A. 1993. *Sexual Violence: Our War Against Rape.* New York: Morrow.

Falk, Patricia J. 1998. "Rape by Fraud and Rape by Coercion." *Brooklyn Law Review* 64 (1): 39–149.

Federal Bureau of Investigation. 1975. *Uniform Crime Reports.* Washington, D.C.: U.S. Government Printing Office.

Field, Hubert S. 1978. "Attitudes Toward Rape: A Comparative Analysis of Police, Rapists, Crisis Counselors, and Citizens." *Journal of Personality and Social Psychology* 36 (2): 156–179.

Field, Hubert S. and Leigh B. Bienen. 1980. *Jurors and Rape: A Study in Psychology and Law.* Lexington, Mass.: Lexington Books.

Fineman, Martha and Martha T. McClusky, eds. 1997. *Feminism, Media and the Law*. New York: Oxford University Press.

Fink, Virginia S. 2003. Review of *Protest, Policy and the Problem of Violence Against Women: A Cross-National Comparison* (2002), by Laurel S. Weldon. *Violence Against Women* 9 (3): 391–398.

Finkelhor, David and Kersti Yllo. 1985. *License to Rape: Sexual Abuse of Wives*. New York: Holt, Rinehart and Winston.

Francis, Samuel. 1997. "Sexual Predator Laws Are Unconstitutional." In *Sexual Violence: Opposing Viewpoint*, ed. Mary E. Williams and Tamara L. Roleff, 171–174. San Diego: Greenhaven.

Francis, Leslie, ed. 1996. *Date Rape: Feminism, Philosophy, and the Law*. University Park: Pennsylvania State University Press.

Frazee, David, Ann Noel, Andrea Brenneke, and Mary Dunlap. 1995. "Gender-Justice Break: A Plain-English Guide to the New Civil-Rights Law Against Violence Against Women." *On the Issues*, Fall, 42–46.

Gaitskill, Mary. 1994. "On Not Being a Victim: Sex, Rape, and the Trouble with Following the Rules." *Harper's Magazine*, March, 35–44.

Galvin, James and Kenneth Polk. 1983. "Attrition in Case Processing: Is Rape Unique?" *Journal of Research in Crime and Delinquency* 19–20 (1): 126–154.

Gardner, Thomas J. and Terry M. Anderson. 1996. *Criminal Law Principles and Cases*. 6th ed. Minneapolis/St. Paul: West.

Gauthier, Jeffrey A. 1999. "Consent, Coercion, and Sexual Autonomy." In *A Most Detestable Crime: New Philosophical Essays on Rape*, ed. Kenneth Burgess-Jackson, 71–91. New York: Oxford University Press.

Giannelli, Paul. 1997. "Forensic Science: Rape Trauma Syndrome." *Criminal Law Bulletin* 33 (3): 270–279.

Gibeaut, John. 1997. "Shield a Prosecution Sword." *American Bar Association Journal* 83 (1): 36–37.

Goldberg-Ambrose, Carole. 1992. "Unfinished Business in Rape Law Reform." *Journal of Social Issues* 48 (1): 173–185.

——. 1989. "Theory, Practice, and Perception in Rape Law Reform." Review of Susan Estrich, *Real Rape* (1987) and Zsuzsanna Adler, *Rape on Trial* (1987). *Law and Society Review* 23 (5): 949–955.

Gregory, Jeanne and Sue Lees. 1999. *Policing Sexual Assault*. London: Routledge.

Gutmann, Stephanie. 1993. "Are All Men Rapists? The New VAWA Is Sexual Politics with a Vengeance." *National Review*, August 23, 44–48.

Hale, Sir Matthew. 1971. *History of the Pleas of the Crown*. Vol. 1. London: Professional Books. (Originally published 1646.)

Harris, Angela P. 1996. "Forcible Rape, Date Rape, and Communicative Sexuality: A Legal Perspective." In *Date Rape: Feminism, Philosophy, and the Law*, ed. Leslie Francis, 51–62. University Park: Pennsylvania State University Press.

Harris, Angela and Lois Pineau. 1996. "A Dialogue on Evidence." In *Date Rape: Feminism, Philosophy, and the Law*, ed. Leslie Francis, 109–131. University Park: Pennsylvania State University Press.

Haxton, David. 1985. "Rape Shield Statutes: Constitutional Despite Unconstitutional Exclusions of Evidence." *Wisconsin Law Review* 5 (September/October): 1219–1272.

Hay, Alex, Keith Soothill, and Sylvia Walby. 1980. "Seducing the Country by Rape Reports." *New Society*, July 31, 214–215.

Hayler, Barbara. 1985. "Rape Shield Legislation: How Much Difference Does It Make?" Paper presented at the Society for the Study of Social Problems, Washington, D.C., August.

Hecht Schafran, Lynn. 1992. "Importance of Voir Dire in Rape Trials." *Trial*, August, 26–27.

Henderson, Lynne. 1993. "Getting to Know: Honoring Women in Law and Fact." *Texas Journal of Women and the Law* 2 (1): 41–73.

———. 1988. "Review Essay: What Makes Rape a Crime?" *Berkeley Women's Law Journal* 3 (1): 193–229.

Henshaw, Stanley K. 1992. "Abortion Trends in 1987 and 1988: Age and Race." *Family Planning Perspectives* 24 (2): 85–86, 96.

Herman, Lawrence. 1977. "What's Wrong with the Rape Reform Laws?" *Victimology: An International Journal* 2 (1): 8–21.

Herman, Susan. 2004. "Rape Shield Laws: Interview with Susan Herman." *Kojo Knamdi Radio Show*, WAMU. www.wamu.org/ram/2004/k1040310.ram. Accessed March 10, 2004.

Hinch, Ronald. 1988. "Enforcing the New Sexual Assault Laws: An Exploratory Study." *Atlantis* 14:109–115.

———. 1985. "Canada's New Sexual Assault Laws: A Step Forward for Women?" *Crime Law and Social Change* 9 (1): 33–44.

Human Rights Watch, Women's Rights Project. 1995. *Human Rights Watch Global Report on Women's Human Rights*. New York: Human Rights Watch.

Hunter, Sharon, Gail Burns-Smith, and Carol Walsh. 2000. "Equal Justice? Not Yet for Victims of Sexual Assault." *Connecticut Sexual Assault Crisis Services (Connsacs) Newsletter.* www.connsacs.org/library/justice.html. Accessed April 6, 2000.

Hunter, Sharon, Bonnie R. Bentley Cewe, and Jamie L. Mills. 1998. "Police Response to Crimes of Sexual Assault: A Training Curriculum (Second Edition). Module 2: Police Investigation, Part 6: Writing Reports and Arrest Warrant Applications, Note about False Allegations and Reports." www.vaw.umn/documents/policeresponse/policeresponse.html. Accessed July 5, 2004.

Iadicola, Peter and Anson Shupe. 1998. *Violence, Inequality, and Human Freedom*. Dix Hills, N.Y.: General Hall.

Jones, Alex S. 1989. "Naming Rape Victim Is Still a Murky Issue for the Press." *New York Times*, June 25, 1989, A18.

Jones, Ann. 1994. "Crimes Against Women: Media Part of the Problem for Masking Violence in the Language of Love." *USA Today*, March 10, A9.

Jong, Erica. 1973. *Fear of Flying*. Austin, Tex.: Holt, Rinehart and Winston.

Judicial Committee on Model Jury Instructions in the Eighth Circuit. 2006. "Manual of Model Criminal Jury Instructions for the District Courts of the Eighth Circuit. 2006 Edition." www.juryinstructions.CA8.uscourts.gov/criminal_instructions.htm. Accessed June 25, 2007.

Kadish, Sanford H. and Stephen J. Schulhofer. 1995. *Criminal Law and Its Processes*. 6th ed. Boston: Little, Brown.

Kadish, Sanford H. and Stephen J. Schulhofer. 2001. *Criminal Law and Its Processes: Cases and Materials*. 7th ed. Gaithersburg, N.Y.: Aspen Law and Business.

Kalven, Harry, Jr., and Hans Zeisel. 1966. *The American Jury*. Boston: Little, Brown.

Kanin, Eugene J. 1994. "False Rape Allegation." *Archives of Sexual Behavior* 23 (1): 81–87.

Katz, Steven B. 1989. "Expectation and Desire in the Law of Forcible Rape." *San Diego Law Review* 26 (48): 21–65.

Kennedy Bergen, Raquel. 2000. "Rape Laws and Spousal Exemptions." In *Encyclopedia of Women and Crime*, ed. Nicole Hahn Rafter, 223–224. Phoenix, Ariz.: Oryx.

Kilpatrick, Dean G., David Beatty, and Susan Smith Howley. 1998. *The Rights of Crime Victims—Does Legal Protection Make a Difference?* Washington, D.C.: National Institute of Justice, December.

Kinports, K. 2001. "Rape and Force: The Forgotten Mens Rea." "Feminism and Criminal Law," special issue, *Buffalo Criminal Law Review* 4 (2): 755–799.

Koss, Mary P., Christine A. Gidycz, and Nadine Wisniewski. 1987. "The Scope of Rape: Incidence and Prevalence of Sexual Aggression and Victimization in a National Sample of Higher Education Students." *Journal of Consulting and Clinical Psychology* 55 (2): 162–170.

Koss, Mary, Thomas E. Dinero, Cynthia A. Siebel, and Susan L. Cox. 1988. "Stranger, Acquaintance, and Date Rape: Is There a Difference in the Victim's Experience?" *Psychology of Women Quarterly* 12 (1): 1–24.

Koss, Mary P., Lisa A. Goodman, Angela Browne, Louise F. Fitzgerald, Gwendolyn Puryear Keita, and Anancy Russo Felipe. 1994. *No Safe Haven: Male Violence Against Women at Home, at Work, and in the Community*. Washington, D.C.: American Psychological Association.

Lane, Charles. 2004. "Disabled Win Right to Sue States Over Court Access." *Washington Post*, May 18, A1.

Larson, Jane E. 1993. "Women Understand So Little, They Call My Good Nature Deceit: A Feminist Rethinking of Seduction." *Columbia Law Review* 93 (2): 374–472.

Lees, Sue. 1996. *Ruling Passions: Sexual Violence, Reputation and the Law*. Philadelphia, Pa.: Open University Press.

LeGrand, Camille E. 1973. "Rape and Rape Law: Sexism in Society and Law." *California Law Review* 61(3): 919–941.

Leive, Cindi. 1994. "The Final Rape Injustice." *Glamour*, November, 198–201, 254.

Leo, John. 1997. "Sexual Predator Laws Can Reduce Sexual Violence." In *Sexual Violence: Opposing Viewpoints*, ed. Mary E. Williams and Tamara L. Roleff, 167–170. San Diego: Greenhaven.

Levine, Judith. 1992. *Juries and Politics*. Pacific Grove, Calif.: Brooks/Cole.

Levinson, David. 1989. *Family Violence in Cross-Cultural Perspective*. Newbury Park, Calif.: Sage.

Lewin, Miriam. 1985. "Unwanted Intercourse: The Difficulty of Saying No." *Psychology of Women Quarterly* 9 (2): 184–192.

Loftus, Colleen M. 1982. "The Illinois Rape Shield Statute: Privacy at Any Cost?" *John Marshall Journal of Practice and Procedure* 15 (1): 157–175.

Loh, Wallace D. 1981. "Q: What Has Reform of Rape Legislation Wrought? A: Truth in Criminal Labeling." *Journal of Social Issues* 37 (4):28–52.

Lonsway, Kimberly A. and Louise F. Fitzgerald. 1994. "Rape Myths: In Review." *Psychology of Women Quarterly* 18 (2): 133–164.

MacKinnon, Catherine. 2001. *Sex Equality*. New York: Foundation.

———. 1991. "The Palm Beach Hanging." *New York Times*, December 15, E15.

———. 1989. *Toward a Feminist Theory of the State*. Cambridge: Harvard University Press.

———. 1983. "Feminism, Marxism, Method and the State: Toward Feminist Jurisprudence." *Signs: Journal of Women in Culture and Society* 8 (4): 635–658.

Marcus, Paul and Tara L. McMahon. 1990–1991. "Limiting Discourse of Rape Victims' Identities." *Southern California Law Review* 64 (4): 1019–1056.

Malamuth, Neil M., Daniel Linz, Christopher L. Heavey, Gordon Barnes, and Michele Acker. 1995. "Using the Confluence Model of Sexual Aggression to Predict Men's Conflict with Women: A 10-year Follow-up Study." *Journal of Personality and Social Psychology* 69 (2): 353–369.

Males, Mike. 1992. "Adult Liaison in the 'Epidemic' of 'Teenage' Birth, Pregnancy and Venereal Disease." *Journal of Sex Research* 29 (4): 525–545.

Mardorossian, Carine M. 2002. "Toward a New Feminist Theory of Rape." *Signs: Journal of Women in Culture and Society* 27 (3): 743–775.

Marsh, Jeanne C., Alison Geist, and Nathan Caplan. 1982. *Rape and the Limits of Law Reform*. Boston, Mass.: Auburn House.

Matthews, Nancy A. 1994. *Confronting Rape: The Feminist Anti-Rape Movement and the State*. London: Routledge.

Michigan Judicial Institute. 2002. *Sexual Assault Benchbook*. Lansing: Michigan Supreme Court.

Michigan Women's Task Force on Rape. 1974. "Background Material for a Proposal for Criminal Code Reform to Respond to Michigan's Rape Crisis." Mimeograph.

Miller, Susan and Michelle Meloy. Forthcoming. *Exploring Policies and Politics of Violence Against Women*. New York: Oxford University Press.

Mullendore, Kristine. 1997. "Federal Court Access for Victims of Gender Based Violence: The Civil Remedy of the Violence Against Women Act of 1994—Post Brzonkala." Paper presented to the Academy of Criminal Justice Sciences annual meeting, Louisville, Ky.

Murthy, Sakthi. 1991. "Rejecting Unreasonable Sexual Expectations: Limits on Using a Rape Victim's Sexual History to Show the Defendant's Mistaken Belief in Consent." *California Law Review* 79 (2): 541–572.

Myers, Martha A. and Gary LaFree. 1982. "Sexual Assault and Its Prosecution: A Comparison with Other Crimes." *Journal of Criminal Law and Criminology* 73 (3): 1282–1305.

National Center for Victims of Crime. 2004a. "Violence Against Women Act Reauthorization: Summary Highlights." www.ncvc.org/ncvc/main.aspx?dbName = DocumentViewer&DocumentID = 32700. Accessed July 13, 2004.

———. 2004b. "Spousal Rape: 20 Years Later." www.ncvc.org/ncvc/main.aspx?dbName = DocumentViewer&DocumentID = 32701. Accessed July 13, 2004.

National Institute of Justice. 2000. "Measuring Violence Against Women: Recommendation from an Interagency Workshop." *National Institute of Justice Journal*, October, 18–19.

National Institute of Law Enforcement and Criminal Justice. 1978. *Forcible Rape: A Literature Review and Annotated Bibliography*. Washington, D.C.: U.S. Government Printing Office.

Nicoll, Christopher W. 1979. "Idaho Code &18–6105: A Limitation on the Use of Evidence Relating to Prior Sexual Conduct of the Prosecutor in Idaho Rape Trials." *Idaho Law Review* 15 (2): 323–342.

N.O.W. Legal Defense and Education Fund and Renée Cherow-O'Leary. 1987. *The State-By-State Guide to Women's Legal Rights*. New York: McGraw-Hill.

Oberman, Michelle. 1994. "Turning Girls into Women: Re-evaluating Modern Statutory Rape Law." *Journal of Criminal Law and Criminology* 85 (1): 15–79.

Odem, Mary E. and Jody Clay-Warner, eds. 1998. *Confronting Rape and Sexual Assault*. Wilmington, Del.: Scholarly Resources.

Office for Victims of Crime. 2002. "Victim Input into Plea Agreements." Legal Series No. 7, OVC. U.S. Dept. of Justice, Office of Justice Programs, Office for Victims of Crimes, November, 1–7.

O'Gorman Hughes, Jean and Bernice Resnick Sandler. 1987. *Friends Raping Friends: Could It Happen to You?* Pamphlet. Washington, D.C.: Center for Women Policy Studies.

Osborne, Judith A. 1985. "Rape Law Reform: The New Cosmetic for Canadian Women." In *Criminal Justice Politics and Women: The Aftermath of Legally Mandated Change*, ed. Claudine Schweber and Clarice Feiman, 49–64. New York: Haworth.

Paglia, Camille. 1994. "Women's Naivete Contributes to Rape." In *Violence Against Women*, ed. Karin L. Swisher, Carol Wekesser, and William Barbour, 67–70. San Diego: Greenhaven.

Pineau, Lois. 1996a. "Date Rape: A Feminist Analysis." In *Date Rape: Feminism, Philosophy, and the Law*, ed. Leslie Francis, 1–26. University Park: Pennsylvania State University Press.

———. 1996b. "A Response to My Critics." In *Date Rape: Feminism, Philosophy, and the Law*, ed. Leslie Francis, 63–108. University Park: Pennsylvania State University Press.

Polk, Kenneth. 1985. "Rape Reform and Criminal Justice Processing." *Crime and Delinquency* 31 (April): 191–205.

Rape, Abuse and Incest National Network (RAINN). 2008. "At Least 180,000 Rape Evidence Kits Backlogged, Awaiting DNA Lab Analysis." *Violence Against Women News*. www.feminist.com/violence/vawnews5.html. Accessed March 24, 2008.

Remick, Anne Lani. 1993. "Read Her Lips: An Argument for a Verbal Consent Standard in Rape." *University of Pennsylvania Law Review* 141 (3): 1103–1151.

Rhode, Deborah L. 1989. *Justice and Gender: Sex Discrimination and the Law*. Cambridge: Harvard University Press.

Rhodes James, Robert, ed. 1974. *Winston S. Churchill: His Complete Speeches*. Vol. 7, *1943–1949*. New York: Chelsea House.

Roberts, Dorothy. 1993. "Rape, Violence and Women's Autonomy." *Chicago Kent Law Review* 69 (2): 359–388.

Robinson, Matthew. 2002. *Justice Blind? Ideals and Realities of American Criminal Justice.* Upper Saddle River, N.J.: Prentice-Hall.

Roiphe, Katie. 1993. *The Morning After: Sex, Fear, and Feminism on Campus.* Boston: Little, Brown.

Rowland, Judith. 1985. *The Ultimate Violation.* New York: Doubleday.

Rozee, Patricia D., Py Bateman, and Theresa Gilmore. 1991 "The Personal Perspective of Acquaintance Rape Prevention: A Three-tier Approach." In Andrea Parrot and Laurie Bechhofer, eds., *Acquaintance Rape: The Hidden Crime,* 337–354. New York: Wiley.

Rozee, Patricia D. and Mary P. Koss. 2001. "Rape: A Century of Resistance." *Psychology of Women Quarterly* 25 (4): 295–311.

Rudstein, Davis S. 1976. "Rape Shield Laws: Some Constitutional Problems." *William and Mary Law Review* 18 (1): 1–46.

Russell, Dianna E. H. 1998. "Wife Rape and the Law." In *Confronting Rape and Sexual Assault,* ed. Mary E. Odem and Jody Clay-Warner, 71–81. Wilmington, Del.: Scholarly Resources.

———. 1985. *Dangerous Relationships: Pornography, Misogyny, and Rape.* Thousand Oaks, Calif.: Sage.

Sampson, Rana. 2008. "Acquaintance Rape of College Students" COPS (Community Oriented Policing Services) Problem-Oriented Guides for Police Services Guide No. 17. Washington, D.C.: U.S. Department of Justice. www.usdoj.gov. Accessed March 26, 2008.

Sanday, Peggy Reeves. 1981. *Female Power and Male Dominance: On the Origins of Sexual Inequality.* New York: Cambridge University Press.

———. 1996. *A Woman Scorned: Acquaintance Rape on Trial.* New York: Doubleday.

Sasko, Helen and Deborah Sesek. 1975. "Rape Reform Legislation: Is It the Solution?" *Cleveland State Law Review* 24 (3): 463–503.

Schneider, Elizabeth. 2002. *Battered Women and Feminist Lawmaking.* New Haven, Conn.: Yale University Press.

Scholz, Sally J. 1998. Review of Leslie Francis, ed., *Date Rape: Feminism, Philosophy, and the Law* (1996). *Violence Against Women* 4 (2): 240–249.

Schulhofer, Stephen. 2001. "Society Needs Better Laws Against Rape." In *Rape,* ed. Mary E. Williams, 143–152. San Diego: Greenhaven.

———. 1998. *Unwanted Sex: The Culture of Intimidation and the Failure of Law.* Cambridge: Harvard University Press.

Schwendinger, Julia R. and Herman Schwendinger. 1983. *Rape and Inequality.* New York: Sage.

Scully, Diana. 1990. *Understanding Sexual Violence: A Study of Convicted Rapists.* Boston: Unwin Hyman.

Searles, Patricia and Ronald J. Berger, eds. 1995. *Rape and Society: Readings on the Problem of Sexual Assault.* Boulder, Colo.: Westview.

Seghetti, Lisa M. 2006. "DNA Testing for Law Enforcement: Legislative Issues for Congress." CRS Report for Congress. Updated January 19. www.house.gov/gallegly /issues/crime/crimedocs/RL32247.pdf. Accessed March 24, 2008.

Sheehy, Elizabeth A. 2000. "Rape Shield Laws, Canada." In *Encyclopedia of Women and Crime,* ed. Nicole Hahn Rafter, 226–227. Phoenix, Ariz.: Oryx.

Snider, Laureen. 1985. "Legal Reform and Social Control: The Dangers of Abolishing Rape." *International Journal of the Sociology of Law* 13 (4): 337–356.

Snow, Nancy E. 1999. "Evaluating Rape Shield Laws: Why the Law Continues to Fail Rape Victims." In *A Most Detestable Crime: New Philosophical Essays on Rape*, ed. Kenneth Burgess-Jackson, 245–266. New York: Oxford University Press.

Soothill, Keith. 1995. "The Changing Face of Rape?" In *Rape and the Criminal Justice System*, ed. Jennifer Temkin, 165–176. Aldershot, England: Dartmouth.

Spears, Jeffrey W. and Cassia C. Spohn. 1997. "The Effect of Evidence Factors and Victim Characteristics on Prosecutors' Charging Decisions in Sexual Assault Cases." *Justice Quarterly* 14 (3): 501–524.

Spohn, Cassia and Julia Horney. 1996. "The Impact of Rape Law Reform on the Processing of Simple and Aggravated Rape Cases." *Journal of Criminal Law and Criminology* 86 (3): 861–884.

——. 1992. *Rape Law Reform: A Grass Roots Revolution and Its Impact*. New York: Plenum.

Staff of Senate Committee on the Judiciary. 1993. "The Response to Rape: Detours on the Road to Equal Justice." 103d Congress, 1st sess. Comm. print.

Stap, Dannielle. 1997. "Students Warned About Rape Drug." *Western Herald*, February 26, 2.

Steinbock, Bonnie. 1995. "Megan's Law: Community Notification of the Release of Sex Offenders. A Policy Perspective." *Criminal Justice Ethics* 14 (2): 4–9.

Tanford, J. Alexander and Anthony T. Bocchino. 1980. "Rape Victim Shield Laws and the Sixth Amendment." *University of Pennsylvania Law Review* 128 (3): 544–602.

Taylor, Ian, Paul Walton, and Jock Young. 1973. *The New Criminology: For a Social Theory of Deviance*. New York: Harper and Row.

Tchen, Christina M. 1983. "Rape Reform and a Statutory Consent Defense." *Journal of Criminal Law and Criminology* 74 (4): 1518–1555.

Temkin, Jennifer. 2002. *Rape and the Legal Process*. 2d ed. New York: Oxford University Press.

——, ed. 1995. *Rape and the Criminal Justice System*. Aldershot, England: Dartmouth.

Tong, Rosemarie. 1984. *Women, Sex, and the Law*. Totowa, N.J.: Roman and Littlefield.

Tracey, Patrick. 2000. "Christy's Crusade." *Ms.*, April/May, 53–61.

U.S. Senate. 2000. *Violence Against Women Act*. S. 2787. Public Law 106-386, U.S. Code.

——. 1993. *The Violence Against Women Act*. 103d Cong., 1st sess., report 103-138, calendar no. 195, September 10 (legislative day, September 7), 1993. S. 1607. Title IV of the *Violent Crime Control and Law Enforcement Act*, September 13, 1994. Public Law 103-322, U.S. Code.

Vachss, Alice. 1993. *Sex Crimes*. New York: Random House.

Valente, Roberta L., Barbara J. Hart, Zeya Seema, and Mary Malefyt. 2001. "The Violence Against Women Act: The Commitment to Ending Domestic Violence, Sexual Assault, Stalking, and Gender-based Crimes of Violence." In *Sourcebook on Violence Against Women*, ed. Clair M. Renzetti, Jeffrey L. Edleson, and Raquel Kennedy Bergen, 279–301. Thousand Oaks, Calif.: Sage.

Vaughan, Kevin, John C. Ensslin, and Karen Abbott. 2005. "It's Over—For Now. Losing Side Vows to Appeal Sex Case at Heart of Scandal." Denver Rocky Mountain News.

www.rockymountainnres.com/drmn/local/article/0,1299,DRMN_15_366713,00
.html. Accessed April 1, 2005.

Walker, Samuel. 2004. *Sense and Nonsense About Crime and Drugs*. Belmont, Calif.: Wadsworth/Thomson Learning.

Walsh, Anthony. 1986. "Placebo Justice: Victim Recommendations and Offender Sentences in Sexual Assault Cases." *Journal of Criminal Law and Criminology* 77 (4): 1126–1141.

Ward, Colleen A. 1995. *Attitudes Toward Rape: Feminist and Social Psychological Perspectives*. London: Sage.

Weddington, Sarah. 1975–1976. "Rape Law in Texas: H.B. 284 and the Road to Reform." *American Journal of Criminal Law* 4 (1): 1–14.

Weiner, Anthony D. 2008. "DNA Justice." www.house.gov/weiner/report4.htm. Accessed March 24, 2008.

Weiner, Robin. 1983. "Note, Shifting the Communication Burden: A Meaningful Consent Standard in Rape." *Harvard Women's Law Journal* 6 (1): 143–162.

Weldon, S. Laurel. 2002. *Protest, Policy and the Problem of Violence Against Women: A Cross-National Comparison*. Pittsburgh: University of Pittsburgh Press.

Weninger, Robert A. 1978. "Factors Affecting the Prosecution of Rape: A Case Study of Travis County, Texas." *Virginia Law Review* 64 (3): 357–397.

West, Robin. 1994. "Men, Women and Rape: Women and the Law Panel Discussion." *Fordham Law Review* 63 (1): 125–174.

Whitcomb, Debra, Gail S. Goodman, Desmond K. Runyanb, and Shirley Hoak. 1994. "The Emotional Effects of Testifying on Sexually Abused Children." Research in Brief. Washington, D.C.: National Institute of Justice.

Williams, Joyce E. and Karen A. Holmes. 1981. *The Second Assault: Rape and Public Attitudes*. Westport, Conn.: Greenwood.

Williams, Susan N. 1984. "Rape Reform Legislation and Evidentiary Concerns: The Law in Pennsylvania." *University of Pittsburgh Law Review* 44 (4): 955–975.

Wolf, Naomi. 1993. "Radical Heterosexuality … or, How to Love a Man and Save Your Feminist Soul." In *Transforming a Rape Culture*, ed. Emile Buchwald, Pamela R. Fletcher, and Martha Roth, 359–368. Minneapolis: Milkweed.

Woolgar, Steve and Dorothy Pawluch. 1985. "Ontological Gerrymandering: The Anatomy of Social Problems Explanations." *Social Problems* 32 (3): 214–227.

Wright, Richard. 1984. "A Note on Attrition of Rape Cases." *British Journal of Criminology* 24 (4): 399–400.

Yancey Martin, Patricia and Marlene R. Powell. 1995. "Accounting for the Second Assault: Legal Organizations' Framing of Rape Victims." *Law and Social Inquiry* 19 (4): 853–890.

Young, W. 1983. *Rape Study: A Discussion of Law and Practice*. Wellington, Scotland: Department of Justice and Institute of Criminology.

Yurchesyn, Kathleen A., Ann Keith, and Edward K. Renner. 1995. "Contrasting Perspectives on the Nature of Sexual Assault Providing Service for Sexual Assault Victims and by the Law Courts." In *Rape and the Criminal Justice System*, ed. Jennifer Temkin, 61–75. Aldershot, England: Dartmouth.

Morgan, Director of Public Prosecutions v.
(Britain), 70–71, 73, 140, 151, 152, 244,
257
Morrison et al., U.S. v., VAWA and, 52–53
MPC. *See* Model Penal Code
M.T.S., State ex rel. (New Jersey), 124, 176,
237, 297n7
Mullendore, Kristine: on civil law, 298n5;
on consent/nonconsent, 100, on
defense of consent, 295–96n3; on
evidence standard, 306n5; on strict
liability, 295n1; on treatment of rape,
303–4n3
Murthy, Sakthi, 204, 220–21
Myers, State v. (Utah), 117
Myhr, Terri L.: on Canadian rape reform,
21–22; Du Mont and, 47–48

Nebraska, corroboration requirement in,
307n2
negligent liability: criminal negligence
and recklessness and, 4, 140–43, 146–
53, 166, 248; Estrich and, 3, 70–74, 83,
155, 164; force/coercion and, 160–62,
305n4; nonagreement and, 149; problems with, 144–46; rape and, 63, 140–
43; rape reform and, 238; recklessness
and, 148; woman's point of view and,
163–65
Nevada, victim history in, 218
New Bedford (Massachusetts) pool table
gang rape case, 61, 264, 280
New Hampshire, nonconsent in, 126
New Jersey: affirmative consent rule in,
32, 76–78, 176, 246, 297n3, 312n3;
force/coercion in, 124; Garron case in,
32–33; Glen Ridge case in, 38, 60, 80–
82, 176, 297n7; Michigan law influence
on, 292n1; M.T.S. case in, 124, 176, 237,
297n7; resistance requirements repealed in, 15; shield legislation in, 280;
victim history in, 253
New York: *Evans* case in, 106–7, 148, 162;
rape in, 59, 61, 264, 280; sexual assault
by fraud in, 196–97

New York Central Park jogger rape case,
59, 61, 264, 280
New Zealand, 21, 293n4
Neuman, Lawrence W., 16, 19, 34
Nicholson, George, 23
1976 Sexual Offences (Amendment) Act,
22
nonaggravated rape, 3; as bulk of rape, 9;
rape reform and, 99, 265. *See also*
acquaintance rape; date rape; simple
rape
nonagreement, 4, 111, 119; as defining
rape, 126; expression of, 181; force/
coercion and, 126, 158–62, 166; inability to indicate, 302n11; "no" as
sufficient indication of, 126–29, 155,
164, 166, 207, 216, 233–34, 236; presumptive, 120–24, 137, 150–51, 154–
60, 166–68, 169, 178, 208, 215–17,
225–26, 228–29, 233–34, 238, 240,
249, 265, 302n7, 311n9. *See also*
nonconsent; involuntariness,
nonagreement
nonconsent: as continuum, 99–101; as
demonstrated by resistance, 143;
determination of, 84–85, 114; as
element of rape, 66, 74; expression
of, 124–29, 131; force/coercion and,
65, 106, 108, 139–40, 308n7; implication of, 120; as involuntariness,
nonagreement, 109–11, 118; need for
rape victims to express, 10, 107, 157;
"no means no," 91–92, 126–29, 134,
137, 146, 155, 160, 166, 207, 236, 253–
54, 283, 312n1; proof of, 80, 139–40;
redundancy of, in presence of force/
coercion, 104, 119–20, 133, 137, 160–
62, 235; semantics of, 109–11; in
trespass, 114, 166; woman's point of
view defining, 134, 146, 168, 210, 214–
15, 308n10. *See also* nonagreement;
involuntariness, nonagreement
North Carolina: *Alston* case in, 106, 148,
235–39; Duke University alleged gang
rape case in, 60, 61, 280, 295n7